MENNONITE SOCIETY

MENNONITE SOCIETY

Calvin Redekop

THE JOHNS HOPKINS UNIVERSITY PRESS

BALTIMORE AND LONDON

The Johns Hopkins University Press
701 West 40th Street
Baltimore, Maryland 21211
The Johns Hopkins Press Ltd., London

The paper used in this publication meets the minimum requirements of American
National Standard for Information Sciences—Permanence of Paper for Printed Library
Materials, ANSI Z39.48-1984.

Library of Congress Cataloging-in-Publication Data

Redekop, Calvin Wall, 1925–
   Mennonite society.

   Bibliography: p.
   Includes index.
   1. Mennonites. 2. Amish. 3. Hutterite Brethren.
I. Title.
E184.M45R43 1989   305.6'87'073   88-32013
ISBN 0-8018-3729-4 (alk. paper)
ISBN 0-8018-3871-1 (pbk.)

Contents

Illustrations

Figures

Tables

Preface

There is something inherently contradictory about a Mennonite writing a book about Mennonites. The powerful tradition of *Demut* (humility) and *Gelassenheit* (submission) that has been etched deeply into the Mennonite soul forbids one from trafficking in self-analysis or attention to the accomplishments of one's own group. It is true that for much of the movement's history, most members quietly accepted their position in a secure though disparaged tradition, probably because the larger world did not seem an option to them.

But in the modern era it is becoming increasingly difficult for Mennonites to unquestioningly accept membership in a minority religious tradition and to derive a sense of identity without looking beyond the group itself. In 1988 alone three books and many articles were written on the Mennonite identity by Mennonites. This book is my own most recent and concerted effort to understand who the Mennonites are. I hope it will help other members of the tradition, but also those who are not Mennonite, to understand the Mennonites better. This latter group should know that nothing flatters the Mennonite ego as much as discovering that someone else is interested in us.

The conclusions stated in this book have been reached after a number of decades of teaching and working in Mennonite institutions. I begin by suggesting that there are now two kinds of Mennonites: the Germanic (the birthright descendants) and the non-Germanic (the converted and convinced nondescendants). The latter are so different and dynamic that it is almost impossible to say much about them—they are probably closest to the original utopian nature of Anabaptist-Mennonitism. The future clearly belongs to them.

Regarding the Germanic Mennonites, I have come to the conclusion that theirs was a religious protest movement, deeply rooted in the utopian tradition that envisioned a society modeled after the plans projected in the New Testament. The movement did not intend to become sectarian; rather it sought to become a pure church, and hence reflect the coming Kingdom of God (for a quick overview of my scheme see Table 1 in Appendix A). But the sectarian phase was thrust on the Anabaptist movement in spite of itself, and this had the tragic consequences of driving the movement underground. Thus the next three centuries were a dark period for the movement during which the prophetic impulse was subordinated to keeping the memory alive.

As the times became more tolerant, the utopian dynamics began to resurface. The original motifs were slowly unearthed, and ultimately the desire to salvage the original utopian ideals and ideology, rather than let the forces of reality compromise or destroy them, won out, according to sympathetic observers such as Rosemary Ruether. That this is not simply a self-pitying and self-vindicating verdict is indicated by the increasing chorus of non-Mennonites who are loudly proclaiming that it is the Anabaptist-Mennonite tradition that has been holding on to aspects of the utopian vision that need desperately to be adopted in our day.

The largest part of the book thus deals with the agonizing attempts of this group to realize its utopian ideals. The Anabaptist-Mennonites faced the vast internal contradictions of people presuming that they could do what few if any other groups have been able to do. They also were subjected to covert and overt resistance and rejection of the surrounding society, which could not stand nor understand this presumptuous movement. (There is no doubt that few Mennonites, if indeed any, have been aware of how presumptuous and arrogant their blueprint for the future of the world must have appeared to others, and how such arrogance must have evoked resistance and even aggression.) Obviously the presumptuousness of the movement was aggravated even more by the humble, submissive, though stubborn, pacifist characteristics of the tradition.

My conclusion is that the Mennonite society of today is comprised of three divergent groups: 1) the utopian restitutionist, which is expressing itself in the recovery of the communal and mutualistic elements of the original; 2) the sectarian/ethnic, which is hoping to protect the birthright by separating and preserving the heritage (This has been and remains a most uncomfortable position; it is rejected by most since it tends to be exclusivistic and hence militates against the "Great Commission" of the New Testament.); and 3) the acculturationist, which under the guise of being a return to faith is actually a return to the pre-Radical Reformation unity of faith and culture where the goals of nation, culture, and faith are subtly, if unintentionally, equated.

A question of prediction inevitably emerges: Does this group known collectively as Mennonites or Anabaptists—so strangely and pervasively divergent within itself—reflect some incredibly durable cohesive principle that can assure its survival for another five centuries? Or will we be witnesses, in the coming century, to its dissolution? This book may suggest some answers.

Should not an outsider have written this book? Perhaps. But until such a happy circumstance occurs we must be satisfied with insiders' attempts. One defense for an insider's view is that no one knows the group as well; but of course the pitfalls of subjectivity exist. Hence the challenge to the insider is to avoid the traps of sentimentality and romanticism and to strive for integrity, objectivity, and balance. A credible description and analysis of the Mennonite society should not be romanticized, nor should it be overly harsh and critical. It must recognize that being aware of the prosaic and commonplace is as fundamental to the whole as is awareness of the noble and the inspiring. It is my hope that this goal has been at least moderately achieved.

IT IS IMPOSSIBLE to appropriately recognize and thank all the persons who have contributed to this volume. My parents deserve my deep gratitude for having interpreted membership in a foreboding tradition in such a way that I could accept it as my own without permanent scars, unlike many of my colleagues. My grandparents, particularly my grandfathers, both of whom were elders and strong leaders in their respective Mennonite groups (Mennonite Brethren and Evangelical Mennonite Brethren), have exercised a profound influence on me. In addition I thank all the faithful members of the Mennonite family with whom I have interacted, either in person or through stories, memories, writings, and the like. They are the ones who in various times and places have expressed in their lives the vision of the essence of the movement. It is to this group of largely unrecognized human beings, especially my ancestors, the Wall and Redekop clans, that I dedicate this book.

I also gratefully acknowledge the contributions of the numerous Mennonite institutions and organizations for which I have worked. These have provided me with a realistic insider's view of Mennonite life. I thank especially Conrad Grebel College for providing the congenial and supportive atmosphere in which this work could proceed. I am especially grateful to the Institute of Anabaptist and Mennonite Studies, which provided support for research time and assistance for publication. Pauline Bauman and Rosemary Smith deserve much appreciation for typing the interminable revisions. I thank Carolyn Moser, my copy editor, for doing an outstanding job of making this book understandable and readable and Henry Tom and the editorial staff at the Johns Hopkins University Press for their cordial assistance and guidance. I extend special thanks to Angeline Polites, production editor, and Chris Smith, designer, for their excellent and creative assistance.

And finally, my wife, Freda, who has cheerfully served as sounding board for the birth and life of this book, deserves thanks for her advice, patience, and support.

Part One

An Overview

Even though the central thrust of this book is an attempt at understanding the contemporary North American Mennonites, a clear review of the origins and dispersion of the movement and of the differentiation of the Mennonite family is necessary. These three chapters present a brief survey of the European origins, the manner in which persecution and survival contributed to the dispersion of the group, and the way in which the Mennonite family has become an "extended" family with many differences.

This historical overview, though by necessity terse, should help orient the reader to the more observable and substantive nature of the Mennonite tradition. Parts 2 through 4 build on the information provided in this first section. For readers who desire more exhaustive discussions of Mennonite history, I have provided references to such discussions in the footnotes and bibliography.

Chapter One

The Origins of the Mennonite Movement

The term *Mennonite* itself muddies the water when one is attempting to describe the Mennonite society because although it is the most general term, it is only one of many that are used. Not all groups who belong to the Mennonite stream accept that designation—for example, the Hutterites in North America or the Doopsgezinde of Holland, although the latter were originally known as Menists. I will, however, use the term *Mennonite* throughout this book to refer to the general movement; it is assumed that readers will develop a clearer picture of the complexity of the phenomenon as they read these pages.

Persons in the original movement were originally and derisively called Anabaptists by both the state churches and the magistracy from the beginning of the movement in 1525 and well into the seventeenth century.[1] In fact, the use of the word *Anabaptism* as a derogatory term moved right into the twentieth century. Derived from Latin, it means "to baptize again." At first it referred only to those who were rebaptized, but quickly the term identified all those who refused to have their children baptized as infants (H. Bender 1955b, 113–16).

Self-designations for the early Anabaptists varied with the area; in

Switzerland they called themselves "the Brethren," a term that included women (Dyck: 1967, 36). In South Germany they referred to themselves as "Brethren"; in other cases, they referred to themselves as the followers of various leaders such as Hut, Denck, Hubmaier, and in the case of Jacob Hutter, Hutterites. In the north, Anabaptists called themselves Melchiorites (after Melchior Hoffman), Obbenites (after Obbe Philips), and Menists, after Menno Simons. The term *Menists* gradually became the name for the entire group, probably because of Simons' extensive writings on faith and doctrine, which have been variously published as *The Complete Writings of Menno Simons*. The Amish name derived from the leadership of Jacob Amman, who was at the center of the Amish division. *Mennonite* is thus a further elaboration of *Menist*, which evolved into *Mennonist*, and finally *Mennonite* (H. Bender 1957b, 586–87).

It has generally been assumed that the Anabaptist movement began in Zurich, Switzerland, centering on Huldrich Zwingli and a number of youthful supporters, including Conrad Grebel, Felix Manz, Georg Blaurock, and Simon Stumpf (Blanke 1961; C. Dyck 1967). Baptism of infants, which seemed to be the heart of the disagreement, was not the only issue at stake. There were others, including (1) the protest against the use of magisterial power to bring about religious reform, as Zwingli was proposing; in the Anabaptist view, this really meant continuing the marriage of church and state instead of effecting a separation of the two; (2) the demand for a pure church with discipline and excommunication of transgressors; (3) standing on the authority of Scriptures alone in matters of faith as well as action; and (4) the rejection of violence in matters of faith as well as action, a position expanded to include rejection of military service.

Although the persons named above, along with others, are recognized by some as founders of Anabaptism, recent scholarship is demonstrating that Anabaptism had no single leader or close-knit group of leaders who gave the movement its character, nor even a single locale from which it spread.[2] This is proven by the fact that the Roman church, the Reformers, and civil authorities alike viewed Anabaptism as a pervasive cancer with cells appearing rapidly in many parts of western Europe, including the cantons of Switzerland, Tyrol, Austria, and South Germany, as well as Moravia and other parts of North Europe (see Map 1.1).

The leaders mentioned above were all young, most in their twenties. With the exception of Pilgram Marpeck and Menno Simons, few lived past the age of thirty and hence could hardly have become ideological or

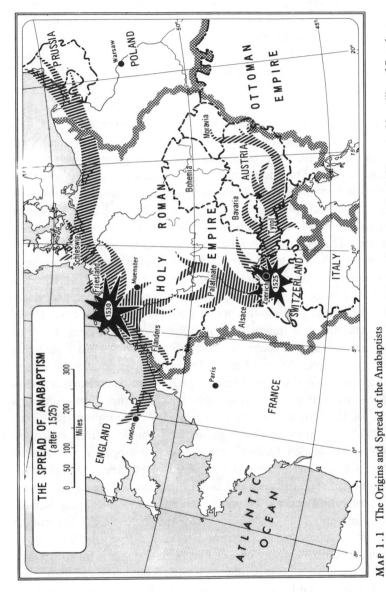

MAP 1.1 The Origins and Spread of the Anabaptists
Source: Frank H. Epp, *Mennonites in Canada, 1786–1920: The History of a Separate People* (Toronto: Macmillan of Canada, 1975). Courtesy of the Mennonite Historical Society of Canada.

charismatic leaders of the movement. In the other parts of Europe where the movement emerged, the spokesmen were also relatively young people.[3]

Non-Mennonite scholars maintain that the movement sprang up and received followers almost simultaneously in many parts of central Europe. Groups emerged early at St. Gall and at Appenzell in Switzerland; both cities were leading centers in the growth of peasant revolt. Almost simultaneously Anabaptist-like groups emerged in middle and northern Germany, Holland, northern Italy, Moravia and Bohemia, Prussia and Silesia, and Lithuania, where social unrest obtained (Williams 1962; Stayer 1972, 1988). The Anabaptist movement emerged at the same time that a major social upheaval was convulsing Germany and other parts of Europe, the social protest movement known in Germany as the Peasants' Revolt. There is increasing agreement among scholars that the Anabaptist movement was related to this revolt in complex ways, with some of the Anabaptist leaders having been involved in the Peasants' War, and some of the members of the Peasants' Revolt joining the Anabaptist-Hutterite society. This interconnectedness underlines the position taken in this book, that the Anabaptist movement was a religio-social rebellion with utopian dynamics. An awareness of the more socially based factors in the Anabaptist revolt is causing a major reevaluation of the origins and significance of Anabaptist society (Stayer 1988).

The amazing and tragic "Münster Rebellion" (see below), which took place in North Germany in 1533–35 and which most Mennonite scholars have rejected as not being "Anabaptist," illustrates the variety of responses within the movement. The movement was clearly a part of the general turbulence and social upheaval in Europe during the first quarter of the sixteenth century (Clasen 1972). Symptomatic of the upheaval was a growing challenge to the Catholic church expressed supremely by Martin Luther, who sparked the open revolt against Rome. As a reformer, Luther was followed by Huldrich Zwingli, Melanchthon, Carlstadt, Bucer, and others. Stimulated by the humanist movement, which was itself a major element in the developing Renaissance Reformation, the new breed of reformers believed that the Roman church was badly in need of reform (Stayer and Packull 1980).

That the Roman Catholic church had been oppressive for a long time is a view that has been generally accepted. The clergy held complete control over the faith and life of the laity. Worse than this control, however, was the great exploitation of the peasants, who had to pay heavy taxes in order to maintain luxurious living quarters for their religious leaders. The sumptuous and riotous living of the clergy and other persons related to the church establishment exasperated the peasants. Beyond that, the clergy's questionable moral and ethical life seemed to demand a strong reaction. Menno Simons, for example, expressed his contempt for the clergy in terms rather uncharacteristic of the ethic of love which he espoused.

In spite of all this, Luther's main attack was mounted against the Roman church's espousal of righteousness through works. The church had become a major social and political institution and dispensed grace as though it were a commercial enterprise. In general terms, the Roman church had done what many organizations learn to do when they "have a good thing going": it struck an alliance with the prevailing power structure to ensure maintenance of position and power. "*Sola fide*," Luther thundered. His words reverberated throughout Europe and added explosive fuel to the fires of discontent already burning. For with the invention of the printing press in the middle 1400s, more and more people were reading the Scriptures for themselves. In part because of this, the authority of the priest was beginning to decline. But along with this decline there was also a growing awareness of economic oppression. Consequently, in many areas, the peasants began to rebel—not only against the princes, but against the church as well.[4]

Of course, the emergence of the Anabaptist movement has had numerous alternative interpretations. Marxist theorists have insisted that the Anabaptist rebellion was a protosocialist revolution, that it was in reality a forerunner of the revolution of the oppressed in religious clothing. They have argued that there was a thread of rebellion and revolution going back into the fifteenth and even fourteenth centuries, and that the Anabaptists were the hardened and remnant facets of a great continuum of unrest which finally surfaced and culminated with the Peasants' Uprising (Brady 1982; Zschäbitz 1958).

Other less ideological theoreticians maintain that Anabaptism was not so ideological in origin; rather, it was more the result of disaffection with the general sociopolitical conditions than of a strict theological dispute with the Reformers (Goertz 1980). Hence, they say, Anabaptism must be defined as a religiosocial movement, arising in various areas under unique and specific conditions, and becoming an identifiable, self-conscious movement only after it began to be defensive, entrenching itself against the counterattacks of the authorities.

Naturally, the more orthodox Mennonite historians and theologians are also part of this debate concerning the nature of original Anabaptism. They argue that the Anabaptist movement was a singularly spiritual attempt to reform ecclesiastical practice, that is, "normative Anabaptism." Others, mainly non-Mennonite but increasingly Mennonite as well, reject this position. This latter group counters that the Anabaptist movement was driven as much by social forces as by theological and spiritual issues.

In any case, the original Anabaptist movement protested the debauchery of the clergy, the oppressive tithes that were being levied against the poor to support church institutions, the lack of disciplined living among laity and clergy alike, the use of oaths in swearing allegiance and truth-telling, and the use of force in coercing belief as well as in achieving national and military objectives. Hence, total nonresistance was espoused. Further, Anabaptists held that Christians could not hold public office because this constituted a compromise with the use of coercion, although they assumed obedience to the state unless the conscience was directly contradicted.

Because the movement challenged both state and church authorities simultaneously, a broad range of opposition and persecution developed immediately. The first Anabaptist martyr was Hippolytus Eberle, who was executed in his home canton of Schwyz in May 1525. The first Anabaptist to be martyred at the hands of those representing the new Protestant faith was Felix Manz, who was drowned in the Limmat in the middle of Zurich in January 1527 (Blanke 1961).[5]

The movement spread very quickly from Zurich to other parts of Switzerland, especially to the cantons of Appenzell and St. Gall, Bern and Berner Oberland, where persecution continued until the latter part of the seventeenth century. In these parts the last Anabaptist was martyred on September 20, 1614, although others died later as a result of mistreatment (P. Schowalter 1957).

From this beginning, Anabaptism spread from other sources in South Germany, the Tyrol, Austria, and Moravia. As early as 1525, Anabaptist leaders were known to exist as well in Germany and even in Holland. The city of Strasbourg quickly became a refuge for various dissident Anabaptists, and for a while it appeared as though Anabaptism would become the dominant religion in that city. Augsburg was also an early center; it was there that Anabaptists held the so-called Martyrs' Synod—given that name because so many people who attended the conference later became martyrs, having committed themselves at that meeting to spread the gospel immediately to all of Europe (Hege 1957).

In Germany many groups were imbued with a strong millenarian[6] emphasis. At least in part, this was certainly due to the unrest and ferment which produced the Peasants' Revolt in 1525. Thomas

Müntzer, a leader of this revolt, was a person with whom the Swiss Anabaptists had had considerable contact.

The Tyrol was an especially important area because of the severity of the persecution and the equally resilient response on the part of the Anabaptists. A tinge of chiliasm[7] probably contributed to a fanatic flavor throughout much of the movement in this area. Some members of the movement managed to flee to Moravia, where Leonhard von Lichtenstein offered asylum to the hunted Anabaptists. The Hutterite sector of Anabaptism emerged in this area in 1528. Though Peter Riedemann was their original inspiration, the group derived its name from Jacob Hutter, who became the leader in 1533. The Hutterites—because they were so quickly and summarily persecuted—pooled their resources by necessity and instituted full community of goods, a pattern which they have preserved until this day (J. A. Hostetler 1974; L. Gross 1980).

The most bizarre and significant expression of millenarianism in Anabaptism developed in the city of Münster. Münster, a leading northern German city which was undergoing great economic and religious conflicts and changes, became a center for humanistic and Anabaptist influences. The Peasants' Revolt had also spread its influences to this area. Because of the mixture of various groups and movements—including defecting Catholics, radical Lutherans, and a variety of Anabaptist groups—the leadership and direction of the Münster movement expressed itself in a variety of confusing, contradictory, and violent moves. The basic issues had to do with establishing a pure society of adult-baptized believers and a community based on social and economic equality.

In 1531, Bernhard Rothmann, a former priest turned Lutheran preacher, provided some unifying leadership for the Münster movement. The movement was intensified and expanded by an Anabaptist convert named Heinrich Böll, who was related to the Melchiorite branch of Anabaptism. Jan Matthys, another Anabaptist, converted by Melchior Hoffman, took over the leadership in Münster and proceeded to institute a new society. He called this new society the New Jerusalem and claimed that it had been prophesied in the Old and New Testaments. With the coming of an even more fanatic leader, Jan von Leyden, a certain collective behavior was set in motion. It reached its final climax with Leyden's declaration that the kingdom of God was indeed now on earth and that people were invited to become members of the New Jerusalem. The Catholic bishop and the local princes did not receive this announcement kindly; subsequently, the city was surrounded and literally starved into submission. The final outcome was the fall of the city and the death of all its inhabitants in an awesome and insane orgy of destruction and murder (Krahn 1957; Stayer 1988). The association of the name *Anabaptist* with the radical chiliastic experience of Münster became a millstone around the neck of the more pacific Anabaptists. To this day Europeans regard Münster as having a vague association with the Anabaptist sect.

The movement in Holland, however, was not totally informed or controlled by the millenarian ideas of Melchior Hoffman, who died in jail in Strasbourg believing that he would be freed to resume the leadership of the final assault to achieve the New Jerusalem. Among the membership of the Dutch movement was Menno Simons, a Catholic priest in Witmarsum in North Holland. Through a long personal struggle, Menno slowly became convinced that he was in need of regeneration, and he experienced conversion. In the midst of the turmoil caused by the spread of Anabaptism throughout North Germany and Holland, he was finally persuaded to assume leadership of the scattered flock in Holland. It was this Menno Simons—apparently somewhat physically handicapped, very timid as well as irenic in temperament—who became an important catalyst and guide for the Mennonites in Holland and North Europe. In his homeland, however, his name was not officially adopted by the Mennonite movement, although its members were called Menists in derision in early years. The factions which emerged in different areas or countries were often identified by various names; today, Mennonites in the Netherlands call themselves the Algemene Doopsgezinde Societeit. In Switzerland they are called the Taufgesinnte or simply the Swiss Brethren.

The Anabaptist movement and its teaching met with great receptivity throughout the Continent; as a result, it became one of the first as well as one of the fastest-growing religious movements in early modern times. Considering its amazing spread and growth, some scholars have designated Anabaptists as the forerunners and beginning of the modern missionary movement. But the reception of the Gospel by the commoners was matched by the equally strong resistance of, and oppression from, the magistrates of the reigning principalities as well as by the established Roman, Lutheran, and Reformed churches. In Holland alone, more than two thousand martyrs gave up their lives for the faith between 1530 and 1578, with women also constituting up to one-third of the roster of martyrs in certain places.

Authorities from the south of Switzerland to the tip of Holland publicly named Anabaptist leaders and put prices on their heads. Especially in Holland and Switzerland, official "Anabaptist hunters" were sent out to catch the hated Anabaptists. The Anabaptists, however, were not intimidated; they responded by going underground and propagating their faith in more informal and clandestine meetings. Hence, the leadership became very fluid, and the organization of the believers developed congregationally, with a lay ministry becoming the norm for leadership. Map 1.1 shows the spread of Anabaptism, the places where strong centers emerged, and the dates.

Any attempt to briefly summarize and encapsulate the essence of Anabaptism would be futile and foolhardy. But a beginning must be made, and this chapter has provided some introduction to the subject. Ernst Troeltsch, probably without peer in his understanding of the sociological and theological forms of Christianity from the Reformation to the present, had this to say about the Anabaptists:

> Under the stimulus of the Reformation, on every hand there sprang into existence an enormous number of small groups of earnest Christians, living apart from "the world," claiming complete civil and religious freedom, whose main ideal was the formation of religious communities composed of truly "converted" persons, on a basis of voluntary membership. Their outward symbol of membership was Adult Baptism, which implied the voluntary principle. They rejected Infant Baptism, with its implications of an all-inclusive, non-ethical basis of Church membership. Another characteristic external sign was the demand for Church discipline, and authority to excommunicate, which was closely related to the demand for "a pure Church." They did not accept the ecclesiastical doctrine of the Sacrament. To them the Lord's Supper was mainly a festival of Christian fellowship, and an expression of personal faith in Christ. Thus they were classed with the "Sakramentierier." Their real strength, however, lay in the emphasis which they gave to the desire to be a "holy community," "holy" in the sense of the Sermon on the Mount, and implying a voluntary community composed of mature Christians. In practice this "holiness" was expressed in the following ways: in detachment from the State, from all official positions, from law, force, and the oath, and from war, violence, and capital punishment; the quiet endurance of suffering and injustice as their share in the Cross of Christ, the intimate social relationship of the members with each other through care for the poor and the provision of relief funds, so that within these groups no one was allowed to beg or to starve; strict control over the church members through the exercise of excommunication and congregational discipline. . . . But in addition to the positive characteristics which have just been indicated—the priesthood of all believers, the central position of the Bible, and their emphasis on personal religion—these movements also contained some negative features—a spirit of criticism, of disappointment with the Reformation, as well as a more thorough emphasis upon its main ideas. (Troeltsch 1960, 695–96)

The Anabaptist-Mennonite movement developed and became enriched as it spread. This story needs to be told in more fullness before a closer look at the nature of the movement itself can be taken; I do so in Chapter 2.

Chapter Two

The Dispersion and Expansion of Mennonite Society

The Anabaptist-Mennonite movement, which sprouted in Europe between the 1520s and the 1530s, has grown and spread its branches into almost every part of the world. This expansion has taken place by way of evangelism, population growth, migration, and divisions. Sometimes these have been interrelated; at other times they have been quite distinct from one another.

Although I have focused on original Germanic Mennonites in my general analysis of "Mennonite society," and will continue to do so in this book, it is nevertheless important to keep in mind the general historical as well as the global unfolding of the group. In this chapter I look briefly at the expansion of the group as well as its dispersion. Schisms and divisions are one of the most obvious indicators that Mennonite society has not been able to weather the stress of change that has confronted it in its various contexts. At the same time, division and subsequent dispersions have also contributed to the expansion of the group, as we shall see in Chapter 15.

Mennonite Migrations

Migrations of major groups reveal that the Anabaptists spread by way of evangelism and by way of division. The former need not involve change of residence, at least not for many people, while the latter concerns itself with movements of people and social segregations. We will follow the various streams as explicitly as possible. For an overview of Mennonite migration see Table 2.1.

TABLE 2.1 The Migrations of the Mennonites

I. SWISS-GERMAN MIGRATIONS

About 8,000 persons of Swiss–South German Mennonite background crossed the Atlantic from Europe to America in about two centuries of migration. The migrations of the Swiss (including the Amish) can be summarized as follows (if the numbers of immigrants are known, this is indicated in parentheses):

1. From Switzerland to Moravia in the 16th century; to Alsace, the Palatinate, and Lower Rhine in the 17th century; to Holland in 1711; to Pennsylvania, 1707–56 (3,000–5,000); to Alsace in the late 19th and 20th centuries; to Ohio and Indiana, 1830–60 (about 500).
2. From the Lower Rhine to Germantown, Pa., 1683–1705 (about 100).
3. From Alsace, Palatinate, and elsewhere to France, Bavaria, and Hesse after 1700; to Galicia and Volhynia, 1784–85; to Pennsylvania after 1700; to Ohio, Indiana, Illinois, and Ontario, 1815–80 (about 3,000).
4. From Galicia and Volhynia to Kansas and South Dakota, 1875–80 (about 400).
5. From U.S.A. to Ontario, 1786–1840 (about 2,000); to Saskatchewan and Alberta in the early 1900s (several hundred); to Ontario, British Columbia, and Paraguay in the 1960s.

II. DUTCH-GERMAN MIGRATIONS

About 55,000 Dutch-North German Mennonites crossed the Atlantic to North or South America over a period of 100 years. The total dispersion of the Dutch can be summarized as follows:

1. From Holland to Prussia beginning in 1530; to Pennsylvania in 1683.
2. From Prussia to Russia, 1789–1870 (about 8,000 persons); to Canada and Uruguay after 1947.
3. From U.S.S.R. to U.S.A., Canada, and Palestine in 1873–84 (about 18,000); to Canada in 1920s (21,000); to Paraguay and Brazil in early 1930s (about 4,000); to Canada and South America via Western Europe after 1943 (about 12,000); to Canada and West Germany in the 1970s (about 6,000).
4. Within U.S.S.R.: to Crimea, Caucasus, Siberia, and Central Asia, 1850–1914; to northern Russia and Siberia, 1930s; to Central Asia, the Urals, the north, 1940s.
5. From U.S.A. to Canada around 1900 and again in 1918.
6. From Canada to Mexico in 1922 and again in 1948 (about 5,000); to Paraguay in 1927 and 1948 (about 2,000); to Bolivia in the 1960s (about 12,000).
7. From Paraguay to Bolivia, Germany, and Canada in the 1950s, 1960s, and 1970s.
8. From Mexico to Canada from the 1930s to the 1980s (about 5,000); to British Honduras (Belize) in 1950s (several hundred); to Bolivia in 1960s to 1980s (about 8,000).

Source: Updated from Frank Epp 1978.

Migration within the confines of Switzerland was diffuse and gradual. As the movement won adherents in the various cantons, small congregations emerged, so that expansion in the first several years resulted largely from missionary activity. "With fiery zeal [Mennonites] promoted the truth they recognized: recognition led to confusion, with the result that the movement expanded to such an extent that in a short time there were thriving congregations not only in such Swiss towns as Zurich, St. Gall, Bern, and Basel, but far beyond the Swiss borders, in the Tyrol and South Germany, and adjoining German-speaking lands" (Geiser 1959, 675).

But the eager evangelism was very quickly interrupted by ecclesiastical and political persecution. Anabaptists fled, especially from the cantons of Bern and Zurich, where the persecution was the most severe. Beginning in 1526, many Anabaptists emigrated into the Tyrol, and eventually many ended up in Moravia, where they experienced relative toleration for some years. The size of these migrations is not fully understood, but evidence suggests that "considerable numbers of families, sometimes flocks or a whole congregation," were included (H. Bender 1959b). The canton of Bern bears the dubious distinction of being the harshest and the most tenacious in its persecution of Anabaptists. It continued to harass Anabaptists until 1820. In 1660 a major effort was made to deport all of the unrecanting Anabaptists, with the aid of "Anabaptist hunters" and many of those who had fled to the Juras finally capitulated and left for the north.

As is implied above, not all Anabaptists fled Switzerland because of the early persecution; many became "evasive" and retreated into the most inaccessible hinterlands where the authorities or "Anabaptist hunters" would be discouraged from pursuing and finding them. For this reason, and because the Catholic prince-bishop of Basel, under whose jurisdiction the Bernese Jura belonged, was more lenient than authorities of the Reformed church (Neff 1955a), the Bernese Jura became a major refuge. A modest number of Mennonite families have remained in the Juras to this day. More families, however, continued migrating into the southern Alsace, while others continued down the Rhine toward the Palatinate beginning in 1655 and went as far as Zweibrücken. In 1711 some even reached Holland.

The movements of these early Anabaptists was thus occasioned by a very complex mixture of evangelistic effort and escape from persecution, and it is difficult to give one motive or the other preeminence as the cause. Among the leaders, evangelism and nurturing the scattered flocks were obviously the greater sources of motivation, but for the rank and file, persecution may have been the predominant force.

In the meantime the South German and Austrian branch of the Anabaptist movement had emerged in the Tyrol and in South Germany in 1526–39 under the leadership of Hans Denck, Balthasar Hubmaier, Jacob Hutter, Hans Hut, and others. Spurred by the preaching of these leaders, small congregations began to emerge in cities such as Augsburg, Nuremberg, Ulm, and Nikolsburg. Because of the violent persecution mounted against them, some of these Anabaptists finally migrated to Moravia and began to settle there, particularly in Nikolsburg. It was they who in turn offered asylum to the Swiss refugees referred to above. Since the Hutterites provided hospitality, many of the Swiss Anabaptists fleeing to Moravia also became Hutterites; hence, the many Swiss names in Hutterite communities. Although the number of refugees is not known, Hostetler states that "the incoming refugees were so numerous that it was impossible to adequately house and feed them" (J. A. Hostetler 1974, 18).

Recent research is indicating an increasing presence of Anabaptists in central and northern Germany, especially in the Hesse, Westphalian, and lower Rhine areas. Although there were local skirmishes pointing to an Anabaptist-like protest, the movement got much of its impetus from missionaries who helped focus the protests, such as Melchior Hoffman, who had come from Strasbourg earlier. There is little evidence, therefore, of Anabaptist-Mennonite migrations from southern Germany or Switzerland; the Dutch–North German movement was largely of the homegrown variety. The Münster Rebellion was the consequence of a substantial migration of early Anabaptists from Amsterdam and Friesland, but it was soon dispersed, so that it does not figure much in later Anabaptist developments (Krahn 1968).

In 1712 the Mennonites were officially expelled from Alsace by Louis XIV; from then on there was a constant migration to the interior of France, as well as into Hesse in Germany, but some Mennonites managed to stay for many generations more (Séguy 1977). The Mennonites who had settled in the Palatinate moved into South Germany, including Württemberg, Franconia, and Bavaria. Others moved from Alsace and the Palatinate to Galicia between 1784 and 1785; still others moved to Volhynia. Anabaptists had been in most of these areas before, but the bitter persecution had forced them to flee or recant (see Map 1.1).

The greatest migration of Swiss Mennonites, however, began in 1683 and lasted for over two hundred years. Beginning with refugees from

Bern, who had stopped off in Holland, this migration represented a major relocation of Mennonites, one which had great significance for their future and has particular significance for this story (see Map 2.1). Though there are not even estimates available as to the number of participants in the earlier migrations, the latter movements, especially to America, are more easily described. The noted historian Harold S. Bender believed that a total of eight thousand Anabaptist Mennonites migrated to America between 1683 and 1883 (1957c, 686). From these initial American settlements came further migrations into new areas of America; they are noted in Table 2.1. We turn now to the other major source of Mennonite migration.

The Dutch and North Germans

Although the Dutch Anabaptist story officially begins a few years later than the Swiss, with the preaching of Melchior Hoffman in 1530 the Netherlands migration patterns are very similar to the Swiss. Anabaptist congregations existed in Amsterdam and surrounding areas as early as 1530 with religious unrest at fever pitch. One of the most celebrated events in Anabaptist-Mennonite history, the Münster Rebellion, had its origins in Amsterdam with the baptism of Volkertsz Trypmaker, a disciple of Hoffman. Hoffman's chiliastic tendencies, coupled with the radicalism of Amsterdam Anabaptists, caused some of the more radical Anabaptists—Jan Matthys, Jan van Leiden, and Jacob van Campen— to lead a migration to Münster to establish the "New Jerusalem" there. Münster had already become a center for revolt and reformation by 1528, with one reformist wing Lutheran in orientation, and the other sacramentarian; the latter became Anabaptist in sympathy. The Münster rebellion involved the formation of a communistic society, in which God would establish his kingdom on earth. The kingdom lasted for two years, and was, as we have seen, finally suppressed and destroyed with brutal carnage and warfare by a coalition of Lutheran and Catholic bishops and princes.

Anabaptist leaders and missionaries, forced to look for refuge, migrated to settle wherever they could. The early Anabaptists from Flanders fled to the northern province of the Low Countries soon after 1530. Menno Simons and other leaders fled to German East Friesland; others fled to Schleswig-Holstein in North Germany. Soon after 1530 Anabaptists were known to have arrived in the Vistula Delta area, including Danzig and the Marienburg sectors. With the settlement in the Danzig-Elbing-Marienburg triangle—which resulted in a continuous commu-

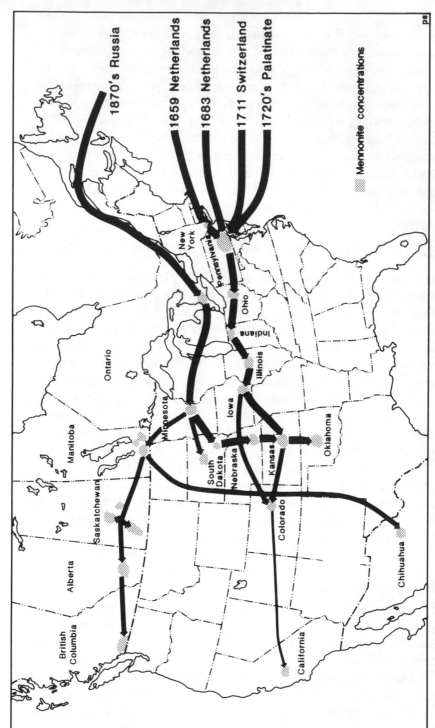

MAP 2.1   Mennonite Migrations to and within North America. Map drawn by Pamela Schaus.

18

nity until World War II—the stage was set for the later major migration to Russia that began in 1789. Although a "commonwealth" form of settlement was already in its early stages in Prussia, it was the migration to Russia which opened wide the opportunity for this type of society. The much later migration of Mennonites from Russia to America, beginning in 1874, presents a development parallel to the Swiss migrations (See Map 2.1).

The migrations of the Russian Mennonites were and have been more extensive than the Swiss, especially in the degree of continuance as well as in the number of people leaving and returning. Thus, between the Russian Mennonite settlements in the United States and Canada there has been a constant moving to and fro, from one country to the other. The Russian Mennonite migration to Latin America from Canada and the United States also has been characterized by a constant return of people to Canada; some estimates indicate that up to one-fourth of the migrational stream in one direction later returned to the point of origin. Patterns of migration have become firmly entrenched in both streams of Mennonites. In fact, one could say that many, if not all, Mennonite families have a history of migration in their not too distant past. This is especially true with respect to internal migrations.

Internal migration refers to the movement of a group to some frontier within a country. Since Mennonites have been basically farmers, internal migrations were often motivated in search of new lands. These migrations have been based mainly on the extension of subgroupings, that is, of family or conference groups. Thus, the migration of major blocks of Mennonites to new areas in Russia were composed of either Kleine Gemeinde, Mennonite Brethren, or Kirchliche, although there was sometimes a mixture of migrants. In Canada and the United States, though there were myriad individual family migrations, westward migrations were mainly of the conference membership types.

An Analysis of Mennonite Migrations

The migration of Mennonites, both externally and internally, has probably been more extensive and complex than that of almost any other religious-ethnic group. These migrations—whether caused by religious, political, or economic factors or by a combination of all three—have had a profound impact on the nature of Mennonite society. Unfortunately, very little information is available on this topic, as little research has been done. However, E. K. Francis, a Jesuit and an authori-

Menno Simons, after whom Mennonites were named, according to the conception of artist Jan Luyken. *Martyrs' Mirror*, 1685.

The *City of Richmond*, one of the many ships that carried Mennonite refugees to North America and other parts of the world in the nineteenth century. Photograph by John Thut, courtesy of *Mennonite Life*.

ty on Mennonite society, has made migration a keystone of his theory of ethnic formation, so it is imperative that the Francis theory be included in our analysis.[1]

After describing the history of the Russian Mennonites in Russia and their subsequent migration to Manitoba, Francis concludes: "The study of the Manitoba Mennonites has provided us with the object lesson of how primary ethnic groups may emerge and maintain themselves in an alien environment. The principal condition for the formation was apparently the effective segregation of a relatively large population from its social environment. The motivation for the withdrawal was religious" (Francis 1976, 183).

Francis maintains that the Mennonites, whose ethnic coherence was first formed by religious faith, forged the ethnic group proper by migration. For when a primary group is transferred from the parent society (its original home) to the host society, the differences become even more marked, "so that the population transferred can be readily identified with the parent rather than the host society" (ibid., 169). The lynchpin in this idea is the next sentence: "After their transfer they will still remain firmly embedded . . . in a web of familiar social relationships" (169). Thus it is that the *religious persecution* which creates the sense of cohesion also results in migration; in turn, migration tends to seal the formation of an ethnic group because the relationship of the group with the new host society becomes one of unfamiliar and strange environments (169). The ethno-religious group encounters the following social factors, which affect its relations with the larger society:

1. A status of special privilege. This is usually the first prerequisite or condition for migration to a given area. Certainly, it has been the case for Mennonites.
2. Unfamiliarity and strangeness with respect to the culture of the host society. Unfamiliarity strengthens the importance and salience of the familiar within the group and sacralizes these traits.
3. Cultural and social differences. These become symbolic bearers of distinctiveness and uniqueness as well as of the unity of the group.
4. A spatially segregated migrating group. Distance interferes with the normal rate of interaction with members of the host society and thereby intensifies the emergence of in-group language, symbols, meanings, sentiments, and other private elements.
5. A nationalization process in the host nation. Resistance to assimilation can start the migration process all over again and further entrench ethnic group solidarity. If the nation leaves the religio-ethnic group free to prosper, it will entrench itself as well, as is

illustrated by the Mennonite settlements in Paraguay (Francis 1976, 168—71).

This process has operated in similar fashion for subgroups of Mennonites who have separated from larger Mennonite groups and departed for other lands, especially since the Prussian Mennonite emigration to Russia in 1789. Thus, migration serves to provide the cohesion for a splinter group to form a new identity. The Amish schism is a case in point. Many attempts have been made to explain their reasons for what one writer called a "family squabble" (J. A. Hostetler 1980, 33). Mennonite historians have commonly assumed that the intransigence and haughtiness of Jakob Ammann precipitated the split of the group (later called Amish) from the main body of Mennonites in Alsace. However, John A. Hostetler argues that it was the differing conditions among the Alsatian Mennonites that were really at the bottom of this schismatic movement: "The Alsatian Mennonites, that is, the Amish, migrants of Swiss background, were experiencing tensions that were different from those they had known in Switzerland. . . . The Alsatian immigrants and their children appeared to have been a well integrated social and self-contained religious community" (ibid., 40).

The process of migration can create conditions in which the original factors that led to the creation of religious movements can become confused with peripheral or even extraneous characteristics. Thus, the web of social relationships is strengthened and may even become sacralized to the point where the group's own survival becomes more important than its original objectives and beliefs.[2] Likewise, the migration itself can serve as a cause of or as a support of schism and division in a religious group. Migration as a cause is illustrated by the Amish division. Migration as the support of a schism is illustrated by the Sommerfelder migration to Paraguay from Manitoba. The more conservative Sommerfelder were unable to convince the rest of the Sommerfelder of the righteousness of their cause, so the migration served to prove as well as to enact the basis for eventual separation (M. Friesen 1977, 1987). Schism is discussed more fully in Chapter 15.

Expansion and Growth of the Mennonite Movement

The Anabaptist-Mennonite movement has spread and grown in a remarkable fashion from its earliest appearance in Zurich in 1525. It was indeed an acorn that produced the oak. And yet, in comparison to many other church groups, such as the Mormons or the Baptists, it has grown hardly at all. It is a very small oak. In fact, the number of Dutch

Mennonites has actually declined in the last two hundred years, and as a whole, the Mennonite church has been growing only slowly (see Table 2.2).[3]

Growth by Evangelism

Precise population figures for the Mennonite tradition during the four centuries since its inception are not available. The early days of the

TABLE 2.2 Mennonite and Brethren in Christ World Membership, 1986

	Membership	Organized bodies
AFRICA	136,930	14
Angola	300	1
Burkina Faso	34	1
Ethiopia	7,200	1
Ghana	854	1
Kenya	2,700	1
Nigeria	5,000	1
Somalia	100[a]	1
Tanzania	14,441	2
Zaire	92,583	3
Zambia	6,000	1
Zimbabwe	7,718	1
ASIA	114,828	17
Hong Kong	40	1
India	52,837	6
Indonesia	55,159	2
Japan	2,942	5
Philippines	2,500	1
Taiwan	1,200	1
Vietnam	150[a]	1
AUSTRALIA	26	1
CARIBBEAN, CENTRAL & SOUTH AMERICA	81,782	72
Argentina	1,516	2
Belize	2,829	6
Bolivia	7,121	6
Brazil	5,064	4
Colombia	2,595	2
Costa Rica	1,026	2
Cuba	35	1
Dominican Republic	1,922	2
Ecuador	80	1
El Salvador	185	2

Source: Mennonite Yearbook 1988–89.
  [a]Membership estimated.

movement boasted a large membership spread across many congregations. Clasen states that there were congregations with as many as 360 members, such as that at Waldhut, Germany, in 1525 (Clasen 1972, 62). Medium-size congregations—by which Classen presumably means fewer than a hundred members—became the norm soon after the movement stabilized. There were many such congregations in South Germany and Switzerland. Although Clasen does not provide figures for

	Membership	Organized bodies
Guatemala	3,018	4
Haiti	975	3
Honduras	2,870	2
Jamaica	390	1
Mexico	31,879	9
Nicaragua	1,822	3
Panama	400	1
Paraguay	15,953	15
Peru	75	1
Puerto Rico	900	1
Trinidad/Tobago	85	1
Uruguay	942	3
Venezuela	100	1
EUROPE	92,500	20
Austria	1,150	1
Belgium	85	1
England	30	1
Federal Republic of Germany	10,975	4
France	2,000	1
German Democratic Republic	244	1
Ireland	10	1
Italy	88	1
Luxembourg	105	1
Netherlands	20,000	1
Spain	63	2
Switzerland	2,750	1
U.S.S.R.	55,000[a]	4
NORTH AMERICA	347,700	21
Canada	104,033	9
United States	243,667	12
WORLDWIDE	773,766	145

North Germany or the Lowlands, the situation there would probably have been much the same. Clasen believes that "most Anabaptist . . . congregations in the second half of the sixteenth century did not exceed thirty or forty members" (63).

Clasen does present some statistics for the spread of Anabaptism in central Europe between 1525 and 1618. Between 1525 and 1529, there were 3,579 new converts to the faith; between 1530 and 1549, there were 3,667 additions; and between 1550 and 1618, 3,767 new converts were added (Clasen, 300). Thus a total of 11,013 Anabaptists had joined the movement during that period in South Germany and Switzerland. This is not a total picture, of course, because Clasen did not obtain figures for the Low Countries, North Germany, the Vistula Delta, and other areas where Anabaptists spread. Nor is this a total tabulation for the areas Clasen studied, since records would not have been available for all the Mennonite groups which emerged during that time period and within the geographical limits that he applies. Since no other statistics are yet available for the rest of Europe, we can only speculate on the population totals for the various time periods. According to the best information, the movement declined in fervor owing to persecution after 1550.

Mennonite society might well have reached a total of 20,000 during the first few years, then declined, possibly, to as few as 10,000. By the end of the sixteenth century, the movement had probably recovered to the 20,000 mark. The quiescent period, from the latter sixteenth century to the beginning of the twentieth century, literally brought expansion by evangelism to a halt. The revived missionary activity of the Germanic Mennonites took the form of officially organized missionary work, beginning in Indonesia in 1851 and in India in 1890 and soon spreading to other regions of the world (see Table 14.1). The church which was established in the foreign countries was at first very closely controlled by the mission boards, but is now developing national autonomy. A major context for the recent establishment of missions has been the relief and service work done around the world by Mennonites since 1920. This will be expanded upon in subsequent chapters.

Biological Growth

After the initial period of intense persecution, the Mennonite movement began a slow general increase because of biological reproduction. After slowly gaining a foothold in Alsace, the Palatinate, North Germany, Holland, Moravia, and other areas, the movement expanded. By the end of the seventeenth century, Mennonites had already spread to America and Russia, and it is safe to say that the movement was on the increase, by birth, if not by evangelism.

After 1600 there must have been continual growth, for by 1900, there were probably as many as 150,000 Mennonites worldwide. The *Mennonite Yearbook* for 1905, reporting for only one major stream of Mennonites in North America, lists 89,377 members even without the four conferences which declined to provide numbers; these four might have accounted for at least an additional 10,000 members.

Mennonites have always had a high reproductive rate: having many children was always a basic value. This is true even today among the more conservative Mennonite families. Some groups, like the Hutterites and the Old Colony, are near the top of any known reproductive rates.[4] In fact, the Hutterites are described as having "a record fertility in all but the 15–19-year-old groups" when compared with figures in the *United Nations Demographic Yearbook* (Eaton and Mayer 1954, 16). Eaton and Mayer continue: "Only 39% as many Hutterite babies would have been born if the Hutterites in 1950 had had age-specific birthrates similar to those of the United States in general" (19).

Mennonite families have been a central element in the fabric of Mennonite congregations, as will be pointed out below; the reproductive process has assured the continuance of both. There is no specific teaching on the having of children, other than the traditional one used by all conservative biblical communions: "Be fruitful and multiply and replenish the earth." It is generally assumed that with the focus on the Mennonite family and community, the emphasis on outreach is undermined (see Chapter 17). Mennonites influenced by modern fundamentalism especially take this position. Thus, many of the more evangelical members of Mennonite churches have criticized the large families and the dependence on reproduction for growth in church membership. Instead, they have stressed outreach to the "unsaved" or the "unchurched."

This lack of concern for evangelism can explain in part the heavy emphasis on conversions and revival work among the young people, which often forces the age at conversion to move dangerously close to what could be called infant baptism. In one research effort, it became clear that in lieu of being able to do mission work among the "heathen," the accepted alternative for certain Mennonite groups was to see the evangelizing of their own offspring as obedience to the great commandment. This, in turn, could feed the justification for having many children (C. Redekop 1984b).

The increasing growth rate toward the end of the nineteenth century must have been the result of both population growth and of missionary work. Table 2.2 for world membership indicates the many lands which now have Mennonites. In some of these countries the increase in Mennonites is a result of missionary work; in others, increases are the result of migrations and internal growth. However, even the missionary-minded Mennonites have expanded their numbers through population increase, so that the importance of the two factors is almost identical for all groups. In 1984, the World Conference *Handbook* listed a total of 730,000 baptized members; it is reasonable to multiply this figure by 2 to get a picture of the entire Mennonite family.

Analysis

The growth of Mennonite society has been uneven. The Hutterites have survived only through reproduction, since they do not practice any evangelism. Among other conservative groups, such as the Old Order Amish, the same tendency has been present. But here and there a new member has joined the group. The more progressive Mennonites have engaged in aggressive mission work and consequently have gained a considerable number of converts. Nevertheless, it is generally true that for church growth Mennonites have depended more on reproduction than on missions, whereas other groups, such as the Mormons, have obviously grown basically by outreach, although their birthrates have helped as well.

Even though some of the major branches of the Mennonite church have had a strong missionary thrust, scholars have long contended that the lack of growth in general among Mennonites is caused by the many defections of Mennonite members from congregations.[5] By contrast, the Hutterite defection rate is very low and relatively easy to determine. John A. Hostetler suggests that it is less than 2 percent for the total Hutterite society (1974, 273). As a result, the Hutterites are the fastest growing group among the Mennonites. The Amish have also grown more rapidly than the Mennonites as a whole, since defection is not as rapid nor as widespread. Defection is highest among those groups which have become evangelical.

In view of the high rate of church growth among the Hutterites and the Amish—a result of large families and low rates of defection—it is plausible to hypothesize that the relatively slow growth rate in "progressive" Mennonite congregations is the direct result of high rates of defection. That is, the reason that Mennonite society (apart from the

Hutterites, Amish, and Old Colony) has grown very slowly is that a majority of the offspring do not remain Mennonites, but rather, join other denominations or leave religious institutions early.

This area has not been adequately studied, but a new source of data is becoming available: a rash of genealogies. These usually provide the denominational affiliation of all the descendants of the original Mennonite family. In one such genealogy, no doubt quite representative, over one-half of the offspring of Mennonite grandparents no longer belonged to the Mennonite faith (F. Redekop 1984). This fact is probably indicative of the sociological pressures on minorities.[6]

The expansion of the Mennonite population to most parts of the globe is seen, therefore, as a result of the triple forces of migration, biological growth, and evangelism. The worldwide dissemination of the *non-Germanic sectors* of Mennonitism, however, is almost exclusively the result of evangelism by Mennonite missionaries and church workers, beginning with the first missionaries sent out by the Dutch Mennonites in 1847 (Shenk 1978). Hence, today, from a global perspective, the majority of Mennonites are non-Germanic and non-Caucasian. This means that the sociology of Mennonites has a bipolar dimension which cannot be comprehended in one paradigm. That is to say, this book self-consciously deals with Mennonites as though they were only Germanic; it would be impossible to include the non-Germanic parts of the Mennonite family using the same social conceptualization (see Chapter 3).

Mennonite polity has solved the problem of conceptualizing the missionary origins of non-Germanic, nonmigrating Mennonitism by referring to the Germanic Mennonites as *traditional* or *ethnic Mennonites,* while the rest are called *missionary churches, missionary Anabaptists,* or simply *nonethnic-Mennonites.* All of these terms are inadequate, but they do identify an obvious distinction which creates a very clear although muted line between the two groups.

It has often been stated that the Mennonites turned inward because of persecution; hence, they lost their missionary fervor. Some have speculated also that the high rate of reproduction among Mennonites has been a response to the threat of extinction. This is not just idle theory; it is known that many overpopulated nations have maintained high birthrates as an assurance of future survival. Among Mennonites the threat against survival is no longer valid, but once a value has become entrenched, the practice may continue long after its original purpose has been fulfilled.

Chapter Three

The Differentiation of the Mennonite Family of Believers

Upon becoming more knowledgeable about Mennonites, most persons will experience the shattering of the image of a unified traditional society. It is appropriate to develop a clear picture of the entire "rainbow" of Mennonite groups early in our analysis, so that the reader can develop a general picture of the Mennonite society and ethos (see Chart 3.1). Division and schism, specifically, are discussed in Chapters 4 and 15, and are referred to in many places in the text.

The Germanic/Non-Germanic Differentiation

A distinction that is becoming increasingly important among Mennonites themselves is that between "birthright" Mennonites (to borrow a phrase from the Quakers) and converts, or the "convinced," as the Quakers would say.[1] The birthright, or Germanic, Mennonite stream—until recently considered the central stream—includes those Mennonites who derive their spiritual, ideological, and biological ancestry from Swiss, German, Alsatian, Moravian, Dutch, Prussian, and Russian origins.

Even though the early Anabaptists were active missionaries, their converts were within the German-Dutch culture, and hence the identity of Mennonites early became synonymous with German-Dutch culture and language. The consequent identification of Germanic language and culture—whether German, Pennsylvania Dutch, or Low German—with Anabaptist-Mennonite faith has produced a great and often acrimonious debate. Many Mennonites, especially those influenced by modern fundamentalism and evangelicalism,[2] have accused the Mennonite church of identifying Christianity with Germanic culture. The Germanic subcultural Mennonitism which has emerged has wrestled with the "in-group" ethos which suggests that non-Germanic converts can never become full-fledged members of the Mennonite family. Thus, unless one came from German parentage and was reared on the heritage of German preaching and Bible reading, enhanced by the sacred mythology of the martyrs, especially as portrayed by the *Martelaarspiegel (Martyrs' Mirror)*, one somehow could never fully identify with the Anabaptist-Mennonite heritage.

The non-Germanic stream of Anabaptist-Mennonites, on the other hand, are those members who have joined the society because of a personal conviction of the rightness of the Anabaptist theology and ethics, but only in the first generation. The division between the Germanic and non-Germanic is so sharp that a knowledgeable Mennonite can tell immediately by a surname alone whether a Mennonite is a birthright or convinced member. The numerous autobiographies that have been written by these converts almost without exception point to the attractiveness of the lifestyle of the Anabaptist theology and ethics, but are often sharply critical of the exclusivity of the Mennonite "family." The second-generation non-Germanic Mennonitism now beginning to emerge will increasingly become a problem.

Worldwide, non-Germanic Mennonites are now in the majority, a direct result of missions and service work around the world (Table 2.2). The international relief and service work of the Mennonite Central Committee has resulted in extensive foundings of new congregations, in Indonesia, Africa, South America, and even Europe. Often, the Mennonite mission boards have continued a work which had been started by MCC. In other cases, such as India, and Tanzania, missions were established in a deliberate way.

Germanic and non-Germanic congregations often exist side by side, and the integration process has taken long, and is not yet complete. Thus, in cities like Chicago, there are Germanic (birthright), Hispanic, black, Chinese, Vietnamese, and other congregations, but only rarely

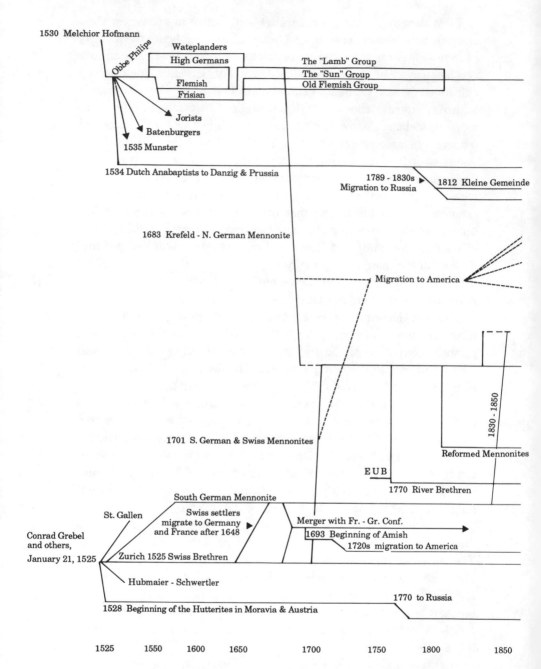

CHART 3.1 The Anabaptist-Mennonite Family Tree
Source: Expanded and revised from C. J. Dyck, *An Introduction to Mennonite History*
(Scottdale, Pa.: Herald Press, 1967).
Note: Vertical lines denote schisms or reunification; diagonal lines denote migration.

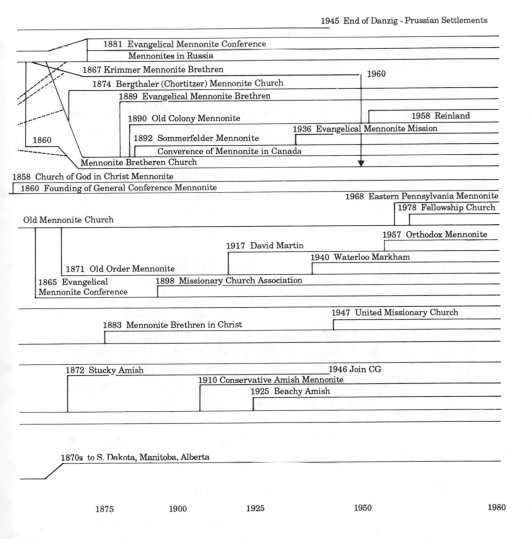

1811 Dutch Mennonite Conference (ADS)

1945 End of Danzig - Prussian Settlements

1881 Evangelical Mennonite Conference

Mennonites in Russia

1867 Krimmer Mennonite Brethren

1960

1874 Bergthaler (Chortitzer) Mennonite Church

1889 Evangelical Mennonite Brethren

1890 Old Colony Mennonite

1958 Reinland

1936 Evangelical Mennonite Mission

1860

1892 Sommerfelder Mennonite

Converence of Mennonite in Canada

Mennonite Bretheren Church

1858 Church of God in Christ Mennonite

1860 Founding of General Conference Mennonite

1968 Eastern Pennsylvania Mennonite

1978 Fellowship Church

Old Mennonite Church

1957 Orthodox Mennonite

1917 David Martin

1940 Waterloo Markham

1871 Old Order Mennonite

1898 Missionary Church Association

1865 Evangelical
Mennonite Conference

1947 United Missionary Church

1883 Mennonite Brethren in Christ

1872 Stucky Amish

1946 Join CG

1910 Conservative Amish Mennonite

1925 Beachy Amish

1870s to S. Dakota, Manitoba, Alberta

1875   1900   1925   1950   1980

have Hispanics, for example, joined a Germanic Mennonite church. In Latin America, as in Brazil or Paraguay, there are Germanic and indigenous congregations in the same areas, but there is little interaction between them. Intermarriage, for example, is almost nonexistent. Theologically and ecclesiastically, there are no reasons for the segregation, but sociologically of course, there are good reasons for the divisions. The missiologists and church leaders publicly deplore these conditions, but in practice there is little that can be done, short of letting the long process of assimilation take its course.

The Swiss-Dutch Differentiation

General theory and parlance assumes that there were two main streams of Germanic Anabaptism—the Swiss and the Dutch. Earlier scholarship seemed to support this view, but recent research maintains that there was a polygenetic birth of Anabaptism, emerging at many centers in Europe including Italy and France (Stayer, Packull, and Depperman 1975), which contributed to a multifaceted Anabaptism.

Even though the latter view is clearly more correct, it is nevertheless true that two "ethoses" have subsequently emerged, and there are some clearly observable differences between them. Little empirical research exists, but recent scholars such as Leonard Gross (from the Swiss branch) and Juhnke (from the Dutch) insist that there are clearly two different orientations toward a number of points. The Swiss are allegedly defined by the Schleitheim Confession, which stressed a dualism and separation from the world, whereas the Dutch followers of Menno are more rationalistic and "high-church" in their policy (L. Gross 1986; Juhnke 1988). Thus, the Swiss Mennonite stream has been more traditional, conservative, and rural in its life than the Dutch stream. For example, the more liberal Dutch stream has been much more prone to be involved in politics than the Swiss (as described in Chapter 13). The same liberal and conservative tendencies obtain for education, which is discussed in Chapter 11. The differences and similarities between the Swiss and Dutch branches will be highlighted in the following chapters.

But the overarching awareness of being "brothers under the skin" has remained firm, as is underscored by the way in which the two branches have cooperated in most institutional and social situations where it was reasonable to do so. Further, it is interesting that the Swiss branch has used basically Dutch confessions of faith (especially the Dortrecht Confession) in their theological life (Neff 1955b, 682ff.).

Recent expert analysis unequivocally maintains that the two streams are basically part of the same source—the Anabaptist.

The Specific Mennonite Groups

Some terminological analysis is pertinent here. Mennonite scholars do not consider the Mennonite church a denomination, even though it is often referred to that way. Anabaptism has increasingly been considered as neither Catholic nor Protestant (Klaassen 1981b), and must be seen as part of the "free church tradition" (Durnbaugh 1968) or of the Radical Reformation (Williams 1962). Mennonites refer to themselves normally by using the term "Mennonite church," or "General Conference Mennonite Church," and so on. Even though Mennonites use the term *denomination,* it is inappropriate, since it refers to sectors and divisions of Protestantism in America, and it is clear that Anabaptism experienced as much conflict with—and persecution from—Protestants as Catholics (Francis 1976, 259–60; R. Friedmann 1955).[3]

Non-Mennonites to this day refer to the Mennonites as a sect, a designation resisted by Mennonites themselves. Nevertheless, this pejorative term has stuck to the group since the Reformation and in fact is more correct than *denomination* for numerous reasons: (1) The sectarian designation has served to remind Mennonites of their historical position as a minority—a not altogether useless technique for encouraging the asking of questions about origins, purpose, and future. (2) As Troeltsch so adamantly maintains, the Anabaptist-Mennonite movement was a sectarian protest movement against the established church in Europe and England, both Roman Catholic and Protestant. (3) Most important, the "sect" type of church represented the voluntary disciplined brotherhood concept, directly in conflict with the tendency toward lowest-common-denominator belief typical of denominationalization in America (Francis 1955; Payne 1957; R. Friedmann, 1955). Wach most clearly stated the nature of the Anabaptist nondenominational sect as "a third type of . . . Christian fellowship" which is "characterized by a three-fold protest," against Roman, reformed, and denominations, against the identity of ecclesia and church, and against external tradition (Wach 1946, 16–17).

There are three major groups of Anabaptist-Mennonites in the Germanic tradition—Hutterites, Amish, and Mennonites.

Because of their uncompromising stance regarding the communality of property, the Hutterites very soon began to believe they were totally correct and to develop an in-group solidarity which tended to cut off interaction with the other Anabaptist-Mennonite groups. The Hutterite branch, numbering about 25,000 persons today, is basically distinguished from the other Mennonite branches by several general traits or emphases: (1) a staunch belief in the biblical teaching of absolute community of goods; (2) an agriculturally based life; (3) life in isolated and segregated communities; (4) little outreach to the world beyond the colonies in activities such as relief, service, or missions; and (5) a very friendly people, aggressively missionary in inviting all non-Hutterites to join their colonies and thus fulfill Christ's commands (J. A. Hostetler 1974; Peter 1987).

The Hutterite way of life has threatened the surrounding society almost without exception, and provinces and states have on occasion attempted to pass laws to restrict their expansion and/or activities (Peter 1987). Normally human rights organizations have come to their aid in cases of human rights violations. Numerous books, pamphlets, TV and radio programs, and films have been produced to interpret the Hutterite way, and it seems increasingly to attract people who are looking for an alternative to contemporary industrial and individualistic society (J. A. Hostetler 1974).

The Hutterites are unique in the Mennonite family for their achievement of unity and avoidance of schism. There have been a few minor divisions involving dissident family groups, one group linking up with a Hungarian communal group in Ontario led by Julius Kubbasek in the 1940s. Another group left in 1950 to form the Forest River colony in North Dakota, which, composed of dissident families, established contacts with the Society of Brothers.

The Society of Brothers was founded in 1922 by Eberhard Arnold, who came to a religious conviction very similar to the Hutterites and succeeded in establishing a "Bruderhof" at Neuhof, near Fulda, Germany, in 1926. Arnold was ordained a Hutterite elder in Alberta in 1930. The attempt to merge the German-culture "New Hutterites" with the "old Hutterites" was beset with difficulties, so that by 1955 there was a total break with the Hutterites.[4] After years of troubled attempts to integrate the two groups, the Society of Brothers and Hutterites eventually agreed in 1974 on a form of unity which respects the cultural heritage and the differences of each group, but which is based on fundamental agreement on the basics of the Christian commitment to community of goods (J. A. Hostetler 1974, 280–83; P. Gross 1978, 352–58).

Hutterites now reside in North America and England, with several colonies in Washington State, more in Montana and South Dakota, several in North Dakota, and the majority in Alberta, Saskatchewan, and Manitoba. In 1974, there were a total of 229 colonies, with a total of 21,521 persons (J. A. Hostetler 1974). By 1984, there were 324 colonies, and a total of 13,201 baptized members (P. Kraybill 1984).

The Amish

There is really little justification for considering the Amish a separate group, since they derive from the Swiss Mennonite group and are not substantially different from the other more conservative groupings in the Mennonite family. But their deletion of the term *Mennonite* in their name and their extreme stress on separation from the world and from other Christians, including other Mennonites, has served to define them as a separate stream.

Amish history is one of the most complex and mystifying in Mennonitism and possibly in Christendom, largely because of the emphases on purity and separation which were the causes for the original split. Originating in 1693 over the issue of strict avoidance of those excommunicated for their faith, the Amish Mennonites, as they were then called, embarked upon a tumultous time of migrations, mutual incriminations for not being strict enough, and divisions. Amish congregations from Switzerland migrated to Alsace, South Germany (basically the Palatinate), Russia (Volhynia), and Holland. Their subsequent migrations to North America and later even to Central and South America is so varied and complex as to defy comprehension.

The "Old Order Amish" is the American term for the most conservative and largest segment of the Amish Mennonite stream. They are also known as the "House Amish," since they worship in private homes. They are distinguished, as Hostetler succinctly states it, by "their nonconformist attitudes and resistance to social change, and characterized by worship in private homes, a strictly rural way of life, a horse-and-buggy culture, the use of a dialect of the German language, and 'plain' dress resembling that of European peoples two centuries ago" (J. A. Hostetler 1959, 43). The Old Order Amish have over 526 church districts, located in more than sixty geographic areas of the United States and Canada, with scattered settlements in a few Latin

American Countries. Ohio has the largest number of Old Order Amish today, with Pennsylvania in second place (J. A. Hostetler 1980).

Completely rural in structure, Amish society centers on settlements, each of which consists of "Amish families living in a contiguous relationship, that is households that are in proximity to one another" (ibid., 93). Every settlement has at least one district, which is "a congregation, a ceremonial unit . . . the size . . . determined by the number of people who can be accommodated for the preaching service in one farm dwelling" (95).

While one-third of the original Amish continued in the "house-church" tradition, the rest developed into the "Church Amish," beginning about 1862–78, which finally merged with the "Old" Mennonites in the 1920s and are no longer identifiable today.

A more progressive group separated from the Old Order Amish around 1880 and became known as Amish Mennonites, consisting of the Eastern Amish Mennonite, Indiana-Michigan Amish Mennonite, and Western District Amish Mennonite Conferences (H. Bender 1955a, 97). These merged with the "Old" Mennonite Church as well. A group which could not accompany the "progressives" formed a new conference, known as the Conservative Amish Mennonite Conference, but a small group broke from this group because the Conservative Amish Mennonites were too liberal.

The Beachey Amish, begun as a "liberalizing" movement by an Amish bishop named Beachey, focused on softening the ban of the excommunicated. Later their adoption of Sunday schools also became an issue. In the meantime the Beachey Amish conference has become a creative and growing movement which has welcomed the growing number of Old Order Amish congregations who are desiring more liberal church life and process. In many areas the Beachey Amish are in the process of merging with the Old Mennonite Church. Numerous other smaller divisions and modernizing groups are present within the Amish tradition, but they are too minute to merit discussion here.

Because of the extreme stress on discipline and separation, the Old Order Amish have experienced continuing loss of members, congregations, and larger groups to more "liberal" groups. This "escalator" to more liberalism has in turn formed the basis for a great sense of loss within the Amish community and thus strained its relationships with the more "progressive" recipient groups. Amish leaders have been under great pressure to maintain discipline and hence risk membership losses while other groups in the Mennonite family can be faithful yet espouse a more liberated way of life (J. A. Hostetler 1980, 274ff.).

Mennonites constitute the largest of the Anabaptist-Mennonite branches, with members from both Swiss and Dutch roots. I will exclude the non-Germanic segments and focus basically on the Western world, especially North America, although Table 2.2 provides the general statistics for the world membership.

As shown in Chart 3.1, there are Germanic Mennonite conferences in the Netherlands, Germany, France, Switzerland, Luxembourg, North America, and South America. The Mennonites all but disappeared in Austria and Italy as a result of the earlier persecutions. There are also Mennonite conferences and churches with some Germanic roots in East Germany, Poland, and the Soviet Union. Present Mennonite World Conferences tend to bring representatives from all these countries, along with the non-Germanic congregations, together and unite the members through bonds of common history and faith. What is noteworthy about European Mennonite society is that there are fewer divisions in the family today: in Holland, for example, the Mennonites are organized in one conference. While Germany still contains two Mennonite conferences, the North and the South, and there are still some feelings of theological differences, there is a movement toward merger. Several new conferences of refugees from the Soviet Union are in the formative stages (P. Kraybill 1984).

The European Mennonites of Germanic origin represent a stable, entrenched, and institutionalized society which makes little effort to proselytize or serve human need, although in recent decades there has been a rebirth of interest and concern, especially in relief and service work in underdeveloped countries. European Mennonite relief and service organizations now cooperate with American relief and service organizations (ibid.).

In North America, the largest Mennonite group or conference is the "Old" Mennonite Church (MC), or simply "the Mennonite Church," as members refer to themselves. This designation, however, irritates members of other groups, who consider themselves no less members of "the Mennonite church." This conference traces its origins back to the Swiss Mennonite migrations, beginning in 1683, to Germantown, Pennsylvania. Today, it totals 145,320 attenders and 97,667 baptized members in United States and Canada (M. Yoder 1985, 311).

The Old Mennonite Church immigrants came mainly from the Palatinate (1707–56) or Switzerland (1710–56) and settled originally in Pennsylvania and Ohio. All other Old Mennonite groups have come from these two migrations. The church is basically derived from 70 percent Mennonites and 30 percent Amish (H. Bender 1957c, 611). The Old Mennonite Church can be described as congregational in structure, although there was a strong centralizing period, beginning around 1840, which placed authority in preachers, bishops, and conferences of bishops. Conservative in theology, it has taken a moderate stance toward separation from the world and church discipline. It has tended to remain rural, although parts of the church, especially in the East, have become urban and cosmopolitan, even while retaining a traditional conservatism and piety (MacMaster 1985).

The Old Mennonite Church has held to a stable course and developed a vast set of institutions and organizations to carry out its goals. It is the strongest partner in many inter-Mennonite organizations and dominates by sheer numbers in many ways. Members of this tradition are normally perceived as relatively low-key, but firm and strong in their faith.

Because of its moderate position in the gamut between liberalism and conservatism, the Old Mennonite Church has experienced a large number of schisms to the left *and* right in North America, including the following: Funkites in Franconia (1778), Reformed Mennonites in Lancaster (1812), Stauffer Mennonites in Lancaster (1845), Eastern District General Conference, or Oberholtzer division, in Franconia (1847), Church of God in Christ Mennonite, or Holdeman (1859), Old Order, or Wisler, in Indiana and Ohio (1871–72), Central Illinois, or Stucky, Amish (1871), Mennonite Brethren in Christ, or Brenneman division, in Indiana (1875). The Old Order Mennonites deserve separate mention because they resemble the Amish in almost every respect, including polity, church organization, and way of life, but they do not express any interest in relating to the Amish. There are a number of other "old-order" groups which have divided from the Old Mennonite Church and also from some of the more conservative groups mentioned above, but their numbers are very small and their reasons for division are almost trivial, often causing embarrassment to the larger Mennonite community (see Chart 3.1).

The second largest group of Mennonites, the General Conference Mennonite Church (GCMC) of North America, is a combination of Swiss and Dutch branches. The Mennonites in Russia, there known as the "Kirchliche" in distinction to the Mennonite Brethren (described below), migrated to North America beginning in 1874 and kept the names of their origins, such as Chortitza, or "Old Colony." However, the Oberholtzer division (Eastern District General Conference Mennonite Church), which had among its objectives the unification of all Mennonites in North America, appealed to the recent Russian Mennonite immigrants, and eventually most of the "Kirchliche" affiliated with the General Conference Mennonite Church. At present there are Canadian, U.S., and Latin American branches of the General Conference. The goal of action has always been "unity in essentials; liberty in nonessentials; and love in all things" (Kaufman 1956, 467).

With a mixture of Swiss and Dutch roots—never in the same proportion from place to place, and with only one root present in some areas—the General Conference Mennonite Church has a much more dynamic and mottled career than other Mennonite groups. Membership varies from conservative to more progressive, from pietist to fundamentalist and even rationalist. Very few schisms have emerged, since the General Conference has been strongly congregational in orientation, so that any Mennonite can find a congregation to his personal preference. The Canadian sector is probably more conservative, and reflects the more recent migrations of Mennonite refugees from Russia (1920s) and Germany (post–World War II) (Pannabecker, 1977).

Strongly ecumenical both with Mennonites and non-Mennonites, the General Conference Mennonite Church has developed a comparably strong institutional and social fabric, and participates as the second strongest member of the Mennonite family in worldwide relief, service, and missionary activities. In comparison to the membership of the Old Mennonite Church, the General Conference membership can be characterized as more individualistic, aggressive, and forthright. The geographical distribution of the GCMC extends from Pennsylvania to California, and from Ontario to British Columbia, with Kansas and Manitoba having the greatest concentrations of members.

The Dutch-Russian Mennonite stream has also contributed its quota of schisms. The first major one was the Kleinegemeinde ("the little congregation"), which broke from the Kirchliche in 1812 in Russia over the questions of restoring purity of life, discipline, humility, and nonconformity to the world. Since 1952 it has been called the Evangelical Mennonite Church (EMC) and is found mainly in Canada, the United States, and Mexico, with approximately 5,500 members. The Evangelical Mission Conference of Canada split from the EMC in 1962, and represents a more aggressive evangelical and missionary emphasis (M. Reimer 1983).

The largest divisions of the Dutch-Russian branch are represented by the Old Colony, Reinlander, ᵒnd Sommerfelder Mennonites. All three are the result of conservative reactions to change in Russia. These groups have approximately 39,060 members in Canada, Mexico, Paraguay, and Bolivia. This total (1984) consists of members in the church, so that the entire community would total at least twice that number. These groups are similar to the Old Order groups of Swiss origin and can easily be confused by the casual observer; the differences are basically the result of different traditions in clothing and farming practices.

One very interesting division is the Church of God in Christ, Mennonite, which represents a fusion of dissidents from both the Swiss and Dutch-Russian branches. Basically the result of the vision of one John Holdeman, culminating in 1858, its main spiritual dynamic was extreme separation from the world and the avoidance of those excommunicated from the church. Very exclusive, these Mennonites do not cooperate with other Mennonite groups, and they promote their own missionary and service program. They are still actively attempting to evangelize among other Mennonite groups, whom they consider in need of salvation. Although membership statistics are hard to come by, they number approximately 9,000 today (Hiebert 1973, 307).

The third largest Mennonite group in North America is the Mennonite Brethren Church (MBC) of North America. This group broke away from the larger "Kirchliche" Mennonite group in Russia in 1859–1860. The circumstances of the division, and the subsequent love-hate relationship between the Brethren and the Kirchliche both in Russia and in the General Conference in North America, have been turbulent, charged, and at times acrimonious. The schism was the unfortunate consequence of a demand for revitalization and renewal in the old church, which was conceded by many Kirchliche at the time and most members on both sides since the schism (P. Friesen 1978).

Encouraged by the Pietist influence which had spread to the Mennonite area by the 1850s, assisted by Baptist and other like groups in the Ukraine, the Mennonite Brethren withdrawal caused strife and suffering in church districts, congregations, and families. The consequences of this division followed the two groups as they migrated to America, and only in recent years has there been conscious effort to heal the wounds and bridge the rift. No basic theological issues were involved; the overwhelming concern was purity of life and a vital religious conversion experience in life and worship, according to Jacob H. Lohrenz. "The early M.B. Church strongly stressed repentance from sin, conversion as a personal experience of faith in Christ, a life of prayer, and a conduct consistent with the teachings of the Bible" (1957, 597). Officially and traditionally, the Mennonite Brethren have adhered to all the basic doctrines of the Mennonites, including nonresistance and separation from the world, although at present larger numbers of congregations are relinquishing some of the doctrines (J. B. Toews, in P. Toews 1977).

The strong emphasis on missions and evangelism has made the Mennonite Brethren Church the most rapidly growing group in the Mennonite family since the mid-twentieth century. The church is strongly congregational, but has an extensive institutional structure, including three colleges, numerous Bible schools, a thriving mission board, and worldwide missionary outreach. Many Mennonite Brethren work for numerous inter- and non-denominational missionary and evangelical organizations; this is especially the consequence of a gradual drifting toward the mainline fundamentalist-evangelical stream in North America. Though some of the leaders and most scholars in Mennonite Brethren circles strongly affirm their Mennonite heritage, the rank and file seem to be increasingly uninterested in the religious heritage.

Numbering about 42,000 in Canada and the United States, almost equally divided between the two countries (25,000 and 17,000, respectively), Mennonite Brethren are found mainly in the U.S. Midwest and California, and in Manitoba and Canada's western provinces, with concentrations in urban centers. The Mennonite Brethren Conference is the most urbanized of all Mennonite groups and is overrepresented in business, commerce, and the arts as compared with other Mennonite groups (Kauffman and Harder 1975, 284).

Aside from the three major groups and their offspring, described above, there are a vast number of smaller groups which have divided and subdivided in specific and complex contexts. It must suffice here to very briefly list and identify only the most important groups. The Evangelical Mennonite Church, originally the Egli Amish, and then called the Defenseless Mennonite Church, was formed in 1864 and emphasized regeneration; it represents a break from Amish traditionalism in Indiana and Ohio. The Evangelical Mennonite Brethren Church, emerging in 1889, was a reform movement separating from several General Conference Mennonite congregations in Nebraska and Minnesota and later spread to Canada. It has in the last several years dropped the Mennonite name and is relinquishing its historical connections with the Mennonite heritage.

One of the most ambiguous schisms and cousins of the Mennonite family is the Brethren in Christ Church (BIC). Originally known as "River Brethren" and "Tunkers" in Canada, it came about as the result of Pietist influences and an attempt to recover congregational discipline. The founders were Martin Boehm and Philip Otterbein, the former being a Mennonite minister. Their attempt to amalgamate Anabaptist emphases and Pietism has created ambivalences regarding their affiliation and attraction to the Mennonite tradition, although there has been continuing interaction, intermarriage, and cooperation with many institutions, such as the Mennonite Central Committee (Wittlinger 1978).[5]

These and other groups too numerous and too small to mention are in varying stages of change and dissolution. Most are either becoming assimilated into the mainstream of North American fundamentalism and evangelicalism or are continuing to turn inward, insisting on ever more rigid adherence to traditional principles. Either way, they are rapidly losing their Mennonite identity and appear to be slowly disappearing. A sociological study and analysis of these "splinter" groups as a whole has not yet been made, but a few groups have been studied (cf. C. Redekop 1981 and K. Rempel 1982 [an analysis of the EMB conference]).

A more systematic and extensive analysis of the schism phenomenon and how it figures in the Mennonite saga is presented in Chapter 15.

Part Two

The Mennonite Ethos

A historical survey is a relatively easy task. Attempting to describe the essence of a movement, however, requires a conscious and deliberate selection of some events and structures as being more essential than others: this is a daunting task. In this section, I present the essential dimensions of the Mennonite movement, namely, the beliefs, the religious practices, the social base of the movement, the personality, the intellectual and creative life, and the context of it all—the community.

The selection of these major foci and the material that has been used to flesh out these dimensions are clearly the consequences of a frame of reference. It is always possible to argue with a frame of reference, but there is evidence for the structure that I am proposing. The subsequent sections will provide supportive material for the profile of Mennonitism presented here.

Chapter Four

The Belief System of Anabaptist-Mennonites

When Mennonites are asked by outsiders what they believe, they usually reply that it is difficult to articulate their faith. They would probably not refer to any of the confessions of faith that have been produced, nor would most of them recite a long list of things "surely believed." The probable response would include a vague reference to the "peace position," that is, Mennonites' nonparticipation in war; to the fact that they do not swear the oath; or possibly to Mennonites' belief in separation from the world.

The questioner might very well conclude from such responses that the Mennonite movement certainly must not have emerged nor flourished on the basis of a clearly defined dogma. And indeed, in contrast to the Lutheran or the Reformed churches, for example, Mennonitism has been identified as a much more complex socio-religious phenomenon composed of many facets, rather than being only a religious movement. However, this does not mean that religious beliefs and commitments were, or are, absent from the movement. On the contrary, they were of central importance in the emergence and growth of the movement, and have remained so until the present. In this part of my analysis I will focus on the way theological and biblical interpretations figured in the emergence of the Anabaptist movement. In the last section of the book, I provide a sociological analysis of the movement, including the broader socio-political and economic factors which figured in the revolt.

There is no better way to highlight the significance of the religious factors than to quote Troeltsch, who described the religious mood at the time of the Anabaptist revolution. He introduces the Anabaptist movement by describing the way the Protestant Reformation had compromised on its original ideals: "It is not surprising that this extreme idealism was grievously disappointed, and that this practical reform did not succeed" (1960, 698). One part of the Anabaptist movement, which emerged in 1525 in Zurich within the radical reform circle, rejected Zwingli's applications of Scriptures because they seemed inadequate (703). In spite of such pointed references to religious issues, however, none of the radical reformers lived in isolation from their culture, nor were they insulated from the other forces in the environment which nurtured the larger movement (Stayer 1988).

It is therefore the relationship between the protest group and the larger society which must be seen as the "context" in which Anabaptist beliefs were developed and forged. "Belief system" therefore refers to the dynamic nature of the formulations of belief and practice on the part of the Anabaptists as they found themselves set "over against" the dominant religious and political structures. "Belief system" could also be defined as an "intersystemic" belief system, by which it is assumed that the conflict between Anabaptists and dominant religious groups helped develop the benefits of the former.

The Anabaptist Protest

As has often been stated, the history of the Anabaptist-Mennonite movement suggests that the cause for its emergence was great dissatisfaction with the gap between actual conditions in the society and the ideals which were expressed in the rhetoric and behavior of the societal institutions, particularly the established church (Latourette 1953, 778–79). Specifically, the Anabaptists saw a total lack of coherence between the ideals and norms expressed in the biblical narrative as well as in the teaching of the church on the one hand, and what they were experiencing in the life of the church and the community on the other hand (Bainton 1952).

The corruption of the church in that period has been extensively documented and discussed. What is important for our purposes, however, is to identify the unique responses of Anabaptists in the context of

For our purposes, we will define *beliefs* as the "acceptance of certain things as being true, real, and/or in the eternal order of reality." In any case, it is much easier to develop a system of beliefs than it is to define the "spirit" or "vision" of a group because both terms assume a synthesis of the social group which is difficult to achieve (H. Bender 1957, 35). Chapter 18, however, provides an attempt.

There has been a recent resurgence of interest in and writings on Anabaptist-Mennonite theology. I will not here present a systematic discussion of the theology of Anabaptism-Mennonitism, since nothing approaching a coherent system is available (Wenger 1956, 77–79), even though fragments or aspects of this theology are appearing from various quarters, and there is increasing debate about the need for a Mennonite theology (A. J. Reimer 1980; Weaver 1984; Yoder 1972).[1] Such a discussion is an ongoing process, and covers the entire range of philosophical issues concerning understandings of God, humankind, creation, and the like.

In this section I will attempt to focus on the positions, beliefs, or practices which differentiated the Anabaptist-Mennonites from other groups and beliefs. This methodology provides us with the extremely salient and central points of *difference* and *disagreement* between Anabaptists and others and hence saves us from having to deal in detail with the total corpus of Anabaptist theological assumptions and understandings. Whether the topics we thereby examine make up the complete body of theology, belief, dogmas, or interpretations of all three is thus not of crucial importance.

Of the many attempts to summarize the religious protests of the Anabaptists, Ernst Troeltsch's seems to offer the sharpest insights regarding the issues that separated the Anabaptists from the rest. He is both a sympathetic outsider and a very perceptive social scientist. Troeltsch lists the following emphases among the Anabaptists:

1. Formation of the church to include only truly converted believers (695).
2. Voluntary membership in the church, symbolized by baptism. Infant baptism was rejected as a contradiction of this principle.
3. The necessity of church discipline for all who had committed themselves voluntarily to join the fellowship. This principle implied the right to excommunicate the recalcitrant.
4. Rejection of the doctrine of the efficacy of the sacraments. Hence, the Lord's Supper became a "festival of Christian fellowship" (695).
5. Emphasis on a holy life that expressed itself as follows: (*a*) detach-

the larger Reformation. These are discussed in detail later in this chapter. Here, I shall outline only briefly the circumstances that triggered the Anabaptist protest.

One of the most pervasive facts which is surfacing from recent research on the Reformation is the great dislike and hatred for the corrupted priesthood. One Anabaptist is quoted as shouting: "May God's passion rape them. They cheated us in the past and now they seduce us more shamefully than ever" (Clasen 1972, 77). "Cleric," "priest," and "monk" were used as swear words and hurled with disdain at the bearers of these titles (Goertz 1980, 40). But the priesthood was not the only focus of reaction that surged into protest.

Many of the issues and practices that the leaders of the Reformation first challenged, then changed, stemmed from the abuses of religious practices in the institutional church. To repeat all of them here would be impossible, but high on the list were the abuse of baptism, of the sacraments, and of the tithe. Certainly not the least would have been the cheapening of grace so that the ethical levels of Christian behavior were practically synonymous with debauchery and degeneration. The baptism of children symbolized the callousness and shallowness with which the institutional church viewed the sacredness (or rather lack of it) of entering into the "body of Christ." By baptizing babies, and by routinely assuming that the baby was forthwith a member, the church simply cheapened and downgraded the meaning of repentance for sin, experiencing forgiveness, and being regenerated by the power of Christ. This was echoed in numerous debates that took place between Anabaptists and their accusers: "In short, I have no regard for my first baptism, for it is not the least use to me. As often as a child is baptized, Christ is slandered, for a child, although it is conceived and born in original sin, is pure in soul until the time when it understands good and evil" (Klaassen 1982, 12).

The abuse of the sacraments, which included baptism, was particularly galling to the common people. Menno Simons recalled with bitterness how he had squandered his time and energy while the "flock" was needing a shepherd. The acceptance of indulgences for relief in purgatory, the misuse of communion, whereby the laity observed the self-indulgence of the priests with the very wine that was to be used for communion, and many other practices simply could not be squared with what was to be found in the Scriptures: "[The priests] themselves do not do what they teach. They do speak of the word and of faith but do not themselves believe and do as they speak. . . . The Lord said, 'Go' and they sit down. He said, 'Give freely, for you have freely received.' Formerly it was sufficient to pay thirty or forty guilders to be a priest. Now it costs a hundred or two hundred guilders. . . . It has come to the point that one preaches one or two sermons a week and it costs a farthing a word" (ibid., 33).

The continuing increase in the amount of the tithe that laboring peasants and artisans were expected to pay was probably the most onerous of all burdens and precipitated much of the rebellion which spread over Europe like a prairie fire in the mid-1520s. On this issue, the Anabaptists were allied with the great reformers of their day. The uprising of the common man was centered to a considerable extent on the unbearable load that was being placed on his back. An eloquent testimony of an Anabaptist states the case unequivocally: "Everyone must give an account for all his words, works and the steps of his feet . . . for every penny, how he has received and possessed and spent it, how he has related to all creation, and how he has eaten his bread. The powerful of this world, princes and lords, bishops and pastors most of all, must account for how they have ruled their subjects as their sheep from which they have taken the world, how they have possessed the kingdom of the earth and how they have used their power" (ibid., 15–16).

Another major issue had to do with misuse of the Scriptures by the official church by making them mysterious and accessible only to the learned doctors and clergy. This was a clear attempt to keep members in the dark regarding the Holy Writ. This became a major point of contention, particularly because the printing press had made the Bible more widely available, so that the peasantry became more insistent on knowing what the Scriptures really said, for many could read: "If the Scriptures are the word of God as you say, why did they become a snare and ground for retribution? To the believer it acts for good and blessedness, but to the impure and to the unbelievers it is impure and brings damnation. . . . Scripture is all good things to the good as also is the law, to those alone who use it correctly" (ibid., 116–17).

Finally, the church's oppression of the poor through its alignment with the nobles and princes was seen as a terrible abuse of power and was strenuously protested by the peasantry. The Anabaptists were no less incensed by it, and the Peasants' Revolt of 1525 was a final expression of the outrage.

Any one of these issues could have been sufficient cause for protest. But underlying all of the issues was a growing impatience with spiritual leaders who seemed to be doing very little to bring about fundamental change. This general reluctance of church officials—both Catholic and

Protestant—to work for reform of the ecclesiastical system was the largest single force that focused the protest of the Anabaptists, along with others. At Zurich, St. Gall, Augsburg, Nuremberg, Leuwarden, Amsterdam, and other places in Europe, the refusal of the reformers to clean house seemed to be the straw that broke the camel's back.

The Anabaptist movement is thus defined as a religious and social protest, and this central factor ties the theological and sociological together. The theological aspects of religious movements deal with substantive issues of faith and doctrine, while the sociological aspects deal with the social aspects of these beliefs and values. Troeltsch, as well as most other scholars, defines the sect as a protest against prevailing value and norm systems, and believes the Anabaptist-Mennonite movement is a classic example. Troeltsch characterizes the Anabaptists as opposing the "whole idea of the Church, and of an ecclesiastical civilization" (1960, 698).

The Basic Beliefs

Even though it may appear to be mere semantics, it is important to "place" the Anabaptists in terms of their theological position. Clearly, the Anabaptists are a product of Western civilization, and although they protested abuses, they reflected faithfully the central values of the Judeo-Christian tradition. The values of truth and goodness, reverence f life, and happiness, among others, are as foundational to Anabaptists to all other groups. In regard to specifically religious beliefs, howe the issue becomes very murky. If one refers to fundamental axiom theological principles such as the belief in an all-powerful God "created heaven and earth," Anabaptists were orthodox and mainstream. Further, if one focuses on doctrinal points, such a tion and the nature of the church, the Anabaptists claime orthodox, and claimed that others were heterodox. "No A ever felt the need for an elaborate system of theology, not e who had the necessary education. . . . The 17th and 18th show distinct changes toward formalization and a slackeni creteness, but even then there is little likeness to the systema of the state churches" (Wenger 1956, 79). In the area of re tice, the Anabaptists claimed that they were right, and o Roman Catholics, were wrong.

This is not to deny that there was theologizing durin the movement. It only means that we cannot presume tively whether there was a conscious system of beliefs

ment from the state, including service to it; (*b*) refusal to swear oaths; (*c*) refusal to engage in violence of any sort, including war and capital punishment; (*d*) taking up the cross and suffering injustice as the Christian disciple's share of the suffering of Christ (696).

6. Emphasis on equality and mutuality. "Church members were to be considered equal" (705). This expressed itself in a number of ways, most notably in an absolute equality between males and females as well as in the lay election of leadership. Equality extended to the offering of mutual aid: a mutual or common sharing and assistance between members (703, 705).

7. Following the precepts of the Sermon on the Mount (703). This belief may be stated more precisely as an attitude toward the Scriptures, but Troeltsch believed that it was central to Anabaptist-Mennonite life. It refers to an acceptance of the life and teachings of Jesus as the norm and model for Christians. However, this view went beyond the *imitatio Christi* of Thomas à Kempis; Anabaptists emphasized the idea of participating in the cross of Christ by sharing in Christ's work.

The emphasis on the Sermon on the Mount is central to Mennonite life and deserves a bit more discussion. This emphasis expressed itself particularly in the Anabaptist stance toward the Christian's life on earth—that is, the relevance of the kingdom that is to come to the present life. The Sermon on the Mount was taken to mean that the Christian was already participating in the coming kingdom of Christ, a form of understanding eschatology as being achieved now. The commitment to the Sermon on the Mount led to specific consequences: it directed the Anabaptists toward a literalistic obedience of the teachings of Jesus, such as "turning the other cheek" (nonresistance) or stressing the importance of humility and *Gelassenheit*—that is, the submission of the human will to the will of Christ. This commitment to the teachings of Jesus also meant "living a life of yieldedness toward others" (Cronk 1981, 7). It also resulted in extreme legalism, which will be treated later.

As I have indicated, many others since Troeltsch have tried to systematize or create summaries of Anabaptist beliefs; most of these have considerable merit. But one seems especially relevant. Donovan Smucker's system focuses on beliefs and theological issues that aligned with, and conflicted with, the larger Christian community, rather than on the group's unique beliefs and ethical responses:

1. The primacy of biblical authority interpreted Christologically (biblicism).[2]

2. The nature of Jesus Christ as divine Lord and Savior, revealing both grace and a pattern of living.
3. The nature of man as a fallen sinner desperately needing salvation in Christ, thus making possible the Christian life.
4. The nature of the church as a gathered, responsible, disciplined, converted, suffering, mutual-aid, apostolic, missionary brotherhood.
5. The nature of Christianity as discipleship.
6. The nature of Christian ethics as the all-embracing application of love and nonresistance.
7. The primacy of the local congregation yet with authority delegated to the elders; the validity of the ordinances as symbols yet without any meaning apart from faith and obedience.[3]
8. The presupposition of religious liberty and toleration for interchurch relationships; but with separation as pertaining to church and state relationships.
9. The nature of theology as biblical, covenantal, confessional, and unspeculative.
10. An eschatology of hope for the church and despair for the world with the presupposition that this is not to paralyze effort in the church, nor to open doors to fanatical chiliasm, nor to destroy loving concern for the needs of the world. (Smucker 1945, 74–75)

A summary of Mennonite beliefs might be the words of Roland Bainton, one of the most sympathetic historians of the Anabaptists: "The word 'restored' would be the most appropriate to apply to those who by opponents were called Anabaptists. Their great word was 'restitution.' . . . The Anabaptist view rested upon pessimism with regard to the world and optimism with regard to the Church" (1952, 95–96). Theirs was a simple belief that they had been called to restore the decayed church to its prelapsarian condition, a clearly utopian idea. This belief in or orientation toward restoration probably best explains the serious attempt at congregational purity and holiness of life. Many of the excesses and schisms that the Mennonites subsequently experienced can be traced, fundamentally, to this emphasis.

These then, I propose, are the beliefs or teachings that the Anabaptists espoused and which have served to bring coherence and direction to the movement. In some significant sense, each of these beliefs set the Anabaptists off from all other groups. Although other groups espoused many of the same beliefs, none held all these beliefs together in the same fashion and with the same intensity as did the Anabaptists.

Yet it needs to be restated that insofar as basic Christian dogmas and theology are concerned, the Anabaptists were traditional Christians. That is to say, the orthodox teachings regarding the nature of God, of salvation, of judgment, and of eternal life were never questioned by Anabaptists. None of the traditional doctrines of historical Christianity were rejected or basically changed. Howard Loewen, in a recent, comprehensive study of the Mennonite confession, states, "What they held in common with the rest of Christendom is taken for granted and not discussed at all" (1983, 270). It is in this context that the "non-creedal" argument must be understood. Mennonite theologians and historians have debated whether Anabaptism was creedal or not (idid., 280). The almost unending discussions and study among Anabaptists have labored over the issue of discovering a "theological center" which creates the unity of the heritage. It is probable that this question can best be resolved if Anabaptist theologizing is seen in the context of a continuing dialectic with the majority of Christendom on the issue of ethic or lifestyle—that is, on the concrete expression of the Christian faith.

Although it may be a matter of emphasis, therefore, it seems clear that Anabaptist-Mennonite beliefs and theology are less a clearly defined and coherent system of beliefs than they are a dialogic and dynamic differentiating over against mainline Protestantism and Roman Catholicism. Thus, the "restitution of the Pure church" (a phrase which Bainton and Littell, to name but a few, have promoted) places this idea in theological and ecclesiological language, but reflects a sociological principle as well, namely a living, changing conflict which defines the antagonists and their positions.

The controversy that ultimately caused the formation of the Anabaptist movement seemed to be basically an issue of accepting the Christian teaching at face value *and living it*. It has often been said that the Anabaptist movement was concerned with "hearing God's word and doing it" (Luke 11:28). Hans Denck, an early Anabaptist, said, "No one may truly know Christ except one follows him in life" (Dyck 1967, 47).

The conclusion that naturally emerges is that the Anabaptist-Mennonite utopian movement was much more an ethical response than a creedal one. The ideological and philosophical dynamic of the movement was a derivative one, focusing on the application of the basic Christian beliefs in personal and social life, rather than an emphasis on abstract doctrine which was then expressed in elaborate ecclesiastical liturgy and litanies. As J. L. Burkholder states, "Throughout their history, Mennonites have sought above all to be holy, pure, and obedient to Christ. In fact the ethical emphasis is so predominant in the writings of Menno Simons and others, that one is sometimes tempted to say that for Mennonites Christianity and ethics are one" (1959a, 1079).

The Search for Spiritual Unity

As has already been indicated, the Anabaptist movement did not emerge from a single source or time, and hence could not have had a unity of belief with which to begin (Stayer 1988). From the beginning, there were Swiss, South German, Alsatian, Middle German, Low German, and Dutch sectors of Anabaptism. In addition, many of the individual emphases were never fully integrated into all the groups. The early period saw numerous conferences instigated basically to find the "unity" which was almost impossible to perceive at the time. Yet attempts to unify were often the cause for further conflict, fragmentation, and schism (Neff 1955c, 669–70). For example, as Stayer (1972) and others have proved, there was not even agreement in the early years regarding an issue that ostensibly was central to the Anabaptists: the use of the sword. These fundamental differences were not differences in basic theological principles, such as the nature of Christ, for the Anabaptists did have firm convictions on that issue, but on the ways in which obedience to Christ was to be practiced or the ways in which restitution of the church was to be realized. Thus, the Amish division, already referred to, developed over a difference of opinion on how the nonconformity to the world was to be expressed.

With time, because of persecution, the Swiss Mennonites retreated and became pietistic. The Alsatian and South German Mennonites also became involuted and pietistic.[4] The Dutch and North German Mennonites, more urbanized, and under the influence of Menno Simons, became more rigid and objective in Christian experience. Ingroup classifications have been extant for years. Normally the Swiss Mennonites and their descendents are characterized as more passive, submissive, traditionalistic, and biblicistic. The Dutch stream is characterized on the other end of the continuum on these characteristics, with special emphasis on legalism in regard to church organization.[5]

This lack of unity led some observers to talk about the "marvelous and manifold divisions and bans" of the Anabaptists (Clasen 1972, 30). Clasen states that contemporary observers did not and could not distinguish related groups from authentic Anabaptists. He proceeds to list those whom he considers to have been authentic Anabaptists and indicates that twenty groups could be identified in the Swiss, Austrian, and

South German areas alone (32). We know that there must have been at least that many different groups in Alsace, North Germany, and Holland as well.

Earlier, I described the Anabaptist-Mennonite movement as being based on a theological system of faith. But in the discussion regarding schisms in Chapter 15, I will argue that schism does not occur simply because of disagreements over orthodoxy and faith, but involves instead a mixture of disagreements over belief on the one hand and various sociological factors on the other, with the latter deriving from the cultural backgrounds, experiences of oppression, and lack of intercommunication between groups. This point strongly reinforces the notion that religious beliefs and commitments are not abstract phenomena but take place in real-life situations, reflecting regional social conditions. For this reason, the sociological factors cannot be separated from theological ones. In Chapter 15 we shall examine the sociology of identity and schism; here, we must restrict our discussion to the causes of the differences in belief. It will be helpful to summarize some of the major reasons here:

1. Anabaptism emerged simultaneously in many areas over Europe. Given the great distances and communication problems, it would have been difficult for Anabaptists in one region to know what Anabaptists in another region were doing; hence, beliefs would not be synthesized (Clasen 1972, 36).

2. The differing contexts also clearly contributed to the variations in belief and practice. Each region involved a different and specific form of religious and social conflict; thus, the responses of Anabaptist reformers in the Bernese highlands were clearly different from those in the Münster uprising in many subtle as well as more obvious ways. Men like Jacob Hutter and Hans Denck had vastly different specific understandings regarding the Christian walk, owing largely to the experiences out of which they came.

3. The absence of a central hierarchical authority prevented the development of a unified theological base. Magisterial Protestantism retained an authoritarian base from centers of learning, and was spearheaded by powerful leaders who promulgated "correct" interpretations of the Scripture and demanded adherence to those interpretations. The direction of Anabaptist orthodoxy was exactly the opposite. Anabaptists believed in and sprang from a congregational locus of experience and authority, that is, a priesthood of believers. This approach guaranteed diversity. If because of their own personal

spiritual experience individuals did not like what one local congregation decided, they could join another. Furthermore, if individuals or groups were still not satisfied, they could create new congregations which reflected their own private insight.[6] Clasen suggests that because the Anabaptists considered their church to be outside political and secular control, there was no restriction on their establishing a new sect if the contending parties could not agree (1972, 37). This view reflects considerable logic, since one of the major contentions of the Anabaptists from the beginning was that the secular authority should have no role in determining religious matters.

4. Closely related to the absence of a hierarchy was the lack of trained theologians in Anabaptism; with some exceptions the movement was composed almost exclusively of untrained preachers and lay members. Thus, the autonomous local congregation could legitimately use the spontaneous experience and understanding of members as the base for authority and defining faith. Some scholars have charged that this was rank individualism. Although there were abuses of the principle, this practice did not really reflect individualism, for the authority of the local fellowship was highly regarded (Weber 1958, 144–50).

5. Given the polygenetic origins of Anabaptism, leaders in various regions developed a kind of spiritual "ownership" in their segment of the movement and asserted autonomy and authority over its direction. This, coupled with personal conviction and sometimes personal ambitions, contributed greatly to differing interpretations. This is certainly applicable to the Amish schism in 1693 in Alsace, and to subsequent ones as well.

6. Honest differences over the application of the central doctrines of the Christian faith also contributed to tensions, disagreements, and finally to diverse interpretations that became dogmatic. One of the clearest examples of this is the conflict between Hubmaier and Hut that developed into an accusation of heresy. The "Schwertler" and "Staebler" split among the Hutterites in Nikolsburg[7] must also be attributed to this type of conflict. Many similar conflicts—including even the Münster schism—must be attributed, at least in part, to different perceptions and interpretations of almost infinitely varied approaches to such biblical issues as "the last times," the role of magistrates in religious affairs, original sin, the nature of sin, and how transgressors were to be handled in the congregation, to name only a few.

In subsequent centuries, with a weakening in the goal of uniformity of beliefs and with increasing interaction with the surrounding society, tension began to emerge as the self-appointed orthodox groups—

Robert B. Graber's "perpetuators"—tried to assert the old norms and beliefs. The attempt to achieve uniformity as well as conformity to traditional beliefs and practices is written large in almost every Mennonite memory as well as in the official documents that record conference decisions (Graber 1983, 60). Pronouncements on the wearing of hats for women, the use of tobacco, or the use of radios—to call to mind only three examples—have confronted almost every Mennonite member in the twentieth century. Each locality has its own specific history of the plague of worldliness, and in consequence, each church had its own response in the effort to constrain the tendency to "follow after strange gods."

The development or the ongoing shaping of beliefs among Anabaptist groups continued long after the formative period. One development with lasting consequence was the Oberholtzer division in eastern Pennsylvania, which took place in 1860; ironically, this was intended as a movement for reform and the unifying of the various groups. Another split with equally significant implications for future inter-Mennonite relations was that of the Mennonite Brethren from the Kirchliche—that is, the established church—in the Russian Ukraine, also in 1860. The motivation of the people in these cases and others was to reform and renew the Mennonite church! With reference to the Mennonite Brethren schism, one of the major historians states: "The Mennonite Brethren Church must actually look upon Pastor Wuest as her second reformer: Menno built the house in which we live on the one foundation (I Cor. 3:11 was Menno's motto). After narrow interpretations, differences over small things, and numerous divisions had weakened Menno's family and diverted it from its central focus—Christ living in the heart of faith, one's life being an open letter of Christ proclaiming his name . . . —rationalism and later indifferences gradually captured . . . the Dutch church" (Friesen 1978, 211–12). Just as the original Anabaptists separated from the corrupt and "spiritually dead" Protestant and Roman Catholic churches, so the new sectarians, spurred on by a new inner experience and influenced by Edward Wuest, left the mother church determined to form the only true and faithful church. The motif of "restitution" reappears here and supports the "intersystemic" belief motif described above.

The extent of schism of a more local nature has been documented by Robert Graber (1982), who studied thirteen schisms among the Mennonites of Pennsylvania between 1785 and 1927. And, it should be noted, Graber's list reflects only one sector of the Mennonites in America. Thus, for example, the Dutch Mennonite divided into Flemish and

Frisian groups, each believing the other was wrong. In his historical analysis of the Holdeman Church, Clarence Hiebert suggests that the seeds go back to the Flemish-Frisian division: "The contempt which the Old Flemish bore against the Frisians is expressed by the following verse cited by Herbert Wiebe: Those with hooks and eyes will be saved by God; those with pockets and buttons will be seized by the devil" (1973, 42). This and other research provides extensive evidence of the proclivity for division among Mennonites. Some have called it "the Mennonite disease"; the designation seems apropos. Of course, this is not to imply that other denominations have not had divisions, but only that the schismatic history of Mennonites shows with what seriousness they have viewed the issues at stake.

·As indicated earlier, Mennonites have been highly concerned with unity in theology and polity, and the many confessions of faith have served to provide a rallying point. In fact, certain Mennonite groups still today identify themselves by accepting, for example, "the West Prussian Mennonite Confession as published in Holland in 1660," or the Mennonite Brethren Confession of Faith (A. J. Klassen 1976, 5). Moreover, in the process of schism, the schismatics would normally appeal to earlier confessions of faith as justification for separation (J. A. Toews 1975, 47–48).

Although deeply ironic, the attempt to retain unity of faith has almost constantly occasioned the possibility of disagreement and schism. In any case, however, Anabaptist-Mennonites were incessantly testifying to the importance of faith and belief in their religious life. We may also remind ourselves here of the oft-repeated statement that Mennonite divisions are not the result of faith and theology so much as of either disagreement over practice or personality factors. With this focus, then, we have come full circle: that is, Mennonite schisms are the result of the complex religious beliefs *as well as* social forces that spawned the groups in the first place. The very religious and social forces which contrived to form the movements were also operative in highlighting differences or creating conflicts between them.[8] So we are led to conclude that the Anabaptist Mennonites share the fate of all religious groupings, namely, the incarnation of spiritual beliefs in earthen vessels creates schism. It is the irony of religious organization that the need to reform repeats itself and reenacts earlier reforms in almost identical fashion.

Chapter Five

The Religious Base of the Mennonite Community

Pietist and mystical Christians have maintained through the centuries that religious belief and expression need not have any type of observable social structure. Some Christian theologians have agreed that structures are not only difficult, but normatively impossible for Christianity. Hence Emil Brunner's pronouncement, "The ekklesia of the New Testament, the fellowship of Christian believers, is precisely not that which every 'church' is at least in part—an institution, a 'something'" (1953, 10).

However, Western sociology and most Christians have assumed that Christian experience does involve the formation of a church—that religious group or fellowship which by definition implies institutional structure (Durkheim 1915). The very presence of structure further implies a division of labor and the positing of authority and leadership as well as the ordering of the group's sacramental life, including worship, communion, and preaching. Thus two churchmen state: "To assert that the church possesses an institutional character and is articulated in a multiplicity of institutions, does in no way imply a derogation of the intensely personal quality of its koinonia—the institutional pattern of the church provides an ordered structure for the common life" (Ehrenstrom and Muelder 1963, 29).

Since Christianity is not simply a mystical and individualistic religion, although it is that too, a social structure has been inextricably involved in its varied expressions, forms, and groupings. This is also true of the Anabaptist-Mennonite movement. Having created an intricate social form, this religious movement has been totally orthodox in its reflection of sociological principles although, possibly, it has had more substructures within its confines than most other Christian groups. In this chapter, we examine both the historical and the contemporary expressions of Mennonite social structure.

The Religious Basis of Organization within the Mennonite Community

The Congregation as the Organizing Principle

On the basis of their understanding of the New Testament, as well as by virtue of their experience during the Reformation, the Anabaptists took literally the significance of Christ's words, "Where two or three are gathered together there I am in the midst of them." From the beginning, when an unordained Grebel baptized Blaurock, this served as a source of ecclesiastical authority to baptize; ever since, these few words have served as a mandate for authority. Although there are modifications and variations among Anabaptist-Mennonites and although there have been cyclic as well as regional deviations, to this day the individual congregation is intended to be autonomous and accountable to no one except Christ.

From the beginning, Anabaptist-Mennonites conceived of themselves as the *Gemeinde,* a "body" or community, a group of people who voluntarily join to share a common life. They rejected the concept of the *Kirche,* which to them meant the ecclesiastical structure that had aligned itself with the state to oppress dissidents (H. Bender 1945). We thus need to constantly remind ourselves of Troeltsch's central dictum: "The main ideal was the formation of religious communities composed of 'truly' converted persons on a basis of voluntary membership" (1960, 695).

The congregation was composed of those who covenanted together to follow Christ; it assumed the authority to baptize, to admit individuals into membership and fellowship, to elect ministers who were to preach and lead the flock, and to determine the very nature of the faith itself.

This characterized the first group in Zolliken, Switzerland; it also describes the typical Mennonite congregation in North America today, rural or urban (Blanke 1961).

After an extensive review of all the Mennonite confessions of faith, Harold Bender concludes that "the priesthood of all believers and the autonomy of the local congregation are held as an indispensable heritage of faith from the fathers" (1955e, 597). Thus, the locus of all other institutional parameters which have emerged in later years was the local congregation, where individual members covenanted together to follow Christ in the full meaning of the words *covenant* and *follow*. This commitment included not only the inner life and workings of the fellowship but also so-called external activities such as evangelization or sharing with those in need through an application of mutual-aid principles.

We are confronted, however, with the problem of both antecedents and consequences of church structure. That is to say, a congregation normally has a beginning before which point the authority issue, for example, is still in limbo. But as soon as a nucleus is formed, a certain congregational autonomy becomes established. Then the issue of individual leadership and authority must be introduced, to be dealt with more fully later. Of course, the creative function which individual missionaries and preachers performed in the formation of the new church cannot be denied; but at the basis of the authority structure of the Mennonite religious institution from the beginning has been the congregation, the "body of Christ" (H. Bender 1955e, 597; Blanke 1961, ch. 2).

From the beginning, nevertheless, the local congregation has been the authoritative social organization which has accepted members by baptism; selected and appointed its own pastors, elders, deacons and other officials; overseen its own educational program; determined the collection as well as the allocation of its own resources; decided if, when, and how it should engage in missionary and evangelistic work; and commissioned its own missionaries—to name only a few of its many fundamental responsibilities. Finally and most crucially, the congregation has decided how it should relate to other congregations, if at all. Mennonite congregations have never really relinquished their hegemony and authority to any other body, at least theologically, although there have been some aberrations, to be discussed below.

This total congregationalism, however, has not expressed itself in the same kind of ecclesiastical polity that other "congregational" religious groups have reflected. This fact rests upon the sociological elements which make the Mennonites almost unique. These elements consist of the following:

1. Because of great persecution and their rejection by the general population, the early Anabaptist-Mennonite congregations very early developed a need to communicate with and assist each other by providing shelter for fugitives, mutual assistance when physical or financial disaster struck, and spiritual support.

2. The precipitous and almost total separation from the established religious institutions (as well as the deaths of many leaders) created a great dearth of intellectual and traditional leadership in areas of theological and ecclesiastical polity; hence, the various and separated congregations found themselves with a great need to consult and confer on a host of issues from points of theology to matters of family discipline.

3. The interlacing of most Mennonite communities—during earlier periods through the high mobility of missionaries and refugees, and later through intermarriage and other family connections—melded most Mennonite congregations with others in an intriguing manner that created a network which historically has tied the entire Mennonite world together. Thus, for example, it is said today that one Mennonite's friendship network at the third level would include Mennonites almost everywhere. That is to say, the friends of the friends of a Mennonite might include up to one-third of all the Mennonites living today. Let us say that Mennonite A has 500 friends. Each in turn has another 500 friends. These friends multiplied together constitute 250,000, almost a third of the entire Mennonite world brotherhood.[1]

4. Geographical dispersion, coupled with marital endogamy and economic and political isolation, has produced a religious-ethnic society which has evolved in almost every region of the world. This society of Dutch-Germans—in Prussia, the U.S.S.R., Canada, the United States, Mexico, Alsace, South Germany, Paraguay, and Bolivia, to list only the most prominent settlements of Mennonites—has created a network almost unparalleled for a group the size of the Mennonites. The dialects that have been developed by Mennonites are in many cases unique and not shared by any other groups. Good examples are the Plattdeutsch, Hutterite, and Amish dialects.[2]

This religious-ethnic-linguistic network created a kind of tough fabric within which the life of a congregation could be maintained. Although congregations were theologically sovereign and autonomous as well as the bedrock of religious authority and power, they did not spin off in every conceivable direction. Instead, there has been within and between congregations a unity and coherence resulting from the historical and sociological needs of the movement as well as from the processes of survival, of preserving its life through the centuries.

While the unifying factors just discussed may seem to contradict my analysis of Mennonite schism in the preceding chapter, they point to the central dynamic and enigma of Anabaptist-Mennonitism: the great coherence initiated by the "utopian movement" has constantly faced the shattering of unity when it has been expressed and institutionalized in actual community life.

Unquestionably, the "body of believers," or "the priesthood of the laity," gave the Mennonite tradition a starting point. Some theologians and historians would suggest that the coherent thread for Anabaptism was simply thoroughgoing biblicism.[3] There was no doubt that biblicism was a characteristic of Anabaptists, but that alone does not distinguish them from any other group, for most Protestant groups, especially the free churches, were biblicists. The principle of the sole authority of the Bible for faith and life was not an exclusive Anabaptist-Mennonite possession, but rather a basic principle of the Reformation beginning with Martin Luther himself (Wieswedel 1955, 323). It must be considered, then, that it was the *substance* of that biblical belief and a particular approach to the Bible—determined and interpreted by the local congregation—which made the Anabaptist-Mennonite religious expression what it was and has become.[4]

The Conference and the Authority Question

After having made the point that the congregation (the voluntary fellowship of redeemed) represents the fundamental organizing principle for the social structure of Anabaptist-Mennonite tradition, I must now qualify that statement with a fact already alluded to: very early there began a process of consulting and sharing between congregations. As I noted in Chapter 3, conferences were held as early as 1527 to discuss matters of faith and practice, such as the one in Schleitheim in February 1527. A total of at least twelve major conferences were held within the first forty years of the movement's life, from 1527 to 1568 (Neff 1955c, 669). The number of conferences held since that time in the various parts of Mennonite lands would total hundreds, if not thousands. This tendency to consult or confer with each other became a significant counterbalance to a totally independent congregationalism.

At first, conferences were ad hoc, the result of specific and urgent problems which needed to be solved. By the end of the 1700s, however, regular meetings for conferring were being held in various areas. It is important to note that these conferences were usually attended by the leaders and elders of the congregation, and fewer lay persons, indicating the role that formalized and institutionalized leadership was already beginning to play very early in the history of conferences.

Among some groups—the Old Mennonites in the eastern United States and Canada and the Mennonite Brethren—these conferences achieved specific positions of authority. In the Old Mennonite church, the eastern U.S. influence flowed westward through migrations as well as itinerant preachers; thus, Old Mennonite district conferences from Ohio westward through the Dakotas and Oregon reflect certain authoritarian positions and experience. In the eastern United States, where the authoritarian attitude developed most strongly, this anomaly is probably best explained as the response of the group to the rapidly developing urban influences and an attempt to cope with the resultant assimilation that was threatening the life of many congregations. In Canada, migration to the cities represented a similar threat. Among Old Mennonites, the Lancaster Conference is a good example of a response to the problem. The conference, organized around 1750 and urbanized relatively early (Wenger 1947, 105), moved from being a periodic meeting of all the congregations in Lancaster County for fellowship and discussion to becoming an authoritarian body able to impose its decisions on local congregations, including both the ordaining and the silencing of ministers. A superficial reading of the Russian Mennonite commonwealth history would imply that these conferences were authoritative, but they were not. The elder of each congregation retained power and leadership (Braun 1955, 678–79).

By and large, however, throughout most of Mennonite history and within most Mennonite communities local congregations have essentially retained their autonomy. This is true also of the Hutterite and Old Order groups. The Hutterite colonies, living as a total social unity, are individual congregations, even though there is a close "conferencing" between the various colonies. The Old Order district is a congregation, and beyond this, there is no official organization.

In general, then, the conference, both historically and today, needs to be understood as being a functional *convocation* serving the need for consultation on matters such as the following:

1. Defining the faith. Most of the confessions of faith were produced and adopted as a result of conferences (Neff 1955b, 679). Periodic revisions and updating of confessions also took place from time to time in these conferences. A present example is the discussion of

the status of homosexuals, which is creating great conflict in numerous conferences.

2. Issues of church polity and administration. Procedures for the ordaining of ministers, for the excommunication of recalcitrant members, as well as for general church disciplines were discussed and debated at conferences. Conferences have also discussed the various influences on church theology, such as higher criticism (J. Peters 1986; R. Sawatsky 1987).
3. Inspiration and fellowship. Because Mennonite churches have been situated largely in isolated and rural areas, periodic conferences have been arranged to provide spiritual inspiration as well as social fellowship. For many people in many times and places, conferences are and have been the high point of being a Mennonite. They provide an opportunity to relate to one's own people.
4. Group action. Conferences have served as the arena within which congregations can do things together that they are unable to do alone. For example, the urge to do mission work among the natives, whether in Russia or in western Canada, necessitated the cooperation of many congregations who might well have had willing workers but who lacked the resources and organization to be most effective.

Thus, with the few exceptions noted, conferences have been functional instead of being ecclesiologically hierarchical and authoritative. So when an outsider asks a Mennonite, "Where are your headquarters?" she or he may not know how to answer that question. There are conference headquarters, but they are not ecclesiastical power centers. There is theoretically no head, no bishop or archbishop, in the Mennonite fabric. Rather, the fabric is woven from the common purpose and history originating in the congregations.

Congregationalism and Leadership

The lay nature of the Anabaptist tradition has been accepted by most authorities of Mennonite history. One leading church historian, Ernest Payne, states: "By their concern for the *koinonia* and the *ecclesia* portrayed in the New Testament, the Anabaptists were challenging what had been the basis of ecclesiastical theory and practice since the time of Constantine. For them the church had become a fellowship of believing people" (Payne 1957, 308). The theological significance of this lay movement was tremendous, according to Payne, but the incarnation of these ideals proved a bit more difficult.

But to emphasize that the Mennonite society has been congregational is not to deny the fact that the congregational principle has faced questions of authority and leadership. It would be less than candid not to explore the ways in which the "theology of the congregation" has been breached, adapted, or compromised.

From its beginning, the movement has been strongly influenced and shaped by individual leaders and prophets. One need not labor the obvious fact that every congregation received at least some of its original help and direction and spirit from its designated or self-appointed leader. Since the process for the selection and ordination of leaders was so clearly outlined in Scriptures—including the selection by lot—there seemed to be little room for debate in this area. But it was precisely at this point—where the collective voice of the congregation intersected with the potentially individualistic or singular perceptions of a God-appointed leader—that one of the essential elements in a classless congregationalism began to break down: in the collective selection of a leader, the collective voice had risked a kind of competitor.

The second influence toward an accommodation of congregationalism has already been alluded to—the Anabaptist-Mennonite tendency to confer. There were obvious needs within congregations, issues that reflected differing theological biases and interests, various factions competing with each other (a typical problem), even the very existence of a particular congregation during times when persecution and migrations made congregational life very tenuous. But the major issues often focused on questions having to do with leadership. What authority did the leaders have in resolving local congregational problems? Who was to decide whether the congregation or the minister was right? What should a congregation do with a person who felt called to be a prophet and who accused the congregation of apostasy? Pressing questions, all, and there were others like them. The history of every Mennonite congregation is littered with conflicts over such questions of position and authority, as well as of faith and practice.[5] And it was precisely during the process of seeking help through consultation that the authority of the local congregation became increasingly ambiguous.

Of course, the congregation constituted the primary group and provided the traditional locus of authority as well as initial direction. But the help of conferences—both as a process and as an emerging leadership structure—became an imperative in confirming or correcting direction as well as in providing a coherence the movement required. The many schisms in the Mennonite church are clearly the result of differences that emerged as either leaders or congregations came into conflict with each other, or as congregations differed on points of doctrine or practice from the conferences. Obviously, some kind of supra-congregational authority, along with a clear definition of leadership roles, was necessary to guide Mennonite society.

The biblical materials regarding church structures included the terminology for deacons, preachers, and elders (variously translated as "servants," "teachers," and "bishops," respectively). At the very beginning, leaders were called *Lehrer* ("teachers"), *Vorsteher* ("guardians"), and *Prediger* ("preachers"). Elders and preachers as official leaders of the congregation existed as early as 1579, when the *Emden Protocol* states that "bishops and preachers [*Dienaren*, or "servants"] are chosen by the congregation under God's guidance by a majority vote with fasting and prayer unto the Lord. Such ministers are ordained by the laying on of hands of the elders" (Krahn 1956a, 178). The "elder" and "preacher" designations were often used interchangeably, while "deacon" was reserved basically for welfare concerns.

The elders-bishops were the senior leaders of the congregation, entrusted with the most important functions of the congregational life, such as conducting communion, baptisms, and ordination of other preachers. Because of the lay nature of the leadership—that is, leadership that was congregationally ordained—and their lack of training, most congregations had a number of leaders in order to lighten the load financially and personally. The bishop (elder) thus was the *spiritual* elder; sometimes he served as the elder for several congregations.

A gradual accumulation and concentration of ecclesiastical as well as spiritual power took place in most of the Mennonite branches, in different ways, and at different speeds. The Russian Mennonite stream developed an authoritarian system whereby the elders (bishops) and the ministers became the overarching religious arm of Mennonite society, on equal footing with the secular offices in the society, namely, the Oberschulze, Schulzen and Vorsteher (Francis 1955; C. Redekop 1969; D. Rempel 1933). These religious leaders were totally in charge of congregational life and dominated it, *but* they were still accountable to the congregation, and elected by individual congregations. The elders sought counsel from other bishops and arranged for conferences among districts of churches, but never did the bishops develop their own power base, separate from a congregation.

The elder-minister leadership pattern in the Swiss-Mennonite branch in North America developed differently. The office of bishop developed more slowly and vaguely, so that only by 1848 is the term *bishop* consciously used. His function was similar to that of the elder, described in 1890 as follows: "The bishop or elder in the Mennonite church is simply the minister who has been ordained to the special charge of caring for, and officiating in the church of a certain prescribed district. . . . He may have a number of fellow ministers in his charge, to preach at the various places, and aid him in his work generally" (H. Bender 1955f, 348).

In eastern Pennsylvania, however, bishops began to assume more authority both in faith and structure, so that a veritable "bishops' board" developed. Harold S. Bender states, "The practice . . . has evolved through the years in the Lancaster Conference, of treating the group of bishops as a sort of upper house in the conference, like the House of Bishops in the Episcopal Church in the United States. This group is called the Bishop Board, and has the sole right to initiate legislation in the conference sessions" (1955f, 349).

The evolution of the ecclesiastical leadership and authority in the Mennonite tradition is a very interesting area for sociological study; until now, it has not been studied extensively. The manner in which the elders—especially the "Bishop Board" of the eastern Pennsylvania Mennonites—have exerted their authority and influence on all aspects of religious and social life has yet to be documented and analyzed. But it can be stated that many issues—such as excommunication, the ban, and women's role in the church, to name only a few—were effectively decided upon and enforced by the elders-bishops; hence, in many congregations for many years the congregational nature of the Mennonite tradition was seriously attenuated. Many Mennonites have left the tradition in response to the arbitrary enforcement of power, and many people carry the scars of embitterment from authoritarian rule.[6]

There still exist vestiges of this authoritarian approach. But the fact that the force of the authoritarian movement has been corrected and its rather widespread application relinquished—especially during the 1950s and 1960s—proves the basic correctness of designating the Anabaptist-Mennonite movement as congregational. The "recovery of the Anabaptist vision" as a general concept stressing congregationalism is a signal development that is almost universally recognized in Mennonite circles.[7] In fact, the return to the congregation of its lost autonomy has been so strong that now there are calls for a reexamination of the emphasis, thought by many to be overemphasis, on the congregational autonomy (Sawatsky 1987, esp. ch. 5).

The Congregation as Social Institution

The social organization of the Mennonite tradition is simple; at the same time it is very complex. In layman's terms, the Bible as the word of God is the religious source for the formation of God's people, and the congregation of born-again believers is the corps of gathered believers who receive and interpret the biblical revelation. This group, in a process of discernment, applies the essence of the faith in daily life and calls forth the spiritual leadership, which then is ordained, by the laying on of hands, to help the flock in its Christian walk.

These leaders are thus the spokesmen, or spokeswomen,[8] for the life of the church in the world. They are to lead and to inspire, but they are not to be obeyed as hierarchical authority figures. Rather, they serve as representatives of the congregation. When the leadership strays from the perceived path, or goes beyond its mandate or the biblical guidelines, the congregation calls it back to the true way. Of course, if the leader is determined to have strayed in ethical or personal matters, he or she is summarily called to account, judged according to the congregational and/or biblical traditions, and excommunicated if necessary.

The Foundation of the Institutional Church

As indicated in other settings throughout this volume, all the related institutional structures have their basis in this central congregational axiom. The missionary activities, the educational functions, the mutual-assistance activities—all spring from the congregational dynamic. The roles of preacher, deacons, teachers, and others in religiously related functions have their basis directly in the biblical authorization of the fellowship of believers. In addition, the great number of related roles, structures, and activities—such as the Sunday school apparatus, the congregational committees, fellowships, study groups, and many similar clusters—base their authority on this foundation.

Within the sociological tradition, a number of bases of authority have been proposed and elaborated. One of the most celebrated is Max Weber's four sources of authority: legal, rational, traditional, and charismatic. If the legal is interpreted to mean the normative biblical base, then the Mennonite organization can be defined as being at least in part legal. If the rational includes the process of interpreting the biblical material in the context of an orderly collective process, then the Mennonite society can be considered rational. If by "traditional" is meant the process of investing authority as it was done in New Testament and early Christian times, then Anabaptist social structure is traditional. Finally, if "charismatic" can refer to a recognition of the gift of the spirit (in this case spiritual leadership), then the Anabaptist-Mennonite social structure represents all of the forms of authority.[9]

The ancillary social structures—the family, informal friendship networks, the community, and cultural structures—are in one sense the consequences of the congregational dynamics; that is to say, religious authority and life have permeated the mundane aspects of life which are necessary for the religious to exist. From another point of view, however, we must assert that the non-congregationally related social systems are the result of the interplay of congregational and secular institutional elements. Thus, for example, Mennonite family structure is shaped and guided on the basis of the biblical norms derived in the congregational life; but it is also influenced and determined by preexistent and ambient cultural norms. This explains why the Mennonite family was (and is) not different from the larger social system, but has its unique Mennonite flavor as the congregational norms influence and help to form that family. The same can be said for educational, economic, and community institutions. Mennonite social organization is like "the world" in many ways, but it is also "skewed" or "bent" in a certain direction because of the centrality of religious dynamics.[10]

The Congregation as Creature of the Social Institutions and Process

The centrality of the congregation in the life of Anabaptist-Mennonitism creates its own dilemmas or dialectics. A critical reading of Mennonite society would indicate a rather turbulent history: powerful families in the congregation, insecure and aggressive preachers and elders, nasty interfamily squabbles and conflicts, competition for leadership and supremacy, and theological debates and confusions brought in from the outside by radio, itinerant preachers, and attendance at Bible colleges (and the list could go on and on) have seemed to be more powerful in forming the Mennonite ethos than the congregational principle.

Of course, there has been a positive mutual interaction between the congregational principle and the way it was structured in the community of real persons, families, institutions, and cultural settings. Every congregation, situated in some form of social community, has been a unique concatenation of its own history in the development of leadership, the experience of family dynamics and interrelationships, the influence of economic conditions and factors, and idiosyncratic factors—such as the family with extensive mental illness which deeply influenced a congregation's life, as the author experienced it in his congregation (see Chart 5.1).

But a few generalizations about how congregationalism has affected Mennonite society can be made, which may be unique to Mennonites, or possibly to those groups as congregationally oriented as the Mennonites but also constrained by the "ideological history" which they carry in their heads in interaction with the larger environment.

One of the greatest forces which has influenced the congregation is the concept of *Gelassenheit* (submission to God) as it is expressed in the economic life of the community. As indicated above, Mennonites' submission to the will of the fellowship affected life in the economic realm, and imposed on economic activities a strict conformity limiting economic progress and deviance. Hence, differences in wealth and entrepreneurial activities were downgraded. But differences did develop,

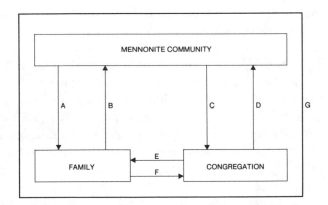

CHART 5.1 The Mutual Reinforcement of Family, Community, and Congregation
A. The community gives the family social status and provides social control.
B. The family provides the community with personnel and resources.
C. The community provides the congregation a physical, material, psychological, and social location in time and place.
D. The congregation provides the community with basic ideology and social reality (reality based on religious beliefs).
E. The congregation provides the family with religious foundations for family socialization and cohesion.
F. The family provides the congregation personnel for membership and socializes the members in the faith.
G. The "Mennonite peoplehood" encompasses the three elements to varying degrees. The Hutterite wing is most enclavic and complete.

and the impact of wealth on congregational relationships did influence congregational life. Since the theology did not allow for these differences, and since there was no overt way to recognize them, they affected negatively the mutuality of Mennonite congregational life for many generations. This is an almost entirely unstudied area in Mennonite sociology. The commonwealth period of the Russian Mennonites is possibly the one epoch which has received some analysis (Kreider 1951; D. Rempel 1933).

The ambiguity of leadership in a congregational structure has been another dilemma for Mennonites, as we have noted. Mennonite history provides examples of deeply entrenched, hierarchically oriented systems of leadership which would seem to directly contradict the emphasis here. The fact is that although most, if not all, Mennonites have accepted the idea of lay ecclesiology, in practice it has not been possible to maintain. The issue of social organization and leadership is of course not a uniquely Mennonite question; the principle was addressed by the early Christian bishops, who agreed that the bishop of Rome, although equal with the others, should still be the *primus enter pares,* "the first among equals."

It is true that the biblical teaching laid out how the church should be organized, but with the nasty distaste for ecclesiastical abuse still strong in their mouths, Anabaptists wrestled, and continue to wrestle, with the problem, with ambiguous results. The discernment of leadership, and the laying on of holy hands is theoretically easy, but in actual practice it has not been possible to avoid the issues of the use of influence, precedent, incumbency, wealth, and personal power. The idea that individuals actually possess power, and use it, even in a religious setting, has not been consciously acknowledged by many Mennonites and Mennonite congregational deliberations (C. Redekop 1976, 138–50). *Gelassenheit* and power are in many ways contradictory principles, and they have not been reconciled to this day (J. L. Burkholder 1976, 131–37). Recent analyses of Mennonite splits are bringing to the surface the role of personal ambitions, interpersonal conflicts, family power struggles, and other factors in the formation of new groups, not merely "principles" of fundamental or biblical truths (Cressman 1980; Felstead 1978; R. B. Graber 1979).

A final factor, although many others could be mentioned, is that of intellectual influences. In rural, traditional congregations like those in Pennsylvania or Russia in the 1800s, intellectual life was relatively static and insulated (J. B. Toews 1979). Little seemed to threaten local congregational life as far as the world of ideas was concerned. But after the movement to more urbanized areas, and with the coming of the twentieth century, the role of outside ideas began to increase. Most Mennonites who have grown up in congregations will recognize the terrible disturbances caused almost everywhere by issues such as Pietism, "modernism," evolution, fundamentalism, dispensationalism, pentecostalism, revivalism, the RSV and the Virgin Birth, harmonizing religion and science, higher criticism, and higher education (H. S. Bender 1953; J. B. Toews 1977).

Although not all these influences affected all congregations equally, there is no arguing the fact that these influences tended to skew and even destroy the congregational ideology which lay at the heart of Anabaptism. The congregational principle was being challenged in its faith and in its structure. Traditional leadership was challenged by the new teachings, and the question of the authority of the Bible was changed from its traditional Anabaptist mode to the axioms rampant in the larger world, such as biblical literalism on the one hand, and rationalism and scientific criteria on the other. In one of the most extensive studies of congregational life yet conducted, Beulah Hostetler refers to the influence of the revival meeting in one community in Indiana: "The meetings held were such prayer meetings in which much ado was made, loud crying and weeping—howling that could be heard a long distance—half a mile. [People were] sitting or lying on the floor and making a great confusion" (Hostetler 1987, 114).

The congregational principle forms the bedrock of the Mennonite authority structure, even though it is elaborated and conditioned in many ways. The way in which it has worked itself out in social life will be more fully analyzed in the following chapters.

Chapter Six

Mennonite Social Organization

In the preceding chapter I proposed the idea that the congregation is the religious basis of organization within Mennonite society. It seems clear that the Anabaptist perspective on the biblical center of this "koinonia" has had a direct bearing on the shape of life in Mennonite communities. Harold S. Bender concurs:

> In the sense in which we Mennonites understand the meaning of words "Church" and "Christian" we might well substitute "church" for "community." . . . For have we not historically, and in our highest thought, always held that to be "Christian" means to follow Christ in *all* our ways including what the world calls "secular," and that the "church" is a brotherhood of love in which all the members minister to each other in all their needs *both* temporal and spiritual? And what more is a Christian community than a fellowship of disciples of Christ sharing a common faith, and under a common lord helping one another achieve the fullness of abundant life which the Saviour came to bring? (1945, 90)

Whether or not one agrees that Mennonites were shaped most by congregational structure, and that conferences in their structural and dynamic forms are social institutions that have emerged to support and express the faith, the fact remains that the Mennonite utopian faith in the lay nature of Christianity has continued to exert considerable influence upon the social forms of this society.

Yet the power and authority of the Mennonite church has not inhered, and does not now inhere alone, in the local congregation supported by the conferences. From the earliest days, the Mennonite faith was also a social entity and consisted of families in various forms. Beyond these primary relationships, the clustering of families in a given geographic area constituted a community, usually including villages and settlements (see Chart 5.1).

As has been true of most other groups in the Christian tradition, the spiritual reality represented in a Mennonite congregation was, at the same time, a part of a sociological community. A Mennonite community has always been different, however, from a Roman Catholic or a Protestant community in a very important sense. The Roman Catholic or Protestant parish has usually embraced a large number of people whose religious interaction has often been limited to relatively brief or segmental activities (the sacred), while their social life has focused in segregated social and economic meanings (the secular). This is expressed by Bender in the same article:

> May I voice the devout hope that [we] may . . . eliminate from our minds the dangerously unscriptural and un-Mennonite duality by which we so often draw a line between sacred and secular, between church and community. In drawing such a line we fall under the influence of three erroneous types of thought—Roman Catholic, popular Protestant, and plain worldly. Since the early Middle Ages Catholicism has taught that only that way of life is sacred which devotes itself wholly to narrowly religious duties and forsakes the common life of man; . . . Popular Protestantism from a different point of view has sanctified only certain limited areas of life, particularly the inward experience of salvation and fellowship with Christ, and has abandoned large areas of the common life to compromise with the prevailing un-Christian world order on the specious plea that they cannot be Christianized in a world such as we live in. (1945, 90–91)

For Mennonites, the congregation or sacred community has tended to be identical with the social, political, and economic—that is, the secular—community. Hence, the religious and secular life became integrally interactive and interrelated. The purest example of this model is the Hutterite community, where the worshipping community was and is identical with the geographic, social, and intellectual community.

Mennonite society offers an excellent field for the study of various organizational modalities. These range from a totalitarian form to a near-denial of the factors that make up Mennonite society. The following typology outlines four models that represent the social aspects of the Mennonite view of reality and organization in the secular setting.

The Theocratic Model

As was pointed out in Chapter 2, the Hutterites instituted a form of communism because of a very unusual combination of beliefs, experiences, and external exigencies. Very early they were brutally ejected from their refuge and forced to fend for themselves in an extremely hostile environment. Thus, the congregational form which ensued evolved into a religious congregation/society. The sacred community extended into a total society, for the worshipping members were also the members of the socioeconomic society. Entire families and congregations became members of both the sacred and secular, thus integrating the religious koinonia and the level of the mundane (Smucker 1976).

This form of integration was not limited exclusively to the Hutterites—who have maintained it through the years—but was found in many other early Mennonite groups as well. The refugee groups which fled from Switzerland to Alsace or America, and the Menists who left Holland for North Germany and Prussia, were very similar. The village settlements that began in Prussia in 1560 were Mennonite by definition, since these refugees were given collective asylum because of their peaceful nature and their reputation as land reclaimers. The same form of collective settlement obtained to a large extent when the Mennonites settled in America in Pennsylvania beginning in 1683.[1]

Three crucial variables distinguish this model from other models to be discussed: (1) the degree to which God was directly acknowledged as ruler; (2) the degree to which religious authority determined economic, social, and political life; and (3) the degree to which members were segregated from people who were not members of the faith.

1. Theocracy can be defined as the degree to which ideological authority is retained by God himself and asserted over believers who are "acting in solidary fashion which is pleasing to God" (Weber 1964, 176), that is, "a relationship of man to God . . . of legally definable relationship of subjection." From a theological point of view, theocracy can be defined as the form of government in which the sovereign is God and the laws are regarded as divine (Pike 1958, 374). A literal theocracy is hard to imagine, since human instrumentalities are inevitably involved. But Judaism under Moses, Mormonism under Joseph Smith,

and Buddhism in modern-day Tibet have been used as examples of approximation (Pike). For our purposes, a theocratic society is one which is patterned after the laws laid down by God as closely as this can be achieved; the Hutterites and Old Order Mennonites fit that pattern rather well (cf. C. Redekop 1969, 84).

2. In a theocratic model, social, economic, and political factors are under the strict and total direction and control of the religious offices and teachings. Whether the norms are explicitly stated, as in the Jewish Torah (e.g., the book of Deuteronomy) or as in the Book of Mormon, or expressed through general tradition as well as priestly tradition and offices, the issue is whether religious norms provide a basis for the governance of the economic, political and social practices. Among the Hutterites, "the members of council hold the key positions in the colony, including that of first preacher, second preacher, steward, and field manager—the actions of the council are directed by the church and are performed neither in the name of God nor for God, but with the help of God. . . . The preacher is expected to assert authority wisely, since he must carry out the collective will as well as God's will" (J. A. Hostetler 1974, 162–63).

3. The Hutterites and some Old Order groups also illustrate the third aspect of the theocratic model: the clear boundary—physically, politically, economically, and socially—between those people subject to the sovereign God and the nonmembers. Mormons, Jews, Doukhobors, and others provide further examples of these tendencies. Membership in a theocracy implies an undivided loyalty to the sovereign. This necessitates the formation of a "people" who are separate from others.

Outside of the Hutterite family and a few more conservative groups, Anabaptist-Mennonites did not approximate the theocratic model very directly or very long. For example, with the development of village governments, the Mennonite colonies in Prussia soon began to distinguish socioeconomic aspects from the religious. In the Alsace, the Mennonite religious authority grew to be pious and separate from the economic and political elements as families became limited by the lords and princes under whom they achieved protection. At present, there is no clearly theocratic Anabaptist movement outside of the Hutterite model.

The Commonwealth Model

In many areas, very soon after the Mennonites emerged, the worshipping community began to relinquish its authority over the people's life in the secular realm (Francis 1955, 20–27; C. Redekop 1969, 84; D. Rempel 1933). The form of community life that resulted has been termed the "commonwealth model" and from 1560 on expressed itself, at least partially, in Prussia, Switzerland, Alsace, South Germany, and Russia.[2] It continues almost totally intact among Mennonite settlements in Mexico, Paraguay, Bolivia, and Brazil, as well as to some lesser degree in Canada and Europe. The term *commonwealth* is doubly pertinent for this form, since it was variably autonomous in reference to the sovereign state in which it existed. Hence, in Russia, the Mennonite commonwealth enjoyed a separate and legal status under the czars (Kreider 1951; J. B. Toews 1982); and in Canada, Mexico, Paraguay, and Bolivia this special status allowed Mennonites almost total freedom, to the extent of levying their own taxes, and forwarding to the sovereign what was demanded. The *Privilegien* which commonwealth Mennonites exacted from the sovereign authorities spell out in detail the privileges and rights the Mennonites were to enjoy. Beginning with William of Orange's *Privilegium* for the Dutch Mennonites in 1577, there were documents issued for Mennonites in the Palatinate, East Friesland, Holstein, Denmark, Prussia, Poland, Russia, Mexico, and Paraguay, to name the most comprehensive documents. Other sovereign states, such as Canada, passed special laws but did not provide for the autonomous operation of a Mennonite society (Crous 1959).

The commonwealth model can be viewed as the transitional stage between the theocratic model discussed above and the individualistic model to be treated below. In the theocratic model, all of human life was subsumed under the domination of God himself; his laws were enacted and enforced. In the commonwealth system, the sacred realm and its institutions—that is, the congregation in its various aspects—began to be separated from the mundane or secular, so that the two realms of experience began to operate simultaneously and side by side, but *within one collectivity of people*. As E. K. Francis says of the Russian Mennonites, "The Mennonite social system viewed as a brotherhood, on the one hand, and the system viewed as a people, as society itself, on the other, became co-extensive as to territory and personnel" (1955, 25). Francis argues, in the context of the Anabaptist teaching on separation of church and state, that when Mennonite society became a political entity, the religious sector could no longer identify itself with it; hence, two parallel institutions emerged—the congregational system (sacred) on the one hand, and the socioeconomic village (secular) on the other. What makes this phenomenon a peculiar commonwealth is simply that the two realms were linked together because the same persons were involved in both; it was impossible to relegate the religious dimension of life to one group (as, for example, the priestly class in Jewish life) and the mundane to another. The religious doctrines and commitments were still operative for all the members of the Mennonite community. However, the norms could not be fully enforced only by means of the religious channels; instead, they had to be governed also by a parallel set of "secular" institutions. Of course, indirectly, these institutions were still under the control and influence of the religious realm.

A significant example of the commonwealth model is the Russian Mennonite experience between 1789 and 1925. In the Russian Ukraine and later elsewhere in Russia, Mennonites lived in a tightly segregated society with a completely autonomous religious practice which consisted of bishops or elders, preachers, deacons, and other church officials. These offices received their authority from the voting membership of the congregation (male), and had total power over all religious matters, including baptism and excommunication (Francis 1955, 28ff.; D. Rempel 1933). But at the same time there emerged a "secular" authority that that was concerned with the regulation and control of the "mundane life" yet was dealing with exactly the same group of people, a miniature *Corpus Christianum*. In terms of religious teaching, there was no distinction between the two realms, and in the early period the religious arm wielded greater moral power. As E. K. Francis says, "In Russia the Mennonites, defined as such by their membership in the brotherhood, constituted the whole of society, not just a section of it. The law recognized them as a corporate body charged with the satisfaction of all, or almost all, human needs of its members" (1955, 24). Membership in the congregation was the prerequisite to legal status in the secular community.

The secular authorities derived their power from the democratic consent of every male over twenty-one who owned property and belonged to the church. They were empowered to control ownership of the land, care for the roads, develop and regulate commerce, conduct schools and hospitals, and, among many other things, control deviance. In short, the secular authorities held all the power and duties of authorities in the modern secular state, but their eligibility for office derived from religious status in the congregation.

The "constitutions" that were in effect specified the following structures: Land-owning males in the villages were entitled to vote in village affairs, including the election of the *Schulze* (mayor), his assistant, and the secretary. The officials were authorized to carry out the will of the electorate in the various responsibilities outlined above. The *Schulzen* were in turn the ex-officio representatives to a colonywide organization headed by an *Oberschulze*, assistant *Oberschulze*, and secretary. The colonywide administration had the responsibility for creating and maintaining colony roads, secondary schools, and all other structures through taxation which promoted the agricultural, commercial, social, and recreational needs of a total society (C. Redekop 1969; D. Rempel 1933).

The Russian commonwealth was mortally wounded by the Bolshevik Revolution of 1917, although that process of destruction was not completed till the latter 1920s. The purest continuation of this model can still be found among the Mennonites in Belize, Mexico, Paraguay, and Bolivia, among the Old Colony Mennonites (C. Redekop 1969, 1973.)

This commonwealth model reflects very well the process by which the Mennonite society experienced a separation of the religious life from the secular or mundane while retaining the biological and social community. Through family structures as well as village and colony membership, the same people still constituted the religious community, but the theocratic aspect was lessened. It was a beginning approximation of the parish church idea, strongly reminiscent of Roman Catholicism and mainline Protestantism. But there was a signally important difference: theoretically, no one who was not a church member was allowed in the Mennonite parish, whereas in the Roman Catholic or Protestant parishes, sectarians, members of state churches, infidels, and foreigners lived among the "Christians." The Catholic and Protestant religious parish was the spatial designation superimposed on a population; not everyone within this area was a member of the church and subordinate to its dictates.

But the homogeneity of the commonwealth broke down for several reasons: (1) contiguous land areas for settlement were often not obtained; (2) outsiders began to infiltrate Mennonite settlements and could not be excluded; and most important, (3) individuals who refused to join the church and submit themselves to the discipline and authority of the church could not always be excluded or ejected. This process was already extensive in the Russian commonwealth; and (4) one of the normatively approved evasions of religious conformity was to leave the colony by moving on to private "estates" to which the congregational discipline did not reach. The Russian Mennonite migrants to Manitoba,

Saskatchewan, and the United States—Minnesota, Nebraska, and Kansas in the 1870s—attempted in various ways to repeat the commonwealth model, but except in Manitoba, the attempts failed almost immediately, because of the magnitude of the migration and because the migrants could not obtain large blocks of settlement land.

The Swiss Mennonites moved rather quickly from the theocratic to the third model, to be described below, because of their migration and settlement pattern in North America; consequently, they did not develop a thoroughgoing commonwealth stage. Their closest approximation to the commonwealth idea occurred among the conservative groups, including the Old Order Mennonites and the Old Order Amish, but these modified forms of the commonwealth are actually closer to the model which follows.

The Community Model

In the Mennonite community model the centrality of the religious authority represented by the congregation remains, and the structures of its life are similar to those of the other two models described. What differentiates this model from the others is the structure of the parish, or in other words, the community. The members of the religious community—that is, the congregation—live dispersed throughout the geographical community rather than clustered within definable enclaves. Further, the economic base is dependent on, and as varied as, the region itself, with the business activities and the occupational pursuits of the members reflecting the economic profile of the area. The Mennonites all belong to one or another of the Mennonite congregations in the area and interact with each other on the basis of congregational, familial, and ethnic factors; they also form a self-conscious entity. There is, of course, the normal interaction with non-Mennonite neighbors and the community political, economic, and educational institutions. The nonreligious aspects of life are under the jurisdiction of the local, regional, and national governments. Of course, the congregation still exercises considerable moral control over the secular life of the community, but the influence is secondhand. Excommunication and the ban are applied in a restricted manner, mainly against spiritual and sexual sins. Obviously, in this model the influences on and control of "secular life" have been attenuated.

None of this is meant to suggest that members of the first two types were not ultimately subordinate to the state in some issues. But in both models the secular claims on both the religious and mundane sectors were mediated through the Mennonite community's special status. In the Mennonite community model, the community has two spheres: the religious, which centers on congregational life, and the mundane, which focuses on the familial and social community. Thus, the Mennonite community reflects the existence of an *in-group*, which is identified by a subcultural network of ethnic elements such as a common language (Pennsylvania Dutch) as well as common folk arts, folklore, and folkways, including food. All of these helped to create a cohesion and a social system that is still fundamentally derived from the religious tradition.

Intermarriage, family inheritance and wealth, attending church schools and religious institutions—all of these tend to create a network of interrelationships, so that most Mennonites of one congregation can identify fellow Mennonites almost anywhere. Often, Mennonites who are strangers to each other or Mennonite groups separated geographically can quickly establish common roots and heritage. Among themselves, Mennonites say somewhat jokingly that "within five minutes we become aware of our Mennonite commonality; within thirty minutes, we are able to establish a family and bloodline relationship."

Even though the church *qua* congregation does not directly influence the activities in the nonreligious sector, certain structures have developed to create in modified form the integration of the sacred and secular found in the other two models. For example, a vast system of mutual aid has emerged; these range from fire, wind, hail, and theft insurance organizations to mutual assistance such as barn raisings after a fire, ploughing a sick neighbor's fields, harvesting bees, or caring for another family's children during a mother's illness. Formally organized health and welfare services, including mental hospitals, have also emerged in Mennonite communities since the middle 1880s. Today, in the United States, the Mennonite Hospitals and Homes Association coordinates at least fifteen major hospitals, including at least ten independent Mennonite hospitals. Mutual-aid services are described in detail in Chapter 14.

The Mennonite community model is the type most prevalent in North America and is also the type most outsiders know. These communities are recognizable by the sober and circumspect life of the church membership and the generally good reputation which they enjoy in the larger community. Outsiders often volunteer statements like, "They are the only people who have it together," or "They present a sane and confident style of life." Such comments obviously reflect idealized and partial information, for Mennonite communities are often riven with inner tensions and difficulties.

The best way to understand the Mennonite community model is to look at a specific community. Even though each community is unique, some similarities exist among Mennonite communities. The Mennonite community in Lancaster County, Pennsylvania, is a good example. Lancaster County is the home of the Swiss Mennonites; they are dispersed rather widely throughout the county. The county also includes Mennonites of various conferences and large settlements of Amish as well—sixty districts consisting of approximately 10,833 persons (J. A. Hostetler 1980, 100).

The Old Mennonites of Lancaster Conference consist of approximately 17,206 members (*Mennonite Yearbook* 1988–89, 65). If one assumes that the church membership constitutes one-half of the total population of Mennonites, there could be as many as 32,000 Mennonites of the moderately progressive branch in Lancaster County. Several smaller groups might total another 4,000—including 1,000 members of the General Conference Church (*Handbook of Information GCMC* 1983, 96–97) and numerous smaller groups.

Although traditionally almost all Mennonites were based on the land, the Lancaster Mennonites are now found in almost every occupational category. Among the Amish, who are still predominantly agricultural, there is an increasingly rapid emergence of small industries and shops related to the Amish agricultural base (Beiler 1977). Numerous blue-collar Mennonites are employed in a variety of industries and service establishments. Many Mennonites have established a great variety of businesses, including construction companies, manufacturing operations, and many types of commercial and institutional ventures.

The Amish still conduct their own schools. There are also still a few private Mennonite schools in the county, although most of the other groups send their children to public schools. There is a church high school in Lancaster created by the Mennonite church to preserve the Mennonite faith. The majority of Mennonite youth in this area, however, do not attend this high school. The Amish, of course, do not attend high school in any case.

The entire Mennonite population cooperates in Mennonite activities like supporting the worldwide relief activities of the Mennonite Central Committee, although the Amish are rather cautious. Mennonite community activities also include local efforts like the MCC Relief Sales. Through yearly auctions of donated materials, these sales raise sizable monies, forwarded to the Mennonite Central Committee for its world-wide relief work. These sales contributions also help to maintain other MCC activities, such as Mennonite mental hospitals.

The Mennonite community in Lancaster County could be described as having no observable or credible identity. Moreover, the Amish and related groups have little overt contact with or sympathy for each other. Even groups within the "liberal" wing may not have much to do with each other. On the other hand, the lifestyle and subcultural system as well as the network referred to above clearly identify the entire group to outsiders (even if they tend to assume that all Mennonites drive buggies).

But from an insider's perspective there is nevertheless a clear coherence and identification; almost all Mennonites remember their heritage and accept its major components, such as the way of peace and a simple life. The church—that is, the religious life of the community—still serves as a tie that binds. If that were not the case, the community known as the Mennonites of Lancaster County, as in other areas, would simply fall apart. This is so because the Mennonites no longer have control over a geographical area which creates a kind of fence to keep the group together and strangers out. The norms of the Mennonite community emanate from the association in the congregational life; if and when that deteriorates, the Mennonite community will slowly die. The ethnic elements of the Mennonite community simply cannot perpetuate the group indefinitely.

The Individualistic Model

It is immediately obvious that an individualistic Mennonite model would be very similar to American society in general; furthermore, it would be premised on the almost total integration of Mennonites into the mainstream. There is a striking paradoxical and limiting aspect to this model. When Mennonites following this model approximate the atomistic, highly mobile nature of contemporary, basically urban society, they usually have relinquished all of the identifying traits of membership in Mennonitism (J. Kauffman 1960; C. Redekop 1957).

There are Mennonite congregations, communities, families, and individuals who have sloughed off almost all emotional and ideological commitments to their roots, have left the structural bonds of membership in Mennonite organizations and institutions, and consider themselves citizens of the nation and members of respectable mainline churches. Individualistic Mennonites are normally assimilated to the prevailing mainstream society. They may appreciate the Mennonite heritage and Mennonite beliefs, but for various reasons they have become alienated from the Mennonite identity. Studies of the dissolution of the "Mennonite bond" are considerable.[3] The only indications that these are genealogical Mennonites are the family names, the family relationships and "tribal" awareness which still tend to persist, and sometimes the nominal identity of the congregation.

These individualistic Mennonites pursue conventional occupations, live in urban neighborhoods appropriate to or commensurate with their income levels and general lifestyle, and are generally concerned with upward social mobility and economic security. Though they may still attend Mennonite churches, they are on the way out; with the likely outmarriage of their children, they confirm the cutting of ties with the traditional community. They consider the Mennonite commitment to the peace position and nonconformity undesirable traits, since these marks identify them as being adherents of a deviant group. Obviously, it is difficult to quantify the members of this individualistic model, but the model is most prevalent in the urban environment.

Many indices can be adduced to define and document the individualistic model. On the more formal level, the best indices are the degree to which congregations themselves have formally or informally distanced themselves from being called Mennonite congregations, or have disavowed the theology of Anabaptist-Mennonitism. The Mennonite Brethren, the Evangelical Mennonites, and the Evangelical Mennonite Brethren conferences are the foremost examples.[4] This separation has been closely connected with the inroads of fundamentalism and the evangelical movement, as several conference names imply (cf. C. Redekop 1981; K. Rempel 1982). In other conferences—such as the General Conference Mennonite Church, the Mennonite Church, and some regional parts of the Mennonite Brethren—individual congregations or groups of congregations have broken away from the main body to form their own organizations, in order to be faithful to the Scriptures, as they see it. Such individualistic-model congregations tend to accuse mainline Mennonite conferences of legalism, ethnicism, traditionalism, and lack of spirituality.

On the other hand, to the sincere Anabaptist-Mennonite, a number of the practices of these evangelicals really represent a falling away from the faith. In one of the most comprehensive studies of one of these groups, the Evangelical Mennonite Brethren, Kevin Rempel states, "The EMB of the 1980s had fallen into what is commonly known as civil religion. Along with worshipping God, the conference had come to also idolize their nation. Threats to their faith were synonymous with threats to their government or economic system. . . . Nationalism and fundamentalism existed alongside Mennonitism" (1982, 70).

In reference to beliefs and personal behavior which point to individualism, little direct empirical evidence has been collected. Unfortunately, the most objective survey ever done of the main groups of Mennonites (Kauffman and Harder 1975) does not deal directly with the subjectivity and piety of Mennonites. Kauffman and Harder do conclude, however, that fundamentalism has made inroads in Mennonite society: "Certainly by virtue of its first rank as a predictor it can be said that few leaders of [the five largest Mennonite conferences] have adequately acknowledged the influence of fundamentalism on their members" (328). They state further: "Our data have empirically demonstrated that fundamentalist orthodoxy undermines the pacifist commitment, racial tolerance, a focused social witness by Christians, concern for the welfare of the poor, ecumenical openness, shared ministry, and support for MCC" (329). The role of fundamentalism in creating a personalistic, subjective piety is well known.

The lifestyles of these individualistic Mennonite congregations and individuals are further indices of the model. Since the congregation no longer carries the scepter of truth and authority, personal behavior is dichotomized into that which is religious and that which is secular, the latter not coming under scrutiny. Thus, in reference to religion, new translations of the Bible came under bitter attack—for example, the RSV—but the issues of concern for the poor and the support of labor unions, reported in Kauffman and Harder, were conceived as "communist inspired" (K. Rempel 1982, 68ff.).

A variable which may also provide some information on the individualism process is the nature of conversion in the Mennonite tradition. Although subjective experience was stressed, conversion had as its end result or objective a high moral-ethical lifestyle. The Kauffman-Harder survey reveals that there is an increasing emphasis on the personal aspects of conversion, including sanctification, so that there is more similarity to the mainline Protestant denominations. "The scores of all five groups in our study are closer to those of the Southern Baptists than the Congregationalists, and are significantly higher than the totals for Protestants and Catholics generally" (95).

Also, in the individualist model, membership and participation in Mennonite institutions has declined or has been forsaken entirely and replaced by participation in the major institutions within mainstream Christianity. Young people no longer attend Mennonite schools and colleges; instead, they attend mainly interdenominational evangelical schools. The intermarriage of young people with non-Mennonites is increasing, with the bulk of these newly married couples joining non-Mennonite churches. Many families and individuals try very hard to obscure their Mennonite roots.

There is little point in extending the description of this sector of the Mennonite community, for, as indicated at the beginning of this section, there is a boundary beyond which one is simply describing mainline American religion; and that is not the focus of this study.

IN THIS CHAPTER and the two preceding, I have tried to present the social and religious basis for the order and cohesion of the Mennonite society. Doing so has not been easy, nor has my attempt provided a totally adequate description. Furthermore, it has not presented a definite theory of Mennonite society, for a number of reasons: (1) An explanation theory of a social group like the Mennonites (let alone a theory of society) is not possible given the present stage of sociological knowledge. (2) Even if a theory about the nature and meaning of Mennonite society *were* possible, that theory would require a massive amount of information qualifying the various aspects of society; that is clearly not possible in this context. (3) Even if the data were available, such a theory would have to include all other perspectives—the theological and the aesthetic as well as an understanding of the "ethos" and "spirit" of a group—and this is precluded for obvious reasons.

In the light of such limitations, we need to be satisfied with the sociological typology presented above. At this point it suffices to say that the Mennonites are a social group united by the religious faith cohering in the religious community, a community which has a unique cast and which provides a "boundary" mechanism for identity. This identity forms the basis for a social bond which elaborates into family, neighborhood, and community systems. The interaction with the environment, however, constantly limits, changes, and directs the development of all aspects of the society.

Chapter Seven

The Mennonite Personality

A sensitive biographer of a Mennonite minister described him as a man with a mission, principled, with self-control. "But," the author continued, "his impatience as well as the single-mindedness . . . made Oscar seem unusually direct, even caustic at times. His son John stated flatly, 'He was never harsh but he could get impatient. Nor did he ever look for an argument. Still, he could get pretty riled up. Only once, on the mail route, I saw father wallop a man who persisted in yelling at him. He got out of the buggy, turned the man around, and sent him packing and told us boys to forget we saw it'" (U. Bender 1982, 107). There is something paradigmatic about the Mennonite personality in this short vignette. In this chapter we shall try to discover whether something like a Mennonite personality type in fact exists.

The character and personality of an individual or a people would probably be perceived in the artistic and expressive stream of a group. And even though Mennonites have not yielded much to self-analysis or speculation, there is an almost clandestine literature and art outlining the subleties of Mennonite personality and character—clandestine in the sense that "good" Mennonites were not to be consuming "worldly" literature or art, much less to be writing or creating it. But there were such people, more in the Dutch stream than in the Swiss, and Arnold Dyck is one of the more celebrated examples. His own lifelong marginality to the Mennonite community, though he never voluntarily forsook it, illustrates the point. Dyck's *Koop en Bua op Reise* have become some of the best-known portraits of Mennonite personality and character extant.

Although various Mennonite communities reflect different stages in the assimilation process, an astute observer of Mennonite society can identify characteristics in family and community that clearly mark these groupings as Mennonite and can also identify a unique cluster of factors with reference to the Mennonite personality structure.

However, there are problems. Not the least of these is the shortage of data upon which could be based certain conclusions, since almost no scientific research exists. But even more problematical is the generally accepted fact that the concept of personality is surrounded with so much complexity and ambiguity. Since this chapter represents largely a description of personality to help understand Mennonite society, we will not need to deal in depth with these complexities and ambiguities of personality theory.

For our purposes, therefore, we will restrict our definition to personality structure defined from a sociological perspective as "the major central tendencies that are characteristic of a sense of individuals who belong to a single society" (Hallowell 1953, 606). In short, we are interested in describing how, in non-institutional contexts, a Mennonite person acts, and how he or she acts differently from a non-Mennonite. In other words, when he or she is not involved in a highly structured and symbolic congregational worship setting, how does a Mennonite behave in ways that are identifiably consistent?[1]

This question can be put concretely and specifically. For example, are Mennonites more passive than others? Are they more prone to express erratic compulsive behavior? Are they more somber and less expressive emotionally than others? Are they more self-deprecating? In something of the same vein, one could ask, Are Mennonites more likely to have mental illness than others? On the casual and informal level the quick answer to all these questions would probably be yes. In fact, as a stereotype of the Mennonite character, affirmative answers to these questions could be confirmed in many in-group conversations on the street corners of most Mennonite villages.

If, however, we wish to move beyond the informal and casual approach, there are at least two ways to answer these questions. The first is historical, attempting to deduce from historical data whether the Mennonites have indeed evidenced characteristic behavior in certain areas. The second is to see what empirical research has shown. We begin with the first.

According to eyewitness accounts, early Anabaptist Mennonites "stressed strongly the idea of *Gelassenheit*—that is, yieldedness to God's will, including a life of submission to others" (Cronk 1981, 7). Although the concept is expressed in the other Mennonite groups, it has persisted, according to Cronk, much more durably in Hutterite society. Relative to personality structure, *Gelassenheit* would influence Mennonite behavior in two directions: toward God and toward one's fellow human beings. Behavior toward God would show yieldedness in attempting to do his will. With reference to humans, Mennonites would tend to submit or defer to other people in such matters as giving others the place of honor at a table, expecting other persons to speak in a meeting, and not asserting one's own ideas or opinions too aggressively. Cronk offers a specific illustration of *Gelassenheit*: "Instead of encouraging a daughter to get a higher paying job in town, a family lets her work for very low wages at the home of a church member to help a new mother with the housework while she recovers from the birth of a baby" (8).

The fact that *The Martyr's Mirror* occupied a place of central importance in Mennonite families for centuries corroborates the importance of *Gelassenheit* in Mennonite personality structure. *The Martyr's Mirror* was a strong symbol of the Mennonite society's approach to life and became a very important socialization mechanism for reinforcing obedience and submission to God and the teaching of the church. Van der Zijpp remarks: "Our whole community has manifested a unanimous desire for . . . the bloody theatre. . . . The book was used very widely in the Palatinate, especially by the Amish. It's seen in many instances as a devotional book" (1957a, 528). *The Martyr's Mirror* became a model and manual for submissive behavior and thus has undoubtedly contributed to those aspects of Mennonite personality structure.

Another aspect of the personality structure which emerges throughout the historical accounts of Mennonites is their dogged determination and perseverance. From the early days of their existence, Mennonites were never known for either flippancy or timidity in matters of faith. In fact, the accounts of some of the trials and disputations tell of brash and taunting, if not insulting, behavior that risked the most serious consequences. Many instances of this could be cited. One case involved a tribunal in which the accused Anabaptist stated, "If I am to suffer therefore, I demand the seven judges." After the interrogators refused his request, John Claess spoke up again, "Can I not obtain the full court? It is granted even to thieves and murderers. Why should it not be granted to me?" (Sauder 1945, 47).

Recent accounts of the early Anabaptists tend to present Anabaptists as being relatively unstable and credulous: "In *Ursula* (1879), included in the *Züricher Novellen*, sixteenth-century Anabaptists are portrayed as perverse enthusiasts who contribute not only to the disorder and chaos in their society but also to the suffering and madness of otherwise sane and morally upright individuals like Ursula" (Harry Loewen 1980a, 210). Other writers, such as Voltaire, Jung-Stilling, Gottfried Keller, Theodor Fontane, Gerhart Hauptmann, Ricarda Huch, and Lulu Von Strauss, tended to take the same direction (209). In Voltaire's *Candide* (1759), for example, the only good person is an Anabaptist named Jacques, but it is generally assumed that Voltaire used the Anabaptist image to present his social critique.

This is not to imply that all of the early Anabaptists were similarly outspoken, arrogant, or fully committed to live out the implications of their new faith. On the contrary, many gave up their new-found faith. Thirty companions who met in the Hottinger House in 1525 decided to "give up baptizing, simply live the Christian life together, and be obedient to my lords" (Blanke 1961, 68). As Blanke says, "With this decision the brothers of Zollikon made their peace with the state and with the church. It was a peace caused by fatigue. The various restrictions and punishments had in eight months undermined their resistance" (69).

These brief references indicate a line of questioning that could yield fascinating answers once the data has been more fully assembled and analyzed. The protocols of both disputations and trials are particularly rich in material relating to the personality structure of early Anabaptists. Although many questions are probably not answerable, further research could provide additional information for a Mennonite personality profile as well as provide answers to such questions as, Was there any selectivity in the people who joined the movement? Did the Anabaptist protest appeal to more impulsive types of people? Were the initiators and leaders of the movement more rigid and humorless than others?

Establishing a typical personality structure for present-day Mennonites is much more plausible. Not only is the field of study more accessible, but the Mennonites of our age are the beneficiaries of isolation and socialization in nearly total communities. Thus characteristics are more likely to be fixed than transient or accidental. Anthropologists maintain that selective isolation does indeed create identifiable personality structures; they point to such Indian tribes as the Hopi, Navajo, Zuni, and Papago as prime examples (Hallowell 1953, 606). Hallowell goes on to state that "human personality structure is the product of experience in a socialization process and that the resulting structure varies with the nature and conditions of such experience can scarcely be doubted" (608).

At this point, several related factors need to be discussed briefly in order to clarify the focus of the term we are using, "Mennonite personality." As used above, "personality structure" impinges on the sociological concepts of role structures and performance, and identity. The first phenomenon has to do with the way a person accepts the norms that are expected of him or her in a given social structure, and the way he or she fulfills the expectations of those roles. To illustrate, most Mennonite youth would be expected to participate in the religious activities of the community, to undergo the normal "conversion to faith," and to join the church at the usually accepted time and in the traditional manner. This response is termed "role performance"; it could be confused with "personality structure." The effectiveness of socialization is the crucial factor in role performance; the success is gauged by the degree to which younger Mennonites adopt the normative beliefs and behavior of the community. This issue is discussed in another connection in Chapter 9.

The other sociological concept which impinges on personality structure is group identity. This latter term refers to the degree to which a person is aware of, and accepting of, membership in a particular group which is set off from other groups. In this case, a more exact term would be identification, which refers to the degree to which a person accepts and internalizes the characteristics of the group. Thus, identification with the Mennonites could also be construed as referring to personality structure, but it is, in fact, different. A person could be totally identified with the ethnic group yet not show evidence of a peculiarly "Mennonite" behavior. The concept of identity is discussed further in Chapters 16, 17, and 18.

How, then, can contemporary Mennonites be described so that they are differentiated from other subgroupings in society? The easiest way, of course, is to describe the personality structure of Mennonites whose socialization is the most intense, namely, the Hutterites, the Amish, and the Old Order Mennonites. There is evidence that these Mennonites have specific characteristics. Furthermore, there is evidence of subtle but interesting variations between these groupings.

One study suggests that the Hutterites have a tendency toward depression (Eaton and Weil 1953, 84, 129). Also, Hutterite children seem to have less propensity for competitive play and behavior. Schoolteachers say that Hutterite children cannot be motivated by self-interest as much as non-Hutterites (J. A. Hostetler 1974, 230). Hutterites also seem to be more oriented toward work as a part of self-identity (ibid.) and are very prone to consider group membership as important to their self-identity. In fact, individuality is downplayed; both group membership and acceptance are central to their sense of well-being. Hosteltler says that "a successfully socialized adult Hutterite gets along well with others and is submissive and obedient to rules and regulations of the colony. He is a hardworking responsive individual" (245). According to the Myers-Briggs personality type system, Hutterites are ESFJ— "*e*xtroverted rather than introverted, *s*ensing rather than intuitive, *f*eeling rather than thinking, and *j*udgmental rather than perceptive" (Hostetler 1974, 246).

A team of psychologists from the University of Manitoba has done extensive in-depth studies of Hutterite children and adults. Although few of their researches compare Hutterites with others, their conclusions indicate that the male and female self-perceptions of Hutterite children is markedly different (Schulderman and Schulderman 1969, 272). They suggest that females tend to perceive their roles in terms of "meek-goodness" or "sociable-potency" modes, whereas males tend to perceive themselves in "potent-goodness" and "useful-activity" modes.

There is less specific information available for the Amish, but some inferences can be drawn. The Amish person tends to be conformist, according to John A. Hostetler, who uses a paradigm introduced by Merton. They are ritualistic rather than innovative, nonrebellious, curious, and desirous of learning (1980, 294ff.). Hostetler concludes that the Amish can be defined as "quiet, friendly, responsible and conscientious. The model Amish person is loyal, considerate and sympathetic. . . . how other people feel is important to him" (185–86).

The Old Order Mennonites of Ontario were studied by Minako Kirokowa Maykovich, who unfortunately did not provide any comparative data with non-Mennonites. However, from her studies she concluded that the conservative Mennonites have a greater sense of isolation, more authoritarianism, more maladjustment, and less of a feeling of personal adequacy than more progressive Mennonite groups

(Maykovich 1976). The Old Colony Mennonites, another conservative group, reflect many of the same characteristics. Members of the Old Colony group may be a bit more individualistic and contentious than individuals in the groups mentioned above; but in terms of personality structure they are in most respects quite similar to the Hutterites, Amish, and Old Order Mennonites. Reticent and cautious, they are shy, suspicious, and shrewd. They have a subtle sense of humor (C. Redekop 1969, 46–55).

The discussion of personality structure among the more progressive Mennonites is a vastly more difficult exercise. There are a number of reasons. In the first place, they encompass a much greater variety of beliefs, due to assimilation to the larger world, and this creates a more complicated model. There has also been the major movement out of isolated communities and interaction with non-Mennonites, with a consequent loss of sharpness in the delineation of characteristics. But the critical reason is simply that so little research has been done on them (B. Dyck 1983). Given the difficulty of maintaining the confidentiality of the persons studied (since Mennonites can quickly figure out who is being discussed), and because there may be very little difference between Mennonites and others, Dyck believes specialized research on Mennonites may be unnecessary (151). This is a debatable assumption at best. There is, however, an awakening interest in some aspects of this question. A clinical study from a psychiatric perspective was recently conducted at Oaklawn Psychiatric Center, a mental health center sponsored by the Mennonite Mental Health Association. In comparing individuals from the Church of the Brethren and from an Amish subgroup (not a very useful comparison for our purposes), the study showed a "higher than average percentage of diagnoses in the following categories: depressive, obsessive, compulsive adjustment reaction to adult life, passive aggressive and marital maladjustment (listed in order of frequency)" (ibid.).

There has also been some informal discussion among Mennonite scholars about the "Mennonite personality syndrome," but little if any hard evidence has been produced. In an unpublished, undated paper entitled "The Mennonite Syndrome," William Klassen—for many years affiliated with the Mennonite mental health movement—suggests on the basis of "phenomenological observation" that Mennonites indeed have some personality characteristics that set them apart. Klassen tells us that clinicians have proposed five characteristics to describe mentally healthy people: (1) they have a wide variety of sources of gratification; (2) they are flexible under stress; (3) they are able to recognize and treat other people as individuals, not merely as a mass; (4) they are able to recognize their own limitations and assets; and (5) they are active and productive in a non-neurotic sense. Klassen suggests that Mennonites tend to evidence characteristics 2, 3, and 4, but are weak on 1 and 5. He continues by saying that the Mennonite emphasis on productive work, rigidity, and dogmatism, as well as the repression of the "joy of living," contribute to this "Mennonite syndrome." The sociological issues of authority and nonresistance (pacifism), it is maintained, form the parameters within which these characteristics express themselves.

In one of the pioneering research efforts conducted in the early 1960s among Manitoba Mennonites, Irmgard Thiessen found that progressive Mennonites express "the awareness of guilt, the threat of authority, the feeling of uneasiness in a non-Mennonite authority, and the apparent suppression of sex" (1966). Since a non-Mennonite control group was used in this research, there is considerable validity in the conclusions. The author makes the significant claim that "religious teaching does form personality characteristics" (61).

Another study has some relevance to the personality topic, although the research itself deals more with values than with personality. Rushby and Thrush (1973) used the Rokeach Values Scale to compare Mennonite students at Goshen College, Goshen, Indiana, with Michigan State University students. They conclude that "the data strongly support our thesis that Mennonite students at Goshen College are both orthodox in religion and compassionate in social attitudes. As such, they constitute an exception to the inverse relationship between Christian orthodoxy and social compassion hypothesized by Rokeach" (23).

Social compassion can be interpreted as a value among Mennonites and as expressing more an expected role behavior than a personality trait. However, as was indicated earlier, it is difficult definitively to separate values and beliefs from personality traits, especially if the values and role expectations have become thoroughly internalized through effective socialization. Thus, in research reporting on Mennonites as compared to Protestants and Catholics, Hunsberger found that Mennonite students attending Mennonite colleges "seem to practice religion more and chose friends from their religious orientation as compared to the Mennonite students attending secular universities" (B. Dyck 1983, 153). Hunsberger found it difficult to separate the personality characteristics from their religious preferences.

Although not focusing on personality structure per se, Clarence Hiebert—in a study of the Holdeman Mennonites—suggested that members of this group have "developed a generally wholesome esteem. . . . The most obvious psychological syndrome . . . is a feeling of guilt for failure to live up to their teachings" (1973, 436). Hiebert goes on to say that casual observers tend to assess the Holdeman people as being overly "humble, asocial, and even austere" (436).

Probably the most sophisticated and recent study of Mennonite personality was done in 1974 by David Augsburger. While its focus is the expression of hostility in its various forms, it does compare Mennonites with others so that a norm is established. Among Mennonites Augsburger finds "sharply lower mean scores on assault and verbal hostility for both men and women; significantly lower scores on irritability and negativism; higher mean scores on guilt" (118).

Possibly the most comprehensive analysis of the Mennonite personality and/or psyche has been presented by Al Dueck. Couching the analysis in the framework of the Mennonite sectarian consciousness which is confronting the devastating forces of modernization and modernity, Dueck has the following conclusions to offer: "The traditional Mennonite self is religious. It is a psyche marked by the memory of persecution religiously defined. . . . Cognitively there is a tendency toward sectarian dualism. Belief tends to be systematized and absolutized. Intolerance is the predominant style. Emotionally, ethnic Mennonites are incapable of deep affect. The vital springs of life are choked given the parental assumption that self-will must be broken. Anger is not given expression but internalized. . . . Behaviorally, ethnic Mennonites are rigid. Traditional Mennonite faith tends to dominate most every aspect of life" (Dueck 1988, 217–18). Dueck cites the research of Dan Forsyth, who maintains that the Mennonites express an unusual need for affiliation and nurturing (218).

Dueck's analysis, and others here reviewed, tend to approach the issue from the standpoint of Mennonite identity. It is rather generally assumed that Mennonites are experiencing a "crisis of identity" not only collectively, but as individuals. A major conference of scholars held in 1986 had as its focus the Mennonite identity crisis, and the keynote speaker stated that "it can help us to understand that the search for Mennonite self-understanding is no mere academic question. . . . The first point I would like to treat is the crisis of [identity of] the Mennonites" (Goertz 1988, 2). The identity theme is prevalent in the literature and poetry of Mennonites as well, according to Peter Pauls. The thrust of Pauls's analysis is similar to that of Dueck and others—it is the difficulty of integrating "the traditions and present circumstances . . . the time-honored values and the more rapidly changing values of a larger society" (Pauls 1980, 256).

Unfortunately, in spite of these few references, well-researched data is sparse. Consequently, any extension of this discussion about contemporary Mennonite personality must be based on a variety of other evidence. As indicated above, one of the best alternative sources is literature, both fiction and nonfiction. Nonfictional historical accounts provide some evidence for personality traits and behaviors. A study of the writings in one of the church papers of the 1800s leads Liechty to conclude that "at one level, in the language of the 1800s' Mennonites, humility frequently found expression. Many articles and letters in the *Herald* and much private correspondence began with self-effacing disclaimers and ended by thanking the reader for kind indulgence. An anonymously written *Herald* article began, 'I will . . . endeavor to make a few brief remarks, although unlearned, and unworthy to make the attempt' " (1980, 12). This quality of humility is clearly reflective of the *Gelassenheit* concept discussed above.

Among fictional sources, the most representative and best-known are Arnold Dyck's writings. His Koop and Bua characters have been widely claimed as "representing some basic Mennonite types" (Al Reimer 1980a, 264). Koop is introduced in skit number two as quoting Dyck himself, "a type which is often found among us as Mennonites" (264). Reimer, in evaluating Koop and Bua, asks, "Did Arnold Dyck have actual models in mind when he created the two brush farmers? There is some reason to believe that he did" (262). Reimer continues: "Like all good artists, Dyck knew how to borrow details from actual experience and character traits from people he knew" (263–64). Reimer believes there were personality and character types in Koop and Bua:

> Koop and Bua . . . represent the two basic sides of the traditionally rural Mennonite character or psyche. Bua represents the liberal, progressive side. He is open, cheerful, gregarious, curious, eager for new experiences, emotional, impulsive, generous, and fun-loving. . . . Koop represents a less attractive side of the Mennonite character: the isolationist, ultra-conservative, pious tradition of "the quiet ones in the land." Koop's negative qualities—his penny-pinching avarice, his suspicions about everything new or different, his crass materialism— . . . are made much more explicit. (264–65)

Novels written for Mennonite children by Mennonite authors also provide us with some ideas about the ideal personality. In an analysis of

Mennonite juvenile literature, J. D. Stahl concludes that "the nexus of a communal consciousness . . . consists of a strong family life, unity of religious experience, and a distinctive minority self-awareness" (1981, 62). In terms of personality, this minority self-awareness expresses itself in "total submission to the divine command, which is interpreted as the imperative of love at all costs, the abnegation of revenge, defenselessness in the face of evil, and more challenge through exemplary action" (64). That this orientation has personality behavior consequences for young readers is self-evident. Stahl concludes: "The principle of nonresistance internalized can turn natural and inevitable feelings of anger, denied external expression, into 'passive aggressive' behavior accompanied by feelings of self-pity and self-righteousness, and issuing at their extreme in self-hatred and despair" (73).

Another source which cannot be ignored are Rudy Wiebe's novels, considered by many critics to be the best representation of contemporary Mennonitism. In *Peace Shall Destroy Many*, Mennonites are portrayed typically as rigid, dogmatic, sullen, humorless, and vindictive. On the other hand, in the same story, there are also Mennonites who are kind, open, optimistic people who enjoy life and are very gregarious—a reflection of the characteristics in *Koop en Bua*. The creation of characters who reflect various traits—contradicted in turn by others—highlights the precariousness of proposing a Mennonite personality structure. At the same time people who know Mennonites would say that they can be identified by their actions. This may be expected, since beliefs should make a difference in people's behavior; nevertheless, determining exactly how a subgroup's beliefs and values become incorporated into individual feelings, thinking, and behaving is a difficult exercise indeed.

One of the least scientific yet most suggestive and interesting ways of determining the personality structure of Mennonites is to note the popular stereotypes advanced by both outsiders and insiders. From the perspective of the insider, the following stereotypes are applied almost universally to Mennonites, Hutterites, and Amish.

1. They are frugal, economizing to the point of penny-pinching and downright stinginess. This trait is illustrated in myriad and ubiquitous stories about Mennonite tightfistedness.
2. They are shrewd and good bargainers, getting the best of most transactions. Again, many stories and anecdotes bear this out.
3. Mennonites are clannish—a very strong stereotype—always preferring their own people; it follows that they are not easy to learn

to know. They are polite to outsiders, friendly to a point but slow to open up to close relationships.

4. They are typically deferential and passive, not prone to express their feelings and attitudes in public. They will respond when addressed but usually do not assert themselves. This is usually the case in meetings and activities within the Menonite circle as well as outside.

5. On the other hand, Mennonites tend to be authoritarian, especially in family matters and congregational issues. Even outwardly passive Mennonites will be authoritarian and possibly even dictatorial within their homes and congregations. This can be documented easily in autobiographical and biographical materials, such as Urie Bender's *Stumbling Heavenward* and *Four Earthen Vessels*. These biographies depict family and neighborhood dynamics as well as religious and congregational ones, and provide evidence that goes beyond stereotypes to reality.

6. Mennonites are unemotional to the point of being somber. Two aspects of this trait relate to humor and open expression of emotion. In the case of humor, "somber" may well apply only to the outsider's perspective; it certainly does not mean that Mennonites have no sense of humor. On the contrary, there is great humor among Mennonites, but it tends to be sly, sardonic, and rather covert. In regard to expressing emotions, typically, in the privacy of their families and interpersonal relationships, Mennonites are often quite open in their feelings. Public expression of emotion has been another matter. Of course, this cliché about unemotional Mennonites is being challenged by the existence of charismatic and pentecostal Mennonites, but these groups are the exception that proves the rule.

7. Mennonites are extremely practical and down to earth. They do not engage in lofty speculation or theorizing. But they are quick to adopt new practices and often innovate in areas which have utility and relevance for their daily lives. This is especially true of the more conservative groups, who are widely known for their clever innovation and inventions.[2]

Undoubtedly, insiders could mention other traits equally as much a part of the Mennonite personality structure. But the ones listed are certainly part of the syndrome. The non-Mennonite general public would certainly list the above traits, and add to them more positive traits which may not be as unique to Mennonites as many assume. Included in this list would be honesty, a willingness for hard work, trustworthiness, charitability, humanitarianism, a preference for privacy, and aggressiveness.

Description and analysis of Mennonite personality by non-Mennonites is practically nonexistent. There are some rather intimate characterizations of the Mennonite psyche, such as Ingrid Rimland's *The Wanderers*. But Rimland is an ex-Mennonite, and it is clear that there is considerable emotional investment in the analysis, not that this detracts from her perceptiveness. A similar description is *I Hear the Reaper's Song* by Sara Stambaugh, a granddaughter of a Mennonite. She describes the Mennonite personality in very much the same terms as Rimland—rather humorless, austere, authoritarian and yet submissive, driven by guilt, hypocritical (Ohm Jasch in Paraguay in Rimland's book), and often occupied by suppressed sexual urges and fantasies. The men are domineering while the women are sullen and tending toward depression and fatalism. Religious orthodoxy and legalism is a strong restriction on a relaxed enjoyment of life. In short, Mennonites are not open and easy-going, free to express their feelings and to enjoy the normal experiences of human life. And the undercurrent which causes this mood is the tenacious, subconscious adherence to the principle of obedience to Christ and his teachings, a principle which is derived in a straight line from the Anabaptists' early faith and experience. These traits are variants of those in the list above; though not wrong, they reflect more of a biased sampling of Mennonite personality structure.

Mennonites' own awareness of personality and of mental health has been conceived traditionally in terms of religious and communal norms. That is, a "normal" person was one who accepted the norms of the Mennonite community and accepted the beliefs of the Anabaptist-Mennonite belief system. There has never been great credence given to "inner" or subjective states. Personality traits thus have normally been attributed to the "inherited" behavior of families. Invariably, when personal behavior or idiosyncracies are referred to among Mennonites the comments are couched in terms such as "You would expect Henry Penner to act as he does; after all, he is from the Peter Penner family line." The view of personality as hereditary has served as a means of avoiding and possibly also ignoring the complex subjective psychosocial dynamics of human personality which would be difficult to handle in a society that has maintained a rather intimate cohesive and homogenous collectivity.

This orientation has thus helped Mennonites downplay or evade the issue of subjectivity and individual idiosyncracies and uniqueness. The religiously based belief in the centrality of the community of believers is emphasized, and any focus on, or acknowledgement of, individual autonomy and personal perceptions and will is strongly contained and subordinated. Yet, it is precisely this factor which has created immeasurable stress on individuals in the community. Every community has its classic cases of mentally ill persons who have been carefully hidden from public view and managed with a collective silence. I spent eight months in a close-knit Old Colony community in Mexico and was not able to make direct contact with a number of people who were rumored to be ill, one being a compulsive swearer, now diagnosed as suffering from Tourette's disease (C. Redekop 1969, 281–82).

Paradoxically, Mennonites have been pioneers of sorts in treating the mentally ill among them, especially in Russia. Already in 1910, the Mennonites in Russia had established a mental hospital at Chortitza to treat patients.[3] The emergence in the United States of the rather incongruous but successful and respected Mennonite Mental Health Movement and the subsequent establishment of eight hospitals was the result of the alternative service program which emerged during World War II. Hundreds of Mennonite boys were assigned to state mental hospitals in lieu of military service; the experiences they had there developed into moral revulsion at the treatment the patients were receiving. From this compassionate response, the Mennonite Mental Health Movement was born.[4]

One dimension which has not been broached, but which is certainly a basic factor in a discussion of Mennonite personality, is the female psyche as compared to the male. Because of the generally partriarchal nature of Mennonite communities historically, the subordinated position, and possibly also the oppressed status and role, of Mennonite women has not been studied or, until recently, even admitted. But that is beginning to change, as is illustrated by the ordination of women, which is at present a major source of agitation and excitement. One of the unusually articulate and forceful voices in the Mennonite community in recent times is that of Katie Funk Wiebe. In an article entitled "The Mennonite Woman in Mennonite Fiction," she states: "There is much misery and little grandeur in the female characters presented in works dealing with the Russian-Mennonite background. . . . Female protagonists are limited in number, and minor characters frequently flat, uninteresting, and unconvincing. . . . As a type [the Mennonite woman] possesses great strength stored in some inner reservoir, but strengths which never threaten men's masculinity or their place in society" (1985, 231).

Wiebe reviews the extensive literature produced by Mennonites about themselves, and concludes, "If this image is realistic and not merely a reflection of a created image of Mennonite women, then the Mennonite experience would seem to deny women the right to full humanity" (242). A chilling observation, this, but it is probably a relatively true description. The role and position of the Mennonite woman, and the resultant self-image and identity, has been quite disturbing and is in dire need of correction, especially in the light of the Mennonite utopian ideology which has stressed the importance and equality of the person-in-community subordinated to Christ the head. The masculine and patriarchal dominance among Mennonites is illustrated by the sermon at the funeral of the widow of an elder who had died several years earlier. The minister spent most of his sermon paying respects to the elder and only briefly alluded to the woman, and then only to commend her for having been faithful and supportive of her husband (M. Redekop 1988).

USING THE DATA available, I have tried to define the nature of the peculiarly Mennonite personality. Mennonites share some personality traits with all other human beings; they also have personality traits that are unique to the Mennonites; moreover, each Mennonite has some personality traits which are totally unique to him or her (Allport 1961, 13). A standard and predictable reaction that can be heard from curious non-Mennonites after they have become acquainted with a Mennonite individual is, "I had not believed that David would be so much like other people, and yet also so unique. He is not simply a product of a Mennonite cookie cutter."

The much more difficult question is left rather unresolved, and that is, Of what importance is the Mennonite personality, and how does it affect the achievement of the Mennonite project? According to the "great man" theory of civilization, the personality of the individual is the critical factor in the process of societal goal achievement. Sociologists by definition are prone to deny this point of view, suggesting that culture and institutions are not built or changed by individuals. Interestingly, Mennonite ideology would agree with this point of view, stressing rather the importance of the group reality and the need of the individual to realize his subordinated place in and to contribute his share to the larger whole, thereby contributing to a synergistic solution—the Kingdom of God, where the whole is greater than the sum of its parts.

It is probably correct to say that the Mennonite ethos would assume that the individual's meaning is achieved fully in the context of the

Gemeinschaft and that the undue concern, even obsession, with the actualization of the separate individual is counterproductive, and maybe even profane. Hans Denck's aphorism has become something of a watchword for Mennonites: "He who would follow Christ must follow him in life." This speaks of subordination of the self to the will of a higher power. It is this which, I submit, lies at the center of the Mennonite understanding of personality.

Chapter Eight

Mennonite Intellect and Aesthetics

Seen from the perspective of one of the enduring themes in Anabaptist-Mennonite life, *Gelassenheit*, or yieldedness to God's will, the topic of intellect and aesthetics is highly suspect, if not pernicious and possibly even evil. Against the background of the "pomp and circumstance," the blasphemy of hypocrisy in "serving God," Menno Simons, in an address to the "learned ones," states: "You break the living images in which the Spirit of God dwells, making and adorning images of gold, silver, and wood. You hate a pious, blameless life, encouraging and defending by your frivolous example an unchecked wild life in the flesh. Dear sirs, where is there a single letter in the Scriptures enjoining all your ritual and worship, . . . etc.? Is not all you do and promote deception, hypocrisy, blasphemy, abomination, and idolatry?" (1956, 207).

From this point of view, it is easier to understand the concept of *Gelassenheit* which has been proposed as being the basic mode of the new life. Learning was for the purpose of instructing members in the humble walk with Christ, and an adorning of the mind or of the flesh was seen as a reversion to "Babylon." Testimonies to this position can be found almost at random in the early writings of Anabaptism.

Melchior Hoffman said, "Therefore I warn all lovers of truth that they do not give themselves over to lofty arguments which are too hard for them, but that they hold themselves to the straightforward words of God in all simplicity" (Klaassen 1982, 148). Bernhard Rothmann echoed the same sentiments: "The divine, unquestionable Holy Scriptures which are called the Bible alone have the fame that they are needful and sufficient for teaching, reproof, correction, and for instruction in righteousness" (ibid., 149). And Menno Simons, who was quoted above, continued: "You say, we are inexpert, unlearned, and know not the Scriptures. I reply: the Word is plain and needs no interpretation" (ibid., 151).

Mennonites early expressed this fear of human pride and worship of human creativity in many ways, and it can be identified in many groups in manifold ways even today. The so-called Plain People—the Mennonite groups who have retained simplicity of lifestyle and thought—have most eloquently symbolized this mode. The groups and/or individuals who sympathize with this tendency in the Mennonite spectrum have thus never been overly bothered with intellectual and aesthetic concerns (Redekop and Hostetler 1977). In fact, Mennonite life of the "humanist spirit" has emerged in direct confrontation with this attitude or orientation.

Most if not all of the artistic and creative impulses which expressed themselves in the history of Mennonitism has broken in through the inherent suspicion of the corruptibility of human nature. The fact that many of the early leaders had been exposed to humanism and had in varying ways been influenced by it does not negate the fact that the orientation toward, and separation from, the world soon included a strong proscription of humanistic expression (Kreider 1952). It is therefore almost impossible to describe influence on Anabaptists of the intellectual and aesthetic climate that prevailed during the Reformation. But a word about the theological, philosophical, and aesthetic environment at the time may be in order.

A Historical Sketch

Theologically, the great ferment of the Reformation centered on the conflict between traditional and classic religious orthodoxy (Roman Catholicism) and the attempt on the part of some of the more courageous to challenge it and to make it more responsive to the needs of the people and to the biblical texts. Philosophically, humanism was beginning to make great inroads into the universities and intellectual strata in the larger cities such as Vienna and Amsterdam. Certainly Erasmus was widely known and was influential even for Menno Simons and other Anabaptists (Kreider 1952). A renaissance of the philosophy of antiquity, which was one of the streams of humanism, also was filtering into the mainstream, and the development of the printing press revolutionized the intellectual life of Europe by 1500. Aesthetically, of course, the Renaissance spirit had long been making its way into all aspects of the society, including the religious institutions, and involved architecture, art, painting, poetry, and music. The role of the Renaissance in the emergence of the Reformation itself has been studied extensively, and it is clear that the Renaissance was a major factor in the emergence of the common man and the belief that society was not a predetermined order of the elite and the slaves (Latourette 1953, 604ff.).

The members of the Anabaptist revolt had obviously been as exposed to the factors described here as had the general population, but how these forces may have energized or influenced the form the Anabaptist movement took is pretty much conjecture since so little information has been available and so little study has been done in this area. Recent scholarship has, however, expanded our understanding of the degree to which Anabaptism was part of the general cultural and social ferment (Goertz 1980).

Historically, for some Mennonites, this subject has been a contradiction in terms. Some contemporary scholars go even farther and point to the utter intellectual and aesthetic impoverishment of the Mennonite mind, while others state that "it is extremely difficult to find 'the thinker' in contemporary Anabaptist Mennonite circles" (Wiebe 1980, 149). In explaining the paucity of the Russian Mennonite intellectual history, Toews states that the educated men "could not expose their modest treasure to the crass minds of a new language and new culture. The intellectual had too much to lose. There would be no niche for him in the villages of the hard frontier" (J. B. Toews 1979, 137). Numerous discussions point to the rather sparse aesthetic and intellectual life among Mennonites. For example, Harry Loewen states that "for all the skills they have shown for centuries in the practical arts, Mennonites have failed to develop among themselves an appreciation for the literary arts and even less for literary artists" (1983, 119). These characterizations are only partially true, however, for it will be shown that Mennonites have produced considerable literary and artistic material.

The description of the aesthetic and intellectual life of Mennonites is one thing; tracing its causes and its consequences is quite another. For example, Don Wiebe suggests that the Mennonite tradition itself is anti-intellectual and inimical to the arts (1980, 160). In this section I want to deal historically with Mennonite participation in the life of the mind as reflected particularly in intellectual and aesthetic activities. The simplest way to get at this subject is to ask whether Mennonites have produced as well as consumed intellectual and aesthetic culture. It is not an easy question to answer.[1]

During the first three hundred years of Anabaptist-Mennonite history there is little evidence of any secular intellectual or aesthetic production except among the Dutch. Most of the intellectual and aesthetic effort was channeled into the nurturing of the religious life. The basic text for living was the Bible, the German translation of Martin Luther. Hence the Lutheran orientation became influential, even though Anabaptists produced a few of their own versions (Bender 1955e). *The Martyrs' Mirror*, published in 1659, was the next most important influence in Mennonite cultural life and was used by a vast majority of Mennonite homes for many centuries (van der Zijpp 1957a).

The production of Mennonite music began with the *Ausbund* (1564), composed by Philipite Hutterites at Passau on the Danube, and considered to be the oldest Christian hymnal in continuous use (Friedmann 1955). The Dutch also produced hymnals as early as 1560. More hymnals were produced in subsequent years; for many years, these probably represented the closest thing to aesthetic activity appearing in the Mennonite tradition. Mennonites have always engaged in singing. Much of this has been congregational, but they have also established choirs which have nurtured the faith through the centuries. Musical expression among Mennonites has thus developed into an amazingly rich and complex tradition, but little writing of original music appeared until very recently, since Anabaptists and Mennonites have traditionally adapted their lyrics to existing sacred or secular songs or folk melodies (H. Bender 1957e, 792).

Singing of various kinds, especially by choirs, was probably most developed in the Russian Mennonite tradition, possibly coming to full flower among the Mennonite Brethren. The numerous singing schools and *Saengerfesten* which were held in Russia and subsequently in Canada, the United States, and major Mennonite settlements in Paraguay, Uruguay, and Brazil attest to this development. In recent years, many musical performers and even virtuosi have come out of this tradition, especially in Canada. There were also Swiss Mennonite singing schools in the eastern United States (Yoder 1959). Usually held in a school, these were community events occurring as often as once a week, normally during the winter, in which the various rudiments of singing were taught. The *Philharmonia*, published in 1875, had thirty-seven lessons on music theory. The most extended and well known of these schools was the one organized at Singers Glen, Virginia, by Joseph Funk, who also pioneered in the development of *Harmonia Sacra,* an early collection of religious music. The same phenomenon was found in Ontario as late as the 1940s. The Amish hymn sing is another example of Mennonite interest in singing; these events still take place.

In the more specifically aesthetic expressive arts—such as non-religious music or the plastic arts, including painting and sculpture—Mennonites have tended to be relatively uninvolved. The Dutch Mennonites are a very significant exception. In the Netherlands numerous Mennonites were represented in the arts early; these included Lambert Jacobsz, Govert Flinck, Jacob van Ruisdael, possibly Rembrandt, and others (there is still disagreement as to whether Rembrandt was actually a member of the Mennonite church). Indeed, H. S. Bender states that Mennonitism in Holland was the source of Reformation art in Holland: "All that Protestantism has contributed to the cultural life of the Netherlands, especially with respect to art, can be traced in principle and in its essence to this Anabaptistically determined Reformation" (H. Bender 1955c, 169). A recent work by Groenveld (1980) for the first time presents in an organized fashion the incredibly creative aesthetic life of seventeenth- to nineteenth-century Dutch Mennonites, which has not generally been recognized.

In literature, practically nothing was produced for many generations, and Mennonites read very little "worldly" literature. Often artists of Mennonite origin produced literature, but left the church, as did, for example, the well-known Dutch poet Joost von den Vondel (1587–1679). Jan Philipsz Schabaelje wrote *Lusthof des Gemoeds* (*The Wandering Soul*), the "most popular Mennonite book ever published" (Jeltes 1957, 355). Jan Luyken (1649–1712), known above all for his illustrations of *The Martyrs' Mirror,* was probably one of the most noted and gifted poets and artists. Here is further evidence that, following 1560, the Dutch Mennonites became the leading producers and consumers of the arts in the Mennonite family for some three hundred years.

Swiss Mennonites produced practically no writing or art of any note apart from music (O. Schowalter 1957, 360). The Russian commonwealth also produced relatively little art, but occasionally good literary works appeared. Among Russian Mennonites, the leading writers would include Arnold Dyck (1889–1970), Hans Harder (1889–1970), Gerhard Loewen (1863–1946), Gerhard Toews (1897–1986), Fritz Senn (1894–1983), and J. H. Janzen (1878–1950) (Al Reimer 1980b,

256; Harry Loewen 1983). Mennonites in North America did not enter into the literary and artistic world until the late nineteenth and early twentieth century, although some *Fraktur* work emerged early in Pennsylvania, even among the Amish.

Generally speaking, until about 1850, it could be said of Mennonites that "with their emphasis upon simplicity, sincerity, and humility, art seemed to them artificial and pretentious, often dangerous and wasteful. . . . Possibly the rural character of these groups and their cultural isolation may account for some of their negativism toward art. In any case, this negative attitude toward art . . . persisted through the nineteenth century among all Mennonite groups except those in Holland, the North German cities, and the Palatinate" (H. Bender 1955c, 167). Since the beginning of the twentieth century, however, there has emerged a collection of Mennonite artists who have established solid artistic reputations. Foremost among them are the German Daniel Wohlgemuth (1876–1967), renowned for his landscapes and portraits; Woldemar Neufeld (1909–), born in Russia, who has a firm reputation as a landscape painter; and Oliver Wendell Schenk (1903–), also known for landscapes. Arthur Sprunger (1897–1972) and J. P. Klassen (1888–1975) are known for their sculpture. Neufeld and Schenk, probably the best-known artists of Mennonite stock in North America, forsook the Mennonite community, although they still occasionally paint Mennonite themes.

An increasing number of Mennonite artists, including composers, musicians, painters, sculptors, poets, novelists, and even playwrights, have appeared among the Swiss and Dutch Mennonite streams. Many of these are employed by Mennonite colleges, but others are employed at secular universities or self-employed. The creativity and contribution of the artistic community among Mennonites is just beginning, and promises to gain acceptance in the larger arena. The *Mennonite Life* quarterly, published at Bethel College by Cornelius Krahn for many years, and now the more recent *Festival Quarterly*, have chronicled the development of this movement.

There developed through the centuries a considerable and varied body of writing *about* Anabaptists and Mennonites—from Voltaire's *Candide* (1759) to Gottfried Keller's *Mennonite Novellas* to Theodore Fontane's *Quitt* (1891) and Josef Ponten's cycle *Auf dem Wege*. But since Mennonites shied away from literature, it is doubtful that many Mennonites read these authors or were even aware of them (Harry Loewen 1980a, part III).

In the more specifically intellectual quest in the academic context,

American Mennonites began to enter the arena at the turn of the nineteenth century. The scholarship began with the serious writing of Mennonite history; C. Henry Smith (1875–1948) was one of the leaders of the movement, being the first Mennonite to obtain a Ph.D. degree from an American university, in 1907 (C. Henry Smith 1962, 238). In Russia at the same time, P. M. Friesen wrote a massive composite history, sociology, and psychology of the Mennonite Brethren and the Kirchliche in Russia, dealing with the period from 1850 to 1910, a volume published in 1911. Later, H. S. Bender, another outstanding American Mennonite scholar, researched and wrote in both history and theology. He spearheaded many significant activities, including the *Mennonite Encyclopedia,* which is the most comprehensive source on Mennonitica available. Many others pioneered in higher education. But it was a difficult terrain, containing many obstacles and setbacks. Mennonite resistance to, and eventual embracing of, higher education is expanded upon in Chapter 11.

Since the 1940s, Mennonites have begun to move beyond mere self-interpretation and self-analysis and make a contribution in the intellectual world beyond the Mennonite pale (Harry Loewen 1983, 123). Most of this intellectual and aesthetic activity has been informed by the prevailing intellectual and aesthetic milieu. Thus, Mennonite Ph.D.'s in history or biology or art have contributed to the world of scholarship on the basis of their professional community's values. Few, if any, of the scholars, intellectuals, and artists have achieved a self-confident status which allows them to use their own history and tradition as the basis for art forms or for discourse, as the Jews have done.

One recent and eloquent statement of the reticence of Mennonites to enter the world of literature and art is John L. Ruth's *Mennonite Identity and Literary Art.* Ruth's message focuses on the fact that Mennonites have tended to want to forget their history because it sets them apart and keeps them from becoming a part of the mainstream: "We fail to know our own past not because it has left no evidence, but because we prefer not to know it" (17). Ruth pleads for a creative expression of the Mennonite faith:

My point . . . is that what will enable us as Mennonites to see our story, let alone tell it, will be . . . a vital imagination. This is our only protection against being zapped from two opposite directions. If, on the one hand, our practical, provincial piety, fearful of the risks of art, has drowned our story in obscurantist inarticulateness, a "liberation," on the other hand, that results in an easy abandoning of the story only substitutes another, more ironic shallowness: ignorance of who one is. A positive, life-affirming energy must drive the delicate craft of our art between the Scylla of the legalistic negations of a narrow communal mind, and the Charybdis of a soul-forsaking shopping about in the macrocultural marketplace for themes and styles. (48)

In conclusion, Mennonite aesthetic and intellectual life has been portrayed as very subdued and sparse. With the exception of the Netherlands, where Mennonite art and philosophy flourished, it has remained relatively quiet for centuries. In the present century North America has had an awakening coterie of people who are becoming increasingly vocal and visible. It is no longer necessary to say there is no Mennonite art, literature, or philosophy; there are now Mennonites who are engaged in the doing of art, literature, and philosophy. The emergence of literary and scholarly journals, several in the last few years, which are receiving general acclaim and acceptance, is an indication of the growing interest in this field of expression. The foremost examples are *Mennonite Life*, the *Journal of Mennonite Studies*, the *Conrad Grebel Review*, and the *Festival Quarterly*, all of which are experiencing wide subscriber support. In general, they deal with scholarly studies, literature, art, and music produced among Mennonites. Whether Mennonite literature and art is quality work and whether it has a peculiarly Mennonite flavor is still being debated (Tiessen 1988). The discussions regarding the reasons for the existence of art, literature, and philosophy themselves become part of the story.

The Traditional Rationale for a Mennonite Stance toward Art, Literature, and Philosophy

Unquestionably the nature of Mennonite art, literature, and philosophy is related directly to Anabaptist-Mennonite beliefs as well as to the history of Mennonites' minority-majority experience. On the basis of this premise, it could be understood why the Mennonites have produced so little intellectual or aesthetic material. On the other hand, it could be argued that the aesthetic life has been very impressive, considering the restrictions under which it operated: "There are those, however, who doubt whether much great art can be produced in a group which has a strict standard of Christian morals and a strong sense of separation from the 'world,' and a relative isolation from the main stream of the national culture, since this might interfere with the freedom required for creative art. There are also those who hold on the other side that the autonomy of art is a danger to a truly profound religious experience and that one or the other must be sacrificed" (H. Bender 1955c, 168).

As indicated in preceding chapters, Anabaptist-Mennonite society has emerged as the result of an attempt to live the gospel message as Mennonites understood it, in direct opposition to their oppressors and to the neighbors who believed differently. As is the case with all minority groups, their view of themselves, of others, of the world, of their own purpose, and of their experience were interpreted in the context of history and of daily life and thought. There was no preexisting charter or constitution. The shape of Anabaptist-Mennonite society emerged through its interaction with and its experience within a mainly hostile environment.

It might be useful here to note H. Richard Niebuhr's attempt to recreate a typology clarifying the religious impulse in its cultural context. His categories are: (1) Christ against culture; (2) Christ of culture; (3) Christ above culture; and (4) Christ and culture in paradox. Niebuhr suggests that "Mennonites have come to represent the attitude Christ against culture most purely, since they not only renounce all participation in politics and refuse to be drawn into military service, but follow their own distinctive customs and regulations in economics and education" (Niebuhr 1951, 56). This characterization of the Mennonites, though helpful, must be rejected. In the first place, it is not true that Mennonites reject culture. They selectively reject certain aspects, but they adapt a great deal of culture and technology. Secondly, Niebuhr's statement is a contradiction in itself, for to reject political participation and military service yet follow one's own "distinctive customs" is a contradiction. Both military service and one's own customs are cultural expressions. Thus, Niebuhr indirectly admits that Mennonites reject certain cultural areas and accept others; this is inconsistent with his term for the Mennonite stand on culture.

The only generally acceptable position is that Anabaptist-Mennonites were not against culture as such, but only certain aspects of it. Loewen suggests that "Anabaptists of the sixteenth century, while rejecting the sinfulness of the world, did not withdraw from the world" (Harry Loewen 1980a, 86). They were "religious and social activists and some of them were political revolutionaries" (87). What stance, then, did the Anabaptist-Mennonites take with respect to the environment, and how does an awareness of this stance help us to understand their cultural life? None of Niebuhr's categories seems to fit, and so I propose another category, namely, "Christ the Lord of culture." In this perspective, the relation of culture to the Christian life is that culture has to be judged by biblical teaching and subordinated to that teaching (C. Redekop 1970, 120).

This position would hold that those things which were not in conflict with the biblical record were condoned, while those institutions, norms, and values which contradicted or ran counter to biblical teaching had to be rejected. In other words, nonconformity to the *evil* in the world was the central attitude. Thus, Christ was Lord over all culture, and those elements which were contrary to his Lordship had to be rejected. "We have been united concerning the separation that shall take place from the evil and the wickedness which the devil has planted in the world, simply in this: that we have no fellowship with them, and do not run with them in the confusion of their abominations," states the Schleitheim Confession of 1527 (Howard Loewen 1985, 80).

It was this view which created the negative and dualistic perspective which has informed Mennonite history for four hundred years. But it was the experience of Mennonites as they tried to follow this counsel that forged the actual stance toward the "world." In the realm of education, therefore, the attitude was created not only by the intrinsic way in which higher education could threaten faith, but by the way the "learned doctors" engaged in persecution of the "faithful flock." Dirk Philips quoted a common proverb—"The more learned, the more perverted"—in support of his view that education was not sufficient to give a true knowledge of theology and Holy Scriptures (Harry Loewen 1980a, 89).

What the Anabaptist-Mennonites considered to be worldly and of the world can be said to be derived from three areas: the Scriptures, Anabaptist experience at the hands of secular and religious authorities, and the Anabaptist "reading" of history in terms of the first two elements. Let us look at each in turn.

First, Mennonites were above all biblicists. Thus, when the apostle John stated, "Love not the world nor the things in the world," Mennonites felt that they were faced with a clear mandate which had to be applied in concrete fashion to the civilization in which they lived. Although the concept of biblicism has been variously defined, it is generally agreed that for Mennonites the Bible was "authoritative for doctrine and life, for all worship and activity, for all church regulations and discipline" (H. Bender 1955d). The influence of external factors (culture) on this stance cannot be denied. But it must be emphasized that the Anabaptists were ultimately concerned about responding to the *substance* of biblical teaching on its own terms.

Second, the interaction between Anabaptist-Mennonites and the authorities in the secular and religious institutions was clearly two-sided. On the one hand, the Anabaptist-Mennonite actions helped, in some degree, to determine the reactions of the authorities. On the other hand, it was this very response of the secular world that became influential in defining the world—that which was against the Christian faith as Mennonites understood it. While it is obvious that their theology was a beginning point, it is just as obvious that the process of conflict contributed greatly to the forging of Mennonite ideas of what was worldly.

Finally, Anabaptists' experience and subsequent "reflexive" reactions to that experience produced a theology of what was worldly and what was holy and significant for the kingdom of God. Hence, for example, the use of power and coercion was seen as futile and was rejected totally, since their own experience had "proven" their conclusion. This argument has been advanced not only by Marxists such as Engels and Kautzky, but also by historians and sociologists (Clasen 1972; Friesen 1974; Goertz 1980; J. Stayer 1982).

Mennonite participation in the "life of the spirit" in the areas of music, literature, art, and intellect was generally weak and discouraged therefore, because the experience of oppression at the hands of the "pagan world" was simply not distinguishable from any of the possibly acceptable aesthetic aspects in the religious part of this culture. Indeed, the institution that was persecuting them was a church replete with religious symbolism reflected in incomparably rich and varied art forms. So it was only a short step to link these aesthetic expressions to the obviously ungodly acts of oppression and persecution. In discussing nonconformity to the world, Menno Simons, a converted Catholic priest, stated: "It would be more in accordance with evangelical requirements, if [Gellius] would diligently point such proud and exalted persons to the humility of Christ . . . that they may repent of their excessive pomp and vanity, and their superfluity and ungodliness. . . . This is not a kingdom in which one adorns himself with gold, silver, pearls, silk, velvet and costly finery, as does the proud, haughty world" (H. Bender 1944, 94). The occasional outcroppings of aesthetic production—such as appeared in Holland, especially in art, as well as the continual emergence of music—indicated that the urge was ever present and that it was the Mennonite ideology of faith and life which kept it in submission.

However, having said all this, one can still maintain that Mennonites have produced a rather astounding amount of intellectual and artistic culture. The Dutch Mennonites have produced an array of paintings, literature, music, and even plastic art, including stained glass windows (H. Bender 1955c, 168; Groenveld, Jacobszoon, and Verheus 1980). Moreover, in 1625 there were Mennonite art collectors in Amsterdam who were famous for their collections of art, both Mennonite and non-Mennonite (Groenveld et al. 1980). The same holds true for Mennonites in North Germany.

At present, there are faithful Mennonites producing intellectually creative literature and art that has no ostensible Mennonite derivation or substance. There are others creating scholarly, literary, or artistic works pertaining to Mennonite themes who—although their heritage and wellspring of creativity is clearly Anabaptist-Mennonite—would not identify themselves as such (Pauls 1980).

The Faith/Arts Dilemma

Having noted the above, it is important to emphasize a major change that is taking place. An increasingly large sector of Mennonites self-consciously consider their work as coming out of a Mennonite experience and speaking to a peculiarly Mennonite perspective. The *Festival Quarterly*, the *Journal of Mennonite Studies, Mennonite Life*, and other journals increasingly portray the conscious Mennonite theme. As a matter of fact, attenders at a recent conference entitled "Mennonite Artists in the Community," in Winnipeg, discussed the tensions Mennonite artists feel as they try to create art, knowing they will experience rejection for it (*Mennonite Reporter* 1983).

Although the content of such aesthetic activities as painting and music cannot be applied too directly or literally in understanding the essence of Mennonite aesthetic and cultural life, it can more easily be done in literature and poetry. The subject and content of much Mennonite art, over a long historical time line, reflect the tensions between belonging to a separated people and desiring to relate to the larger world. Bender concludes that art was produced mainly by those Mennonite groups who had integrated rather closely with the national culture (1955c, 169). In describing contemporary Russian Mennonite poetry, Peter Pauls states, "Much contemporary Mennonite poetry reflects the clash of the past European-Russian culture with the present more urban and more urbane way of life" (1980, 250). Later, in describing ethnic poets in general and Mennonite poets in particular, he states: "All of them observe, comment on and/or dramatize the clash between traditions and present circumstances, between time-honoured values and the more rapidly changing values of a larger society" (256).

This reference to a particular type of aesthetic expression may provide a bridge for the contemporary situation. Mennonites have found themselves in a separated world, a world which tended to provide its own *Weltanschauung*. But the continuing dialogue with the larger world, even though it was often discouraged, continued to develop. The extremely complex ambiguity about "worldliness"—which did not really stipulate that the larger society was innately sinful but nevertheless suggested that it should be avoided since mixing with it would mean breakdown of the solidarity of the Mennonite community—tended to produce a love-hate attitude toward the development of the mind and the creative instincts. Thus, both the creative person and the consumer of arts within the community were caught in a bind. Both were attracted to certain creative aspects of life, but because creativity was seen as glorifying humankind, both needed to avoid those attractions. In writing about the Mennonite community, one Mennonite author who now considers herself an outsider, stated, "Once upon a time, my Mennonite grandmother Katja peered at me sternly over her glasses and asked in great consternation: 'Why in the world would you want to write about something that all of us know anyway?'" (Rimland 1980, 267).

Traditionally, if a thought, act, or feeling contributed to the *Gelassenheit* of a Mennonite community, it was sanctioned and accepted. Whatever went beyond that, however, seemed to smack of *Hochmut* ("pride"), a concept which is still very much alive among Mennonites in its various names ("pride," persons who are "high and mighty," etc.). The one reason for excommunication that still applies within the Old Colony Mennonite community is *Hoffart*, which means a haughty spirit. Thus, humility, a more observable dimension of *Gelassenheit*, became the norm for general Mennonite demeanor. Joe Liechty, in a thorough study of midwestern Mennonites states: "All the evidence insists that humility had much deeper, stronger roots than a mere inferiority complex resulting from a lack of education. For most Mennonites, the humble style was only the literary extension of their deepest beliefs about how people should relate to each other and to their God" (Liechty 1980, 16). The Old Colony Mennonites still reflect the hard core of Mennonite ideology, and it is common to hear the phrase *Daut es nicht to brucke* when an unusual development or practice is discussed. Translated it says, "That is not useful" or "That cannot be usefully employed." The Anabaptist-Mennonite sectarian position vis-à-vis the world was a practical view of the Christian life in the Kingdom of God. A great amount of sophistication or obfuscation only served to intervene in or even sidetrack Christ's call: "He who would come after me, let him deny himself, take up his cross and follow me."

But the last century in North America presents a changing picture of how worldliness was defined and controlled in the aesthetic and intellectual arena. There are several typologies of Mennonite intellectual life that can be discerned, although there will be considerable deviance in specific cases. These might help us understand the present conditions.

The Retreatist Approach

The first type, the retreatist approach, considers the world of contemplation and expression a sign of pride and deceit. The conservative Old Order groups and Hutterites fall unequivocally into this category. Even though they support some education, education is very rigidly controlled to function as an agent for socialization, for the purpose of handing down *the faith once delivered* and nothing more. Schoolteachers are prohibited from getting higher education, and the school curriculum is restricted to the utilitarian subjects of Bible reading, writing, and arithmetic. An outstanding Old Colony intellectual, one of the few who has ever put anything in writing, has published a little booklet entitled *School and Community*. In it, David Harder states: "If I have been called to be a Mennonite, the faith of my fathers, insofar as it is consistent with the word of God and true to his will, then I am not free to follow other [worldly] teaching (1969, 2).

Although there are clearly very artistic and intelligent people among the Old Order groups, the expression and consumption of artistic and intellectual interests are stringently restricted. Expressions of art are severely stylized—as, for example, in the quilting done by women. In some groups, sermons are read and often handed down from one generation to the next. Very few, if any, original ideas or artifacts are allowed or developed.

This sectarian cognitive orientation recognizes two worlds. The one is ruled by Satan, the other by God: "Everything falls into one or the other category. There is never any doubt into which kingdom a certain thing falls" (C. Redekop 1959, 140–41). It is only when questions arise about where the boundaries should be that sectarian structure breaks down. Much of sectarian life thus is focused on keeping the sense of boundaries very clear and specific. Any intellectual foray that explores the heart of self-identity must be carefully avoided. The work of art and of the intellect is a part of this category, for both of these tend to call attention to nontraditional perspectives, feelings, and concepts. This is not to deny that poets and philosophers have emerged among the retreatist types. Beyond question there have been many of these, but they have expressed their creativity in normatively subtle and approved ways.

The second approach is represented by those Mennonites who have considered the aesthetic and intellectual spheres in no way inimical to the Anabaptist-Mennonite way of life. This position is at the opposite end of the continuum from the first and is probably not really adhered to by many North American Mennonites. In Europe, the Dutch Mennonites would characterize this position, but in the United States and Canada no Mennonite group has considered the aesthetic and intellectual life fully compatible with religious experience and involvement (Loewen 1980a, 92). There is no Mennonite congregation in North America which would allow free rein to intellectual and aesthetic expression. The closest approximation to such freedom of practice might be found in the church colleges, where more artistic and intellectual endeavor is possible because college communities are not congregations and consequently not subordinate to congregational discipline. But even there, the aesthetic and intellectual product has always been carefully evaluated and monitored. Many "heresy hunts" have taken place on church college campuses, and even today, only a few colleges have been able to hire non-Mennonite professors.

Freedom in aesthetic and intellectual activity is probably exercised only by individuals who are moving or have moved out of the Mennonite community and are, to all intents and purposes, operating as non-Mennonites in the context of the larger society. Mennonites who have achieved much aesthetic and intellectual renown in secular society are usually no longer members of the Mennonite community. One such person, recently portrayed in a fascinating biography, is Gordon Friesen, who became a left-leaning reformer during the Depression and wrote some very good short stories and feature articles (Teichrau 1983). His wife, also a well-known reformer, and he—now living in almost total obscurity—have only memories of their very protected Mennonite childhood. Probably the best example of a person born and raised Mennonite who left the Mennonite faith and community with a great deal of dislike, yet harbored contradictory longings to return "to the fold" is Menno Duerksen. In his book *Dear God, I Am Only a Boy,* Duerksen, a journalist who served with the U.S. army as a journalist-reporter, portrays the intellectual and aesthetic restrictiveness of the Mennonite community and takes considerable pleasure in pointing out the foibles of Mennonite society. Though much of what he says is true, there is a clear undercurrent of anger which indicates a still unresolved love-hate relationship with Mennonitism.

The Cooptative Approach

The intermediate position might be termed the *cooptative approach*. This approach entails the idea that the aesthetic and intellectual life is not evil so long as it is used for the right objective. Thus, churches could sponsor and utilize church magazines and support publishing houses as well as colleges and seminaries. Poetry could be useful for expressing faith, and fiction could make a religious point, if carefully monitored. This position best describes the stance of most North American Mennonites during the last one hundred years. No conferences reject the mass media, literature, and art as such. There is much optimism that the use of the intellect for the propagation of the faith and the building of the kingdom of God can be helpful. John Ruth, who has captured much of this spirit, has stated, "In the recent words of Irving Howe, 'A sense of national piety towards one's origin can live side by side with the spirit of critical detachment' " (1978, 62). Ruth continues, "For my part I should like to hear my heritage expressed by voices 'artistic' or otherwise" (65).

The floodgates literally have been opened to this approach in recent years. There are artists, poets, and intellectuals in every area of North America's landscape. Some are creating within the Mennonite context; others find they need to work beyond its boundaries. The existence of this latter group points to the factor which brings us to the heart of the cooptation typology.

The cooptation position is premised on the assumption that critique also involves commitment. Thus, the life of the intellectual cannot be given free rein, but must be tied to an ultimate foundation or faith, in this case, the Mennonite heritage (Sawatsky 1983). This situation is not unlike the status of the artist intellectual under Soviet communism. To be totally free to express oneself would lead to the forsaking of or, worse still, the undermining of the tradition.

This is the paradox many Mennonite artists and intellectuals find themselves in, and it explains the bitter diatribes which Mennonite artists and intellectuals have directed toward their own communities. But it is based on Mennonite society's subconscious as well as conscious awareness that unrestricted involvement in the intellectual and aesthetic life can lead to a dissolution of the body. Wiebe says that the "supposed irrationality of our 'Christian' (Anabaptist) 'identity' does not seem to bother us. Instead of grappling with the problem, we attempt to evade it by 'fracturing' the very notion of rational thought; we invoke the 'tu quoque argument' " (D. Wiebe 1980, 163).

The cooptation model has accepted the validity of the aesthetic and intellectual life, but it has strongly attempted to subordinate it to the control of the belief and value system of Mennonite society. This has created a tension which has alienated many creative people, some of whom never return to the Mennonite community.

The cooptation approach is clearly the most unstable of the three models presented. In effect, it is an attempt to keep together two cultures—the culture of self-expression and humanistic endeavor, and the culture of self-denial and *Gelassenheit*. These two cultures tend to want to separate or become alienated. Robert Redfield has suggested that there is in every society a "great and little tradition" which tend to become alienated from each other. The "great tradition" is usually composed of the artists and the learned, and the "little tradition" is concerned that values be preserved. "In a civilization there is a great tradition, of the reflective few, and there is a little tradition of the largely unreflective man" (1956, 70). Whereas the "little tradition" is concerned with the preservation and transmission of values, the "great tradition" is constantly concerned about evaluating, testing, and expanding the given culture; it is this latter factor which is threatening to the "little tradition" (76ff.). This metaphor may be helpful in understanding the tension in Mennonite society, not only between the artists and the laity, but also between the laity and the theologically trained and generally educated "elite" in Mennonite institutions, especially institutions of higher learning.

The Future of the Faith /Arts Dilemma

The threat to churchly identity which aesthetic and intellectual investigation creates has been expressed time and time again through the emergence of sectarian division and conflict. One such example is the running battle between the establishment Mennonites in the intellectual centers, namely, the colleges, and those in the conservative hinterland, as represented, for example, by the *Sword and Trumpet*. This organ, established in 1929, describes itself as a "faith-defending drift-opposing religious quarterly" whose goal is the "unmistakable and uncompromising expression of Mennonite conservatism" (H. Bender 1959f, 677). It continues to join battle with "liberalizing" tendencies in the church. There is considerable conflict as to whether its position is a reflection of reality or a reactionary and romantic retreat. That this one example could be supplemented with countless others points to the critical significance of this issue.

A growing sector of artists and scholars are suggesting that the Mennonite sectarian position creates an incompatibility between the life of the mind and the life of faith. In this interpretation, it is not the traditionalism of the rural-folk-ethnic culture which is inimical to the freedom of the creative mind and imagination, but rather the nature of the faith itself. Hence, the dualistic authoritarianism which has been a seeming consequence of Anabaptist belief has tended to repress all "frivolity" and "worldly" activity. A recent collection of autobiographies entitled *Why I Am a Mennonite* includes a number of artists who propose this theme (Harry Loewen 1988).Women, especially, appear to be the victims of this dynamic.

Another closely related issue is the problem of needing to separate the cultural (ethnic) aspects of Mennonite life from its faith. Many Mennonites—in fact, a good proportion—having been influenced by fundamentalism and evangelicalism, have come to the conclusion that the Mennonite preoccupation with Mennonite art and thought is a sign of secularization and apostasy. These people approve of Mennonite art so long as it is totally and categorically separated from faith. This orientation presumably would say that it is perfectly all right for a Christian to be an artist, but that for a Mennonite to deal with Mennonite subcultural themes would be mixing faith and the world (J. Redekop 1987).[2]

In another context, it has been proposed that the sectarian point of view can be understood as having the following characteristics: (1) it emerges from a rational frame of mind where ideas precede action; (2) it is a categorical frame of mind in which everything is either black or white; (3) it is a closed thought system in which changes are very threatening, in which "there is no point in reopening old issues or reexamining issues that have been decided earlier" (C. Redekop 1961, 42–46). The main issue in the Mennonite intellectual and aesthetic process is the question of identity formation and socialization. These two are interwoven, yet the latter—when it moves beyond mere transmission of the heritage—begins to affect identity. Identity formation is far more complex, and the intellectual and aesthetic process is far more open-ended and critical.

Socialization

The process of handing on a tradition or a system of faith is self-evident and self-justifying. No Mennonite group has questioned the process for a minute, especially that segment of Mennonite society which was largely nonliterate and oral. The heritage was conveyed through an informal communication system and a minimal formal educational program. At this level the challenge and tension of the aesthetic and intellectual world hardly existed, for there was little possibility of its emerging. This observation is applicable for all traditional, nonliterate societies: they do not change much, and if they do, it is mainly in response to external conditions. There is little need for innovation, and consequently there is little deviance.

But with the emergence of formal aspects of socialization, especially among the more progressive and "coopational" types, a serious dilemma has been created for Mennonites. For with the acceptance of formal education—elementary and Bible schools, secondary schools, and colleges—the canons and norms of the scientific approach to knowledge have made inroads. This is true especially in the case of those teachers who have been exposed at least minimally to these new vistas while they work for degrees, even when they return to safe Mennonite classrooms. The strategy of very careful control over who is hired and the very rigid control of the school among Hutterite and Old Order Mennonites attests to their awareness of this danger.

Insofar, therefore, as Mennonite groups have found themselves required to participate in formal educational systems—and almost all Mennonite groups are now so constrained—the seminal seeds of intellectual and aesthetic inquiry and expression are being introduced. The control of the process is probably best illustrated by the prestige teachers have in Mennonite communities. In the Old Order groups the schoolteacher has a very low status, while in the more progressive groups adhering to the cooptational model the teacher, especially the intellectual, is given highest esteem; by this process the role of the aesthetic and intellectual expression is enhanced. For Western educational institutions today reflect a high regard for the intellect and for its nurturing by so carefully protecting its freedom.

Of course, a basic intellectual contradiction exists for sectarian groups like the Mennonites who strongly support socialization of the next generation in the "truths" handed down: They do not consider the fact that all social groups and their "truths" had a beginning, and beginnings imply emergence, growth, and change. There is no necessary contradiction in the fact that the theological accounts of creation are seen as final—since there, we are dealing with the supernatural—and religious traditions are seen as manmade institutions.

In any case, if the informal socialization process works well within the sectarian frame, then such groups do not need to be concerned about the loss of the identity: it is already there and simply needs to be handed down. Thus identity does not really become a conscious issue. When, however, groups utilize the formal socialization process, which imports new elements, the identity question does arise; that is the next issue to be discussed.

Identity

Clear boundaries contribute to identity. Throughout its history, Anabaptist-Mennonite society was clearly set apart by the process of dialogue and subsequent disagreement with the larger society. Of course, this boundary was enhanced and solidified with the persecution and oppression of later years. Only after higher education became accepted, with its consequent relaxation of boundaries, did identity questions began to arise for Mennonites. This process operated in two ways: (1) with the relaxing of boundaries, the issue of identity became an existential issue; (2) with the disappearance of persecution and oppression and other boundaries, the developing intellectual life began to introduce the conscious awareness of the need for a new identity, and a search for its meaning and validity (C. Redekop 1984c).[3]

The question of Mennonite identity thus has been raised with increasing urgency in the last half-century, especially with the advent of World War II when the issues of national patriotism, alternative service to war, economic success, and other related questions confronted Mennonites and created deep divisions among them on many issues. As Peachey noted in 1968, "Thanks to the runaway pace of change in American life the cultural and psychic substance of Mennonite solidarity is rapidly dissolving" (243). The need to recover the Mennonite identity produced what has been broadly called "the recovery of the Anabaptist vision"; this "recovery" was spearheaded by some church historians and social scientists at Goshen College. This movement legitimated and introduced a vast amount of historical and theological research and serves further to enhance the image of the learned people in the Mennonite society (Hershberger 1957a).

But the search for identity did not limit itself to the narrow disciplines of history and social science. As indicated earlier, artistic and literary expressions began to burgeon after World War II, and artists began to produce and create within and without the traditional media and norms of the Mennonite community. Shows for Mennonite artists and even Mennonite art began to be held here and there. One illustration of this movement is the appearance of the *Journal of Mennonite*

Studies, which deals with the Mennonite self-image, including history, literature, and criticism.

A central dilemma of Mennonite society with reference to intellectual and aesthetic life is that self-conscious reflection—by way of the arts and through giving free and creative rein to the intellectual impulse—eats at the very heart of the sectarian commitment. The intellectual and aesthetic impulse, nurtured both in the process of handing on the tradition *and* in the process of maintaining and defining the boundaries of a society, tends, however, to question both. Based on the premise that the inquiring mind is the highest achievement of human existence, the intellectual thrust will continue to gnaw at the heart of the sectarian world view.

As long as Mennonites could move freely to new environments where education was allowed to remain totally utilitarian or where boundaries remained both spatially and symbolically strong, the identity issue did not emerge or express itself through creativity. However, when Mennonite society chose to stay put or when retreat was no longer possible, the issue was joined. It is this factor which is at the basis of the threefold typology presented above.

Mennonites have produced both intellectuals and artists. Often these persons have felt forced to leave the Mennonite community because of the strong pressures toward conformity in the community. When they have stayed, their creativity has often been restricted. This observation is hardly novel and applies to many other groups as well. Mennonites are not ready yet for their version of *Fiddler on the Roof*, although many people are hoping the day will not be too far off. One very creative but alienated Mennonite artist states: "What I would like to do at one and the same time is affirm that one can be a complete human being and be a Mennonite at the same time. Because I grew up with a community that said you had to essentially deny one or the other" (Reimer and Tiessen 1985, 250).

Mennonite society has long been based on a functional and utilitarian perspective—that which helps Mennonites achieve their way of life is good, and everything else is suspect. The dilemma is doubly poignant because the freedom of aesthetic and intellectual experience that is craved by many, if not most, Mennonites may well prove to sound the death knell for the Mennonite ethos and reality.[4] As is indicated in Chapter 14, the "dilemmas of institutionalization," or "structural disequilibrium," theory is a very helpful orientation in understanding the role of the intellectual and aesthetic life in the maintenance and change of Mennonite society.

This structural dilemma has been examined and described by Urry in reference to the Russian Mennonites. After evaluating the changes in the educational system which emerged in Russia, Urry states: "The alteration in the education system had many effects, some of which were difficult to measure. It was not so much that new ideas and practices were taught in school, but rather that the younger Mennonites were provided with an opportunity to escape from the restrictions of the old order and so follow new ways. What was given to the pupils was not only a body of new knowledge but also the skills with which to gain knowledge beyond the boundaries of the old Mennonite order. If these effects were to be characterized by one phrase, it would be that the Mennonites moved from an attitude very closed towards knowledge to a more open and receptive attitude" (1983, 318).

It is with good reason that, from the earliest decades, Mennonite leaders have called upon Mennonites to "resist in a manly and fatherly way the refinement in tastes, novels and the reading of enticing world news. These lead people, like busy ants, from the Word of God, and lead people slowly and insidiously into a desire for the theatre comedies and the loose entertainments of the world" (ibid., 307).

Chapter Nine

The Mennonite Community

✛

Among many Mennonites, there exists the common assumption that "you can spot a Mennonite anywhere." This is thought to be true even if one is referring to a so-called progressive Mennonite, in which case clothing would not be an indicator. Standing at an airline desk in Asunción, Paraguay, in February 1983, I noticed a man whom I identified immediately as a Mennonite. Later, on the plane I sat down beside him and addressed him in Low German; without a moment's hesitation, he responded in the same dialect. Such identification is based upon demeanor, body language, and other subtle behavior traits. This attitude about a Mennonite collective personality is pervasive whether one is speaking about Mennonites in North America, South America, or even Europe, though, for obvious reasons, it would not apply to those of non-Germanic origin or those who have been converted to Mennonitism in recent years.

Mennonite individuals, families, and communities possess a unique cast; as persons and groupings, they are different from almost every other subsystem. For this reason, it is possible to speak about their personality characteristics. As indicated in Chapter 8, Mennonite folklore illustrates this point, especially the fiction produced by such

Mennonite writers as Arnold Dyck and Hans Harder (Al Reimer 1980).[1] How Mennonitism expresses itself with regard to the community is treated in this chapter.

A Definition of Community

On the basis of his analysis of the predominant thinkers in social science, Nisbet concludes that "the most fundamental and far-reaching of sociology's unit ideas is community" (Nisbet 1966, 47). He believes that the concept of community impinges on more than sociology; it extends into philosophy, history, and theology. The rediscovery of community, he maintains, was the greatest concern of nineteenth-century social thought and even spills over into contemporary thought. Nisbet defines community as that which "encompasses all forms of relationship which are characterized by a high degree of personal intimacy, emotional depth, moral commitment, social cohesion, and continuity in time. Continuity is founded on man conceived in his wholeness rather than in one or another of the roles, taken separately, that he may hold in a social order" (47).

All the leading social thinkers concerned with community have been motivated by the conservative view. They say that community is in danger of being lost, and that everything possible must be done in order to preserve or recapture it, even though they do not agree on what community was like or should be. The man best known for his position on the loss of community is Ferdinand Tönnies (1957), but others have echoed his and similar concerns.

Tönnies suggests that human society can be described on the basis of a typology termed the *"Gemeinschaft-Gesellschaft* continuum." The term *Gemeinschaft* has been generally defined as "community," but this begs the question. Tönnies says that the requirement for relationships of the *Gemeinschaft* type is the natural will, normally exemplified by kinship or friendship and neighborhood. The *Gemeinschaft* relationship is most naturally described by the family. The *Gesellschaft* relationship is based on rationality and calculation. All activities and relationships are restricted to a definite means of achieving them. *Gesellschaft* is fostered in the modern economic enterprise. The city nurtures *Gesellschaft*, whereas rural areas tend to support *Gemeinschaft* relationships. The *Gemeinschaft* relationship is based on common spirit, mind, beliefs, and goals. The *Gesellschaft* relationship, however, depends upon the basic heterogeneity in all things except the one factor which produces the relationship, such as the exchange of desired products.[2]

The concept and reality of community has been discussed and debated extensively in the social sciences. No consensus exists as to the exact nature of community. For our purposes, the definition proposed by Nisbet above is comprehensive enough yet also has enough specificity.[3]

The concept of community has been equally important, if not more so, within the Christian tradition. It can even be considered the central purpose of the Christian faith. In reference to the original Christian fellowship, C. H. Dodd states:

> Here . . . was in actual being that holy commonwealth of God for which the ages waited. Here was a community created not by geographical accident or by natural heredity, . . . but coming into existence by the spontaneous outbreak of a common life in a multitude of persons. The free, joyous experience of God had created a family of God, inseparably one in Him: "one person in Christ Jesus." . . . A community of loving persons, who bear one another's burdens, who seek to build up one another in love, who "have the same thoughts in relation to one another that they have in their communion with Christ." (1920, 140, 145)

A leading theologian states, "At the same time that they are a community of faith the churches are also a community of love, but this must be understood within the ambiguities [human divisions] of religion and the Spirit's struggle with these ambiguities" (Tillich 1963, 177).

A Mennonite theologian and ethicist applies Tillich's idea to the Mennonite context:

> Even as Jesus gathered sinners unto Himself, so the apostle followed the example of the friend of sinners and planted the little colonies of heaven in the midst of a pagan and hostile world. It was the evil of this world that the community of saints was commissioned to overcome with good. That was the social task of the church in Paul's day; and it is the social task of the church in our own day. Christians are not called to the defensive, in a losing cause, only to be overcome by evil. They are called to the offensive, fighting the good fight of faith, overcoming evil with good—with love, nonresistance, and the way of the cross, even as Christ overcame the world by going to the cross. (Hershberger 1958, 155)

The Mennonite Community

Mennonites throughout their history and wherever they have lived have displayed in most explicit ways the very central concept of the Mennonite community. Community has always been an influential factor in the thought and life of the whole Mennonite society.

The nonestablishment origin of the leaders of the Anabaptist movement and the group nature of the movement led them to stress the concept of brotherhood, which Troeltsch and others have said was significantly typical of the Anabaptists. The Anabaptist movement has stressed a concept of the church as a gathered people, a covenanted community, in which everything is centered in the gathering of a people around the presence of Christ.

Franklin Littell quotes with approval Friedmann's characterization of the Anabaptists:

> Now then, the central idea of Anabaptism, the real dynamite in the age of Reformation, as I see it, was this, that one cannot find salvation without caring for his brother, that this "brother" actually matters in the personal life. This interdependence of men gives life and salvation a new meaning. It is not "faith alone" which matters (for which faith no church would be needed) but it is brotherhood, this intimate caring for each other, as it was commanded to the disciples of Christ as the way to God's kingdom. That was the discovery which made Anabaptism so forceful and outstanding in all of church history. (1957, 123)

Littell further asserts:

> The Anabaptist rediscovery of peoplehood and rejection of the institutionalized mass establishment, their reassertion of the biblical role of the laity and the local congregation, were related to a view of history which I have elsewhere termed "primitivism." (126)

Thus, the Anabaptists formed a "community of discipleship" which is "the needed word and witness today" (127). Emile Durkheim first introduced the idea that the theology of a group is derived from the group's own structure and experience. The "egalitarian" nature of the early Anabaptist movement hence should have produced a theology which stressed such concepts as brotherhood and the significance of the laity (Durkehim 1915). Although the emphasis on community relates to our basic understanding of Mennonite society, it is also true that the Anabaptists developed a new form of theologizing and thought: the group or community nature of thought (C. Redekop 1970, 100 and passim).

There can be no doubt whatsoever about the existence of a Mennonite community. People know when they belong to it, as well as when they don't. For our purposes here, "Mennonite community" has a unique meaning, in addition to the definitions already given: it refers to the network of interrelationships among persons who share the same history, who have the same symbolic system, who feel emotionally one with other Mennonites, and who tend to live in spatially defined areas. This network derives from and is the functional form of the life of the congregation, which has been discussed above.

In the first three organizational models described in Chapter 6 (excluding the individualistic), the Mennonite community functions similarly—although with varying degrees of influence—in providing the context for individuals and families to live and interact together so that the norms become entrenched.[4] Furthermore, the community provides the basis for the economic, political, and social activity which allows for the emergence and perpetuation of the Mennonite congregation as well as its expansion. For example, economically, the Mennonite community among the Hutterites (theocratic) and among the Amish (modified commonwealth) provides the resources for the creation of new Hutterite colonies or for the Amish barn raisings (Bennett 1967; J. A. Hostetler 1974).

The community performs these and many other functions and is the foundation for the existence of Mennonite society. Most Mennonites have taken these functions almost totally for granted throughout their history, seldom realizing or being able to articulate how important community is to their way of life together. However, the centrality of community for Mennonites is not lost on most outsiders who observe them, and although Mennonites have assumed the existence of community and do not bother to analyze it, others have discussed some aspects of it. For example, E. K. Francis, a Catholic sociologist who has spent many years studying Mennonites, states: "The traditional Mennonite term for their religious bodies is *Gemeinde*, which literally means 'community' but is commonly translated 'church.' . . . Due to their typically loose and spontaneous organization, brotherhoods tend to be confined to rather small localized, at best regional, communities, which on occasion, however, enter into larger associations with like-minded groups" (Francis 1955, 256). The importance of community as explicated by Francis provides helpful directions for the analysis which follows: "As long as a Mennonite remains part of a local community in which such values are still dominant, neither secularization nor even apostasy are able to destroy his religious heritage entirely, or eliminate altogether the social controls exercised by the church. This connection is further strengthened by a keen and wide-spread sense of historical and biological continuity. History, more than anything else, provides the Mennonites with an intelligible explanation of the fact that they have remained distinct from their neighbors" (ibid., 277).

Let us now examine some of the functions the community provides in more depth:

1. In all three types of Mennonite societies, the community has served as the context for social interaction, work and leisure, and the relationships needed for a full life. In this context the definition of community of Effrat is appropriate: he suggests that a community is "a population who are differentiated from others because of their common participation in specific institutions and their interaction with one another in friendship and kinship relationships" (1974, 20). The Mennonite community can be seen as providing a major perspective on the Mennonite society in its entirety.

2. The community provides affirmation for the world view and specific goals of the local congregation. Community acceptance of individuals becomes a stamp of orthodoxy and legitimacy in the religious fellowship. The best illustration of this is the existence of shunning in Mennonite community life at various times and places in Mennonite history. Shunning served as a prime expression of disapproval and, as such, strongly reinforced the group's religious norms. But the existence of a strong sense of community was fundamental for this sanction to have any power against the sinning individual. Shunning was based on blocking the normal interactions of an individual with his community, with his support structure. But if the sinning person did not interact, or did not wish to interact, with the "elect" or "the saints," shunning was of no consequence; it was literally not possible. Outside of the community context, the practice of shunning had absolutely no power. The same is true of lesser forms of community approval or disapproval.

3. The community supports the family. One of the many ways it does so is in providing mates for marriage. Among the Amish and Hutterites, for example, young people are systematically helped to find mates in other communities if none is available in the local community. Assistance and resources for family business ventures are also promoted and provided for in the community. One area is agriculture; expertise in farming has been a mark of Mennonite communities for centuries. Young families who wish to begin farming often need financial and other types of help. In the theocratic and commonwealth types of community especially, these young families rarely, if ever, need to utilize banks or other outside secular institutions for resources, for the resources are available in the community.

4. The Mennonite community provides surrogate status roles which

normally are provided by the secular social system for members of the local congregation. Since the worldly norms and standards are eschewed in Mennonite congregational life, some alternative is required. A religious status in the congregation is not quite enough, for there are many other social relationships beyond those expressed in the congregational life and worship. One can say that a person is "a child of God and the church," but this truism does not offer the full range of social identity normally desired; to be a member of the abstract "body of Christ," although very important, does not by itself provide the necessary identity as a social being.

For a Mennonite Christian, to be a member with a "name" or standing in the social community is very important. More specifically, to be known as a good farmer or as a resourceful housewife is an especially important social placement. This principle is even more important within the theocratic type of community. John A. Hostetler writes, "The adult Hutterite has identified with the group since childhood and his self-esteem depends on his complete acceptance by the group" (1974, 245). Among the Old Colony Mennonites, a more commonwealth type of community, "a second ultimate goal . . . is to live the Old Colony way of life or to be in full fellowship with other Old Colony people" (C. Redekop 1969, 35).

The power of this need to be accepted and given a place in the community is tremendous. The best proof of this power is the fear of sanctions used to keep members in line (see point 2 above). If memberships were not important, sanctions such as shunning or the ban, as it is sometimes called, would be meaningless and irrelevant: "The ban, when it is observed, is effective as a sanction as long as people feel that the Old Colony offers them the only tenable way of life. For them excommunication and ban would mean annihilation" (Redekop 1969, 111).

The Structure of the Mennonite Community

Although the early Anabaptists were dispersed throughout the general population, most later Mennonites have lived in rural and village settings in enclaves of spatially proximate families, neighborhoods, and congregations. Jean Séguy's description of the French Mennonites in Alsace are paradigmatic: there were a number of families, usually interrelated, living on one or several estates, forming a social, economic, and religious unit. The same situation obtained in the Vistula Delta area of

Prussia, later Russia, and of course in North America (Séguy 1977; Penner 1978; MacMaster 1985).

It is difficult to provide an adequate historical and sociological description of the community and its great variety as it existed throughout four centuries. But if we restrict our focus to North America, we can discern several types of sociological communities that have existed for a considerable period of time. Since the concept of community as here described impinges on the analysis of the social foundations of the Mennonite system presented in Chapter 6, and since it will be discussed further in Chapter 12, only a brief discussion will be presented here.

1. *The Mennonite Total Community.* In this form the members of the religious fellowship and their offspring live together in spatially segregated areas, and religious, social, and economic activities are inclusively contained. At present, this type of community is exemplified by the Hutterite communities, including the Society of Brothers (who have in recent years become a part of the Hutterite community), and the various Mennonite-related communal groups existent today (Fretz 1979). This type compares to the "theocratic" type discussed in Chapter 6 and the communal type discussed in Chapter 12.

In a "total community," beliefs, values, norms, structures, and relationships are involuted—that is to say, the orientation is inward. There is little if anything of significance which can be achieved by turning outward. Granted, there is economic interdependence, but this is seen as a natural necessity, not as a substantive constituent of life. This community is self-disciplining and normally isolationist, although some of the newer total communities, such as the Society of Brothers and urbane communes, are concerned about evangelism.

2. *The Mennonite Social Community.* Social community expresses Mennonite peoplehood in less than total geographic enclavement, but with many of the same elements described above. In this type of community the members may live in geographically exclusive areas, as the Russian Mennonites did in Russia, as the Old Colony continues to do in Mexico and in Latin America, and as the Amish and similar Old Order groups do in Canada and the United States. Members may, however, also live in spatially concentrated farmsteads and homesteads, as Mennonites do in many geographical centers in Canada and the United States.

There is in this type a very obvious centralization of families and congregations around certain centers of life, an expression, most always, of the congregation. In social community, the religious dynamic has not been separated from the familial and congregational unity, and the issue of whether religious life can be and should be separated from familial and social life has not been seriously raised. The community of faith is unconsciously assumed to be the social group. The majority of the Old Order and more conservative Mennonite groups do not question the propriety of the religious community (the congregation) being identical with the social and the familial. To belong to the community means to be a member of the congregation and a member of a family which is a part of the community.

When the problem of the identification of religious congregation and family and community emerges, it can be assumed that assimilation to secular values has occurred. The Mennonite social community type can be generally assumed to be similar to the "commonwealth model" discussed in Chapter 6, but it is not the same as the "radical confrontational model" described in Chapter 12.

3. *The Mennonite Ideological Community.* There is no doubt that many Mennonites have considered themselves perhaps even more faithful to the Mennonite faith and vision than those in the total or social communities described above. These persons may live in an area with concentrations of Mennonite congregations or families, or they may live in locations isolated from other Mennonites, such as downtown New York City. But their central focus is a belief in the rightness of the Mennonite faith and way, so that they maintain strong connections with other Mennonites and with the causes and activities which Mennonites promote.

While such individual Mennonites may not even be affiliated with a family, they are committed to the ideology of the Mennonite enterprise, and relate to the Mennonite tradition through various institutions, such as colleges and seminaries, through service activities and organizations like the Mennonite Central Committee and Mennonite Mental Health Services, or through congregational activities. There is a paradox in this type of community, since it is in some ways a downgrading of the Mennonite stress on corporate life, but this form, a concession to the individualism in North American society, is increasingly challenging the viability of the Mennonite stress on community. This model corresponds fairly well to the individualism model of Chapters 6 and 12.[5]

The Meaning of Community for Mennonite Society

As has been indicated in numerous contexts, there is little agreement on the nature of community, nor is there total agreement among Mennonites on the nature of community; but what is nearly universally accepted is the fact of community and its importance. From the beginning, community has been central to Mennonite society's formation and life. Because of that fact, it has been easy for Mennonites to perceive sociological community as the fundamental reality. In fact, some Mennonite and non-Mennonite scholars and writers have tended to reduce the Mennonite faith to its community dimension. In terms of understanding Mennonites, however, this is deceptive and can lead us astray. Mennonites as a whole—even those belonging to the theocratic forms, i.e., the Hutterites—object to the idea that the Mennonites are basically a sociological community.

Rather, Mennonites would agree with Fretz when he writes, "When applied to the Mennonites, then the term 'community' is basically a religious concept with certain sociological implications" (Fretz 1955, 656). It is much more correct to say that adherents to the Anabaptist-Mennonite faith have formed groups who because of their congregational theology and polity interact a great deal more with each other than with nonbelievers. This perspective tends to influence people as to where they will live, what they will do, and what their goals are.

The theological dimensions of the peoplehood concept have not yet been thoroughly analyzed in the Mennonite community, predominantly because the task of developing an identity has necessitated focusing on the ideology which provides the kernel of the society, as has been indicated above. However, there are sporadic statements. One such is that presented by Harold S. Bender in *These Are My People*: "The new 'people of God' are of course under the new covenant and order with a new mode of organization and administration, a new standard of ethics, a new relationship to the world, and new resources in Christ and the Holy Spirit for their life under the lordship of Christ. . . . The essential meaning is the same, namely that a given historical group stands in such a relationship to God as to belong to Him as His people" (1962, 4–5).

The problems of identifying the nature of the Mennonite community are vast because of the theological, ecclesiological, and sociological aspects involved. Mennonites are conditioned by their self-conscious heritage to think of their identity as entirely religious; most of them strenuously resist any implication that they constitute an ethnic group, a race, or a nationality group. On the other hand, it is perfectly obvious to thoughtful Mennonites as well as to outside observers that Mennonites are more than a religious fraternity or even a denomination.

To achieve familiarity with the Mennonite movement in its historical and geographical perspectives is to be convinced that Mennonites constitute a complex religious, historical, psychological, sociological, and cultural phenomenon (Driedger and Redekop 1983). To define it as a purely religious, or sociological, or cultural, or national, group does violence to all the other aspects not mentioned. In this chapter, however, the emphasis is on the relational or interactional aspects, and it is in that sense that the word *community* has been used. In order to facilitate the discussion at this point, it might be simplest and most appropriate to talk about the Mennonite community as the *Mennonite peoplehood.*[6]

The common beliefs and history which are the foundation of the Mennonite community include both oral and written traditions which have been handed down from generation to generation, as well as the contemporary experiences of tensions and conflict with the surrounding environment. These include the dramatic writings of suffering and martyrdom, especially during the early days, such as *The Martyr's Mirror* and the *Ausbund*; the retelling of stories of expulsion and/or migrations because of beliefs, such as the Old Colony experienced; the retelling of, and participation in, heroic achievements of family, ancestors, and church leaders, as in the case of Mennonite pacifists who suffered during World War I but who also made great contributions to human rights; and the continuing experiences of being or standing over against the rest of society.

The concept of peoplehood has been used to refer to the Mennonite community especially in its theological aspects, but it has been creeping into the sociological discussions as well. Thus, Frank Epp, who has written extensively about Mennonite self-consciousness, says:

> Our first and always the most important common denominator was the new-found faith. The differences among the Anabaptists were many, but so central and so significant was the commonly-held core that it was sufficient to tie us together. The rediscovered Christ and other newly-discovered truths were so powerful in the social-political context of the times that they seemed to set in motion a dynamic movement whose fires could not easily be quenched. . . .
>
> Similarly, the same persecutions which decimated us also united us. And when we heard about each other at unexpected times or when we met in unexpected places, we found that our common suffering created a bond so strong that we knew we belonged to each other. And that is why, next to the Bible, the stories of our suffering in the *Martyr's Mirror* and the songs of our suffering in the *Ausbund,* became the ongoing symbols of our common peoplehood. (1977, 23)

The migrations that scattered the Mennonites also brought them together. Epp continues:

> The movements across oceans, through valleys, over mountains, and to new frontiers were experiences akin to the sufferings of the persecution. Where we needed each other we helped each other and where we helped each other we knew that we belonged together. . . . In all kinds of ways we walked our separate paths, but mutual aid and neighborliness knew only a single road and a single peoplehood.
>
> Indeed, in some areas our neighborliness was so complete, our communities so solid and continuous, that we developed the characteristics of ethnicity and cultural uniformity. The strongest manifestations of this trend were in the so-called Mennonite commonwealth of Russia, but the German settlements of Ontario, the reserves of Manitoba and Saskatchewan, and the colonies in Latin America all allowed the ethnic character to develop. (28–29)

A more "folkish" commentary on the same theme is this statement by Louise Siemens:

> The children of Israel had their manna. The French carry long, crusty loaves under their arms. The Swedish have given us *limpa*. Thanks to the Russians, we have rye bread. The Mexicans enjoy their tortillas. As Mennonites from Russia we have our bread—*Zwieback*.
>
> In my childhood blur, I confused the Saturday ritual of baking *Zwieback* with the holy sacraments of the church—baptism, communion, and marriage. Didn't every important function have its ever-present *Zwieback*? After a bit of maturing, I was able to separate *Zwieback* from the plan of salvation, but for many years the gospel and the Saturday baking blended into one. (Epp 1977, 36)

This peoplehood aspect of community has been expressed in classic form by Milton Gordon, undoubtedly reflecting his own Jewish experience and membership. For him, a sense of peoplehood defines the ethnic group, but it is coterminous with the Mennonite community as here defined:

> Common to all these objective bases, however, is the social-psychological element of a special sense of both ancestral and future-oriented identification with the group. These are the "people" of my ancestors, therefore they are my people, and they will be the people of my children and their children. With members of other groups I may share political participation, occupational relationships, common civic enterprise, perhaps even an occasional warm friendship. But in a very special way which history has decreed, I

share a sense of indissoluble and intimate identity with *this group* and *not that one* within the larger society and the world.

Once these attitudes of special ethnic group identity develop, it is obvious that they reinforce each other through the system of mutual expectations that grow up. (Gordon 1964, 29)

In summary, the Mennonite community includes the following dimensions, but in a very particular sense:

1. *Geographical.* This ranges from the Hutterites, where the religious dimensions of community are identical with the physical community, to the urban Mennonites, where geographical boundaries are nonexistent.
2. *Ideological or spiritual.* This encompasses a common allegiance to a faith and the consequences of that faith as it has been lived.
3. *Emotional.* This dimension involves feelings of pride and respect for heritage directed, not toward an abstraction, but toward living members of the Mennonite community, who embody that tradition in a most tangible form.
4. *Relational.* This dimension refers to the complex structure of human relationships, which include marriage networks, friendship structures, organizational friendships and affiliations resulting from working together for common causes, and economic interdependencies which stem from mutual assistance and obligations.

From this perspective the Mennonite community can be defined as that collectivity of persons who have a special and cohesive system of interrelationships, not necessarily limited to or identified with a geographical locality, but based on common experiences and common beliefs and norms which produce a utopian ideology (Bell and Newby 1973). This Mennonite peoplehood is recognized by Mennonites themselves in a unique way, in the "Mennonite Your Way" organization which has been in existence for some years. This is a voluntary association of people who provide hostels for fellow Mennonites. One can travel from coast to coast and always be welcomed and provided for in the Mennonite family. Mennonites sense a feeling of solidarity with each other which goes far beyond neighborly solidarity; it is that ultimately essential feeling of belonging that is the Mennonite community.

Ideologically, Mennonites have been concerned about building community, if it is normatively defined. The concepts of church, congregation, fellowship, *Gemeinde, Gemeinschaft,* and colony of heaven all allude to dimensions of the ideological community espoused by Mennonites. Menno Simons himself said, "What is the church of

Christ—A community of saints" (1956, 742). The church, defined as that group of persons who have committed themselves by repentance and confession of faith to each other, is thus the Mennonite community.

Equating the visible, sociological, and especially rural aspects of Mennonite experience with the church of Christ, the community of saints, has been the great temptation, however, and, I might add, has expressed the capitulation to sociological community in the life of Mennonite peoples. Thus the "rural bias" of Mennonite life and faith, as it has expressed itself in the Germanic Mennonite tradition (notably different from the recent non-Germanic groups), especially in Europe, Russia, North America, and Latin America, and the assumptions that Mennonite faith could survive best in the rural arena. The "Mennonite community" emphasis and the Mennonite Community Association of the 1940s and 1950s are concrete illustrations of this movement (Fretz 1955; Hershberger 1957b).

Dirk Willemsz, Dutch Anabaptist, turning back to rescue his pursuer. Engraving by Jan Luyken, in *Martyrs' Mirror*, 1685.

142

Maria van Beckum, Dutch Anabaptist, burned at the stake for her faith on November 13, 1544. Engraving by Jan Luyken, in *Martyrs' Mirror*, 1685.

The Anabaptists in Switzerland were persecuted longer than those in other countries. Catherina Müller was imprisoned in Zurich in 1639. Engraving by Jan Luyken, *Martyrs' Mirror*, 1685.

The Mennonite congregation, a central anchor of Mennonite life and thought, at worship: an Old Mennonite service in the 1940's. Courtesy of Mennonite Publishing House.

An Old Order churchyard. The Mennonite Old Order groups, constituting a substantial part of Mennonite society, today still emphasize community and separation from the world. Photograph by David L. Hunsberger.

Mutual aid, which has been a central tenet of Mennonite faith, is seen most dramatically in an Amish or Old Order barn-raising. Photograph by David L. Hunsberger.

The Mennonite family in North America has lived its life mainly on the rural farmstead. Photograph by David L. Hunsberger.

148

The modern family farm is much bigger than its antecedents, but is rapidly disappearing as mechanization continues. Photograph by David L. Hunsberger.

A college graduation ceremony is becoming a community event, symbolizing entrance into the intellectual domains. Courtesy of Eastern Mennonite College.

A Mennonite-owned business, producing products invented and designed by Mennonites, with Mennonite employees, is a general norm for the industrialization of Mennonite communities. Courtesy of Excel Industries, Inc.

A delegation of Mennonites from various conferences discussing their position with U.S. government representatives. Such activities indicate a more aggressive stance toward government. Photograph by Reg Toews, courtesy of the Mennonite Central Committee.

A rural development program in Chad conducted by the Mennonite Central Committee reflects the worldwide concern and outreach expressed by North American Mennonites. Courtesy of the Mennonite Central Committee.

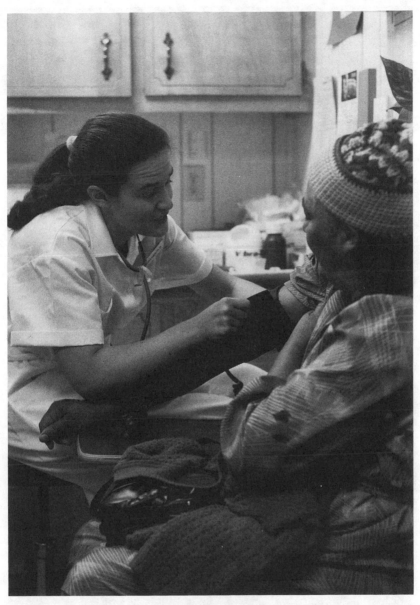

A Mennonite mission medical worker in Mississippi. Photograph by Phil Mininger, courtesy of the Mennonite Board of Missions and Charities.

The first joint communion service of two major Mennonite groups meeting in joint session, the Old Mennonite Church and the General Conference Church, in 1983. Courtesy of the *Mennonite Reporter*.

A youth conference in Banff, Alberta, with a Mennonite speaker. Mennonites are facing considerable difficulty in keeping young people within the Mennonite ethos. Courtesy of the *Mennonite Reporter*.

Part Three

Mennonite Institutional Life

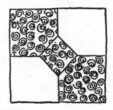

Robert Bierstedt has suggested that "the concept of institutions is one of the most important in the entire field of sociology" (1963, 340). He defines an institution as "a formal, recognized, established and stabilized way of pursuing some activity in society" (341). Most sociologists agree that the activities enveloped in institutions are recurrent and pertain to basic human needs. Thus, government, family, education, and economics, especially as the Mennonites have experienced them, are institutions.

In Part 2 we examined how Mennonites developed and expressed their faith in cultural, social, and personal form. This process obviously has had to deal with the recurring human, social, and cultural aspects of living. Even the most utopian communities have to solve basic physical, social, and cultural needs; Mennonites have discovered this, though there has been very little self-conscious attempt to deal with this.

There can be little doubt, however, that institutions have emerged in the Mennonite community and have allowed it to achieve many if not most of its objectives. On the other hand, institutions have also created some of the greatest difficulties and dilemmas for the ideological and religious objectives. The following description and analysis of the five major institutions is not exhaustive, but it does inform the reader of the most central structures and dynamics operating in the Mennonite community.

Chapter Ten

The Family in
Mennonite Life

The Mennonite family has expressed itself in a wide variety of forms, from a bizarre polygamy in the Münster chiliastic experiment in the 1530s to the very traditional authoritarian family of the Hutterite, Amish, and Old Order varieties, still existing today. It is no exaggeration to state that the family has been a bulwark of the persistence of the Mennonite movement in spite of the persecution and the corroding forces that have acted on it (Marr 1987, 351ff.).[1]

A Historical Survey

In the early period of Anabaptist history, the family was under considerable strain, since persecution often disrupted families and sometimes literally tore them apart. Torture and execution of family members was the most severe form of persecution, but the constant prospect of at least harassment, or of flight from authorities or imprisonment, also created much anxiety in Anabaptist families during this time. There was often also the need to do one's work surreptitiously to avoid discovery; this separated husbands from wives, parents from children, and families from extended relations. Women were very active in the early movement, so much so that almost one-third of Anabaptist martyrs were women (John Klassen 1986).

But after the initial period of persecution, the Mennonites began to achieve asylum and protection and were able to pursue their own way of life. In these protected settings, the family quickly became the basic element in the congregation and thus also the means for the preservation of Mennonite society. The establishment of Mennonite congregations in Alsace, the Swiss highlands, Holland, North Germany, and Prussia's lowlands, as well as the eastward movement of Mennonites into Bohemia and Volhynia, were dependent upon the migration and settlement of sufficient Mennonite families to allow a congregation to emerge (Krahn 1956b; Séguy 1977).

Recent research on early Anabaptist families suggests that the family structure and action system reflected the prevailing milieu with some variations. The male was clearly superordinate, but there often existed genuine love and respect. According to Clasen, husbands and fathers were dominant in their homes, and women were excluded from voicing their consciences in religious affairs (Clasen 1972, 202ff.). Even today, in some of the more conservative Mennonite communities like the Old Colony in Mexico, women have no voice in religious affairs, while in more progressive congregations, in general, they still have only a limited voice in church affairs.

However, since the women were very much involved in the religious protest and were victims in the ensuing persecution and violence, they were prone to have a more equal role in the rearing of children and the planning of family life and survival. Indeed, many wives were left with the rearing of children when fathers were apprehended and martyred, or left home to escape capture (Marr 1987, 394ff.). The marriage ceremony itself was also sacralized more, with the ceremony taking place in the middle of the congregation in a private home or other hidden place.

In fact Krahn has maintained that only if the sacredness of marriage among Anabaptists is understood, is the importance of the contemporary Mennonite family meaningful. He states: "An early characteristic among the peaceful Anabaptists . . . was the emphasis on a union of heart and mind and a common loyalty to God. This emphasis on the devotion to a common cause, ideal, and community, transcending the personal preferences, was an outstanding feature of early Anabaptist family life. . . . For this reason marriages outside this covenant [church] were not desirable nor permissible" (1956b, 293).

After the Mennonite congregations were founded, whether in the

Swiss Juras or in the Vistula Delta in Prussia or in Russia, the family functioned as a central element in the building of the Mennonite community. Very little explicit information is available on early Mennonite family life. But the available evidence, whether through the sparse family accounts or in the little Mennonite literature that exists, makes clear that the family—basically the extended family—was the powerhouse, along with the religious leadership of the congregation, during the heroic migrations and treks from Western Europe eastward and westward across the Atlantic to America. If there is an epic tradition among Mennonites, it would be the trial of hardship and suffering Mennonites have undergone as they migrated for religious, economic, and political reasons through the centuries. Al Reimer's *My Harp Is Turned to Mourning* and Rudy Wiebe's *The Blue Mountains of China*, while both referring to the Russian Mennonite tradition, represent the Mennonite saga in general.

In spite of the closely knit families, however, a great strain on the Mennonite family was created historically by a theological factor which was part of the earliest understandings of the faith. That factor was the sacred community's commitment to the teaching of an adult faith as well as the limiting of church membership to adults. That problem has never been solved.

In other traditions, a child would be baptized while still an infant and would immediately assume a place in God's realm and within the Christian community. Later, at puberty, the confirmation of the child affirmed the covenant the parents had made and provided recognition by the community that the person indeed belonged. But Mennonite families, by their understanding of Scripture, considered their offspring in a saved condition but not as members of the church. "The Mennonites consistently insisted that children were innocent. They found it utterly inconceivable that God would condemn a child at death simply because baptism had not taken place" (W. Klassen 1980, 90). Membership in the church, however, always meant an adult conversion experience—in other words, an acceptance of the Christian way and baptism upon the adult confession of faith. The child, as long as it was innocent, was a natural child of God, but when that child entered adolescence and began to express his or her own will and autonomy, he or she moved from a "saved" condition to one of being "pagan." This ambiguity during the adolescent years created great concern for Mennonite parents and tended to develop pressures upon children to experience a religious conversion, and quite early to minimize the period of the "uncertain group" (G. Yoder 1956). Especially during the first centuries, when families were often isolated and forced to turn in upon themselves for fellowship, the intimate nature and social flavor of the relationship between church members and those not yet a part of this tight community must have created tremendous tensions.

It was natural, therefore, that the Mennonite theology on adult baptism and its practice in actual life began to diverge rather quickly. In the close Mennonite society, there was little opportunity to rebel and become apostate; thus, there seemed to be less need to be converted. In the theocratic and commonwealth models, especially, there was great ambiguity regarding the status and behavior of the unconverted. These children were part of the Christian community, they lived intimately with members of the congregation in the same community, yet they could not be considered a part of the covenant (Francis 1955). So behavior and conformity to community norms became irrelevant for the adolescent. Thus H. S. Bender states, "Increasingly church membership was based on family connection and catechetical instruction and became conventional, with much of the original idea of conversion and vital personal experience lost" (1955g, 596).

This helps to explain why the congregation in the theocratic and commonwealth models tended to institutionalize the "rebellion" of youth, so that conversion could be more easily encouraged and realized. Particularly was this true within the Amish and Hutterite communities, where "sowing wild oats" was ritualized to serve this purpose (J. A. Hostetler 1974, 222ff.; 1980, 240). In most other groups the requirement that baptism and church membership must take place before the church would marry young people has served as a control to keep youth in line and institutionalize the conversion procedure (C. Redekop 1969).

There were few formal ceremonies in family life. Clasen suggests that during the early period some Anabaptists may even have been casual about having legal marriage ceremonies, since they "were already married in the sight of God" (1972, 202). John Klassen (1986) states, however, that the Anabaptists were rather progressive, in that they began to "sacralize" their marriages even more than was the case in Protestantism by making the marriage a central part of a congregational worship process. What Anabaptists were uniformly insistent upon was that believers and unbelievers could not be married. Since there were sometimes conversions on the part of one spouse but not the other, there were instances of divorce taking place.

In spite of this problem, the Anabaptist-Mennonite family structure has not deviated much from the conventional family structure prevailing in early times. Historically then, until recent decades, the family has been predominantly authoritarian, strong, patriarchal, and large. Among some groups, like the Old Colony Mennonites in Mexico, families have been extremely large, with some families having up to eighteen and even twenty-five children (J. Kaufmann 1960; C. Redekop 1969).

The Contemporary Mennonite Family

Central to our concern is the role of the family in providing cohesion for the Mennonite church. The cohesion of the Mennonite society was and is based on the way the congregation received its substantive support from the family. The family was the consituent population for the congregation, while at the same time the congregation served as the source for construction of the social reality of the family—an image illustrated in Chart 5.1.

The congregation thus provides the referent or reality structure for the beliefs, norms, and values, as well as in fact the entire world view, of the individual and the family. This can be stated so emphatically because the alternative secular individualistic view was seen as "worldly" or "of the world." Hence, the "will of the congregation" expressed and symbolized by the office and authority of the leadership, which presumably spoke the truth of the church, by regulating the family provided and became the shaper of the charter of the entire Mennonite society.

In turn, the family provided the raw material for the ongoing life of the congregation: that is, the children in every family became potential recruits for the congregation, so that it could continue and flourish. The parents also served the purposes of the congregation in a less direct but certainly profound way: they acted as surrogate church leaders. In fact, this concept was extended to the point that parents actually constituted a kind of surrogate congregation. They were expected to carry responsibility for the socialization of the children's belief and behavior and help their children achieve conformity by means of physical and moral sanctions. Again, in turn, the congregation rewarded family performance in terms of orthodoxy by offering esteem and prestige in the Mennonite community on the basis of faithfulness.

In the contemporary context, the Mennonite family is largely conventional and Western, although its variations need to be described by referring to the four typologies noted in Chapter 6 above.

Theocratic Societies

In "theocratic societies"—basically the Hutterites and the Society of Brothers, which have recently merged—the family is clearly subordinated to the community. In Hutterite society, "the function of the family is to produce new souls and to care for them until the colony takes over" (J. A. Hostetler 1974, 203). The production of children and their socialization in the early stages of life are the major functions of the family. Since so much of social life is conducted communally, the Hutterite family is really an extension of the communal Hutterite society (ibid., 204; Huntington 1965).

But this is not the extended family as generally understood by anthropologists—that is, the extended biological family. Even though blood relationships are revered and supported, the Hutterite family is really an extension of the Hutterite colony: "The Hutterite nuclear family of parents and their young children do not really form a social unit. Rather they form one essential aspect of an indivisible unit—the colony. The question of freedom of the nuclear family has little meaning in the context of Hutterite culture" (Huntington 1965, 111).

In any case, the foundational structure is that of traditional European society. The father is considered the head of the family; the children are to be obedient and supportive in the family's private life. The mother stands somewhere between, possessing authority over the children, but being submissive to the husband. Since the family is subordinated to the communal structures, the husband-wife relationship is relatively restricted to more personal facets and of course the conjugal dimensions. The entire procedure of courtship and marriage is rather standardized and publicly controlled. When the issue of intermarriage with relatives emerges, the colonies initiate intercolony visits to allow young people of marriageable age to become acquainted and develop friendships which eventually end in marriage (J. A. Hostetler 1974, 237ff.). The decision to marry is a concern of the colony: "No formal acknowledgement is made of the intention of a young couple to marry until the prospective groom, accompanied by his father or other close relatives, makes a trip to the girl's colony and seeks her permission and the consent of the colony" (239).

In the "orthodox" Hutterite theocracy, the idea of a nuclear family has hardly existed, although it has appeared at various times with the infiltration of secular values (Peter 1976b). In practice, however, there has been considerable variation in the way the family has been subordinate to the communal ideology. In fact, Karl Peter, in a very interesting article, "The Dialectic of Family and Community in the Social History of Hutterites" (1976a), suggests that Hutterite society was inherently unstable because of a dialectical tension between the "harsh" demands of centralized authority with its community of goods and the desire for autonomous family life with the kind of structures which Hutterites could observe in the host society. The tension arose basically over the question of "whether the family or the community ought to control property, socialization and mate selection" (1976b, 342).

From a sociological point of view, it is understandable why the pressure for centrality and supremacy have created such a tension, as well as why the Hutterite family pattern has varied through the centuries as external or internal factors highlight either family or colony supremacy. There were times when Hutterite society became almost defunct, and the ideal community structure was relinquished. However, in the main, the Hutterite model has reflected family subordination to colony.

Commonwealth Societies

In the commonwealth typology of the Mennonite family—which still obtains among rural conservative Mennonite groups such as the Old Order Amish and the Old Colony Mennonites—the family can be described as quasi-extended. That is to say, the biological family tree, consisting of grandparents, parents, and children, is very important. Property is transferred by way of the family line, and the individuals receive their stamp and identity as members of the family. Nevertheless, they are still members of the Mennonite "community," or church, and the community determines the overarching self-identity and social status.[2]

Members of the Mennonite commonwealth family receive major status and assistance on the basis of family standing. Further, prestige and social standing as well as the general standing in the church of the Mennonite family is transferred to the offspring. Election to Mennonite institutional offices and leadership generally depends upon membership in prestigious or important families. In the same vein, a Mennonite born to a poorer Old Colony Mennonite family will probably never achieve financial independence unless he or she marries well. But, as was indicated above, "family power" is limited considerably by membership in the commonwealth, which asserts church norms over all in a way that families cannot supersede.

In terms of the inner family structure, the family is ordered very traditionally; the authority is entrenched in the father, who has veto power in family matters as he does in the community. Children work at home until they marry, at which time females can expect a "dowry," and males can expect to be helped to set up a farm or a related business. In cases where there are no boys, the daughters inherit the farm, a circumstance which helps to give marriages in the Mennonite community certain political and economic overtones (J. A. Hostetler 1980; J. Kaufman 1965; C. Redekop 1969).

Courtship in the Old Order groups begins in a very casual and stylized way. Among the Old Order Amish and related groups, the hymn sing and other community festivities have traditionally served as the format for courtship. Among the Old Colony and similar groups, informal visiting along the village streets among groups of girls and boys provides the setting for increasing attraction and intimacy (C. Redekop 1969, 70ff.). Family visits to friends in other villages or communities provide the opportunity for interaction between boys and girls in the entire gamut of semicommunal groups.

There is considerably more private initiative in the decision to marry and more freedom from community permission to marry than in the theocratic model. The families of the two young people are naturally directly involved in the negotiations, though an uncle or aunt often becomes a broker—the *Schtecklimann* among the Amish or *Umbitter* among the Russian (J. A. Hostetler 1980, 192; Krahn 1956b, 294). The publishing of the banns is a tradition practiced in most of the semicommunal groups; among the Old Colony this amounts to a public announcement of the intention of the two members to marry. During the following two weeks, before the marriage, the couple visits relatives and friends in the congregation. For many centuries, ministers were asked for permission to marry (Krahn 1956b, 294).

The traditional view of marriage indicates that it is basically for the promotion of the social and economic requisites of the community which include the bearing of numerous children. Large families have therefore been a trademark of Mennonite families of almost all times and places. Hence, birth control has been almost universally condemned, as it has been both in the communal groups discussed above and in commonwealth societies. In fact, having children has usually been expressed as being a commandment from God (J. A. Hostetler 1980, 101; C. Redekop 1969, 52). Family size, as a result, has been above average. An intensive study of Mennonite family size in Kansas by Gustav E. Reimer provided the statistics shown in Table 10.1. These statistics are very representative of the Old Order Mennonite groups—

including the Hutterites, the Old Order Amish, and the Old Colony Mennonites—even though they were based on a General Conference Mennonite group; indeed, birthrates among these conservative groups are, if anything, higher (Eaton and Mayer 1954; J. A. Hostetler 1980, 1974; C. Redekop 1969). Eaton and Mayer wrote, "Among the Hutterites, the 1950 fertility ratio was 96.3 per hundred women. It is greater than that of any other human population" (15).

Among commonwealth groups, the family is the reinforcer of Mennonite community values. If a family begins to deviate, the offspring are often lost to the church. Occasionally the church may be able to exercise its authority to counteract the secularizing family influence on the children, but it is clear that the commonwealth operates most effectively when the family and the church are in harmony. The key seems to be the Mennonite woman. If she is totally submissive, the harmony seems complete. "The only occupational role for the Old Colony married woman is that of housewife. If a woman does not get married, she remains in the parental home, caring for her parents when they get older" (C. Redekop 1969, 72). The same condition obtains in the other commonwealth Mennonite groups, such as the Amish; however, indications of resistance to this pattern are increasing. "An Amish woman knows what is expected of her in the home and in the church, and her attitude is normally one of willing submission. . . . In practice, the farm is the Amishman's kingdom, and his wife is his general manager of household affairs" (J. A. Hostetler 1980, 153–54). In fact, occupational opportunities are so severely restricted in this Mennonite sector that before marriage, or if she never marries, a woman can look only to housekeeping, occasional nursing, or teaching as outlets.

TABLE 10.1 Average Number of Children per Couple in Whitewater, Kansas, Mennonite Community, 1876–1924

| Years | No. of children | Marriage age | |
		Male	Female
1876–1884	7.45	—	—
1885–1900	6.11	28.20	22.85
1901–1910	6.21	28.16	22.74
1911–1918	7.11	28.65	23.78
1919–1924	3.50	—	—

Source: Krahn 1956b, 294.

The Mennonite family in the Mennonite community type is generally similar to conventional American families. The family is almost totally nuclear, with few, if any, grandparents living within the home, as is the case in theocratic and commonwealth communities. Although family tradition and property are still handed down, the family unit of parents and children is autonomous and neolocal—that is, the new family moves to its own home independent of extended family connections. Church membership is transferable and negotiable, meaning that modern Mennonite families often change denominational affiliation if they move to an area where there is no Mennonite church.

The occupation of the male has traditionally been the basic determiner of where the family will live, how they will live, the type of community in which they will live, who their friends will be, what roles they will fill in society, and what their social status will be. But, as is true in the larger society, in Mennonite community societies the role and importance of women are changing. Children are socialized into the economic and intellectual milieu of the parents and develop friendships often not Mennonite because of school and other contacts.

The marriage and family structure of this segment of the Mennonite "family" is almost identical with that of the prevailing North American system. Courtship practices are for all purposes those of society at large: dating involves movies, recreational activities, and church activities. Courtship and the decision to marry are individual choices, with parents increasingly uninvolved in the process. Marriage counseling is strongly promoted in the congregation, but not all participate in it. Weddings, honeymoons, setting up housekeeping, and starting careers are modeled after the surrounding society although congregational influences operate in varying degrees in the various communities (J. Kauffman 1956b, 297–99).

The Mennonite family in this rubric is basically endogamous, with most people marrying other Mennonites, a practice derived from the teaching on separation: "Be ye not unequally yoked with unbelievers" (2 Corinthians 6:14). The kinship systems and the strong community life of the Mennonites are also causes for such high endogamy (J. Kauffman 1956b, 296). Divorce has been strongly disapproved, and has been very rare until recent times; this will be expanded upon below (Corell 1957, 502–10).

Very few records are available regarding family size and birthrates among Mennonites. The major congregational study of 1972 does not provide information on Mennonite fertility and fecundity. A recent survey taken among the Old Mennonites, one of the groups in the community typology, reveals that the family size is below average for the United States at present, although the earlier cohorts exceeded the U.S. percentages (Table 10.2).

The congregation is important in the community type but the degree of importance depends upon the history of the individual family itself. Some families who nurture a close identification with the Mennonite heritage and faith will send their children to church high schools and colleges and Mennonite camps. They will also encourage them to volunteer for foreign relief service under MCC or for missionary service as one way to carry on the heritage. Such families slow the secularizing influences flowing around the Mennonite congregation, and their attempts help to maintain basic sociological and religious ties.

In extensive studies of Mennonite families, J. Howard Kauffman has placed Mennonite families on a continuum from the "traditional" type of family to the "emergent." He defines "emergent" to mean the more modern type of family in which authority is shared more equally between husband and wife and in which the relationships are more democratic and permissive. The "Mennonite community" family type would approximate Kauffman's emergent type, which reflects traits characteristic of the emerging urban American family patterns (Kauffman 1965, 82). Kauffman concludes from his studies that the more conservative Mennonite groups (the commonwealth types in my classification) are more traditional and thus authoritarian, and by "authoritarian" he

TABLE 10.2   Children Ever Born per 1,000 Women Ever Married, Mennonite Church Members, 1982, and United States

Age group		Children ever born per 1,000		Difference	
Mennonites, 1982	U.S., 1978	Mennonites	U.S.	Menn. − U.S.	%
20–29	20–29	1,157	1,221	− 64	− 5.2
30–39	30–39	2,327	2,438	−111	− 4.6
40–49	40–49	3,231	3,219	12	.4
	Age, 1970				
50–59	40–49	3,920	2,967	953	32.1
	Age, 1960				
60–69	40–49	3,642	2,486	1,156	46.5
70–79	50–59	3,487	2,420	1,067	44.1

Source: M. Yoder 1985.

means "the exertion of authority in a rigid or strongly controlling manner. In family relationships an authoritarian husband is one who expects that his wife will always or usually yield to his viewpoint in case of difference of opinion" (77). Kauffman is of the opinion that authoritarian family structures tend to produce conflict and unhappiness, especially among those families moving into urban areas, where members become aware of greater freedom and equality in human relationships. A "sacrifice of emotional and interpersonal relationship values" (87) results. "Whether this is too great a price to pay, depends, of course, on how strongly sectarian viewpoints are held" (86).

But the basic profile is clear: the Mennonite family in this third typology is almost totally bereft of geographical or neighborhood supports, and must encourage and nurture the Mennonite "network of relationships" if its commitment is to survive. The Mennonite congregational life, on the other hand, is geared very strongly toward retaining the loyalty of the offspring of the families, and efforts to retain youth are not as dependent upon family authority and programs as on congregational age-graded activities and enticement.

Individualistic Mennonites

The individualistic Mennonite typology should of course have a counterpart in the family structure, and indeed it does. But there is practically nothing to distinguish it from contemporary American family structure. According to Kauffman's typology, this type of family has completed the "emergent" trend and reflects full adaptation to the prevailing patterns. Clearly there will be remnants of traditional family life in the individualistic system, but in the main there will be little uniqueness. As indicated earlier, the individualistic typology means that the family has adopted the values and norms of the surrounding society and therefore models itself after that system. In this case the "Mennonite" family would be such only by living in a Mennonite community or by historical ties to a Mennonite congregation.

Mennonite Family Changes

The tendency of Mennonites to adapt to the host society is beginning to be debated and studied rather extensively by Mennonite scholars. There remains considerable ambivalence about the trend, but it is clear that urbanization has changed attitudes toward numerous traditional views. This assimilation trend obviously has great implications for the

Mennonite family. In this section I provide some indicators of what is happening to the Mennonite family, based on information from census material which was not available in earlier periods.

One of the most important indicators of family structure and change is divorce. Mennonites, along with other religious groups, have always assumed that the marriage bond is indissoluble. But divorce is making inroads into the Mennonite society. Thus, in a recent national sample Driedger and Kauffman found that 39 percent of rural Mennonites thought divorce was always wrong, as compared to 24 percent of urban Mennonites. The authors conclude that "there is evidence here that fewer metropolitan Mennonites hold to some present and past norms of personal morality, and that there is somewhat more urban tolerance toward family breakdown" (1982, 287). It is clear that the Mennonite family, especially among individualistic Mennonites, is headed for increasingly profound changes, if separation and divorce are any indication (see Table 10.3). Of course, this heralds changes for the Mennonite congregation as well, to say nothing of the Mennonite community. Although changes in the family structure are observable even there, the theocratic and commonwealth model families will change less radically. These family models will continue to perpetuate the traditional Mennonite way of life. In the Mennonite community and the individualistic family types, changes are increasingly apparent. The prevailing tendency toward individualistic life styles will affect more and more the way these families support and complement the congregational life of Mennonites.

As important as these effects may appear to be, there is one other powerful agent of change that has only barely begun to seep into the Mennonite society which will have much more profound significance—the revolution in the status of women.[3] As women begin to become active in congregational life in a sense not known heretofore and as their traditional submission in the Mennonite community decreases, forces and influences will be unleashed that will strain and ultimately change the traditional patterns.

The revolution in the status and role of women in the Mennonite society is in its infancy, but the rumblings and storm signals are beginning to emerge. It is not unrealistic to propose that it will present probably the greatest crisis and cause for change that the Mennonite church has faced, and will face. There are a number of reasons for this. For one thing, despite their relatively prominent role in the Anabaptist beginnings, women's status and role soon became that of the conventional practices in the society. A recovery of the relatively important

TABLE 10.3 Marital Status by Sex and Age, Adult Members Only, Mennonite Church (percentage distribution)

Marital status	Men					Women				
	20–29	30–44	45–64	65 +	All adult member men	20–29	30–44	45–64	65 +	All adult member women
Never married	45.6	7.1	3.0	1.7	15.5	36.9	11.1	11.7	13.7	18.2
Separated	.7	1.0	.7	.4	.7	.9	1.2	.9	.4	.9
Divorced	1.2	2.5	.5	.2	1.3	1.6	3.4	1.7	.4	1.9
Remarried after divorce	.3	3.9	2.1	1.0	2.0	.9	3.8	1.5	.7	1.9
Ever separated or divorced[a]	2.2	7.4	3.3	1.6	4.1	3.4	8.4	4.1	1.4	4.6
Widowed	.1	.4	.8	15.8	2.8	.1	1.5	5.3	36.6	8.9
Remarried after widowhood	.0	.2	2.0	10.9	2.3	.0	.5	1.2	3.5	1.1
Married to original spouse	52.0	84.9	90.7	70.1	75.3	59.6	78.6	77.6	44.8	67.1
Total	99.9	100.0	99.8	100.1	99.9	100.0	100.1	99.9	100.1	100.0
Number	10,568	12,165	10,324	6,136	39,193	11,672	13,204	12,622	8,855	46,333

[a]Totals of rows 2–4.

Source: M. Yoder 1985, 333.

Note: Heaton (1986, 58) gives the following figures for the marital status of ever-married males and females in Canada:

	% ever married	% divorced or separated
Mennonites	71.7	3.3
Hutterites	56.9	0.2
Total population	72.2	7.7

status they held earlier could give contemporary women added determination and power. Second, the rather strongly subordinated role of women in Mennonite society, especially in its rural context from 1550 to the present, has placed women in a more rigid and restricted role than they hold in most other religious groups. This was exacerbated by the symbolic functions women played in the separation and nonconformity emphasis that motivated Mennonites for several centuries (J. Klassen 1986; Klingelsmith 1980; Kraybill 1987). The slowly emerging consciousness that women have been especially subordinated in this way will create all the more attempts to compensate for past wrongs.

Third, the recent urbanization of Mennonite families and the increase in the education of women will accelerate the move for revolution and the rectification of wrongs perpetrated through the centuries. The achievement of relative freedom that Mennonite women experience will create demands for more, expressing the general axiom that once a bit of freedom is achieved, more is demanded—that is, that rising expectations and their achievement cause revolutions (Cohan 1975, 194–96). Thus, intellectual emancipation will produce an increasingly insistent and aggressive demand for equal access to community life.

Fourth, the "rediscovery" of the relevance of Anabaptist-Mennonite faith and life by rank-and-file Mennonites, especially young people, will increasingly produce energy for the achievement of a consistent and biblical expression in all areas of life, which will include the role of women in the religious life of Mennonite society and hence will place increasing pressure on Mennonite institutions to allow women fair access to all aspects. The strains that are presently spreading through Mennonite society as a result of theological, ethical, and ecclesiological debates regarding women's status will not be resolved until Mennonite women have achieved what they feel is a just and equal role.

Finally, the structural and temporal aspects of this phenomenon guarantee that the struggle will continue for generations. Structurally, the status of women presents a spectrum, from groups which are already undergoing a revolution (the Old Mennonites, the General Conference, and the Mennonite Brethren), to the groups which will soon be facing the same revolution (the smaller groups like the Evangelical Mennonite Church, the Church of God in Christ–Holdeman, and others), to traditional and communal groups (the Old Order groups and the Hutterites). The temporal aspect of this structural variation guarantees that the battle will be staged in the order presented in the preceding sentence, with the time frame of the changes very difficult to predict. It is clear that the Hutterites and Old Order groups will be the last to undergo any revolution in women's status. What complicates the issue even further is that individual women in the various groups will experience the revolution on a personal basis, so that there may well be an individual "ladder of accommodation" as each woman moves to a more "progressive" segment of Mennonite society or moves totally out of Mennonitism to a more friendly religious group. This latter phenomenon is already taking place in isolated cases.

The implications of this revolution for the structure and functions of marriages, for the structure and functions of congregations, and for the life of Mennonite society can only be imagined; it will be dramatic. It involves changing the traditional view of the Holy Scriptures, which through long rehearsing, propounded a hierarchical order of authority, with God at the apex, men next in line, women below them, and children at the lowest levels. The shift in this traditional world view will be thoroughly resisted, even by women themselves, as is attested to by letters to the editors of the various church papers when the topic of women's emancipation is broached. One example is the spirited and hard-hitting way in which a newly ordained young woman responded to a Mennonite theologian who wrote an article entitled "The Contemporary Fathering Crisis, the Bible, and Research Psychology" (J. Miller 1983; Steiner 1984).

As if the religious authority question is not enough, the sociological structures of power and domination in the Mennonite community will be challenged, and the resistance is already expressing itself, although there is evidence that men, on the basis of the general retreat of male chauvinism and the discovery that the Holy Scriptures do teach equality of the sexes, will capitulate relatively quickly. But the struggle will take time, simply because it will take time for the psychological ethos and the institutional practices to develop so that women will in fact be able to compete on an equal level.

A relatively new organization in Mennonitism (now ten years old) has been bringing women's issues into focus and publishes a paper entitled *Report: MCC Committee on Women's Concerns*. One leading female writer states, "In our Mennonite Churches, we've taught the servanthood and priesthood of all believers. We have a natural base with which to begin the second ten years. One decade is too short a time to measure progress or to indicate defeat. The only way is ahead" (K. Wiebe 1983, 6). Although not strident, such statements imply a calm determination to forge ahead.

Although the questions cannot be pursued fully here, it is entirely possible and probable that, with the assertion of female leadership and authority, the locus of authority and cohesion asserted earlier by an arbitrary and often ruthless masculine hegemony could well return to the family and congregation in a natural way. In any case, if such an inevitable and probably salutary transition is resisted by the male sector of the community, it seems clear that a strongly patriarchal Mennonite society will face great dangers of dissolution.

THIS NECESSARILY BRIEF and schematic review of the family points to its centrality and significance in the life of Mennonite society. Subsequent chapters on education, economics, and service will illustrate the intricate and intimate ways in which the family is intertwined with other facets of the Mennonite movement and will make clear how difficult it is to analyze the family without bringing into focus for discussion the other institutions.

Chapter Eleven

Mennonites and Educational Activities

Central to Anabaptist self-awareness was the role of religious and secular authorities in their persecution. It was the "learned professors and doctors" who provided the rational justification of the rejection, prosecution, and oppression of the Anabaptists. The almost unnumbered disputations, hearings, debates, and inquisitions that Anabaptists experienced at the hands of Catholics and Protestants alike were given legitimation by the representatives of learning. Menno Simons, who managed to live out a natural life, experienced this conflict and expressed himself: "I repeat, Do not hear, do not follow, and do not believe the many learned ones who let themselves be called doctors, lords, and masters, for they mind but flesh and blood . . . therefore do not hear those who are after fat salaries and a lazy life. They deceive you. They teach you according to the lust of your hearts. They implore for the sake of filthy lucre; they preach to you empty inventions out of their own imagination and not out of the mouth of the Lord" (1956, 195).

This statement, along with many others from early Anabaptists, provides the context for a general attitude which Mennonites have had toward worldly learning and sophistication. The mixing of truth and error, the craftiness of deceit, clothed in the robes of genteel learning, alienated Mennonites from almost all semblance of knowledge. To quote Menno again "The craft and subtlety of the devil, who can clothe himself with the radiance of an angel of light, are not known by some. . . . It was done through false prophets against whom I say we have been faithfully warned by the mouth of the Lord" (198).

This is not to ignore the fact that many of the early leaders of Anabaptism were well educated. Conrad Grebel, Menno Simons, Balthasar Hubmaier, Pilgram Marpeck, Hans Denk, George Blaurock, Michael Sattler, and numerous others had been trained at universities, monastery schools, and the like. Hubmaier had earned a doctorate in divinity; Marpeck had an engineering degree (Horsch 1950).

In Chapter 8 we considered the impact of the misuse of knowledge and learning in the oppression of Mennonites upon their attitudes toward learning and aesthetics. In this chapter we focus on how Anabaptist-Mennonite society has socialized its offspring so it could perpetuate itself and thrive. It is nevertheless important to realize the role that history played in the development of the educational program.

A Historical Review

For the first several decades of the Anabaptist movement, the issue of establishing an educational process or structure hardly emerged, for the members of the movement were busy sharing their faith and struggling to preserve their existence. Children, who are the central focus of socialization, could not in the early years receive the attention they deserved. It is natural, therefore, that the earliest indications of institutional socialization occurred among the Hutterites, who were the first to have some control over their own lives and activities. But in Switzerland, France, Germany, Austria, Holland, and elsewhere children were presumably trained informally in the home.

In the 1540s and possibly even in the late 1530s, the Hutterites were already conducting their own schools: "In every Bruderhof there was a 'little school' and a 'big school'. . . . from the age of six to twelve [children] attended the big school supervised and taught by a man" (J. A. Hostetler 1974,55). In 1542, Peter Riedemann described Hutterite schools in the Brotherhood Rechenschaft, "where children learned the meaning of *Gelassenheit* (the quality of yieldedness), a central Anabaptist teaching [which] defined in large part the Hutterite Community" (L. Gross 1980, 32). The philosophy of Hutterite education was simple and forthright: "The schoolmaster, with the entire Brotherhood, was to raise the children in the honor and fear of God, and to subdue any evil inclinations from the time of their youth" (ibid., 34).

The Hutterites have managed to maintain an educational process throughout their entire existence, even though it began to become rather traditional and lose its early creativity and innovativeness. Speaking of the contemporary school system, John A. Hostetler states that "Hutterites accept the English school but restrain and bridle its influence so that it will serve colony ends. . . . the further the child goes in English school, the less he is said to learn. From the colony's point of view this is correct" (Hostetler 1974, 219). Before the schools were required to conform to the host society's norms, the educational process had become very inward-looking and was concerned mainly with propagation of the Hutterite tradition: "Since human nature is sinful from birth, Hutterites value education not for self-improvement but as a means of 'planting' in children 'the knowledge and fear of God'. . . . The individual will is broken primarily during the kindergarten years" (ibid., 144).

The growth of the educational thrust in the rest of the Mennonite family is a patchwork, although the Hutterite philosophy and practice of education can be generalized to the other Mennonite groups to a large extent. As can be deduced from the history of the movement described above, the Swiss Mennonites who remained in Switzerland, France, Germany, and Austria did not develop their own educational institutions. The same can be said for Holland, with one exception, Haarlem, established in 1792 (M. Harder 1956, 150).

The Mennonites who migrated to West Prussia, and subsequently to Russia and North America, provide a different story. The Dutch Mennonites who went to West Prussia established private schools as early as the 1550s, very soon after their arrival (Ratzlaff 1971, 15; M. Harder 1956, 924). The earliest *Privilegium* (the first being given by Sigismund II [1548–72]), and all subsequent ones, granted the right to Mennonites of providing for their own schools and, of course, the right to employ their own teachers (Ratzlaff 1971, 15). Very little information is available about these early schools, but the later school system as established in the Russian Commonwealth period and extended forward for over two centuries to Canada, Mexico, and South America provides us with information about the thrust of the schools and their structure.

While the West Prussian schools were very informally organized and operated, in the Russian Commonwealth system each village developed its own school and hired its own teacher. The village was responsible for the employment and payment of the teacher and for the laying down of curriculum and related matters, but the religious institution (the congregation) through its leaders was responsible for the central function of the schools—to instruct the young in the life and faith of the Mennonite tradition. All substance was to focus on humility, obedience, and reverence to God and his holy order—the Gemeinde, which was an earthly model of the Kingdom of God: "We have practiced the belief from olden times, that the teachers and students become deeply involved in the scriptures . . . that it may serve the life of the Gemeinde" (D. Harder 1969, 22).

During their commonwealth period in Russia, the Mennonites not only institutionalized basic education, but they also developed an extensive secondary system which, in every aspect, served to pass on their traditions to the next generation. The high school, or a comparable level of secondary education, developed in the Russian Mennonite commonwealth to a rather sophisticated degree. It was expanded to include women. It also had professional dimensions, as, for example, was reflected in the *Kommerzschule* (M. Harder 1956). When they emigrated to America, these Mennonites from Russia continued the educational practices they had already developed.

The elementary level of formal education among the Swiss Mennonites in North America is more difficult to explain. It is clear, however, that the Swiss Mennonites lived in somewhat dispersed communities—in direct contrast to the Mennonites in Russia, who lived in villages and colonies that were exclusively Mennonite (MacMaster 1985). Thus, in the earliest stages of new settlement, the fledgling state was generally not directly responsible for the formal education of their children, so private schools emerged.

An early example was the school of Christopher Dock, the "pious schoolmaster of the Skippack," who by 1718 "was teaching a subscription elementary school among the Mennonites of Skippack settlement north of Germantown, Pa." (Leatherman 1956, 76–77). Such schools were the rule in Pennsylvania and Virginia, where the Swiss Mennonites migrated; usually the church was used for the site of the school. By 1771 at least sixteen schools were conducted by Mennonites in the new settlements. The Old Order Amish were slower in adopting the formal elementary school system (M. Harder 1956, 182).

Historically, there was relatively little Mennonite participation in middle-range or secondary schools, as we know them today; only recently has education at these levels become a movement. Mennonites developed no secondary schools in Switzerland, Holland, and France, and only one in Germany, at Weierhof in 1867 (H. Bender 1959d, 491). Those in the Russian commonwealth did develop a specialized high school in the latter part of the nineteenth century. A type of Bible school which also provided academic training above the grade school level was introduced among Russian Mennonites in the United States and Canada beginning in the 1880s in relatively primitive and limited circumstances (H. Peters 1925). Swiss Mennonites did not enter the field of secondary education until well into the twentieth century.

The more conscious entrance into the secondary school movement began through the preparatory schools, the first of which was founded in Kansas in 1879 at Goessel and eventually became Bethel College. Minnesota and Nebraska also produced such schools very early. These were originally called academies, and several of these academies retained their secondary-school arm as well as expanding into colleges (e.g., Hesston College and Eastern Mennonite College). Today there are a number of Mennonite high schools: the Old Mennonite church operates nineteen, the General Conference has nine, and the Mennonite Brethren sponsor four. The Old Mennonites, the largest Mennonite group, sponsor, in addition, ninety-four elementary schools. That number must be considered partial, since conservative groups like the Old Order Amish and the Old Order Mennonites administer their own elementary schools and do not report their number. According to H. S. Bender, these conservative schools "maintain a strong emphasis on their Christian character, and most of them also emphasize their Mennonite character and their particular denominational loyalty" (1959d, 493).

Post-Secondary Education

The *Mennonite Yearbook* states that there are twelve Mennonite colleges in the United States and Canada. Mennonites also support three seminaries. Beyond these categories, numerous other educational institutions exist. There are nursing schools—often affiliated with secular hospitals not listed in the roster of Mennonite institutions—as well as numerous regional Bible schools, short-term schools for ministers, and Chautauqua-type schools, such as the Keystone Institute of Pennsylvania. However, the discussion here is limited to seminaries and colleges. A variety of educational institutions will be described briefly and analyzed from a functional perspective.[1]

Seminaries

Although a Mennonite seminary called Witmarsum was founded in Ohio as early as 1868, it was really a Bible school. A similar school was initiated in Halstead, Kansas, in 1883: "At the founding of the school the desire was strongly emphasized that teachers should be trained in it for our church and district schools" (H. Peters 1925, 75). Other local teacher-training schools emerged in Russian Mennonite settlements (ibid.; Hartzler 1925).

Mennonite Biblical Seminary, a General Conference school, was initiated in 1945, in conjunction with the Church of the Brethren. The first autonomous Mennonite seminary on a graduate level was founded at Goshen College, Indiana, in 1946. In 1970, these two seminaries joined hands on a common campus in Elkhart, Indiana, under the name of Associated Mennonite Biblical Seminaries. Two other seminaries— Eastern Mennonite Seminary of Harrisonburg, Virginia, and Mennonite Brethren Biblical Seminary of Fresno, California—were established subsequently.

It will be obvious immediately that the seminary as a specialized institution has arrived on the educational scene only very recently. This was because Mennonitism was a lay movement; it was not concerned about intellectual and ecclesiastical development. However, the modernization of the Mennonite society, especially the influence of two world wars, created the beginnings of a confrontation with the world which demanded increasingly sophisticated leadership. With the increase of outside influences because of war and growing economic linkages, as well as through mass media and Bible conferences (to name only a few factors), it became clear that Mennonites needed to develop their own trained leadership if their society was to survive. Exacerbating the situation was the increasing attendance of aspiring ministers at seminaries and schools outside the Anabaptist frame of reference. It was this latter seepage which had, and continues to have, major impact on Mennonite society and is largely responsible for the increasing shift toward fundamentalism and evangelicalism, as well as for the strands of liberalism among American Mennonite churches (Sawatsky 1987; J. E. Toews 1978).

The seminaries were established, therefore, to provide firm grounding in biblical teaching and church history for Mennonite leadership. It is possible that this need was perceived more by the leadership than by the laity, for the laity was becoming rampantly assimilated, adopting the values of the larger society (Baehr 1942; M. Harder 1986; C. Redekop 1978b). Today the seminaries function in a number of ways to preserve Mennonite faith and practice: (1) they provide a biblical and historical orientation for the maintenance and recovery of the Mennonite faith and heritage; (2) they train potential ministers and teachers in the orthodox Mennonite faith; (3) they serve as a recruiting device for supplying pastors to local congregations; and (4) they help congregations become more vital in their inner life by assisting in research, study conferences, and the like (H. Bender, 1959b).

Colleges

One of the reasons for the late emergence of the graduate seminaries had to do with the existence of Mennonite colleges, which had developed somewhat earlier. For a time the Mennonite colleges performed some of the functions of the seminaries, particularly through their Bible, missions, and service departments. Indeed, although Mennonites had been in America since 1683, it was not until 1883—two hundred years later— that a "seminary" was erected at Halstead, Kansas. This school became the precursor of Bethel College of North Newton, Kansas, which was begun formally in 1887. Goshen College, established in 1903, also had a precursor, in the Elkhart Institute, begun in 1894. As indicated above, twelve Mennonite colleges are now in existence (M. Gingerich 1955).

Although unique local conditions and conference factors contributed to the emergence of each of the colleges, there were several factors or concerns common to the founding of each.

Probably the most important of these was to keep Mennonite young people from learning strange doctrines and beliefs elsewhere. Because of the Mennonite doctrine of separation from the world and the often strenuous attempts to escape from its influences, Mennonites had developed an attitude of anti-intellectualism and an anti-education bias. Hence, no higher education had been instituted for many generations. One notable exception existed in the *Zentralschule* in Russia but the consequences of this very movement in Russia, proved, according to many conservatives, that this secularization process was destroying the faith. James Urry quoted Balzer, a Russian Mennonite bishop who maintained that "the desire to seek 'knowledge' as a form of revelation could only lead men further from God and the proper way of Life" (Urry 1983, 307). In Balzer's vivid words, Mennonites who sought such a path were at risk of being caught "stealthily in the snares of reason. We must not exceed the necessities of our faith!" (307).

Nevertheless, as Peters noted in his history of Mennonite education in Kansas, "No church discipline, no resolutions of conference could keep our rising generations free of getting that educating elsewhere, which was denied them at home, for the desire to learn and to know is implanted in the human soul by our creator" (H. Peters 1925, 108). The founders of Hesston College were more blunt: "Many bright young minds have been lost to the church by going out into the worldly schools to acquire an education" (M. Miller 1959, 5). It is an intriguing irony, therefore, that one of the major reasons for higher education among Mennonites was to protect their members from higher education in the more dangerous and worldly setting.

A second reason is reflected in the positive side of the same argument—namely, to carry on and preserve the religious heritage, which was in need of rejuvenation and upgrading. Tabor College, begun in 1908, had as one of its three objectives the training of leadership for the benefit of the church: "It is not enough simply to have trained leadership. The question then is: in what direction do they lead the people? Whither are we going as a church or denomination?" (Lohrenz 1928, 9). With the gradual awakening to the missionary obligation, which came in the late nineteenth century, Mennonites realized that they needed to make an impact on the larger society, and that church colleges constituted a kingpin in this move. A statement of this impulse provided the foundations of Hesston College: "The schools are the most powerful instrument in working out [the church's] mission" (Miller 6).

A third reason for starting the colleges was to prepare people for certain vocations within the context of a particular view of the Christian life. Again Lohrenz states, "A third of the early aims for the founding of Tabor College was to give preparation for certain vocations." Persons who receive this preparation "are to be used of God on the mission fields at home and abroad, in the ministry, in the teaching professions, . . . and in many other vocations" (ibid., 8–19). The similar purposes of Bethel College were stated very precisely: "It will . . . be the high and noble aim of Bethel College to give an opportunity to the sons and daughters of Mennonite families to obtain their education within the pale of their own church" (H. Peters 1925, 109). The secularization of higher education was clearly understood by the Mennonite pioneers. At the same time, they understood well that not all young people would want to remain farmers, or would be able to. By calculated design, the Mennonites felt that there was more chance of controlling secularization by coopting higher education than by allowing young people to attend non-Mennonite or secular schools. However, that position was arrived at finally only amid great controversy.

All of the colleges experienced a typical history of being formed by private, forward-looking and progressive members, only to be opposed by the more conservative members, who felt that the thrust of schools and their end result would be secularization. Indeed, attempts at higher education in all sectors and periods of North American Mennonite history have been accompanied by intense emotion and struggle. The greatest point of contention has been over maintaining the "orthodoxy of the faith," focused especially on the Bible and religion departments. A number of the schools—Bethel, Tabor, and Goshen, for example— had difficulties or were closed because of the controversy over whether the teachers were espousing heretical doctrines. The closing of Goshen College in 1923–24 left such bitterness in its wake that the controversy dissipated only as the principals slowly went to their graves.[2] A recent furor indicates that the struggle of the schools is not over. In a pamphlet entitled *A Crisis among Mennonites: In Education, in Publication*, George R. Brunk II states, "The historic positions of the Mennonite Church are seriously threatened from two directions, education and publication" (1983, 81). The broadside itself created a crisis of sorts which is now unfolding in the Old Mennonite Church.

In time, the membership at large saw the utility of the colleges and became ardent supporters of them, especially after their own children began to set their sights on advanced training. Now all but one of the colleges (Bethel College) are controlled by conferences or boards of education elected by the conferences. The colleges, though varied, are flourishing generally and are in many ways the nerve centers of their respective conferences. They seem to have achieved a good degree of trust among the various constituencies and are considered to be the mainstay of the mission of Mennonite society. After reviewing Mennonite higher education, in particular the colleges, Melvin Gingerich, one of the foremost experts on Mennonite education, concluded: "Rural life conferences, Mennonite historical society programs, Anabaptist theology seminars, Mennonite cultural problems conferences, Christian life conferences, and other similar programs largely sponsored by the church colleges have given the future Mennonite leaders an appreciation of and a loyalty to the basic New Testament principles, which in the thinking of the patrons of the colleges, are sufficient reasons for their continuation" (1955, 639). The rather cautious tone of this definitive statement on colleges in the *Mennonite Encyclopedia* and the reference to the "patrons" of the colleges give a little insight into a very contentious area which is only now beginning to receive more open discussion.

Comparative Analysis

A curious difference exists between the "Swiss" Mennonites and the "Russian" Mennonites with reference to the formal education thrust present in each group. As indicated above, apart from the early elementary grades, the Swiss Mennonites did not organize any major formal education institutions for the better part of two centuries after they arrived in North America. That is not to say that there were not concerned educators; among the most noteworthy was Christopher Dock, an outstanding Mennonite schoolmaster who taught in eastern Pennsylvania in the early 1700s. But as a rule, the push for general education was less focused and less mature than among the Russian Mennonites. By contrast, the Russian Mennonites established formal educational institutions beyond elementary education within ten years of their arrival in America. What can explain this difference? Is it significant?

Several explanations are quite obvious. In the first place, when the first Mennonites, the Swiss, arrived in North America, practically everything was raw frontier. There were certain survival concerns that claimed a higher priority than education. Secondly, one could say with some justification that the Mennonites in North America during the first century or two were not as advanced as their host culture, in terms of educational sophistication, while the Mennonites living in Russia were superior to the host culture. Of course, the goal of the Swiss Mennonites was the same as that of their Russian counterparts, namely, separation from the world. So the Swiss Mennonite stance, in general, reflected minimum cooperation with secular programs of education and that usually only at the elementary grade level. Thus the vitality of the Swiss Mennonites rested all the more heavily on strong congregational teaching and discipline, as well as on the home. For two hundred years the need for schools among the Swiss Mennonite communities did not appear to be as great as it was for the Mennonites in Russia, who—in their commonwealth form of Mennonite society—carried responsibility for the full gamut of social and religious life.

It is interesting to note the coincidental development of colleges and seminaries among both Russian and Swiss Mennonites—in the late 1800s—in North America. Within twenty-five years of the major emigration of Mennonites from Russia (1874), both groups were busily engaged in such formal education developments; the emergence of high schools came somewhat later. Apart from the possible influence of the exemplary educational developments in Russia, there was undoubtedly another factor that motivated the Swiss Mennonites. By the late 1800s and certainly by the turn of the century, the dangerous forces of acculturation were beginning to make powerful inroads into the Swiss Mennonite communities. It was becoming increasingly obvious to church leaders and to parents that the protection of their young from secular influences could be realized only by providing higher education (beyond elementary) within the aegis of the religious community (Mac-Master 1985, 150ff).

Accurate data on Mennonite education before the 1950s and 1960s are not available. But the indications are for a continuing increase in the percentage of Mennonites attending higher levels of schools. Table 11.1 shows the educational achievements as of 1971 for the five major Mennonite groups. Until 1966, the colleges collectively kept statistics on their own attendance, and these data provide some picture of the growth in attendance since 1930, when records were begun (see Table 11.2). A comparison of the educational levels of U.S. Mennonites and non-Men-

TABLE 11.1 Distribution of Church Members by
Educational Attainment and Denomination, 1971

| Educational attainment | Percentage distribution for | | | | | |
	MC	GCMC	MBC	BIC	EMC	Total
Less than eight grades	7.5	6.6	9.9	6.5	3.9	7.4
Eight grades but not more	20.8	12.6	13.8	13.7	10.6	16.7
Some high school	20.8	16.9	25.2	21.8	16.3	20.4
High school diploma but not more	24.9	24.6	15.4	27.4	33.0	23.5
Some college	11.8	16.2	13.4	12.7	14.4	13.4
College degree but not more	4.9	6.1	6.2	6.0	9.6	5.6
Some graduate work but not a degree	3.3	4.8	4.8	2.6	3.4	3.9
Graduate degree	6.0	12.3	11.4	9.3	8.7	9.0
Total	100.0	100.1	100.1	100.0	99.9	99.9
No. of respondents	1,193	610	710	614	436	3,563
Median no. of school yrs. completed	12.0	12.6	12.1	12.3	12.1	12.2

Source: Kauffman and Harder 1975, 59.
Note: MC   = Mennonite Church
  GCMC = General Conference Mennonite Church
  MBC = Mennonite Brethren Church
  BIC = Brethren in Christ
  EMC = Evangelical Mennonite Church

Year	Mennonite students	Non-Menn. students	Total	College students	Below college
1930–31	1,515	655	2,170	1,234	946
1940–41	2,101	608	2,709	1,581	1,128
1950–51	5,575	1,111	6,686	3,464	3,222
1964–65	4,490	1,969	6,459	—	—

Source: Gingerich 1955, 638.

nonites is difficult to make because the U.S. Census does not allow religion to be used as an identifying characteristic. The situation is different in Canada, and Table 11.3 indicates how Canadian Mennonites compare with other groups. It is probably fair to assume that the Canadian statistics would be representative for U.S. Mennonites as well.

The types of education sought by Mennonites—whether religious, secular, helping, or theoretical—are not easily ascertainable, but it has always been assumed that Mennonites, at least in the Mennonite col-

TABLE 11.3 Comparative Level of Education among Religious Groups in Canada

Religion	Post-secondary	11–13 yrs.	Less than grade 11
Roman Catholic	35.9	25.0	39.1
Ukrainian Catholic	32.8	20.8	46.4
Anglican	41.4	27.2	31.5
Baptist	37.5	24.7	37.3
Jehovah's Witness	26.3	29.1	44.1
Mormon	48.3	27.9	23.8
Lutheran	40.4	24.5	35.1
Mennonite	31.3	19.3	48.9
Hutterite	1.1	1.4	97.5
Pentecostal	32.1	23.3	44.1
Presbyterian	39.5	28.7	31.9
Reformed bodies	40.6	26.6	32.8
Salvation Army	26.2	21.1	52.7
United Church of Canada	40.7	27.7	31.6
Other Protestant	46.6	24.3	29.2
Eastern Orthodox	32.0	20.6	47.4
Jewish	55.6	22.3	22.1
All other religions	59.7	18.8	21.5
No religion	50.8	25.2	23.9
Total population	39.1	25.5	35.4

Source: Heaton 1986, 60.

leges, tended to choose majors which were oriented toward service professions. The most intensive study of Mennonite higher education was conducted by the Mennonite Church in the early 1960s. Since the Mennonite Church is the largest group, its findings are significant and probably rather representative of the other groups. Medicine and nursing majors composed 181 out of a total of 219 medical science students, namely 82 percent, while in applied sciences, education accounted for 114 graduates out of a total of 263, for 42 percent. In applied sciences, majors in home economics, social work, and agriculture would also qualify as service majors. Majors in social work, an overwhelmingly popular major among the general population in the 1950s and 1960s, were not very numerous since none of the Mennonite colleges were accredited in this area until the mid 1960s. The totals for medical sciences and applied arts and sciences are unusually large, and indicate how strong the service motivation was, since the medical science majors were basically nursing and medicine, and the applied arts basically education.

A host of comparisons could be made in the educational enterprise in Mennonite society; I have described only the tip of the iceberg in terms of the tremendous variations in the actual practice of the Mennonite population regarding formal education. A profitable study could be made, for example, of the percentage of Mennonite children attending Mennonite grade schools (and these grade schools vary tremendously in quality among the Mennonite groups) as opposed to public schools; of the number of Mennonites attending Mennonite high schools (again, extremely varied among themselves, some with outstanding academic standards), as over against those Mennonites attending non-Mennonite schools; the number of Mennonites attending church-supported versus non-Mennonite colleges and seminaries, a statistic extremely significant for the Mennonite vision. Not only a "Mennonite" education, but also the type of training received would make great differences in the life pattern of graduates.

Education and Mennonite Faith

The differences and variations just reviewed need to be placed in some sort of perspective to make sense or become useful. One perspective that can be used is the degree of conservatism of the Mennonite body sponsoring the school. The Old Colony or Sommerfelder schools as they exist today in northern Mexico or in Alberta are of the conservative type, while those primary schools now being launched in Alberta by conferences of Canadian Mennonites are more foward-looking. In the former, the purposes are to retain the old ways with the most minimal educational advance or intellectual openness; the purpose is basically to keep the Mennonite community functioning as it is. In the latter, the objective is to provide the best and most up-to-date education but one carefully informed by the values of the Mennonite community in order to prepare young people to confront and to withstand the almost overwhelming persuasion of mass and popular culture.[3]

Mennonite high schools and colleges can be seen as more similar in purpose—the preparation for leadership in the work of the Mennonite church or in its outreach and service. In fact, the struggle for survival by Mennonite secondary and postsecondary schools is premised almost entirely on the need to support institutions which are the basic hope for the survival of Mennonite society (Regehr 1972, 114). The massive effort in public education by the respective boards of education responsible for the high schools, colleges, and seminaries through the years, and the annual budgets of the entire educational enterprise, attest to the centrality of Mennonite formal socialization as it became increasingly obvious that the Mennonite community was losing the boundaries that separated it from "the world." It is equally clear that far-sighted leaders had concluded that only by coopting and guiding the desire to learn, as well as controlling its consequences, could the church be guaranteed a future.

These objectives became a powerful motivation in the life of Mennonite society. Vast amounts of energy have been expended in maintaining educational systems that protect and propagate the way of life to which Mennonites are committed. Often, this drive to keep Mennonite young from the ways of the world required "double taxation." It is clear that congregations, communities, and families have joined in a significant display of support for their Mennonite traditions and spiritual concerns. One proof of this is the noteworthy array of Mennonite educational institutions and their continuing survival during the student and financial crunch of the 1960s, '70s and '80s.

The function of education in the Mennonite community, and the philosophy on which it is based, is sparsely discussed in the Mennonite scholarly sector.[4] It is curious that the significance or effectiveness of transmitting the faith has received so little from academics. In a survey of Mennonite research, Driedger and Redekop state: "How Mennonites have transmitted their faith to the next generation has been of great interest. Most research has dealt with this topic, but only indirectly, mainly when the family and the community are discussed, the two major bearers of the heritage" (1983, 59). Yet, this must not ignore the mass of discussions, study conferences, committees, and documentation that have been produced by and for the Mennonite institutions for the purpose of clarifying the goals of the institutions and the means to achieve them. Hence, what scholars have tended to neglect has intuitively been of great concern to church people at large. Faculty members of Mennonite educational institutions from grade school through college and seminary can attest to the seemingly unending self-analysis and "futuring," which has created near psychic exhaustion at times. Much of the urge has of course been motivated by the struggle for survival, which almost all Mennonite institutions have faced from the beginning. Thus, for example, C. Henry Smith describes the emergence of Goshen College in the following mood: "Even then there was very little sentiment in favor of such an institution. . . . Goshen College owes its existence to the foresight of a small group of progressive men" (1950, 759).

Despite a general dearth of scholarship in this area, a few theoretical and analytical studies have been published. In a provocative article, "A Century of Private Schools," Rudy Regehr concludes his survey with the question, "Education for what end?" He states: "The most frequent question asked about church schools is 'How are these students different from those in other institutions?' The tacit assumption is that schools influence people, and Mennonite schools influence them differently. . . . Adequate documentation for the value of Mennonite public schools is hard to come by" (1972, 114–15).

There have been several empirical studies conducted to gauge the effectiveness of attendance at Mennonite high schools, and the results seem to indicate that there is some positive effect. Don Kraybill summarizes several of these studies and their findings:

> Hooley found statistically significant differences between students who attended the Mennonite school more than two years and those who attended less than two years on five scales: church involvement, religious activities, human relations, theological justification, and theological forgiveness. . . .
>
> When Hess compared graduates of Lancaster Mennonite High School with young adults who never attended a Mennonite high school, he found that the Mennonite high school graduates were closer to Mennonite ideal values on sixteen scales. . . .
>
> In contrast to the Mennonite school pupils, the public students [surveyed in Kraybill's own study] indicated that higher proportions of their five closest friends were members of their church youth group. This fact, in addition to other results in the study, suggests that public school Mennonites tend to

be more involved in their congregational youth groups than the Mennonite school students, who may find more of their social and spiritual needs met in their school experiences. There were no significant differences between students in Mennonite and public schools in the following scales: self-concept, spirituality, and support of church institutions. (D. Kraybill 1978, 46, 48, 52)

The last of these studies, done by Kraybill himself, indicates the lack of clarity of the empirical results, and suggests that further analysis is necessary.

One of the most specifically sociological researches concerned the Manitoba Mennonites. In this study, Leo Driedger (1967) evaluated the functions of education from a sociological point of view and divided the experience of Mennonites into three periods—the period of conflict, that of accommodation , and that of assimilation. The last period refers to the increasing degree to which Mennonites attend public institutions, and the degree to which Mennonite institutions themselves are affected by secular norms and values. Driedger then proposed some models of how Mennonites, through their educational activities, can make a greater contribution to the larger society, while still retaining their faith.

A final study of education is John A. Hostetler's extensive and thorough study of socialization practices among the Hutterites (1965). Since this book deals with a very specialized approach in the very segregated setting of Hutterite society, the study is not as relevant for an understanding of education among the broad stream of Mennonites, who are of the semi-communal and Mennonite community models described in Chapter 6.

A review of the research on Mennonites and their educational pursuits indicates that most of the energy has been spent in describing the history and philosophy of educational institutions and their changes, rather than in taking a hard look at whether education in the Mennonite context actually achieves its goals. College and seminary attendance, of course, is even more pertinent, but very little evidence is available (Smucker 1977).

As CAN BE deduced from this discussion of education, Mennonite society has always recognized the importance of education—that is, the socialization of both the young and converts in the faith of the fathers. Even the most traditional groups, such as the Old Colony and the Old Order Amish, have conducted their own schools to educate children in the rudiments necessary to perpetuate their way of life. So education itself has never been disparaged or avoided; clearly, therefore, there has probably always been a modicum of intellectual and aesthetic activity in the schools (Urry 1983).

But without question, the educational system has always been seen as basically utilitarian—as a means of perpetuating the way of life. An Old Colony bishop stated it well: "The question of conducting schools is for us a religious issue. Hence we cannot submit the schools to governmental control" (D. Harder 1969, 3). The operators of one church school founded in 1893 on the frontier in Minnesota stated that "[the] only purpose of this school is to create interest in religion and the church" (Hartzler 1925, 115). An elder in Russia admonished: "Resist in a manly and fatherly way 'worldly' tendencies in the Gemeinde, in the refinement of school instruction and in the expansion of 'worldly' knowledge. We must not exceed the necessities of our faith" (Urry 1983, 307).

But the contrary role of education in turning people outward and causing them to be concerned about expressing the mission and service aspects of faith has been slowly gaining ground. It is this dilemma which may best characterize the structural paradox of Mennonite education: the conscious transmission of a precious heritage by its very nature causes people to examine what is being transmitted and unintentionally serves to open the doors and windows to the world. And as the Old Order cousins in the Mennonite family have so incessantly shown the rest, "If you give a finger, they will take the hand." This dilemma has not been very generally voiced and understood (C. Redekop 1961).

Chapter Twelve

Mennonites and Economics

The tensions between the economic order and the Christian faith have been one of the persistent issues in Western thought. Throughout Christian history, churchmen and theologians have wrestled with the way faith affects economic activity and vice versa. The tendency for the Christian heritage to integrate with the sociopolitical institutions during the period of medieval Catholicism, a trend which was carried on by Protestantism, was, according to Troeltsch, a signal difficulty for the true expression of Christianity. "After all," Troeltsch said, "it is not so simple to build up a civilization and a society upon the supernatural values of the love of God and the brethren" (1960, 202). Numerous positions have slowly taken shape, so that now, for example, it is possible to talk about a Roman Catholic view regarding economic activity. Protestant groups have also developed extensive and varied interpretations. In fact, critics maintain that, in many ways, capitalism and socialism are the result of the Christian involvement in economic activity.[1]

Social scientists, especially economists and sociologists, have also investigated the relationship between religion and economics. Numerous theories and interpretations regarding the religious-economic nexus have been propounded, the most familiar being that of Max Weber in *The Protestant Ethic and the Spirit of Capitalism.* H. R. Niebuhr's "economic disinheritance" theory of sect life has attempted to combine a discussion of economic activity with sectarian theory. Of course, Karl Marx's view of religion and economics is well known; in fact, to a considerable degree, his ideas have stimulated much of the more recent theory and research. And, to name just one more, R. H. Tawney has attempted to present a more balanced view of the interplay between economics and religion.

Although many theories and explanations have been advanced to suggest how religion and economics affect each other, the interrelationship can probably be summarized by the following axioms or propositions:

1. In most of its forms, Christianity has limited its members—or even directed them very specifically—in their pursuit of economic activities and values.
2. At least in part, economic institutions have developed independently of Christian influence and very likely sometimes, in spite of it.
3. Economic institutions have influenced and continue to influence change in a society and thus often blunt Christian beliefs and teachings in economic affairs.
4. Christian traditions have tended to "rationalize" their adaptation, or submission, to the hegemony of the economic institutions.

All of these positions are best illustrated through reference to the relationship between Christian groups and social stratification systems. The massive research on this topic has proven unequivocally that religious groupings are reflective of social stratification; furthermore, it has proved that religious beliefs—in equality, for example—do not snuff out the invidious factors extant in the society at large. Gardner, in a very thorough analysis of the Christian "fellowship of class" (the title of a chapter), states: "Many careful studies have been made of religion and the class structure in a variety of American communities over the past three or four decades. Although they differ considerably in their detailed findings, they consistently show that membership and participation in specific religious bodies are closely related to the patterns of social stratification in various communities. Taken together these studies reveal a picture of the churches that differs sharply in many respects from the images as well as the norms that the churches hold concerning themselves" (1967, 32).

Probably one of the most definitive works which attempts to test the reciprocal influences of the Christian-economic relationship is Gerhard Lenski's *The Religious Factor*. He concludes his section on economics by stating that "on the basis of our data we cannot assert positively that the religious orientation to which a man is exposed and to which he becomes committed actually influences his actions in the economic field. . . . Nevertheless our findings create a strong suspicion that this fact is the case" (1961, 114). He does not test in his research the obverse of his equation—that economics affects religion—but perhaps in his view, the conclusion is so obvious that it needs no empirical proof.

The Anabaptist-Mennonite relationship to economic behavior, however, is a different story and may well be unique. For in this tradition there has been and continues to be both strenuous teaching and tradition regarding economic behavior; these have created most unusual lifestyles and institutions. In this chapter I will describe as adequately as possible the typologies of Mennonite economic relationships as well as provide an analysis of the dynamics that have produced the accommodations and the stances that are being so earnestly debated by Mennonites today.

A Typology of Mennonite Activities in Economic Life

It is difficult to present a simple and coherent picture of Mennonite economic activity because there have been a wide variety of understandings and expressions. It is possible to describe Anabaptism as a "communal economics," and there are analyses that take this point of view (e.g., Goertz 1984; P. Klassen 1964; R. Vogt 1980). But even if this point of view is accepted, it is clear that there are numerous variations which must be included and explicated. In this first section, that variety is organized under three rubrics.[2]

The Community of Goods Model

Although Mennonite historians and theologians have resisted including the Münsterites and a few other radical chiliastic groups in the Anabaptist movement, recent scholarship and opinion have increasingly assumed that they have to be included in the original movement. Theoretically they fit in the first—that is, economic communism—model; it is the extreme to which they went which creates the problem for Mennonites. Because their revolt was so short-lived and developed under such chaotic conditions, little of a reasoned and coherent picture of their theology emerges, though it is clear that the basic issues, including total community, were the same. In this discussion I can only allude to the central importance of communism. I focus on the more peaceful groups which survived and established a stable structure.

The community of goods stance toward economics is the most original of all Mennonite positions and is most easily described. First enunciated methodically by Peter Riedemann, an early Hutterite, it had seven basic tenets: (1) materialism is unchristian; (2) material goods—which, in themselves, are neither good nor bad—are to be used by Christian stewards as a means of doing good; (3) Christians should trust God, who supplies all our needs; (4) the sinful state of the world is due to unchristian attitudes toward material possessions; (5) extremes in riches are wrong; (6) true Christian fellowship involves economic as well as spiritual equality; (7) this orientation requires a strict community life of sharing and cooperation (Hershberger 1958).

This model—promoted by many early Anabaptists (P. Klassen 1964) and followed by the Hutterites as well as occasionally by other sympathetic groups, such as the Society of Brothers and Mennonite-affiliated modern communal groups (Fretz 1979)—is premised on the idea of *Gelassenheit:* the surrender of the will and personal ambition to God. "Supremely it means complete self-denial and voluntary surrender to the will of God (*Gottesbegebenheit*). Through it suffering becomes the royal road to God in witness, martyrdom, and subordinating material and physical needs to the spiritual" (Smucker 1976, 226; see also P. Klassen 1964, 77).

It is clear that the implications of this model are different today than they were in the sixteenth century. Then there was greater need for both self-reliance and mutual dependence; hence, the objective appeared to be more consistent. Today there have emerged a number of new communities which can be classified under this model, but whose theorizing and articulation are rather different as they attempt to respond to modern conditions. These factors have been extensively described by John W. Bennett (1967) in his analysis of Canadian Hutterites. However, the general profiles of the two streams are similar: one finds (1) the downgrading of, if not the abolition of, private property (though not private consumption); (2) the subordination of economic activities (production, consumption, and lifestyle) to the will of the fellowship or congregation; (3) the elevation of the essential life of the society—that is, the congregation—to a position of supremacy so as to subordinate all economic activities to it; (4) the formation of an extended family as the unit of economic activity rather than the nuclear family; and (5) the refusal to accumulate property and wealth beyond the necessity of moderate consumption needs. Among the Hutterites, the surplus is utilized to create more communities, and in the new community movement it is used for various neighborhood and larger social causes.

The argument that these societies have not really opted out of participation in the capitalist system and that they are contributing to it is true, of course, but irrelevant. The object of the community of goods models is not to "destroy capitalism" or any other system, but rather to be faithful to an understanding of the teaching of Christianity regarding economic life. Further, I have no argument with the view that convictions regarding the community of goods model have undergone considerable change since the sixteenth century. The Hutterite colonies still adhere to these beliefs rather rigidly, but their success in articulating them in economic life is varied. The question of the loss of consistency cannot be addressed here. In any case, in general terms the Hutterite economics needs to be understood as adhering faithfully to total communism.

The Radical Confrontation Model

The approach of the mainstream of Anabaptism confirms *Gelassenheit* as having a posture of *confrontation* with the religio-social-political establishment, rather than one of forming separated communities (Smucker 1976, 225). This confrontation model has also been termed the "nonresistant approach in economic life" (R. Vogt 1972, 160). According to Guy F. Hershberger—whom Vogt defines as the main spokesman of the radical confrontation model—"Christians oppose not only clearly immoral acts of stealing and cheating, but [also] the use of force which appears to be an implicit part of the functioning of many economic institutions" (ibid., 161). Hershberger states, "The coercive methods and powerful maneuverings of modern agricultural organizations, labor unions and industrial corporations are of such a nature that today Menno would hardly classify them as innocent procedures of men with an essentially Christian calling" (Hershberger 1958, 227).

The confrontation model may have been mostly an ideal and may never have been approximated in any extensive way. Nor can it be. In fact, Smucker says, "this model is no longer an option" (1976, 225). But Hershberger maintains that it has been enacted in some degree in certain parts of Mennonite history and should be the goal of all Mennonites. In essence, this view contained the following objectives of "brotherhood economics" (Hershberger 1958, 223):

1. Although private property is not rejected outright, materialism is strongly condemned.
2. Christians will strive to help their neighbors through the use of their own possessions, which are theirs only in trust from God: "Above all, a brother known in the congregation should always have a box of money, a bag in hand, so that during the meeting or later, every member, when admonished by the Lord, may bring his frugal offering and blessing there, in order that whenever necessity arise, the poor may be given according to their needs of that which is available" (P. Klassen 1964, 121). This statement, among many that could be cited, refers to the broad concept of mutual aid in which material possessions are to be shared as need arises.
3. Christians are committed to the concept of stewardship of all resources and possessions, thus modifying or taking a middle position between a total communal stance and the extremely individualistic concept of private property. By stewardship, Mennonites mean that Christians are trustees and caretakers of their God-given blessings. Thus, they are responsible for material as well as nonmaterial resources, recognizing that they are not the sole determiners or dispensers of these resources.
4. Christians avoid economic practices which undermine the ethic of the kingdom of God. Translated into practice, this means rejecting usury or any kind of coercive activity in business affairs. It also means the avoidance of many occupations and economic pursuits where coercion and violence might be applied. It was for this reason that, for many years in North America, membership in labor unions was forbidden. At the same time, the violence so easily perpetrated by management and owners was condemned with equal vehemence.

While this second model was probably never fully realized in any period of Mennonite history, the ideal was held up, and in many Mennonite communities these principles were illustrated in the lives of individual Mennonites. The Old Order groups are in some ways representative of this model. To the extent that they approximate the principles outlined, they represent the confrontational model. Many of the more traditional Old Order Amish, Old Order Mennonite, and Old Colony Mennonite communities operate in this orientation, though they may not be able to articulate this stance. A critical measure of the confrontational nature of the conservative groups would be to evaluate what is done with the surplus wealth created in the community. If it is used basically to perpetuate a way of life that protects the belief system, as is the case in many Old Order groups, then it could be described as attempting to promote and fulfill the biblical commandments of Christian discipleship. To an increasing extent, however, the Old Order types are approximating the model described below, and hence they can also be at least partially included in the analysis.

The Conventional Economics Model

A third way of describing some segments of Anabaptist-Mennonite economic activity is "conventional economics," by which is meant Mennonite behavior in economic institutions that reflect the system operative in the wider society. Soon after the earliest period of Anabaptism, there was strong evidence that Mennonites in certain circumstances participated in almost every phase of economic life as it was then being practiced in the larger world. In some analyses this means that Mennonites reinterpreted and compromised the "faith of the fathers" with respect to economic behavior. But it also implies that there have been Mennonites who have not considered the existent economic norms and values inimical to the expression of the Christian faith (Fretz 1957a; Hershberger 1958; R. Vogt 1972).

The Mennonites in Holland illustrate this position, for after the persecution abated, there developed in the Netherlands a wealthy Mennonite society which included family dynasties in fishing fleets, whaling businesses, and trading companies (Groenveld, Jacobszoon, and Verhew 1980; Hershberger 1958, 284 et passim; van der Zijpp and Bender 1955, 483). In Germany, extensive weaving and related industries emerged. In South Germany, Alsace, Lorraine, and even Switzerland, larger landholdings emerged after the Mennonites were given freedom to own land. And, as we saw in Chapter 5, the Mennonite communal society that emerged in Russia and North and South America expressed the conventional economic model in many ways.

This conventional economic model typically has the following characteristics:

1. A support of private property as well as private initiative in the accumulation of wealth.
2. An acceptance of and participation in prevailing economic activities—including the charging of prevailing interest rates by

lenders as well as engagement in various entrepreneurial pursuits such as merchandising, manufacturing, and commerce.
3. The creation of linkages with non-Mennonites and non-Christians in business associations and dealings; such associations apparently presented no problem and were not subject to restrictions.
4. An assumption that mutual aid and stewardship are not paramount ideals or objectives, since competition and free enterprise are basic in the effort to provide for human needs.

In other words, in this model, the dominant economic values and institutions of the host society are seen as both appropriate and normative for Mennonite behavior within the economic realm.

One of the most detailed personal accounts of the conventional economics model, already blossoming in the nineteenth century, is that of David Epp, of a Russian Mennonite family in the Ukraine. The rise to power of the Neibuhr family in the economic and industrial sector of Mennonitism of nineteenth-century Russia is the focus of the study, entitled "The Emergence of German Industry in the South Russian Colonies" (D. Epp 1981). The analysis of how craftsmen became owners of large flour mills is truly in the best "self-made man" tradition (P. Friesen 1978, 866–84).

The conventional economic model could be described simply as the expression of economic life in full articulation with the prevailing society. However, any total realization of this stance has rarely been achieved in Mennonite circles. Even in the Russian Mennonite situation, where this model was highly developed, P. M. Friesen states, for example, that Mennonites' "ultimate craving" for land prevented them from becoming fully committed to learning the techniques and secrets of trade, commerce, and manufacturing. Admittedly, there was no trade school in the Mennonite colonies until late in the Russian Mennonite saga. But Friesen, who is not an economic or social theorist, states, in regard to the lack of educational support for business, that "an important reason may be that the Mennonite questions the ethical standpoint of the merchant" (1978, 882).

The Mennonite Economic Enterprise

Some specific aspects of Mennonite economic life may help us understand better the life of Mennonites in economics.

Probably the most comprehensive observation that can be made about the entire Mennonite family—Hutterite, Old Order, and Mennonite—is that typically Mennonites have been more successful financially, more secure, and better established than the populations among which they have lived. Empirical evidence for this is not lacking. The Kauffman and Harder study suggests that Mennonite farmers have a 29 percent higher median family income than the U.S. national average (1975, 285), while the average income for Mennonite families in 1971 was $9,608 as compared to $8,583 for the American population as a whole. The economic status of Mennonites has certainly not changed since that time. A survey conducted in 1981 in Canada provides the most recent objective data (see Table 12.1).

Another study by Gingerich (1953) reports that in 1951 the median income for non-Mennonite farmers was $3,111, while for Mennonites it was $3,305. In studies done earlier in central Kansas by Lloyd Spauling, the evidence indicated that the Mennonites were representative of the middle income level and tended to be underrepresented in the lower

TABLE 12.1   Average Income of Religious Groups in Canada, 1981

Religion	Ave. income of persons with income	Adjusted ave. income of persons with income
Eastern Orthodox	$12,395	$11,749
Roman Catholic	12,293	12,452
Ukrainian Catholic	12,421	13,271
Anglican	13,661	14,000
Baptist	11,740	12,230
Hutterite	11,392	a
Jehovah's Witness	10,309	10,347
Lutheran	13,303	13,322
Mennonite	11,809	11,468
Mormon	12,412	11,827
Pentecostal	10,782	10,909
Presbyterian	13,334	13,815
Reformed bodies	12,306	12,678
Salvation Army	10,317	10,866
United Church of Canada	13,693	13,839
Other Protestant	12,586	12,471
Jewish	19,529	19,329
All other religions	12,734	12,384
No religion	14,854	13,903
Total population	12,993	12,993

Source: Heaton 1986, 63 (1981 Canadian Census Data).
Note: Comparable census data for U.S. Mennonites is not available, since the U.S. Census does not allow religious identification.
aCell sizes too small for adjustment.

as well as higher income levels (Spaulding 1953, 83). Other, more informal surveys indicate that, in recent years, many Mennonites have become wealthy. One writer suggests that, at present, there must be at least 700 Mennonite millionaires if one assumes that Mennonites are at least as successful economically as the North American population in general (*Marketplace*, December 1979). This assumption is probably correct, given what we know of Mennonites in business.

It is well known that the early Anabaptists were not basically agricultural during the first decades of their existence as a movement, but that they became agriculturally based through subsequent development (Fretz 1956, 303–13; Peachey 1954). By the nineteenth century in Russia and Europe, except for Holland, Mennonites were overwhelmingly people of the land. Where commerce and industry did develop, as in the Ukraine, it was within the context of the agricultural community, with commercial enterprises gradually venturing out beyond the perimeter of the Mennonite geographical community (Krahn 1955; D. Rempel 1933; Urry, 1978).

In North America, the turning point with reference to Mennonite predominance on the land has come only very recently, far behind the national profile. In a survey done of the Old Mennonites in the 1940s, 66.75 percent of the male membership was engaged in farming. In 1950 the number had dropped to 62.9 percent. By 1973, according to the Kauffman-Harder study, the total for all Mennonites had dropped to 27 percent. The 1963 census of the Old Mennonites indicates that only 38.9 percent were farmers. Thus, between 1940 and 1970—probably around 1960—the majority occupation of Mennonites ceased to be agriculturally based. The comparison with the overall picture in the United States indicates the imbalance between Mennonite occupations and those of the general population even for the year 1971, at which time only 2.7 percent of the total labor force was engaged in farming (Kauffman and Harder 1975, 61).

A recent survey conducted among Old Mennonites recorded the changes for 1983. Table 12.2 shows that the percentage of Mennonites in occupations related to agriculture had slipped to 11.8 percent. The urbanization of Mennonites, and the increasing sprawl of urban settlements and development into Mennonite areas, especially in the eastern United States, is further contributing to this trend (Driedger and Kauffman 1982). The Canadian data (Table 12.3), based on the 1981 census, shows a greater percentage still engaged in farming, though the categories are too broad to be fully comparable.

The Second World War may be called the turning point for Men-

TABLE 12.2 Percentage Distribution of All Adults in the Labor Force by Sex and Occupation: Old Mennonite Church, 1983

Occupation	Men		Women		Economically active adult men and women	
	Members only	All adult males	Members only	All adult females	Members only	All adults
Professional and technical	15.6	16.2	26.8	27.7	20.2	21.1
Manager	15.5	15.0	5.1	4.9	11.2	10.7
Sales	4.1	4.1	3.7	3.7	3.9	3.9
Clerical	2.0	1.9	22.1	22.2	10.3	10.3
Skilled worker	19.6	19.9	2.6	2.6	12.6	12.7
Semiskilled worker	7.5	7.8	6.6	6.8	7.1	7.4
Transport equipment worker	6.2	6.0	1.5	1.5	4.3	4.1
Laborer, except farm	7.2	7.3	2.5	2.6	5.3	5.3
Farmer; farm manager	16.4	15.7	.9	.8	10.0	9.6
Farm laborer; foreman	3.2	3.2	.7	.6	2.2	2.2
Service worker, except private household	2.6	2.8	19.1	18.4	9.4	9.3
Private household worker	.2	.2	8.3	8.1	3.5	3.4
All occupations	100.1	100.1	99.9	99.9	100.0	100.0
Total no. economically active	31,271	35,550	21,846	25,151	53,117	60,701
% of adults in labor force[a]	—	79.0	—	47.2	61.7	61.8

Source: M. Yoder 1985, 322.

Note: Figures include all adults employed full- or part-time or unemployed but looking for work.

[a]These are conservative estimates, since persons for whom information on occupation was missing were counted as not in the labor force. If those persons are excluded, the percentage of adults in the labor force becomes 82.8 for adult men, 49.2 for adult women and 64.7 for all adults.

201

Religion	Professional	Clerical/sales/ service	Blue-collar/ farm
Eastern Orthodox	18.9	44.5	36.6
Roman Catholic	22.4	40.2	37.5
Ukrainian Catholic	22.9	38.8	38.3
Anglican	27.1	42.1	30.8
Baptist	22.4	40.4	37.2
Hutterite	10.4	1.4	88.2
Jehovah's Witness	11.9	45.4	42.7
Lutheran	22.3	37.8	39.9
Mennonite	21.0	29.5	49.5
Mormon	24.4	41.5	34.1
Pentecostal	17.7	40.4	41.9
Presbyterian	24.4	41.6	34.0
Reformed bodies	21.6	30.7	47.7
Salvation Army	17.3	39.0	43.7
United Church of Canada	25.6	40.4	34.0
Other Protestant	27.8	37.8	34.4
Jewish	45.6	43.4	10.9
All other religions	36.2	36.1	27.7
No religion	30.4	35.2	34.3
Total population	24.4	39.9	35.7

Source: Heaton 1986, 61.

nonite economic activity from agriculture to commerce; this was the period when labor shortages and factory work opportunities enticed Mennonites off the land into the urban areas. The complex issue of labor union membership emerged, and the 1950s and 1960s saw study conferences and committees while Mennonites tried to find their way into participation in the nonagricultural society. One such committee was the Committee on Economic and Social Relations, founded in 1951 and sponsored by the Old Mennonite Church. Its original aim was to "assist the working men of the church to maintain the stand of the church (on grounds of nonresistance) against joining labor unions" (Hershberger 1955, 650). It soon went beyond this narrow concern and addressed the broader issues of Mennonite movement into the economic arena and the retention of Mennonite beliefs such as mutual aid (651).

Some of this change was also the consequence of the closing of the frontiers for new land (1940), so that surplus children, especially sons, had to look for employment elsewhere. This process had already been in progress in the East—that is, in the Pennsylvania and Ontario areas—for some time; there, young men had already worked in dairies, feed mills, trucking, and other activities. Also, the 1930s saw the emergence, in these areas, of Mennonite entrepreneurs, engaged in extensions of the agricultural process, such as feed mills, creameries, farm deliveries, farm machinery repairs, sales, and the like.

The emergence of Mennonite entrepreneurship can be attributed to the same ethos and dynamics. Thus, young men who could not get started on the land, or who were more interested in the world of commerce and industry, slowly began to establish agriculturally related industries, such as meat processing and packaging or grain and other produce transportation. Many Mennonite trucking firms were established as well as construction companies, which built many Mennonite churches and other related Mennonite edifices. Along with these and many other activities, there was a surge in the manufacturing of farm machinery and farm supplies. One of the most spectacular manufacturing developments was the New Holland Corporation, founded by a young conservative Mennonite in the 1940s; he developed a time-saving invention, an automatic twine-knotter, into a multinational business presently listed on the New York Stock Exchange.

Almost every Mennonite geographical settlement has its typical Mennonite-owned and -operated businesses. This trend is developing very rapidly now, especially in the Old Order territories, where the pinch in land is causing many Mennonite young people to begin family-based enterprises, some of them very sophisticated. A new listing compiled by the Old Orders themselves identifies approximately 450 businesses in the eastern United States and Canada (Beiler 1977). The shops cover the gamut from buggy manufacture to producing power-generating equipment.

A comprehensive treatment of Mennonite industry—including agriculture as well as the trades, service sectors (such as sales and distribution), and manufacturing—is tantamount to describing some parts of the general economic landscape. The literally hundreds of Mennonite settlements and communities, Hutterite, Old Order, and Mennonite, originally agricultural, span the North American continent including Mexico and are articulated into the economic mainstream. The GNP of the combined Mennonite economy is substantial. The production of food and fiber among Mennonites is widely known wherever Mennonites have lived and has built a reputation for Mennonite competence and contribution.

The broader involvement in the areas of services, technical and otherwise, and production, especially in foodstuffs and farm-related machines and services, has increased dramatically. In eastern Pennsylvania and Virginia there are several large poultry processing plants; several more are emerging on the West Coast in Oregon and California. The manufacturing sector has been growing with rapid strides, with industries in Winnipeg, Manitoba, Lancaster County, Pennsylvania, and Kansas representing considerable variety, strength, and size. A 1978 catalogue of Mennonite businesses and industries, although not totally comprehensive, lists 237 different vocations. Out of a total of 7,637 members of the Mennonite Economic Development Associates, 22.4 percent were farmers, while the rest were distributed over a broad range, and included manufacturers and contractors.

Possibly the best way to provide a picture of the nature of the Mennonite business project is to look at specific Mennonite communities. One Mennonite community that has been thoroughly studied is Altona, Manitoba. Established soon after the 1875 settlement (in 1880), Altona soon became one of the major trading and service centers in southern Manitoba. A similar study has been conducted for Mountain Lake, Minnesota, founded in 1875. Both of these studies present the proportion of Mennonites and non-Mennonites in the community, pertinent information for Altona as well as for Mountain Lake because both were situated in almost homogeneously Mennonite areas. Table 12.4 indicates the occupational distribution in these two communities.

This movement from the farm has shunted Mennonites into the mainstream of the industrial and commercial world, where they must encounter the norms and values of the larger society head-on. Some Mennonites are now becoming identified as laborers and/or employees, while others are becoming owners and managers. Many Mennonites have entered the professions, especially service professions like teaching, social work, nursing, and medicine (in the order given, the highest majors in Mennonite colleges). Income differentials and differences in residential patterns, to say nothing of lifestyles, are beginning to show up strongly in Mennonite congregations. Some Mennonite congregations can now be identified on the basis of their "class structures"; that is to say, some congregations appeal to laboring types, while others have wealthier or more professionally oriented members.

The strains and tensions this creates can well be imagined. The seminaries and the clergy are trying valiantly to maintain a good level of harmony in the life of the Mennonite community in the face of the socially divisive factors. Strictures on the spending of money and diatribes against materialism and affluence and ostentatious lifestyles flow from the pulpit and the printing presses. But the "materialist trend" seems unstoppable. It is quite apparent that it is not the theology of

TABLE 12.4 Mennonite and Non-Mennonite Entrepreneurs in Two Mennonite Settlements

	Altona, Manitoba 1880–1930			Mountain Lake, Minnesota 1875–1985		
Business	Menn.	Non-Menn.	% Menn.	Menn.	Non-Menn.	% Menn.
Auto sales	5	2	71	7	2	70
Bakery				2	5	28
Bank	0	3	0	5	0	100
Barber shop				2	0	100
Butcher shop	0	1	0	4	2	66
Blacksmith	2	2	50	5	2	71
Construction	—	—		11	4	64
Creamery; hatchery	—	—		4	3	57
Delivery and livery	4	1	80	6	3	66
Elevator	0	1	0	3	2	60
Garage	2	0	100	2	0	100
Hotel	0	1	0	2	0	100
Industry	2	0	100	7	2	70
Lumber	0	4	0	3	0	100
Machinery sales	3	0	100	8	2	80
Mills, feed	1	0	100	1	1	50
Newspaper	—	—		4	2	66
Photography	—	—		6	2	75
Printing	2	0	100	—	—	
Repair and serv.	—	—		10	1	90
Restaurant	1	1	50	5	5	50
Store, gen.	9	9	50	14	6	70
Dept.	—	—		5	1	83
Drug	—	—		2	4	33
Hardware	—	—		7	3	70
Furniture	3	1	75	3	1	75
Services (ins., real estate)	2	0	100	4	3	57
Telephone	—	—		6	1	85
Undertaker	—	—		3	2	60
All businesses	36	26	58	141	59	71

Sources: Centennial Committe 1986; Epp-Tiessen 1982; C. Redekop 1953.
Note: Because the two studies used different categories, these figures are not fully compatible. Dashes indicate that information was not available for the particular town.

Mennonites that has been changing in recent decades, but that there has been a major breakdown in the area of boundary maintenance, particularly in the rural agricultural community. A spate of recent sociological and economic research by Laurence, Appavoo, Bennett, Felstead, Graber, Martens, Nafziger, Vogt, and others speaks to various aspects of this issue.

I have not dealt with Hutterite economic prosperity in this discussion. It is difficult to provide any comparable data on Hutterites' economic advances, since their capital is collectively held. In the most extensive analysis of the relative efficiency of Hutterite and other farmers, Bennett concludes that Hutterite colonies are as efficient as other, more conventional farming arrangements but that per capita income was typically higher on conventional ranches and farms than among the Hutterites (1967, 227ff.).

To summarize, the causes for the shift from the agricultural to the industrial sector include (1) the two World Wars, (2) labor demands, (3) the developing shortage of land for settlement and the related surplus population, (4) the emergence of creativity which did not have an outlet on the farm, and (5) the urban sprawl which literally invaded the countryside. The consequences of the breakdown of Mennonite agricultural economics and consequent urbanization are manifold. Among them are:

1. A decline in the functions of the *community* as the enforcer of norms and socializer of values and beliefs. This means that *congregational* teaching and support becomes ever more important.
2. An increase in the importance of the nuclear family as a social, religious, and economic unit of Mennonite life. Yet, the family is becoming more isolated all the time.
3. An increasing stress on jobs and occupations as the means to achieve community standing and economic security. Hence, a formal education is becoming increasingly important in maintaining economic freedom or as a means of climbing the economic ladder.

In one of the early analyses of Mennonite economic activity, Ernst Correll stated, "As a cultural group in history, the economic significance of the Mennonites is a distinct by-product of their religio-sociological existence" (1942, 162). Correll then went on to explain why he took that position. First, Mennonites have consisted of voluntary groups. They were able to live "in accord with the teachings of the Sermon on the Mount." Secondly, these volunteer groups produced "responsible personalities." "They declared their conscientious objection to a variety of forces levelled against their patriarchal or kinship groups." Further, Correll stated, the formation of "beloved communities" served to exert ethical guidance while Mennonites were facing "ridicule and disgust" by the neighboring society. Finally, there emerged able religious leaders who "directed as well as conditioned" the attainments of the Mennonites in the economic realm (ibid., 162–63).

This is an optimistic and probably unrealistic picture of the role that beliefs played in economic affairs throughout Anabaptist-Mennonite history. A later scholar stated the case differently: "What has happened when twentieth-century Mennonites become conditioned to commercial insurance with its profit features to such an extent that the Anabaptist tradition of mutual aid and 'helping each other faithfully' is neglected, or when some in a position to profit personally by commercial insurance programs may even use their influence against the effective operation of brotherhood mutual aid?" (Hershberger 1958; 289). Hershberger raises other questions which are just as stinging in their import.

That economic patterns affect, and are affected by, religious principles is a logical assumption. But questions such as how and to what degree are not susceptible to quick answers. Obviously—among Mennonites as well as among non-Mennonites—there are differing opinions on these points, specifically on the way the Mennonite tradition has related the Christian Gospel to the economic sphere. Naturally, the approaches to this question are varied as are the perceptions. The scholar approaches the issue from one direction and may well disagree with another scholar who brings different background to his queries. On the other hand, rank-and-file Mennonites may not even be aware of any anomaly. What is more disturbing than this ignorance is the fact that many may not care.[3]

General Orientations

In the context of the broad variety of economic practices among Mennonites, what, if anything, can be said which will describe the essence of Mennonite economics, yet take recognition of the differences?

The first and most obvious generalization is to suggest that Mennonites have never fully agreed as to the form Gospel obedience should take in economic activities.[4] The "community of goods" model has been stubbornly adhered to for many centuries, and as indicated above, recently there have emerged some new communities which believe that the Gospel teaching in reference to economics demands an alternative lifestyle. Vogt states, "On the . . . restriction of Christian socio-economic ethics to practices within a distinctly separate Christian community, there is profound disagreement among Mennonite scholars" (R. Vogt 1983, 67). Interestingly, members of none of the three models have aggressively attempted to convert Mennonites who take other positions, so a form of comity has emerged.

None of the three models has been totally enacted in its purest form. Thus, it is true that there has been no "pure conventional" economic practice among Mennonites where at least a trace of the mutual aid thrust has not been expressed. Conversely, even the Hutterite economics has usually reflected some degree of slippage and dissolution. John A. Hostetler notes that "the dangers of Hutterite affluence are twofold: it adversely influences the colony as a corporation, and it tempts individuals to acquire some economic independence" (1974, 268).

By and large, the economic–religious faith issue has not been a great issue of conscious or rational concern among Mennonites (M. Gingerich 1953, 89). In a recent survey of Mennonites, Roy Vogt concludes that "regardless of the ideology, modern Mennonites have largely bypassed this Christian love aspect of the Anabaptist vision and are very deeply involved in society's structures" (1983, 68). Trained Mennonite economists and sociologists have not given much attention to studying and interpreting the way Anabaptist-Mennonite faith has expressed itself in economics. Most scholarly concern has been with the promotion of community and mutual aid; both are commendable objectives, but the more careful and critical analysis of Mennonite economics has not been done. A recent illustration of a beginning, however, is Al Koop's article "Some Economic Aspects of Mennonite Migration," in which he argues that the Mennonite migrations from Russia to North America were to a considerable extent motivated by economic concerns rather than by the traditional reason of religious freedom (143ff.).

One other predominant thread that has produced considerable discourse and research is the assumption that Mennonite entry into economics has corroded and corrupted Mennonite faith. To illustrate, frequent mention is made of the way the Dutch Mennonites became wealthy and "lost their faith." A statement which has become almost apocryphal is one attributed to Pastor Theo Hylkema, who is reputed to have said on numerous occasions, "After the devil failed in his attempt to destroy Dutch Anabaptism by means of persecution, he almost succeeded when he changed his tactics and made them rich" (Hershberger 1958, 284–85; see also M. Gingerich 1953, 91). There is still considerable conviction and "gut-level feelings" that riches and Anabaptism don't mix, and sermons by the thousands are presented annually admonishing the wavering faithful to beware of riches that corrupt. But research for understanding the vital relationship between Christian faith and wealth, property, profit, production, resources, and religious economic issues has not developed.[5] Mennonites are thus to be described as being a major economic force in the larger social setting, but as having a very much underdeveloped theology of economic behavior.

When a Mennonite becomes financially successful, he leaves the Mennonite Church; if he remains religious at all, he will join a more liberal denomination. John Eby states: "With a bit of thought, I can compile a long list of persons, who, along with their success financially and professionally, chose to leave the Mennonite Church. . . . To be sure, not all persons who become successful leave the Mennonite Church. . . . However this phenomenon is common enough to deserve further reflection" (1986, 11). The traditional explanation for this phenomenon by Mennonites is that the person in question became wealthy by "bending the Christian business ethic" and by flouting the counsel and direction of his Mennonite heritage. The successful business person, however, usually has a different story; he suggests that members in the pew became jealous of his success or resented his wife, didn't understand the problems he was dealing with, or were unwilling to recognize or acknowledge the contributions he had been making (C. Redekop 1988a).

Mennonite encounters in economic life present a fascinating but often confused picture. Mennonite economic life is difficult to classify. Marxists have tried to coopt the communalism of Mennonites but have given up. Capitalistic theorists cannot understand the Mennonite rejection of private enterprise or their tendencies to create communities. Then why have Mennonites become so affluent? There are various possible answers. Many Mennonites would be quick to say that their affluence simply reflects proof of God's blessing upon the committed. Sociologists would point to other reasons, the most obvious being the "Protestant work ethic" idea proposed by Max Weber, namely, otherworldly asceticism, the idea of the calling to work hard as a proof of salvation. Aside from the fact that the thesis has fallen into considerable disfavor in recent years, a study by an economist of the Mennonites in Illinois concludes that Mennonite achievement has not been attributable to the work ethic. Nafziger, in fact, concludes that the Anabaptist-Mennonites do not fit the Calvinistic typology (1965). Appling draws the same conclusion from his study of the Amish (1975). Mennonite economic success and achievement must be ascribed to a *number* of factors:

1. The concept of stewardship, which has included the idea of saving and of frugality in general. This involves a rejection of expensive homes or households and avoidance of conspicuous or self-indulgent expenditures, such as alcohol. This emphasis on stewardship is derived not only from a literal biblicism but also from Mennonites' historical experience, for it was the working out of this principle in the reclamation of land that served as the means for toleration of the Mennonites and Amish by nobles and other landowners.
2. The Mennonite penchant or predilection for hard work. This trait is directly derivative from the process of individual members and families gaining acceptance and toleration of landowners and authorities on the basis of their hard and creative work. The Protestant "work ethic" expressed in the "calling," however, has no historical basis in Mennonite ideas of work.[6]
3. Community support for economic involvement and development. The Old Order farmers today probably symbolize most clearly the communal support theme. The Old Orders, for example, consider it their highest priority to help their children get established. Therefore, they purchase farms for their children, often paying for those farms in cash. In 1983 a banker told me of an Old Order Mennonite who had bought a farm for his son for $375,000. When it came time to pay, this Old Order Mennonite peeled off 375 one-thousand-dollar bills. Community support is not only in the form of money, but also in the entire socio-psychological nurturing system, which is geared to producing economically successful entrepreneurs.
4. The need for economic security. Especially among recent Mennonite refugees from Russia, Europe, and South America, the drive to achieve financial security has resulted in phenomenal economic successes and accumulations. It is well known among Mennonites, for example, that the Mennonite refugees from Russia in the 1920s and 1930s have been unusually aggressive in securing financial resources so as not to become dependent on others. Mennonite immigrants to Canada from Paraguay in recent years have also been especially aggressive and successful.

In general, Mennonites have come from a stock which has been on the move; in the process, the group has lost the feeling of security and stability which presumably the human family desires. A trip through Lancaster County farming areas, with all its substantial farm complexes, tends to reflect that human desire; these farms convey an almost total stability. There can be little doubt that much of the animus for this new reality is the result of overcompensation for homelessness in times past.

The Secularization of the Mennonite Society

Almost everyone associated with the Mennonites—either as a member or as an outside scholar—has assumed that the Mennonites are becoming secularized as they become more integrated into the economic mainstream. Indeed, in July 1942 Karl Baehr published an article, "Secularization among the Mennonites of Elkhart County, Indiana." The editors of the publishing organ, the *Mennonite Quarterly Review*, praised the author for a perceptive article, but Baehr's article reveals little conclusive evidence for making such a claim; the author seems to express more of a normative evaluation which the editors *assumed* was correct.

Other authors have echoed the claims that the entrance of Mennonites into the economic mainstream has contributed to their secularization as well as to their wealth and worldliness. That Mennonites have become wealthy and powerful owners of considerable fortunes as well as productive capacity is indisputable; that their lifestyles increasingly have approximated those of their neighbors is also beyond doubt. The question that remains to be answered, therefore, is, Has this increasing cosmopolitanization caused Mennonites to move from the confrontational economic model to the conventional? This dilemma is illustrated by the response I received in an interview with a Mennonite entrepreneur:

> I was influenced a lot by . . . my father or . . . Roy Vogt, from the *Mennonite Mirror;* they all had similar principles on which they worked. . . . With everything they did they had the public welfare in mind. Well, I'm not quite that philanthropic or altruistic. I actually believed . . . that if I promoted business—which I suddenly realized that I was very good at—I was beating the realtors and the attorneys and all the assorted vultures at their own game. . . . I thought that . . . if you created wealth through legitimate means, you could endow the fantastic institutions that we [Mennonites] do have. That dream has faded slightly because I have gotten so close to the principals in our institutions and I see so much infighting and backbiting that I don't even know why I'm doing it. I'm doing it because I have momentum. I still have it in my will if I should die there are substantial endowments to five basic categories of institutions that we have. But I think that many entrepreneurs lose that sense. It's a kind of a vision, because we are a cohesive whole, and you know, I'll stay and die a Mennonite. You know, sometimes you almost wish you could join People's Church, the mega-church here in town, where I don't know, 2,500 members, and you'd really go into business with them, you know. We can't do that.

Assuming that the confrontational model was descriptive of early

Anabaptist-Mennonite society, how can the contemporary situation be defined, and what are the prospects? Several propositions can be advanced.

1. The tendency is for Mennonite economic practice to move either in the direction of the community of goods model or toward the conventional model. The Hutterites are maintaining their traditional economic system in a general way, and the new communities are approaching the community of goods model from various directions, attempting to be relevant to the modern conditions while at the same time remaining biblical. One scholar considers these new communes to be a "reaction by Mennonites to . . . secularization, especially economic," and therefore as an attempt "to restore historic purity" (Chesebro 1982, 53ff.). The proliferation of modern Mennonite communal groups is truly phenomenal. An affiliation of communes has already developed; in addition, the Shalom Covenant of Communities in Elkhart, Indiana, publishes a journal entitled *Coming Together: A Journal about Christian Community*. Annual "Community of Communities" are planned, and a grand network of "communards" is developing.

2. The confrontational model approach is inherently unstable and is therefore prone to dissolve. The attempt to subordinate materialist values to religious communal values without the presence of the strong community boundaries and authoritarian strictures is largely futile. Relationships with nonbelievers and the consequent corruption of values through influences from the outside are almost impossible to control. The external pressures described above, such as urbanization, are introducing economic opportunities totally unlike those experienced in the rural context; there, the producing of good crops for sustenance and the buying of farms for the next generation comprised the limits of economic objectives and opportunities. And, of course, these activities and decisions were watched over closely by the community.

Short of absolute communism, a religious economic system which attempts to subordinate the economic impulses to religious constraints has never worked; furthermore, it could not work especially in a society as materialistic and individualistic as that in North America. An "economic man" theory does not need to be posited in order to predict the pressures of accommodation and assimilation. It is clear that the Mennonite institutional objectives present in either one of these areas are premised on the production of massive amounts of wealth to support them. Whether the capitalists supported institutions as a way of justifying their wealth, or whether the institutions caused the Mennonites to become capitalist so that their support for these institutions would be available, is almost a moot question. The fact is that they do complement each other (Smucker 1976).

3. The triumph of the conventional economics model in the Mennonite community is virtually assured. Today the bulk of Mennonites, in their economic lives, are almost completely integrated into the prevailing North American system. Typically each family has become an independent economic unit in which the father, and increasingly the mother, function as the source of economic participation and consumption, by means of the all-important job. Further, the entrance into economic activity is dependent, almost totally, on professional training through a professional or management training track; beyond such training, access to capital is often gained through family wealth or family connections. The borrowing of high-risk capital and the financing of ventures is the route through which many Mennonites enter the economic sphere and remain in it (C. Redekop 1988a).

But, of course, the transition is not complete. The whole field of Mennonite economics is still circumscribed by ethical concerns, which are still being promoted—congregationally, educationally, in the religious media, and in many homes. In addition, there are movements and associations that attempt to keep the ethical ideal operative in the bosom of the Mennonite enterprise. The credit union movement emerging in Mennonite communities is one example of this effort to maintain economic life in the brotherhood mold. There are also emerging associations of Christian Mennonite business people, such as Mennonite Economic Development Associates, that work hard to maintain an economic conscience and create significant challenges for those who wish to use their affluence in positive ways. But, in general, the forces of sociology and history are against these efforts.

The access to affluence has been too easy. The social and economic base for the confrontational economic model is no longer present. Short of having utopian communities, the contemporary economic system does not allow for a subsociety which subordinates the economic to an ideological system. At the same time, the very existence of massive efforts to retain some semblance of the early ideals does offer some hope—hope that possibly a quasi-confrontational model could appear again.

4. With the emergence of the present economic crisis, caused in part by the ecological limitations, there is a growing recovery of the understanding about the validity of cooperation and decentralization. It is possible that the move toward cooperation—covering the entire eco-

nomic gamut from production to consumption and including all of the requisitive services—will become the avenue for Mennonites to recover their confrontational economics to some degree. As the larger secular context forces people to cooperate in order to achieve the "good life," the same influence may yet turn history around for North American Mennonites.

Obviously, the Mennonite economic experience cannot be fully explained by any single-viewpoint economic sociology, such as the Weberian, Marxist, or even Niebuhrian framework. In some ways, each of these theories, as well as others, helps to explain the Mennonites. It is clear that the economic factor and even class factors have affected Mennonite economics and religious convictions; conversely, values and beliefs have been strongly present in the way Mennonites have done economics. The sectarian disinheritance has been fairly discernible as a factor in Mennonite religious life; but the Mennonites' economic life cannot be understood without reminding ourselves of the importance of their historical background. Their minority stance, their persecution, suffering, exile, settlement, and migration in search of peace and freedom have all contributed to forge a unique socioeconomic orientation.

It is thus most appropriate to suggest that the economic life of Mennonites is a "part-economics," to borrow a phrase from Robert Redfield (1956). Part societies, according to Redfield, are "parts of large societies" (34). In the economic realm at least, Mennonites represent "so incomplete a system that it cannot well be described as a social structure" (37), but on the other hand, the Mennonite system is not totally integrated into the larger economic system. It is simply not possible to generalize. Mennonites participate in the economic system at different levels and in varying degrees. In most cases, they are very obviously involved in it; at the same time, many of them manage to retain certain distinctives that set them apart.

In other words, today's North American Mennonites reflect a rather pervasive ambiguity. That may best be described, in conclusion, in the following manner: (1) economic practices are to some extent constrained and informed by the Anabaptist-Mennonite faith and teaching; (2) the values and practices of Western postindustrial economics are finding increasing acceptance among Mennonites; (3) Mennonites have not yet taken a conscious and concerted look at how economics and faith affect each other. This is a challenge that cannot wait very long.

Chapter Thirteen

Mennonites and the Political Process

No other social institution has figured more prominently in the life and thought of Mennonite society than what was called the "sword" in early Anabaptist thought, or the "state" in more recent times. With its institutions of government—including its demands and its expectations—the state has had a great significance in the subconscious life of the Mennonite movement, to say nothing whatsoever of overt encounters.

Of course, it is not correct to suggest that this is unique among Mennonites. In fact, from its very beginning, the Christian church has had to deal with the fact of the secular state and with the reality of government authority. In *The Early Church and the World* Cadoux states: "The highwater mark of Christian antipathy to the state was reached in the Apocalypse; and no subsequent author exhibits the same fierce and bitter antagonism as is expressed in that work" (1925, 247).

But the early church survived the oppression of Rome. Not only did it survive: it became the official religion under Constantine. But ironically, the church found itself in a new kind of struggle–that of spiritual leadership of the society. The ensuing history was one of a continued struggle with the state and its authority. The story of the emerging papacy provides some enlightenment as to how the Christian church dealt with the state. Hobhouse suggests that "the greatest struggles of the papacy were directed against the institution which stands out as both linked and contrasted with it in medieval thought, the Holy Roman Empire" (1910, 184). Quite obviously, what the church could not destroy, it incorporated: in wonderfully complex ways the Church of Rome and the Roman Empire became the Holy Roman Empire—a mixture of heavenly and temporal powers.

When the Reformation churches in their varied forms protested against the Roman Catholic Church, they were not only protesting its domination of religious and social life but also its alliance with secular power. The fundamental motivation of these reactions, in different settings and with somewhat divergent theological understandings, spawned a variety of additional groups. The attitudes of these groups toward the state ranged across a full spectrum from that of the Church of England, which realigned its relation with the state, to that of the sects, who rejected any sovereignty of the state in matters of faith and life.

So church and state was early and continues to be a broad and pervasive issue. Numerous ways of describing and analyzing the relationships have been proposed, including the most comprehensive, Ernst Troeltsch's justly famous church-sect typology. Other images and typologies that emerged include sacred and secular, church and world, Christ and culture, the City of God and the city of man, and spirit and institution; but all dealt with the question of heavenly and temporal power.

From a sociological perspective, the intention of these typologies is to understand the nature of religion and how it operates in human society. In other words, it asks the question, Is religion a phenomenon that deals only with subjective and transcendental states, or does it affect human and observable institutions as well? If religion does affect human institutions, then there is the implication that religion must become involved in regulating and promoting human relations and structures. As will be indicated below, the Mennonite commonwealths in Russia and Paraguay, to name only a few, illustrate this process of involvement. As I use the terms, *state* and *government* refer to operation of the political process—that is, to the self-regulation of human societies; it is to this that we turn now.

I began this chapter with a reference to the significance of the state in early Mennonite thought. In some sense that significance remains but with a somewhat different content and expression because of the history of change. In the course of their pilgrimage through the centuries, Mennonites have changed dramatically in their experience of, their involvement in, and their attitudes toward, political institutions. In this section I will focus on the dialectical process that has produced some of these noteworthy changes in the Mennonite view of politics.[1] A typology of relationships in historical perspective will be presented first to assist us in our analysis. This typology of political structures and relationships, even though brief and very general, will include both historical and geographical perspectives.

The Typology of Mennonite Political Relationships

The Two-Kingdom Position

The "two-kingdom" theology refers to a dualistic view of the relationship between the Christian and the non-Christian spheres. Juhnke notes: "At the heart of the Anabaptist view of the state as it grew out of the left-wing of the sixteenth century reformation was the doctrine of the two worlds" (1975, 10). Although ordained of God, the state was the secular institution responsible to contain the evil in the world. On the other hand, the "new community of regenerated believers was part of the kingdom of Christ" (ibid.). These two existed together, were interdependent in a sense, but were certainly never to be identical.[2]

Although they would not participate in the activities of the state, Anabaptists did not deny the state's legitimacy; rather, they submitted themselves to it in those spheres where it had legitimate existence. They recognized that the state was ordained of God for the restraint of the evildoer and the protection of the innocent. In this, the Anabaptists followed Pauline teaching closely (Rom. 13).

The earliest formulation on this question was the Schleitheim Confession, which has influenced Mennonites considerably since: "The sword is ordained of God outside the perfection of Christ. It punishes and puts to death the wicked, and guards and protects the good" (Wenger 1947, 210). Even though the state is off limits for Christians, it is nevertheless God's instrument for social order. The Dortrecht Confession of 1632 fully reflects this approach to the state: "God has instituted civil government, for the punishment of the wicked and protection of the pious: and also further, for the purpose of governing the world . . . and . . . to preserve its subjects in good order and under good conditions" (Hershberger 1958, 165).

Actual participation in state functions, however, has varied greatly;

in general, there has been a refusal to participate in the state in any form or setting where coercion or violence might be used. In more recent times and less clear-cut situations, such as state social welfare services, Mennonites have differed in their degree of participation. At the same time, most Mennonites have adhered to the fundamental principle that "laws are to be obeyed as long as they do not require a violation of the laws of God" (ibid., 166).

Thus, for many years and even centuries, most Mennonites have attempted to live under the protection of the political institutions and have benefitted from them, but have not directly acted in the political process; nor have they often supported it or attempted to influence it indirectly. All branches of Mennonites have illustrated variations of this position throughout most of their history. The Hutterites, Old Order Amish, Old Order Mennonites, Old Colony, and related groups still hold to the extreme separatist and dualist position. This view expressed itself in nonparticipation in voting, in the holding of any political office, in any informal support activities such as serving in political parties or speaking on behalf of government, or in activities such as marches, civil disobedience, and protests against governmental activities.

Other more mainline Mennonite groups have held the same theological position for many centuries as well, but gradually these rather absolute applications have been modified. In general, the Mennonites in Pennsylvania have not been actively involved in politics, although at times they have voted and occasionally even held office (Bender 1959a, 615). The Russian Mennonite migrants to Kansas and Nebraska were much quicker to become active in local, state and national politics. A noteworthy example in that setting is Cornelius Janzen of Beatrice, Nebraska, who was active in state and national offices (H. Bender 1959a, 616). This practice fits into the typology discussed next.

The two-kingdom position, as expressed by the more thoroughgoing Anabaptist-Mennonites, is probably illustrated best by the Old Order groups, who do pay taxes but refuse to allow their men to serve in the military and have normally refused to accept Social Security and medical benefits, or unemployment insurance. These groups also have strict regulations regarding the acceptance of certain benefits of technical progress. Furthermore, although they pay public school taxes, they conduct their own private schools. Nor will they serve in local county or village offices. Moving from the Old Orders toward the more liberal groups, there was and is a gradient of participation in local, regional, and national politics.[3]

Selective Cooperation with the State

From early times some Anabaptist-Mennonite groups have participated in varying degrees in certain political activities. For example, as early as 1570, the Dutch Mennonites became active in holding political offices, but they were careful not to hold offices whose duties conflicted with their convictions—such as city magistrate positions, since magistrates had to implement capital punishment (H. Bender 1959a, 611–18).

The development of "selective participation" usually allowed the holding of offices only in local political structures; however, on occasion, it included officeholding in regional and national political bodies. A good example of this modification is found in the central United States, where numerous Mennonites have served in state legislatures. In Canada also, provincial legislatures have had many Mennonite representatives. In recent years, this selective political participation has broadened, especially in the larger urban centers of Mennonite populations, such as Winnipeg, Manitoba; Vancouver, B.C.; and Kitchener, Ontario; as well as in the central United States, especially in Kansas. Particularly among the Russian Mennonites in Canada there has been increasing involvement (J. Redekop 1983). At present, in many Mennonite communities, limited political involvement has become practically taken for granted. A U.S.-Canadian survey of Mennonites carried out during the early 1970s suggested that 46 percent of them vote in most or all of the elections, with only 39 percent not voting in any political elections (Kauffman and Harder 1975, 161).

As a concept, however, "selective participation" is not easily defined; clearly, it means different things to different groups at different times. This fact is illustrated particularly well in a comparison of the phenomenon between the United States and Canada. In Canadian Mennonite settings, selective participation can include provincial and even federal officeholding. In the United States, selective participation implies greater reluctance to serve on the state or national level; it refers more to local and regional political activity as well as active participation in issue-oriented matters and problems (J. Redekop 1983).

But whether in the United States or Canada, it would seem that the selective-participation typology is a relevant and appropriate stance because very few Mennonites have participated at all levels of the political spectrum. Very few Mennonites have served as sheriffs, jailers, and/or police officers. Similarly, few have served as professional soldiers; generally, the majority of Mennonites have refused to serve in the military. Only 16 percent of a recent United States and Canada sample would accept military service if called (Kauffman and Harder 1975, 133), and 12 percent would even support withholding taxes that are earmarked for war purposes.

Selective participation is probably motivated basically by the increasing awareness of the ambiguity of the nature of the state and of the subtle ways in which all citizens, including Mennonites, find themselves involved, whether they want to be or not. As John Redekop states:

> True, the state continues to function outside of "the realm of God's perfection" (which, of course, hardly implies that the church is perfect!) but many of its more recent ventures bear a striking likeness to the humanitarian concerns that Jesus expressed and that have always characterized the true church. . . . Much of what governments now do closely resembles what socially aware Christians have always done, for the simple reason that governments have taken over many humanitarian projects first initiated by Christians. (1976, 188)

Selective participation, therefore, is a stance taken by the middle stream of Mennonites and has been the position for most Mennonites. However, this viewpoint remains a cause for continuing concern, for many radical members feel strongly that members of the Anabaptist-Mennonite tradition should not be supporting national ideologies, war preparations, and international isolationism in any measure whatsoever.

By definition, the selective participation model would exclude those Mennonites who are totally supportive of national and political aims. For all practical purposes, this type of Mennonite stands outside the pale of the general Mennonite congregational understanding of Mennonite faith and polity, and this type of person rarely remains in Mennonite society.

The Mennonite "Churchly State"

Mennonite society has also produced a most curious hybrid of church-state relationships—one which must be almost unique—that is, the creation of a state within a church, inherent in the theocracy and commonwealth society models described earlier. In these two models, Mennonites have rejected almost totally any participation in the political process of the whole society, and have achieved this goal through spatial, cultural, and ideological separation. But in a paradoxical fashion they have nevertheless found themselves harnessed with a comprehensive system of political institutions.

The "churchly state"—illustrated very well by the Mennonites of Paraguay—is a model of paradox. Even though these Mennonites have refused to serve in national political institutions, through voting and officeholding, they have become deeply involved in the political affairs and practices of their own churchly state. This sort of a society that has become a churchly state, represented so fully in the Paraguayan Chaco, was expressed also in other settings: by the Mennonites in Russia, Mexico, and Bolivia, and in a lesser form in Canada among the Russian Mennonites and the Hutterites (H. Bender 1959a; Kreider 1951; C. Redekop 1973; Rempel 1933).

In Paraguay, the religious bond still serves as a basis for a comprehensive and almost totally autonomous social system in which the society assumes responsibility for its own social control and institutional structures. Within their own enclave the Mennonites in the Chaco are responsible for their own educational system from grade one through graduate school. They have also structured their own system of government, thus regulating and controlling all political, economic, and business affairs, including a system of monetary exchange. There is an autonomous taxation system, a police force, a road maintenance organization, and an agricultural development and extension service (Fretz 1953; C. Redekop 1973, 1980).

Although there are some differences, a similar profile obtains for the Hutterites in North America, who have a theocratic type of community. Since the members of the colonies live in contiguous households and since the colonies are dispersed more widely, some general public services such as mail and electricity are accepted from the host society (J. A. Hostetler 1974, 296 and passim). In principle, this is true for every Mennonite churchly state: certain larger host society services are still used. Also, naturally, the requirements that residents pay necessary taxes and abide by regulations such as the vaccination of cattle are fully adhered to.

The Mennonite churchly state poses a fascinating dilemma for Mennonites. At issue: how is the "Kingdom of God" theology and belief system reconciled with the actual expression found in the churchly state model? Granted, no Mennonite colony has inducted members into its own armed forces in order to make war on a neighboring society; yet, there are many activities that do raise serious theoretical, theological, and practical concerns. One of the most pressing problems is the control and punishment of deviants. On occasion, physical violence has been used to constrain colony miscreants in most Mennonite commonwealths (Rempel 1933). Incarceration has also been found to be necessary at times. Possibly the most ambiguous and implicating is the situation in the Paraguayan Chaco, where Mennonite "Ordungsmänner" are literally called upon to perform the functions of police and militia within the Mennonite colonies by the Paraguan government, especially when a fleeing Paraguayan is being pursued for criminal acts (C. Redekop 1980).

What has been most ironic is that the religious authority—that is, the church as embodied in and expressed through the officially elected leadership—is often called upon to provide ultimate sanctions for the decisions of the secular officials, including the enforcement of punitive actions judged to be appropriate. On the other hand, in the midst of the bitter feuds during the schism of the Mennonite Brethren from the Kirchliche in Russia in the 1850s, the religious officials often found themselves calling upon the secular authorities—that is, the colony *Schulzen*—to carry out the "cease and desist orders of religious recalcitrancy" (P. Friesen 1978).

Nevertheless, there is little evidence in the Mennonite commonwealths of any serious concern about reconciling the very obvious paradoxes in the churchly state model for its own members. An excruciatingly poignant example of this dilemma, at least for me, was the annual meeting of the Fernheim Colony in February of 1983. As is the custom, a colony minister conducted a religious exercise to open the secular business of the reports of the last year's social, educational, economic, and governmental activities, of presenting the plans for the coming year, and of the election of the colony officials. The minister used as his text and exhortation the classical Scripture uttered by the apostle Paul: "Let every person be subject to the governing authorities. For there is no authority except from God, and those that exist have been instituted by God" (Rom. 13:1). In subsequent casual conversation, no persons seemed to sense the astounding irony of the moment.

Typically, the commonwealth and theocratic model societies have not been involved in much higher education, so that the level of political dialogue is not very high. Further, as would be expected, Mennonites have stressed ethics above theology; thus, as long as the society is able to be free of outside intellectual challenges, it will continue as though there is no contradiction present.

However, the most complicating factor which perpetuates the commitment to these seemingly paradoxical systems is the conviction that the end justifies the means. That is, if separation from the world is the goal for Christian disciples, then that must be achieved even if it means becoming involved in things which would seem to be as secular as the society outside, namely, operating a state apparatus (H. Bender 1959b; Juhnke 1975; Kreider 1951; C. Redekop, 1973).

There have, however, been some attempts at opening up the subject, particularly through the literary efforts of Mennonite members in poetry and fiction. Recent examples are Ingrid Rimland's *The Wanderers* and Rudy Wiebe's *Peace Shall Destroy Many*. But there is a price to be paid by such keen observers of Mennonite society. Hypocrisy and moral decay are often so painfully portrayed that the author of this kind of critique normally is ostracized from the community. Whether or not such forthright prophetic utterances will lead to lasting changes in these communities remains to be seen.

Mennonites in the Political Arena

Having looked at the three types of positions Mennonites have taken and are taking with reference to political activities in general, we shall now focus on the contemporary situation among the "selective participation" group, which is the most dominant and is undergoing the most rapid changes in North America.

Officeholding

An overall picture of officeholding or voting behavior among Mennonites does not yet exist (J. Redekop 1983). Therefore, local or regional studies have to be resorted to for the documentation of this topic. A study of the Kansas Mennonites from 1870 to 1940 by James Juhnke indicates that there was relatively early a sprinkling of officeholding at the county level, such as county commissioner (Juhnke 1975, 80). The first Mennonite to become a state legislator in Kansas was H. P. Krehbiel; he was elected to that office in 1908 (ibid.). Other Mennonites have been elected to state office in Nebraska and Minnesota. Two Mennonites have served in the United States House of Representatives from Iowa—E. W. Ramseyer, from 1915 to 1933, and E. C. Eicher, from 1933 to 1939 (H. Bender 1959b, 616)—as well as one from Ohio, B. F. Welty, from 1917 to 1921 (J. Redekop 1983).

The picture is different in Canada, however. In the Canadian provinces, more Mennonites have been elected to provincial parliaments; as John Redekop notes in regard to political involvement in the state, "This activity seems to be considerably more pronounced in Canada than in the United States" (1983, 84). Redekop includes a roster of political officeholding among Mennonites in Canada and the

United States. The Canadian roster is extensive, and includes all levels of provincial and national positions (96–99). A comparison of Canadian and U.S. officeholding derived from Redekop's list of officeholders is shown in Table 13.1. The much higher percentage of elected Mennonites in Canada is doubly significant when compared to the percentages of Canadian and U.S. Mennonites in the general population. A basic reason must be the lower salience of the separation of church and state in Canada and the more urbane character of the recent Mennonite immigrants from Russia.

The Mennonite *attitudes* regarding political officeholding are fairly clear from the Kauffman-Harder international study. In response to the statement "Members of our denomination should not hold any local, state, provincial, or national government offices," only 13 percent agreed, while 64 percent disagreed, and 22 percent were uncertain. The percentage rejecting federal officeholding could have been higher if all levels of officeholding had not been included in the one question, while the percentage supporting local participation would probably have been higher as well.

It is probably safe to say that the greatest participation in political office by Mennonites is at the local village and county levels. Many Mennonites have served with distinction—and for long terms—as village and town mayors, or as reeves, county commissioners, and members of school boards and related institutions. Many Mennonites also have held appointed offices in local advisory committees and departments. Draft boards would be an exception; there, very few Mennonites have served (Juhnke 1975; J. Redekop 1983).

Service in the Military

There is more evidence regarding attitudes and activity in this area, since it has always been a concern of great importance for Mennonites. In World War I, in Canada and the United States, almost all Mennonite men who were drafted refused induction and served in alternative service camps. In World War II, the situation had changed considerably, indicating a shift in thinking. Of a total of 9,809 Mennonites of draft age, 4,536, or 46.2 percent, took the conscientious objector position, while 5,273, or 53.8 percent, joined the armed forces (Hershberger 1951, 39). The situation has changed again in more recent times; by the end of the Vietnam War, only 5 percent in the Kauffman-Harder sample said they would choose military service if faced with the military draft (Kauffman and Harder 1975, 133). Other statistics indicate that

TABLE 13.1 Mennonites Serving in Political Office in Canada and the United States, 1905 to Present

	Held federal office	Failed to win	Held provincial or state office	Failed to win
Canada	7	13	21	na
United States	3	2	8	6

Source: J. Redekop 1983, 96–99.
Note: The data are approximate, since some persons elected were no longer Mennonites when they took office, and some cases were not reported, even though persons are known to have held office.

certainly a strong two-thirds of the Mennonites would take a conscientious objector's position in a new draft. Military service has had high salience and symbolic importance in American Mennonitism. Among many congregations and conferences, serving in the military has resulted in excommunication. Many congregations have had serious divisions over this issue, and it probably has contributed to the breakdown of the practice of excommunication and the ban. A novel portraying those tensions, based upon real persons, is Solomon Stucky's *For Conscience' Sake*.

A scholarly analysis of the effect of deviance from the nonresistant position in the life of Mennonite society has not thus far emerged. Juhnke's analysis of conscription among Kansas Mennonites does not discuss congregational tensions resulting from young men entering military service (Juhnke 1975). A major research work of the early fifties discussed the "intensification" of the nonresistant ethic among Mennonites but did not refer to the struggles it created in the local setting. The only reference in this work to the subject was an inquiry by a mother to the editor of a church periodical as to "why a brother who joins the army is set back from communion, while another who has received a draft deferment because he is engaged in the manufacture of guns . . . has nothing said to him about his inconsistency. The editor's comment was, 'The mother may well be puzzled.' Sometime earlier an article by a concerned layman had appeared in the same periodical warning the brotherhood against 'a looseness in the discipline of members who are violating the Word of God and ignoring the position of the Mennonite church in such things' " (Hershberger 1951, 127–28). It is highly probable that the great ideological significance of the refusal to serve in military institutions has caused strong proponents of the peace witness to avoid the great divisiveness of the tenet; further, the Mennonite aversion to overly and publicly discussing conflict and expressing dissension has caused Mennonites to downplay the subtle but serious fragmentation of congregational unity brought about by deviance from nonresistance.

Voting

Although Mennonites have argued that voting and officeholding are equally problematical in terms of relation to the state, their behavior does not bear this out. Almost without exception, a greater proportion of Mennonites have voted in all levels of the electoral process than have participated in government activities. Thus, in the conservative eastern regions of Pennsylvania, Mennonites voted for many years but did not run for office (H. Bender 1959a).

Mennonites in the United States and Canada have generally been very active in local elections (Juhnke 1975, 116–25). In state and national elections—depending upon the group of Mennonites in question—numerous Mennonites have voted. Even the conservative Old Order Amish have voted on occasion. "It is claimed that the Mennonites in colonial Pennsylvania [still relatively conservative] along with other non-resistant German groups helped to keep the Quaker assembly in power years after it would have otherwise lost at the polls" (ibid.). In fact, on numerous occasions when their interests were seemingly at stake, Mennonites have played a significant role in elections. Over three-fourths of the sample in the Kauffman-Harder study felt that "members of our denomination should vote in public elections for state and national offices" (Kauffman and Harder 1975, 161). In numerous local option elections, such as referenda on liquor sales, Mennonites have "packed the polling booth" (H. Bender 1959a, 860).

One of the better researched areas in Mennonites and politics concerns the ideological leanings of the Mennonite voter. U. S. Mennonites have tended to vote conservative in most elections, thus indicating their economic and political loyalties. In the United States, 74 percent chose the Republican party, while only 14 percent chose the Democratic party in the Kauffman-Harder survey (165). In Canada, 58 percent checked the liberal parties—that is, the Liberal, Social Credit, or NDP (ibid.). Especially in the United States, there are indications that Mennonites have identified with the politics of the far right. Thus, for example, in Kansas between 1928 and the later 1940s, during the heyday of Gerald B. Winrod, Mennonites supported his anti-Communist, antiliberal campaigns (Juhnke 1975, 137ff.). But in general, Mennonites did not become heavily involved in the religious far right.

Informal Political Influence

Even though Mennonites have not been aggressively involved in the standard political processes, one should not assume that they have not attempted to influence political institutions, or that they have not been "used" by political leaders. Dating approximately from the time the Mennonites began to migrate to North America (1683) there has been an obvious and increasing interdependence. John Redekop states, "Attempting to influence government decisions very quickly became standard Mennonite political practice" (1983, 83). Beginning with the settlement of Mennonites in the Ukraine in the 1780s, Mennonites have negotiated with governmental offices and officials extensively. The negotiation for land purchases in Canada, United States, Mexico, and Paraguay—to list only a few examples—entailed literally hundreds of letters, trips of delegations to government offices, and visits by officials to Mennonite communities. The story of the negotiations Sommerfelder Mennonites carried out with the Paraguayan government in the 1920s has just recently been published; these transactions involved intense closed-door sessions as well as open parliamentary debates (M. Friesen 1987).

But land was only one of Mennonites' concerns. The issues of exemption from military service and freedom to conduct their own schools, along with a number of other issues, have involved Mennonites in a vast array of petitions, requests, and visits to governmental institutions. By the 1960s, the tradition had become so widespread that both the Canadian and U.S. branches of the Mennonite Central Committee had established permanent offices in Ottawa and Washington, D.C., in order to maintain close contact with their governments and legislative bodies. Although these offices maintain a strong presence, a continuing debate persists among Mennonites about such formal lobbying efforts. The questioners are asking whether such efforts are really consistent with the "two-kingdom" idea which is central to Mennonite theology. Proponents counter that the question of formal lobbying is really moot, since Mennonites have for centuries influenced and "lobbied" governments in many other ways. Even though Mennonites tend to evade the fact that they are involved deeply in the political process, they are often secretly proud that they are a force to be reckoned with. As John Redekop notes, "The inherent contradiction between these two stances"—that of maintaining a "two-kingdom theology" and thereby considering the state imperfect, versus that of supporting it—"seems to have been recognized or ignored" (J. Redekop 1983, 83).

In one of the few empirical studies of Mennonite political attitudes and behavior, Driedger and Zehr conclude:

> We suggested that items related to peace would be supported most strongly by Mennonite leaders. Leaders seemed to perceive the peace issue largely in historical, theological terms relating to the church, and to support action issues related to the State less strongly. Youth seemed more willing to add an element of outreach (to get involved in witness to, and participation in, the State) to the peace position, which the leaders seemed more reluctant to do possibly because of their negative attitude toward the State. . . . Mennonite university students were more willing to participate in issues related to government and the State. (1974, 524–25)

As we have noted, Mennonites in the "selective participation" sector of the spectrum have become more involved in the political process of the host society, but the degree of involvement has not increased dramatically during recent times. Especially after World War II and Vietnam, countervailing forces of theological education and renewal have contributed to a chastened view of the ineffectiveness of the political arm in achieving the stated objectives of the kingdom of God. Hence, it is possible to say that Mennonite political participation is more sophisticated than it was earlier.

A Sociological Interpretation of Mennonite Political Activity

From an overall perspective, Mennonite participation in the political process has been, and is, minimal and very cautious. If the churchly state typology is excluded, Mennonites have considered aggressive political activity in the state to be in conflict with their goals as members of the kingdom of God. Serving the goals of the kingdom of God seemed to preclude using the political process as a means of achieving it. Thus, Mennonites have diametrically opposed the Reformed and Lutheran position, which assumes that the political process is a means to help achieve the goals of the Christian life.

Mennonite theology and practice have consistently and strongly advised against becoming involved in and being supportive of the political institutions. Guy F. Hershberger, one of the leading proponents among Mennonites of the "colony of heaven" approach, has written extensively on the futility of attempting to build the kingdom of heaven through political means. He argues that "the Anabaptists were not political non-participants because they were social outcasts. They were social outcasts because the way of the Cross, which they espoused, did not permit them to participate in the violent methods of the state. The Anabaptists produced their fruits by challenging the social order, not by accepting its way" (Hershberger 1958, 183).

Mennonite teaching regarding political participation continues to take the position that the Mennonite community is to criticize, and witness to, the secular order and to model the "new kingdom" in its socioeconomic life in Christian communities. In spite of this position, however, as has been seen above, Mennonites do take part in political life, at least to some degree; it appears as if the incidence of such involvement is increasing. To what can this be attributed? A number of social forces can be cited, although little empirical data is available to support these conclusions:

1. The evolution of the military state into a welfare state. Whereas the state in earlier centuries was largely a legal-political-military type of institution—presumably necessary for the evolution of stable govern-ment—the state of today has expanded its functions to include pro-grams that affect almost every facet of private and public life: social welfare, health care, mental health care, education, employment, retire-ment, regulations of marriage and family, regulations of support, of economics and the economic order, and many more (J. Redekop 1976; J. Yoder 1972).

Since many Mennonites are becoming increasingly integrated into society, they are finding it increasingly difficult to retain their tradi-tional theory regarding the state and to carry it out in their daily lives. The more conservative groups, such as the Old Order Amish, are still making valiant attempts to remain aloof, as is evidenced by their refusal to accept social security and health benefits, even though they pay the taxes that support the programs. But even they recognize that the state is now providing more services and also exacting more cooperation than was the case in earlier times.

So, as the movement of history has inexorably increased the integra-tion of Mennonites into their host societies, Anabaptist-Mennonites are finding that their political involvements are also increasing, by degrees. In some sense, this constitutes a major retreat. However, the retreat is being made along the lines which seem least threatening to the faith, while the significant issues, such as refusal to serve in the military, are still being staunchly upheld.

2. The economic linkages to the state. The modern state and the political process increasingly concern themselves with the regulation and promotion of economic matters. Indeed, sometimes politics is spoken of as being basically concerned with the regulation of business and economics. "The role of government [in business] has expanded enormously in response to new expectations and new attitudes in our society" (Banner 1979, 194). Mennonites, along with the rest of the citizens of North America, are increasingly and deeply involved in many business and government interdependencies, including subsidies, production incentives, rebates, and tax breaks, to name only a few. Most Mennonites participate fully in governmental health, welfare, and retirement programs. These realities create an awkward context from which to reject the state and its political processes. Few fail to see either the irony or the possible contradictions inherent in the Anabaptist-Mennonite separation theology and its actual implementation in a time when the interfacings between a religious viewpoint and a host society are so extensive.

3. The economic exchange syndrome. Since the first migrations to and settlements in America, Mennonites have benefitted greatly from North American economic opportunities. For example, refugees from Russian Communism have come to the United States and Canada and have become millionaires within a few decades. In general, Mennonites have improved their lot tremendously. As they have become wealthy, they have also become conservative politically; they have thus also become more prone to support government and political activities. This is especially true in the economic sector, which champions private property, private enterprise, and freedom from governmental interference.

To put it bluntly, Mennonites have become quietly patriotic and nationalistic as they have benefitted from the opportunities to "make it." This stance can be inferred from the following statistic noted in the Kauffman-Harder study. About 49 percent of Mennonites agreed with the statement that "it is not the business of the church to try to influence the actions of the government in regard to such issues as war and peace, race relations, and poverty, etc." (Kauffman and Harder 1975, 159). This observation concurs with Reitz's conclusions: "The index of political participation is negatively related both to in-group interaction and to ethnic identification. Those who retain strong ties to an ethnic group are less likely to participate in Canadian politics than those who have abandoned such ties" (1980, 227).

4. *The desire to maintain and protect their own beliefs and practices.* In Russia, in the 1870s, when the Russification policy was promoted, Mennonites very quickly became active in making representations to the czarist regime. In early Pennsylvania, Mennonites went to the polls to keep the Quakers in office. During World Wars I and II Mennonite delegations went to Ottawa and Washington to lobby for favorable legislation for conscientious objectors and alternative service opportunities (Keeney 1965; MacMaster 1985).

One of the most controversial and at the same time most creative activities of contemporary Mennonites, already alluded to, has been the officially sponsored and supported federal offices at Ottawa and Washington. The Mennonites, through the Mennonite Central Committee, have maintained, for example, in Washington a Peace Section office, which "informs and expresses Mennonite concerns on national legislation and policy related to peace and justice concerns," according to the *Washington Memo,* published by the Peace Section, Mennonite Central Committee. This bureau has developed an extensive program of education and lobbying of U.S. congressmen on issues related to peace and justice, especially as they pertain to Mennonite concerns. The same type of office exists in Ottawa (C. Dyck 1980b, 52ff.).

Many other such organizations and activities are operative and serve subtly to bring the Mennonites more deeply into the political stream. It is the motivation to permeate the body politic with the Mennonite peace and justice concerns which is the explanation some contemporary Mennonite aspirants to political office give for political activity. But according to other, more moderate Mennonites, this is the ultimate subtle seduction in a capitulation of the Anabaptist-Mennonite commitments to the kingdom of God to secular goals. In a paraphrase of E. K. Francis, Guy Hershberger writes, "Instead of the church-centered community maintaining a sense of mission challenging the world in which it lived, it was transformed into a secular world of its own, of which the church was only one of its institutions" (1958, 201).

IT IS PROBABLE that the Mennonites in North America today are more selectively involved in political activities than are most other religious groups. This peculiar profile is clearly the result of their attempt to keep their dualistic belief system intact in the process of adapting to the various environments in which they have lived. The great variety of participation in the political process—ranging across the spectrum from almost total withdrawal to full participation in the churchly state model—is to a large degree the consequence of the dialogical relationship of the various Mennonite groups in their various settings. For many obvious reasons, it is clear that the political participation of Mennonites in Nebraska or Manitoba is different from the Mennonite political stance in the Chaco in Paraguay. Although members living in both contexts would identify themselves as brothers in the faith, their underlying presuppositions are extremely varied and disparate.

But the pull of nationalism is still present. In 1975 James Juhnke wrote: "The tragedy of the Mennonites was not that they became American so slowly, but rather that they so desperately wanted to be good American citizens and could not fulfill the requirements without violating their consciences or abandoning the traditions of their forebears" (156). This conclusion may come close to being a value judgment, but it does explicate the conflict between a religious impulse and its political expression. The voices calling for national involvement are episodical and usually express the burden of personal agendas. But the mood is getting stronger. One such voice is Frank Epp's: "Organizations . . . like the Mennonite Central Committee and the General Conference Mennonite Church might long ago have been adjusted structurally to allow for vigorous pursuit of the national mission. As things stand, they try to serve national, continental, and international interests, but they are not properly structured for any of these. . . . What is needed now are not new patches on an old garment but a more deliberate restructuring for national mission" (1977, 58).

There is a subterranean but powerful ambivalence and ambiguity regarding the Mennonite attitude toward, and participation in, the affairs of the state. The close interdependence between economic well-being and political responses is well known. The great material largesse that has fallen to Mennonites is bound to effect some expression of gratitude and reciprocal support. In the context of these multifarious pulls toward assimilation into the predominant society and culture, the contemplation of more political participation strikes fear in the hearts and minds of reflective Mennonites.

Chapter Fourteen

Mennonites in
Missions and Service

"Early Anabaptist missions (1525–
1600) though conducted against opposition of both Protestant and Catholic authorities and eventually suppressed, represent an attempt to introduce an apostolic sense of mission 200 years before the Protestant
church as a whole was ready. . . . In them was developed to a higher
degree the logical reformation emphasis on individual conversion, apostolic call to witness, and voluntary church fellowship. Early Anabaptist
missions, thus, were a pre-cursor of the modern missionary movement"
(Pannabecker 1957, 712). These words, spoken by one of the veteran
missionaries and later historians of missions among Mennonites, S. F.
Pannabecker, express what has generally been assumed to be the
unique missionary thrust of the early Anabaptists.

The Mennonite expression of missions, of propagating the Gospel,
thus has been an inherent aspect of its ethos, as was noted in Chapter 2.
This same orientation is taken toward service, which has expressed
itself more as mutual assistance to its own members. The historical and
theological aspects of missions and service cannot be treated here, but
there is an institutional dimension which requires specific treatment and
is treated here in depth.[1]

Missions

The Missionary Dynamic

The extent of Mennonite missionary work was described in Chapter 2. One of the major reasons for the impressive mission has been the lay nature of missionary work, as Schäufele noted: "The missionary activity of the ordinary members of the Anabaptist brotherhood was an important factor in the spread of the movement. . . . Anabaptism would not have been able to spread so rapidly and to take such firm roots if the missionary activity of the leaders had not been vigorously supported by the missionary activity of the ordinary members" (1962, 99). This lay emphasis derives directly, of course, from Mennonites' basic understanding of the nature of the church and membership in it, alluded to above by Pannabecker.

Lay support was based directly on the missionary commission, which was incumbent on all, as contrasted with baptism and administering the Lord's Supper, which could be done only by the ordained brethren. The missionary mandate, implicit in numerous protocols of trials and disputations, is illustrated by the testimony of one Anabaptist: "Another rebaptised person, of the Markgrafschaft Ansbach-Bayreuth, reports in a trial record that 'he had been commanded to speak the gospel to others.' The members were commonly challenged by their spiritual leaders 'to confess the Lord,' and 'to be stewards' of the truth that had been committed to them" (Schäufele 1962, 101).

The natural channels of missionary work among the early Anabaptists consisted mainly of (1) family members, both intimate and more remote, (2) neighbors and other acquaintances, and (3) occupational connections. Schäufele (103) believes that these channels provided most of the early converts. Another channel was women's missionary work, which Schäufele believes was substantial. He maintains that "the woman in Anabaptism emerges a fully emancipated person in religious matters and as the independent bearer of Christian convictions" (108). That women thus served as a significant element in the missionary outreach hence becomes an interesting but not fully researchable proposition.

As non-Mennonite observers have often stated, the Anabaptist-Mennonites were some of the staunchest missionaries in the Christian church (Bainton 1957; Littell 1947; Schäufele 1962). The spread of the Anabaptists across Europe was considered almost a miracle. Bainton states, "The documentation now in progress of publication reveals an amazing dissemination and indicates a real possibility that Anabaptism, if unimpeded by the sword of the magistrate, might have become the prevailing form of church in Germany" (1957, 321). Fundamentally, the rapid acceptance was due to the view that the Christian Gospel calls for a voluntary acceptance of Christ's forgiveness for all mankind and the belief that Christendom was in great need of restitution.

Of course, this seminal missionary thrust was soon suppressed and then terminated by the secular and religious authorities. Wilbert Shenk, long active in missionary promotion among Mennonites, states: "Wherever the Anabaptists went throughout Europe, they were opposed and persecuted. Under unrelenting pressure the Anabaptist movement was transformed into a search for domestic tranquility where adherents might live quietly without compromising their consciences. For the next 250 years mission lay dormant among Mennonites and Brethren descendents of the Anabaptists" (1978, 20). The resulting quietism from toleration, so earnestly sought, prevailed until the 1850s, when— almost simultaneously in Europe, Russia, and North America—an awakening took place that produced numerous mission activities and organizations (Shenk 1984, 162ff.).

The earliest organized mission activity emerged in Holland when the Dutch Mennonites allied with the English Baptist Mission Society in 1834. By 1851, the Dutch Mennonites had established their own missionary organization, which began sending missionaries to Java (Kaufman 1931, 49). In 1858, discussions about missions began in America, and in 1866 the General Conference Mennonites created a mission board, which had as its object the raising of funds to send workers into the field. Actual work began among the Arapahos in Oklahoma in 1880 (Barrett 1983; Schlabach 1980).

From these rather recent beginnings, the missionary impulse slowly spread to other Mennonite groups. Today, almost all groups of Mennonites sponsor missionary activities; exceptions are the Hutterites, Old Order Amish, Old Order Mennonites, Old Colony, Sommerfelder, and a few small, conservative splinter groups (see Table 14.1). The largest conference, the Old Mennonite Church, at present has a mission organization whose 1987 budget was just over $5 million. In 1987, its staff consisted of 450 workers serving in fifty-seven countries; staff included 81 office staff located at Elkhart, Indiana, and Harrisonburg, Virginia; 131 workers overseas; and over 290 volunteers (*Mennonite Yearbook*, 1987; see Table 14.2). The other Mennonite conferences are engaged in commensurate types of activities.

The mission organization in Mennonite society is a fascinating, if complex structure. It is a part of the official church program in each congregation and has had much less struggle to gain acceptance than the

TABLE 14.1 Development of Mennonite and Brethren in Christ Missions

Year begun	Country	Sponsoring group
1851	Java	Dutch
1871	Sumatra	Dutch
1890	Hyderabad, India	Russian MB
1898	S. Rhodesia	BIC
	Turkey	MBC
1899	India, M.P.	MBM
	India, A.P.	MB (American)
1900	India, M.P.	GC
1901	China	KMB (later with EMB, MB, MCA as China Mennonite Mission Society)
	Shantung	
1904	India, Bihar	BIC
1905	Nigeria	MBC
1906	Zambia	BIC
1908	India, W. Bengal	MBC
1909	China, Hopeh	GC
1911	China, Fukien	MB
	Zaire	CIM/AIMM
1912	Zaire	MB
1917	Argentina	MBM
1921	Inner Mongolia	KMB
1932	Paraguay	LI
		(MB Board 1946)

Year begun	Country	Sponsoring group
1953	Cuba	BIC
	Austria	MB
	Germany	MB
	Japan	BIC
	France	MBM
	Israel	MBM/EMBMC
1954	Somalia	EMBMC
	France	EMBMC
	Cuba	FMC
	Taiwan	GC
	Mexico	EMC/C
	Brazil/South	MBM
	Uruguay	MBM
1955	Jamaica	VMBMC
	Brazil	MCA
	Brazil/North	MBM
1956	Uruguay	GC
	Ghana	MBM
1957	Algeria	MBM
	Germany	EMBMC
	Vietnam	EMBMC
	Luxembourg	EMBMC
1958	Mexico	FMC
	Panama	MB
1959	Paraguay	EMC/C

Year	Country	Agency
1933	Mexico	CGCM
1934	Tanzania	EMBMC
1935	Paraguay	MB
1940	India, Bihar	MBM
1943	Argentina, Chaco	MBM
1945	Colombia	MB
	Colombia	GC
	Dominican Rep.	MCA
	Ecuador	MCA
	Sierra Leone	MCA
	Puerto Rico	MBM
1946	Dominican Rep.	EMC
1947	China	MBM
1948	Ethiopia	EMBMC
1949	Irian Java	Dutch
	Italy	VMBMC/MBM
	Jamaica	MCA
	Japan	MBM
1950	Chad	French
	Japan	MB
	Mexico	GC
	Belgium	MBM
	Germany	CMBMC
	Honduras	EMBMC
1951	Japan	GCM
1952	Haiti	MCA
	Alaska	MBM
	England	MBM
1960	Nigeria	MBM
	Mexico	PCMMB
	Belize	EMBMC
1962	Costa Rica	CMBMC
1963	Nigeria	CGCM
1964	Kenya	EMBMC
1965	Nicaragua	BIC
	Hong Kong	EMBMC
1966	Nicaragua	EMC/C
	Haiti	CGCM
1968	Nicaragua	CMBMC
	Guatemala	EMBMC
1969	Guiana	VMBMC
1971	Bolivia	Arg/MBM
	Trinidad-Tobago	VMBMC
	Philippines	EMBMC
1974	Bangladesh	MB
	Philippines	CGCM
1975	Indonesia	MB
	Upper Volta	CGCM
	Germany	EMC/C
1976	Indonesia-Borneo	PIPKA/EMBMC
		MCC
1951	Spain	MB
	Spain	MBM/Belgian Mission
1952	Dominican Rep.	CGCM
	Guatemala	CGCM

Source: P. Kraybill 1978, 29–30.

Note: This list includes only those new missions begun with a view toward developing an organized church. Service projects or instances where personnel have been seconded to another agency were not included.

(continued)

TABLE 14.1 (*continued*)

Key to Abbreviations:

Arg	Argentina Mennonite Church	GC	General Conference Mennonite Foreign Mission Board/Commission on Overseas Missions
BIC	Brethren in Christ Board of Missions		
CIM/AIMM	Congo Inland Mission/Africa Inter-Mennonite Mission	KMB	Krimmer Mennonite Brethren
		LI	Licht den Indianern
CGCM	Church of God in Christ, Mennonite	MB	Mennonite Brethren Board of Missions/Services
CMBMC	Conservative Mennonite Board of Missions and Charities	MBC	Mennonite Brethren in Christ
Dutch	Dutch Mennonite Mission Association	MCA	Missionary Church Association/Missionary Church
EMBMC	Eastern Mennonite Board of Missions and Charities	MBM	Mennonite Board of Missions
EMC	Evangelical Mennonite Church Commission on Mission	MCC	Mennonite Central Committee
		PCMMB	Pacific Coast Mennonite Mission Board
EMC/C	Evangelical Mennonite Conference of Canada Board of Missions	PIPKA	Indonesian Evangelization Committee
FMC	Franconia Mennonite Conference Mission Commission	VMBMC	Virginia Mennonite Board of Missions and Charities
French	French Mennonite Missions Committee		

educational institutions. There is a sense in which the reasons for this acceptance should be obvious: (1) Given the biblical mandate to "go ye into all the world to preach the gospel," faithfulness demanded missionary activity. (2) With the Anabaptist-Mennonite heritage rooted in missionary activity, reaching out would simply be renewing the traditional heritage. (3) The missionary awakening which was taking place in the larger Christian society influenced Mennonites as well "to get on board."

But apparently, these elements represent only part of the picture, for substantial segments of the Mennonite church have not launched a missionary effort. What would explain the difference? A very creative and plausible explanation has been offered by E. G. Kaufman, one-time president of Bethel College, who suggested that Mennonites, having undergone intense persecution and repression, developed a serious antagonism against the world and entrenched themselves as a "sect" of a very isolationist and separatist nature. As the persecution waned and the sect received acceptance and recognition, the general hostility and consequent separation broke down. Yet coupled with this development was the tendency of Mennonites "to resent the inference of inferiority. . . . Nothing is harder on a sect as a sect than toleration by the world mingled with pity" (Kaufman 1931, 46).

Kaufman suggests that as the tension weakens between a sect and the larger world, the sect becomes increasingly interested in mission work because (a) economic and social conditions make missions possible, (b) the environment encourages interpenetration, and (c) the original mission drive is able to reassert itself. One could add to his list that (d) the missionary effort can also be interpreted as an expression of superiority and taking the offensive—that is, as an inversion of the inferiority complex which had earlier caused a retreat from mission. This last factor is undoubtedly operative in many of the more conservative Mennonite groups, which have been moving into missionary activity on a scale quite out of proportion to their numbers.

The missionary outreach of Mennonites expressed a major conflict within the Mennonite family on a theological and philosophical level. The conflict exists between the polar extremes of those who believe that the essence of Anabaptism and Christianity is outreach and those who maintain that Anabaptism is a "hard road" and for the few, echoing Jesus' statements about the narrow road. Hence, those who believe that the Mennonites are too self-contained, ethnic, or concerned about social forms stress the missionary and evangelical thrust. This group includes many Mennonite Brethren, the Evangelical Mennonite Brethren, the

TABLE 14.2 Mennonite Outreach Overseas, 1986

	Workers	1986 investment
AFRICA	97	$845,043
Algeria	1	7,200
Benin	2	18,782
Egypt	—	6,000
Ethiopia[a]	9	107,419
Ghana	1	51,983
Ivory Coast	4	83,408
Kenya	26	107,022
Mozambique[a]	2	1,071
Niger[a]	2	—
Somalia	15	159,073
Swaziland[a]	2	33,238
Tanzania	31	269,847
Zaire	2	9,000
ASIA	55	$884,432
Afghanistan	—	16,830
China	4	36,284
Hong Kong	5[a]	45,682
India	4	191,983
Indonesia	4	100,219
	—	2,971[b]
	—	5,717
Israel	8	99,346
	—	33,349[a]
Japan	14	226,954
Muslim ministries[b]	2	4,389
Nepal	11	106,753

	Workers	1986 investment
Jamaica	—	22,000[c]
	—	5,462
Mexico	3[d]	76,000
	2[e]	18,695
Nicaragua	2[b]	26,792
Puerto Rico	—	45,671
Trinidad	2[c]	37,000
EUROPE	43	$852,901
Belgium	6	79,814
Eastern Europe	—	3,861
England	7	110,173
France	4	42,389
Germany	4[a]	56,578
	2[b]	22,371
	3[a]	55,065
Ireland	5	42,458
Italy	6[c]	10,000
Luxembourg	—	80,000
Portugal	—	16,266
Spain	4	490
Sweden	2	40,655
USSR	—	—
	—	22,771
SOUTH AMERICA	60	$665,299
Argentina	8	127,951
Bolivia	8	76,733

Location	Workers	Contributions
Philippines[a]	2	13,955
Yemen	1	—
AUSTRALIA	—	322
CENTRAL AMERICA	61	$870,420
Belize[a]	10	121,799
Caribbean[a]	2	1,409
Costa Rica[b]	2	47,455
Dominican Republic[a]	2	74,017
El Salvador[a]	—	5,867
Guatemala	15	174,199
Haiti	2[c]	10,000
Honduras[a]	6[a]	64,200
	15	178,864
Brazil	9	116,160
Chile	4	74,631
Equador	9[b]	65,611
Peru	2[a]	—
	2	—
	—	11,536[a]
Surinam	2	—
Uruguay	6	98,818
Venezuela	4	56,859
Paraguay	4	—
OVERSEAS GENERAL AND ADMINISTRATION		$807,198
TOTAL OUTREACH OVERSEAS	316	$3,848,095

Source: Mennonite Yearbook 1988–89.

Note: This table summarizes mission activities by agencies which are a part of the Mennonite Church General Assembly, Lombard, Ill. If not footnoted, the relationship is through the Mennonite Board of Missions, with offices in Elkhart, Ind., and Harrisonburg, Va. Footnoted agencies are as follows:

[a]Lancaster Mennonite Conference, Salunga, Pa. (Eastern Mennonite Board of Missions and Charities)
[b]Conservative Mennonite Conference, Irwin, Ohio (Rosedale Missions)
[c]Virginia Mennonite Conference, Harrisonburg, Va.
[d]Franconia Mennonite Conference, Souderton, Pa.
[e]Pacific Coast Mennonite Conference, Portland, Ore.

The agencies' contributions to the Overseas General and Administration Fund were as follows:

Mennonite Board of Missions	$346,210
Lancaster Mennonite Conference	413,483
Conservative Mennonite Conference	20,505
Virginia Mennonite Conference	19,000
Franconia Mennonite Conference	8,000

Evangelical Mennonite Church, the Evangelical Mennonite Mission Conference, and some sectors of the General Conference Mennonite Church. This emphasis derives in part from the inroads of fundamentalism and pietism, which have been discussed above. Those emphasizing the Anabaptist ethic claim they are more in line with traditional Anabaptist theology. Feelings run so strong that some Mennonite conferences and congregations are dropping the Mennonite label and affiliation, claiming Mennonitism is "dead" and opposed to evangelism.[2]

The dilemmas created by the inherent pulls in opposite directions, namely evangelization and separation, have been thoroughly analyzed by Leland Harder, who refers to this issue as "structural disequilibrium," which he defines as "an opposition in the social structure itself, over what that structure is to become. It is a structural inconsistency affecting every social position, every law, every logical limitation and every convention" (1962, 28). Harder concludes that the basic dilemma is the result of the missionary thrust versus the thrust to self-preservation: "The voluntary dimension of this definition tends to give the sect a conversionist character as it seeks to propagate its principles among all men. . . . The separatist dimension tends to give the sect an avoidance character as it seeks to divorce itself from worldly evils. In their subsequent development, sects tend to sacrifice one of these dimensions in the preservation of the other" (334). Harder is not optimistic about the ability of the Mennonite society to retain its identity because of this contradiction: "It can be said, in conclusion, that these inner tensions, called structural disequilibrium, . . . are coming more and more to be positive forces of deliberate and legitimate change in the sect group under study" (342).

In any case, the Mennonite missionary thrust of the last century has grown phenomenally and has resulted in an aggressive and substantial church-building program around the world that belies the size of the sending community. For example, there are mission churches and conferences in Africa and India that consist of more members than many of the smaller Mennonite conferences in North America (P. Kraybill 1978, 385). There are nineteen official mission boards in the United States and Canada (see Table 14.1), five regional cooperative organizations of mission boards, and eight inter-Mennonite agencies which assist and promote missions in their various forms (Shenk 1978, 30). A great deal of mission work is done by individual Mennonites under non-Mennonite auspices as well.

Mission work is proclaimed as being one of the highest callings of the Mennonite church, both collectively and individually. Mission boards which are responsible for the administration of the program are totally dependent on voluntary contributions from congregations, usually budgeted as "askings," and for personnel. Mission program and financial planning is the responsibility of a board elected by the conferences which is empowered to carry out all the functions. However, the congregations exercise their ultimate power by supplying the "called-out ones" and by supporting the askings. If a program is not acceptable, the congregation will withhold its support. Another control mechanism is the informal and formal influence applied at the annual meetings and mission conferences where programs are planned, officers elected, and budgets approved.

Sociologically speaking, it is appropriate to suggest that the missionary institution functions (1) to express for Mennonites a feeling of superiority over, or at least of equality with, members of societies and other denominations at large; (2) as proof of having something worthwhile to offer to the world, since it is being accepted; (3) to provide an activity and outlet for young people and others to be related to the Mennonite community in a highly approved way, especially persons who cannot find a niche through other acceptable roles in the Mennonite community; (4) as an opportunity to participate in and support the norms and beliefs of the society as well as to increase the cohesion of the fellowship; and (5) as an acceptance of the "cultural imperialism" which has accompanied most religious systems in the West.

Sociologists and anthropologists have long held that universal religions are constituted to "capture" the minds of all men. In the West, Christianity has supported this universalist mode. To some extent at least, Mennonites who have engaged in mission work would seem to indicate an acceptance of the religious cultural imperialism. "Missionary activity is a manifestation of ethno-centrism. . . . It reflects an attitude of contempt for the values of a different culture and denies the dignity and worth of [these other] people" (Fathauer 1964, 190).

On the other hand, it can be argued (and is by most Mennonites) that the missionary spirit among Mennonites is the result of the central dynamic of the Christian movement. J. D. Graber, a Mennonite missionary statesman with many years of experience in the field, describes the essence of the missionary thrust:

> The fundamental concepts of evangelical Anabaptism made the movement universal, i.e., unhampered by national or territorial limitations. Franklin H. Littell writes: "The gathering of small congregations by believers' baptism went on apace, and Anabaptism spread in many areas closed to the state churches by their acceptance of the principle of territorialism. The Anabap-

tists represent thereby an early Protestant vision of a world mission unrestricted by territorial limitations, and in a unique fashion foreshadow the later concept of the Church as a community of missionary people."

Quite apart from the binding nature of the Great Commission itself . . . , because of the acceptance of the authority and centrality of the Bible in the life of the church, the evangelistic (missionary) motivation of the Anabaptists lay in their concept of the nature of the church. They considered the state church as the "fallen church" and understood their mission to be that of the restitution of the true apostolic church. (Graber 1957, 154–55)

This argument carries considerable force. At the same time, however, a close analysis of the missionary activities of the Anabaptist-Mennonites causes us to conclude that along with these theological or faith issues, the sociological dynamics at work in society helped to determine much of the missionary character of Mennonites during four and a half centuries.

The Missionary Form

There were of course other influences at work in Mennonite society informing the missionary movement. Although this book cannot undertake a history of the missionary movement among Mennonites, we must note that the nineteenth-century awakening of missions was the result at least in part of the larger missionary movement in Europe and America (Shenk 1984). Without a doubt the continuing strong emphasis on revival and mission in the twentieth century was in some measure the consequence of the modern fundamentalist-evangelistic movement.

Although most of the larger groups organized their own mission boards, smaller groups, who also felt the pressure to become missionary, responded by sending their candidates under the aegis of other missionary organizations. Mennonites have served in an amazing variety of denominational and nondenominational organizations. Many of the missionaries who went to serve under other organizations were influenced by the fundamentalist movement, which led them to believe that the Mennonite body was too liberal or unbiblical. There is practically no reference to this phenomenon in missionary literature. Another area which is now coming to light is the role that women have played in mission work, although they were severely limited. In one case a Mennonite woman who had been called to do mission work left for another denomination when she was discouraged from doing the same kind of work under a Mennonite mission board (Klingelsmith 1980, 173).

There are two basic forms of missionary activity—foreign and home missions. Foreign missions among Mennonites have been conducted in the classical style of choosing a foreign country, establishing a permanent residence among the chosen peoples, and conducting a program of Bible study, evangelism, education, counselling, and material assistance. Even though the Mennonite missionary "compound" has approximated in many ways the stereotype disparaged by many social scientists, it is nevertheless true that Mennonite missionaries by and large have tended to pursue a goal which was less exploitative and more responsive to the indigenous people's total needs than many. The fact that many Mennonite Central Committee relief and service activities in the Third World were often the result or cause of missionary activity attests to the responsive roles.

The consequences of missionary work in foreign lands cannot be summarized in this brief survey, but as Table 14.1 shows, indigenous churches have emerged in many nations. In many of these countries, the church is almost self-supporting and self-directed, while in many others, it is still very much dependent upon fraternal support and direction. For a number of Mennonite groups, the foreign membership is greater than the home membership, and this will no doubt mean a dramatic shift in the years to come for the Germanic Mennonite stream. Already the missionary church is challenging the mother church in many ways, criticizing the latter's self-satisfaction and unconcern about the needs of the Third World (Juhnke 1979).

Home missions developed in most Mennonite groups after the beginning of the twentieth century. Even before the turn of the century, some Mennonite groups were involved in "home missions" in the sense of revival meetings among the membership, aimed especially at reaching and reclaiming younger people who were not joining the church. But early in the twentieth century, concern about the inner city and its wretched masses launched a city missions program which saw the creation of missions in major cities such as New York, Philadelphia, Cleveland, Chicago, Minneapolis, Winnipeg, and Vancouver, and in many smaller cities all over the United States and Canada. Schools like Moody Bible Institute and preachers like D. L. Moody and Charles G. Fuller were very influential in "girding up the loins" of Mennonites for action in these areas (Barrett 1983; Erb 1920). These city missions did not take root very easily, however, and few of the original ones remain as established urban Mennonite missions. It appears that cultural differences were too great: the rural Mennonites were not equipped to establish a viable urban congregational life (Driedger, Fretz, and

Smucker 1978). This of course is not necessarily an indication of impotence, since many inner-city churches of mainline Protestantism were busily moving out into the suburbs about this time, forsaking the commitment to the inner city illustrated by the famed Hull House of Chicago, inspired by Jane Addams (Winter 1961).

A more modern version of home missions has been the strong conference-wide church-planting and growth campaigns adopted by every Mennonite group in recent years. In this approach, conference mission committees or boards develop a strategy for promoting evangelistic and mission thrusts with slogans like "Doubling membership in ten years" or "Every congregation an outpost for missions," or through a "ten-year plan" which proposes that each congregation sponsor a new congregation. While most of these programs have been only moderately successful, some conferences have experienced a rather remarkable growth, even though many of their congregations are very small.

The increasing stress on missions, especially in church growth, has caused considerable ambivalence on the part of many, and even some covert conflict among others. At issue is the feeling on the part of those with a more overt commitment to the Anabaptist emphasis that an emphasis on "church growth" is more an unconscious expression of the North American growth, progress, and numbers mentality than of the central message of the New Testament of sharing the good news of salvation, peace, and mutual compassion and assistance (Juhnke 1979, 207–15). From a sociological perspective, the Mennonite "growth syndrome" is more a symptom than a cause: it is the evidence of an acceptance of the values and norms of the predominating Christian milieu and a recognition, as Kaufman reminds us, that the "sect" has recognized that it is now a member of the "club." Yet, the fact that there are many—probably still a majority—who are not wholly supportive of this growth mood undergirds the basic orientation of this book, namely, that the Mennonite Peoplehood exists and is struggling for renascence.[3]

The Mennonite Commitment to Help Others

During the past century or so, rather intricate support systems have appeared among the various segments of Mennonite society—for themselves regionally or as total societies. These systems of supporting and assisting one another have not so much been *created* as they have slowly and informally evolved and then have become more formal; in fact, in many settings, they are now highly organized and institutionalized.

Possibly the most noteworthy of these has been the practice of mutual aid. The term seems to imply a kind of in-group approach to need. In fact, this is often the case, but from the earliest days Mennonites were also mindful of their neighbor who was in need. This concern for both one's brother and one's neighbor has been extended rather naturally from the local community into national and international settings. The Mennonite health and welfare organizations have been primarily national, while the relief and service efforts have responded to both national and international needs.

One of the most noteworthy expressions of the "helping" idea has been the Mennonite Central Committee, which will be described further below. It was formed in 1920 as a response to an urgent crisis among Mennonites in Russia. The statement which was released at the time of the formation of MCC provides an insight into the thinking of Mennonites regarding mutual assistance and concern: "An Appeal to the Brotherhood. The report of the brethren who have come from the stricken country is a touching one, and presents to us a great need of such proportions that merits cooperation of every one of the brotherhood in the U.S. . . . We trust that the brotherhood, which has always rallied to the assistance of the needy when their cry has reached them, will not neglect this opportunity of rendering help to those who are of the 'Household of Faith'" (C. Dyck 1980a, 18).

Among the Hutterites, the concept of mutual aid was originally applied in a total fashion; it was extended to include common ownership of all property as well as a complete communal responsibility for the physical needs of the individual. Among the Mennonite descendants of Anabaptists, however, this all-encompassing pattern of mutual aid is seldom found. Although there has been much sharing of material aid as well as nonmaterial resources among Mennonites, they have usually stopped short of communal property arrangements. Nor have they organized so highly as to guarantee various forms of aid to every member of the society.

At the same time, among Mennonites, there can be found a great variety of applications of the mutual aid principle. Many of these have been developed formally and are expressed in relief efforts to Third World countries, service in times of disaster, the forming of health associations including health plans and burial insurance, community service projects including fire and storm insurance agencies, emergency help such as barn raisings, credit unions, farm cooperatives, and cooperative stores—to name some of the areas in which more formal applications have been made.

Before we go on to look in more detail at the three areas which service work has encompassed—mutual aid, relief and service, and health and welfare—it will be helpful to note an intriguing phenomenon within the Mennonite society. "Support systems" as such are generally viewed as existing for the benefit of a given group; often they are shaped with this objective clearly focused. This is true among Mennonites as well: both informal and formal patterns of response have continued or emerged with the obvious intention of expressing and maintaining patterns of support for the sake of the group itself. At the same time, however, the concern for neighbors—nearby or around the world—has drawn forth responses from Mennonites and helped to create organizations that in themselves have strengthened and extended, or even multiplied, the support systems. In other words, the common mutual aid activities among Mennonites began to include needs outside of the Mennonite society, and became so meaningful that altruistic activities and institutions have become significant energizing systems for the whole Mennonite society. It is difficult to think of Mennonites in their various communities existing without these elements of "worldly" concerns serving as positive reinforcement of identity. It is even more difficult to assume that Mennonites could have continued to exist as a society without the cohesive dynamic provided by these mutual aid and service concerns that have reached far beyond the group itself.

Mutual Aid

Anabaptist-Mennonites have always assumed that mutual assistance was a part of the New Testament teaching. Fretz provides an illustration: "Hans Leopold, a minister of the Swiss Brethren Church in Augsburg and one who suffered martyrdom in 1538, said that 'If [the brethren] know of anyone who is in need, whether or not he is a member of their church, they believe it is their duty out of love to God to render him help and aid'" (1947, 25).

Probably the most widespread application of the mutual aid principle is the voluntary and informal assistance given to needy members of Mennonite congregations when misfortune strikes. For example, when a farmer becomes ill during a spring planting, his friends and neighbors get together to help their brother seed the land. Or, when a mother bears a new child during the canning and freezing season, her neighbors and relatives take over her kitchen to prepare vegetables and fruits for the family freezer or for canning. Or if some member of the Mennonite community has a major and unexpected illness, the congregation will set up a fund to take care of the costs (Fretz 1957b).

But there are many forms of mutual aid which have been institutionalized to take care of the needs in the community. Probably the most traditional of these mutual aid organizations are the fire and wind insurance organizations, which operated in Russia as early as 1850. In North America, most Mennonite communities, especially those in rural areas, have organized fire and wind insurance companies; in reality these are a form of cooperative. As early as 1882 Mennonites in South Dakota organized a fire and storm insurance company called the Mennonite Aid Plan (Fretz 1947, 3). Today more than twenty-five such organizations have banded together to provide re-insurance services so that they can offer more competent and more economical services. This cluster of agencies is called Mennonite Indemnity Incorporated. By 1983, M.I.I. was re-insuring property worth many millions of dollars with Lloyd's of London. There are probably fewer organizations today, since a number of them merged because of geographical redundancy.

These mutual aid societies are unofficial in the sense that they are sponsored by members who adhere to Mennonite beliefs and practices rather than by conferences. Usually, participation is limited to members of a Mennonite congregation and their families. Often, groups of congregations band together to serve each other in this way. Typically, a board of directors elected by the membership of such a mutual aid society employs a staff and provides oversight of the operation. Even though there is no direct congregational or conference control, the mutual aid organizations are controlled indirectly by persons who are members in good standing in their congregations and thus reflect the principles of Mennonite society.

A new area of mutual aid which has quickly become centralized as well as powerful is Mennonite Mutual Aid, a health and life insurance program owned officially by the participating Mennonite conferences. Members recommended by their respective congregations, through conferences, make up the board of directors. The board of this organization is responsible for administering a health and welfare insurance program which supplements Blue Cross, Blue Shield, and other secular plans. A significant feature of Mennonite Mutual Aid is the catastrophe fund; this becomes operative for those members who experience unusual or massive health and hospital expenses. In another feature of this program, needy members are given premium support and made eligible for insurance benefits by congregations who sign up a certain number of people so that a designated member or family can come into the plan free. Numerous burial aid and other types of mutual aid societies also operate.

Of all forms of mutual aid practiced by Mennonites, perhaps the most dramatic is Mennonite Disaster Service, an international Mennonite organization which moves into communities that have been devastated by natural disasters like floods or tornadoes. MDS can send cleanup and rebuilding crews to any part of Canada and the United States and, on occasion, to other countries. Totally voluntary, the organization and its programs are coordinated by a central MDS office. The resources needed for working in a given community may be supplied by agencies in the communities being helped, by the individuals who serve, or by the sending committee. When a flood strikes, for example, the organization swings into action informing local MDS organizations what type of service is needed, where to go, and whom to contact in the community being served. Many people give at least one day a year in voluntary service to Mennonite Disaster Service (C. Dyck 1980c, 114–22; Hershberger 1956).

Finally, Mennonite communities have also organized credit unions which, beyond normal financial services, provide special financial assistance to indigent members. Thus, for example, the Ontario Mennonite Credit Union—whose total assets exceeded $70 million as of December 1988—has a $600,000-plus no-interest or low-interest loan fund for needy families. Again, credit unions are not officially owned by the congregations or conference. Rather, they are composed of individuals who are members of the Mennonite church and operate such credit unions on the basis of Mennonite principles and practices.

Relief and Service

Since Anabaptist-Mennonites have accepted the Sermon on the Mount as a kind of extended recipe for the life of the Christian, they have tried to follow these teachings in a literal fashion. This has included "a cup of cold water" given in the name of Christ. Even while they were being persecuted during the Reformation, Anabaptists practiced relief and service to needy people. The Dutch Mennonites in 1553 "at Wismer in North Germany gave asylum to a group of English Calvinist refugees who had been driven from home by the Catholic queen" (Hershberger 1956, 284).

Through the years Mennonites have provided a spontaneous type of relief and service when occasions of need presented themselves. One such occasion within the last hundred years was the famine in India during the last decade of the nineteenth century. But the landmark example of institutionalized relief work took place with the formation of

Mennonite Central Committee (MCC). Formally organized in 1920 to come to the aid of desperate Mennonites under the new Communist regime in the Russian Ukraine, MCC grew steadily. Today it has an annual budget of over $19 million. The MCC is supported by almost every conference of Mennonites in North America—which at the present time total seventeen—and has approximately 944 workers in 44 countries of the world. Along with other work, the MCC has distributed at least $50 million worth of material and relief supplies to victims of war and other disasters around the world.

There exists a voluminous written record describing the service of Mennonites in various MCC activities. One such activity was the Pax program, developed following World War II as an alternative form of military service for conscientious objectors. Many Pax projects were carried out in Europe, and later in Africa and South America. One such project, a community development program in Greece, operated for a number of years. The response of the community to this service is indicated in the following testimony by the local villagers of Panayitsa:

> We always bear in mind the remarkable and praiseworthy philanthropic work done by you in our village. Your work showed us and proved by example the progress of cultivation, the improvement of all kinds of products for a better income, and the systematic and proper plowing of the fields with the cost of gas only paid by the villagers. We remember the help you gave to every seriously sick person and the transportation of them to Edessa or Salonika free of charge, in the night and in any time after midnight. . . . We also remember your various and good vivid Christian examples: your politeness, meekness, forbearance, patience, love in Christ, prudence, humility, charity, and benefaction. You are the great benefactors of our village.
>
> We feel and understand your concern and sincere love and are moved with today's Godly and precious gifts of the Word of God which is the New Testament. . . . We will never forget, as long as we live, the eagerness and the Godly zeal you portrayed to decorate our holy church with the icon of the annunciation of the Archangel Gabriel to the Holy Mother. . . . We must grant justice and praises, honour and gratitude for all the above. We assure you that your names will remain ineffaceable in our memory and that it will pass to future generations. (U. Bender 1969, 71–72)

As the MCC has matured, it has branched out not only in foreign countries but at home as well; by this point in its history it has become the most ecumenical organization in Mennonite history, bringing together Mennonites in North America from every part of the historical stream. Its program at home and abroad now employs volunteers and paid workers in programs of community development, reconstruction of devastated communities, relief and human assistance in natural disasters, teaching in underdeveloped countries, and many other similar activities. In the United States and Canada, the MCC is the official agency which administers and supervises the eight mental hospitals, and sponsors the work among the native peoples; in South America it gives leadership to the settlement of native peoples in Bolivia and Paraguay (Neufeld 1983).

The foregoing is just a sampling of the work that MCC has done and is doing in various parts of the world. The Mennonite Central Committee has its main offices, including its Material Aid Center, in Akron, Pennsylvania. It maintains U.S. and Canadian national offices in Akron and Winnipeg, as well as four regional offices in the United States and five in Canada. These offices are responsible for administering the entire MCC program described above, at home and abroad. The total effort—including constituency contact as well as programs—obviously involves a labyrinthian organizational structure and resource allocations rivaling that of some modern business corporations. The MCC has also developed subsections which serve special functions. The Peace Section nurtures issues relating to peace, including legislative matters. Another subsection in the Canadian office, the Peace and Social Concerns Section, deals largely with native rights and related matters. The Mennonite Mental Health Services coordinates and contributes to the functioning of the eight mental hospitals. The Self-Help Program is a network of stores promoting North American sales of products from developing nations.

Of course, many aspects of the MCC are not even hinted at in this brief report. For example, the MCC helps to sponsor an annual two-week Third World Development Seminar in cooperation with the Council of Mennonite Colleges. This is a major event that involves both returned and newly appointed relief and service workers—not only those working under the MCC but also those involved in other Mennonite and non-Mennonite missions and similar programs.

The MCC is connected so integrally with the life of the Mennonites that many people conceive of it as the official structure of the Mennonite society. But this is a misconception of the Mennonite social structure. The Mennonite Central Committee is the expression of the Mennonite congregational ethos, while the MCC support, direction, and personnel are the expression of the congregations that support it. In no way is MCC a "super church."

What is the MCC from a sociological perspective, and what are its functions?[4] The organization has never been analyzed sociologically, but any analysis would probably need to include the following factors:

1. The MCC is a very effective mechanism for Mennonites to serve in an approved and fully sanctioned manner. That is, the biblical mandate to Christians to feed, clothe, and help the world's poor is supported handsomely by this organization (Unruh 1952, 356).

2. The MCC serves as a mechanism to help Mennonites relate to and experience the secular world in an approved and well-supported manner. A Mennonite youth who has been protected from the world in his isolated home community is able to "see the rest of the world" in a way that is still protective of his faith and relationships.

3. The MCC provides the context for a broad spectrum of experimentation and innovative service programs which a local congregation would not be able to carry out. Thus, it dissipates the onus of change and secularization which would create severe conflict were it to be done by members of a local congregation in their local setting.

4. It provides an opportunity for the expression of individual creativity and the development of new ideas within the Mennonite context. If such an opportunity were not available, the personal drive for innovation would probably have to be expressed outside of the denomination because of the church's conservatism.

5. The MCC provides a significant mechanism for a degree of cooperation among Mennonites which has not proved to be possible in any other way. Mennonites from various conferences and of various theological stripes can work together in the MCC because the MCC is not involved in theology or mission work, but, rather, deals exclusively with the expression of faith. Yet, as anyone who has ever worked in the MCC can attest, the organization has exerted a far greater force in mission work and in theologizing than most persons in the pew would be willing to admit (Unruh 1952, 357).

6. In terms of the individual member from a local congregation, the MCC functions as the surrogate symbol as well as the actual expression of the desire to be relevant and effective in the world. In some settings, a creative response to need would not be possible, because of local conditions, conservative postures, isolation, and a sense of inferiority that infects congregations as well as individuals. Almost everyone in the Mennonite society is proud of the MCC and what it is doing "in the world." One barometer of this grassroots pride and support is the pattern of annual relief sales which has emerged, recently and suddenly, in almost every major Mennonite settlement in North America. For

example, the Michiana MCC relief sale in Goshen, Indiana—in existence for over ten years—now raises over $300,000 annually for the MCC program. The funds are raised through the donation of almost anything valuable, such as antique furniture, crafts, and various kinds of handwork and needlework, especially quilts, which are bought at auction or from sales stalls by an interested public. Also, many types of ethnic foods are available for sale—for immediate consumption or for take-home. Among a number in North America, this particular relief sale has become so institutionalized that various clubs, such as the Airstream Club, plan a camp at Goshen each year so they can participate in the relief sale and its activities.

7. The MCC provides a center of identity for the larger Mennonite society as well as a rallying point for interaction and the exchange of ideas. This identity role moves beyond an ecumenical function; often the MCC is the only visible, meaningful entity that keeps some people loyal to Mennonite society. Many marginal people who have become alienated from Mennonite society because of its parochial narrowness remain Mennonites because of the fraternity of MCC people who share a common experience and world view.

MCC performs other functions for the Mennonite society as well, but these are among the more important. It is clear that this equation can be turned around to ask how the congregation functions for the MCC. The congregation support of the MCC is reflected in many ways, similar to the mission program discussed above. Basically, the congregation provides personnel, resources, direction, and controls. The ideological roots which determine the basic attitudes and values of the congregations as well as the MCC itself move us outside of the context of this discussion and must be dealt with elsewhere.

Health and Welfare

One could assume that the MCC is the ultimate Mennonite structure. This is not the case. An extensive health and welfare thrust also exists. There are many hospitals, retirement homes, nursing homes, children's homes, and other such programs administered and supported by Mennonites. Some are sponsored by local congregations; others are run by conferences; still others are run by private associations of Mennonites. (The mutual aid organizations which provide some of the funding for health and welfare were described above.) To take only one example, the number of retirement homes sponsored by Mennonites is proliferating rapidly, with such centers now being found in Pennsylvania, Virginia, New York, Ohio, Indiana, Kansas, Arizona, and elsewhere; no tabulation exists giving the totals. Boys' and girls' homes, sometimes sponsored by the MCC, are found in many Mennonite population centers.

The health and welfare structure is so large that, in recent years, coordinating associations have emerged to keep the organizations informed of each other's activities. The following list of such coordinating associations helps to provide a perspective of the range of services provided: Canadian Mental Health Assembly, Developmental Disability Service, Inter-Mennonite Council of Aging, Mennonite Chaplains' Association, Mennonite Disabilities Committee, Mennonite Health Association, Mennonite Health Resources Incorporated, Mennonite Medical Association, Mennonite Mental Health Services, Mennonite Nursing Association, and Mennonite Nursing Homes Association.

Only one thrust can be discussed here, and that only briefly. The Mennonite Mental Health Services, which operates eight mental hospitals in the United States and Canada, began in 1948 as the result of the experiences of conscientious objectors who served in state mental hospitals during World War II. The first meeting of the Mental Hospital Study Committee on December 28–29, 1945, stated, "The Civilian Public Service program has awakened our Church to the whole area of need which we have somewhat neglected—the care of the mentally ill" (C. Dyck 1980c, 80). This program of service to the mentally ill has become a pathfinder through the maze of mental health care practices and is now a model of secular and religious programs (Neufeld 1983).

The health and welfare structure is so extensive simply because the Mennonite concern about mutual aid has so thoroughly permeated the Mennonite consciousness; thus, taking care of the needy and the dependent continues to be a major concern, reflecting more formally now what has been present informally for hundreds of years. The percentage of Mennonites serving the health and welfare services is higher than the national average, presumably for this reason (Kauffman and Harder 1975, 241).

Other Mennonite Support Institutions

There are numerous other institutionalized structures which contribute to the life and function of Mennonite society. Only a few of these can be mentioned. One is an intricate institutionalized structure for communications. Each conference has at least one official magazine or paper along with numerous other subsidiary papers promoting other causes; one such subsidiary publication is *The Marketplace,* which is sponsored by the Mennonite Economic Development Association (MEDA), an organization of business and professional people concerned with applying Christian principles to business management and helping persons in underdeveloped countries to get started toward self-sufficiency and self-determination. There is also the mass media sector, which includes radio and television work, much of it sponsored by the conferences working together in Mennonite Media Ministries—now called Council on Church and Media. There is the camping and recreational thrust, with dozens of camps owned and operated by Mennonite conferences or groups of congregations. Some are private, begun when the churches were still opposed to this "worldly movement"; one example of this is Laurelville Mennonite Church Center of Mt. Pleasant, Pennsylvania. This private camp, owned by members, has served as an innovative leader in Mennonite values for many decades. There are also travel agencies, such as Menno Travel Service and Tourmagination. There are youth organizations and heritage centers, such as the Meeting Place.

Overarching all of this organizational activity is the Mennonite World Conference, which, to the casual observer, might appear to be the central nerve of the Mennonite society. But like MCC, this world body is nonlegislative and dependent on voluntary contributions for the one major activity it performs—namely, a gathering of Mennonites from around the world every five or six years for fellowship, inspiration, and teaching. A significant reflection of the desire to keep in touch is a newsletter published by Mennonite World Conference, which keeps Mennonites informed of each other's activities in their various locations around the world.

A PERUSAL OF the (Old) *Mennonite Yearbook* (there are many conference directories, none totally comprehensive) indicates the variety of the organizations and structures which support the Mennonite society. The participation of congregations and conferences in the network of interagency organizations and structures is both labyrinthian and mixed. The more conservative conferences exclude themselves almost totally from such cooperative ventures. Thus, for example, the Old Order Amish do not participate in any of the structures listed, although they have their own elementary schools, mutual aid groups, and other organizations. However, although they do not participate formally in the structures set up, in some regions they may become involved in certain programs sponsored by the MCC—such as canning beef for relief purposes—or in assisting MDS clean-up and reconstruction crews following a natural disaster. Also, during World War II, the Old Order Amish utilized the various forms of alternative service that were available to reflect their conscientious objection to war.

In any case, the *Mennonite Yearbook* proves that contemporary Mennonite society is no longer a pre-twentieth-century pastoral community. It is structured in a variety of ways to carry out objectives which include, fundamentally, the sharing of the faith and helping those who are in need. How the structurally autonomous congregational ideal can be integrated with a vast bureaucratic system has never been fully resolved. The more pietistic and evangelical Mennonites would say that these structures are really irrelevant and possibly a sign of secularization or even apostasy. Others would maintain that the structures of Mennonite society such as the mission boards and the MCC have become the hands and feet of the Gospel message.

There is, of course, a scholarly concern and a mood of critique growing among Mennonites; these voices are beginning to raise serious questions about the institutional aspects of the Mennonite heritage. Thus, one sociologist states: "Never in the history of the Mennonite Church has the work and activity of the church been as highly institutionalized both at the level of local congregations and in churchwide agencies as it is today. . . . We need . . . analysis and reflection on the way in which the church has structured its activity in order to develop organizational patterns which are consistent with our theological assertions" (Eby 1976, 1). From a sociological perspective, the organizational structure of Mennonite society represents the inexorable institutionalization of religious impulses. In fact, the book *Kingdom, Cross, and Community* (Burkholder and Redekop 1976) is an attempt to understand the institutionalization of the Mennonite movement—the fact that "gospel and the Christian movement . . . embrace two orientations that are in tension: the message of a new being (a new status) and the message of a mission (a goal-achieving system)" (C. Redekop 1976, 139). The goal-achieving dimension of the Mennonite movement necessitates the creation of institutions that promote positive social patterns. Scholars have concluded that all institutions consist of (1) values, symbol systems, and goals; (2) the norms that help achieve these goals; (3) the status role system which harnesses human efforts in a systematic way; and (4) the material facilities which are needed to accomplish the above objectives.

How has the institutional complex of the Mennonite movement affected its goals and its development? Does Mennonite theology—specifically its congregational orientation—make any difference to the institutional structure? Are the evangelistic motif and the mutual aid concept compromised by the vast plethora of organizations which have emerged? If so, what difference does it make? These questions will be addressed more explicitly in the remainder of this book.

Part Four

Stresses and Changes

It is tempting to say that no socioreligious group has wrestled as much as the Mennonite community has with stability and change. Schism, the subject of the first chapter in this section, can to a large extent be ascribed to change and the difficulties in coping with it. Schism clearly involves more than a reaction to change, however; it reaches into the heart of the concern with orthodoxy, faithfulness, and relevance. And if schism is any indication of a vital and involved society, then the Mennonites have shown where they stand.

But change is inherent in all human systems, and Mennonites have encountered and experienced change in manifold ways. In this section, ideas and social structures are analyzed as the contributors to change, indicating that Mennonites have not had to deal with just the influences of change from the outside, such as technology, but have had to deal with internal variables and dynamics as well. This is especially difficult for the Mennonites because the attempt to define and enact a lifestyle that is close to the teachings of Jesus has tended to result in fixed and legalistic interpretations.

Even though the discussion cannot do justice to all the variation within the Mennonite family, the reaction to change, especially as it expresses itself in lifestyles, is a basic criterion for distinguishing many of the Mennonite groups in North America today.

Chapter Fifteen

Schism among Mennonites

Mennonites have disagreed among themselves and fought one another since the earliest conventicles, and yet they have banded together in an almost mysterious way. The earliest fledgling congregations or groupings, such as the early Hutterites, were conceived in disagreements and differences, and to this day the gradients distinguishing the various emerging groups from each other are built on subtle distinctions that escape the outsider entirely. A central difficulty with any attempt to present a coherent understanding of the Mennonite movement is its variety and diversity. It seems that any further characterizing of its essence and core is doomed to fail because of the paradoxical centrifugal and centripetal tendencies.

Typical of this tendency to disagreement, conflict, and schism is the famous *Lammerenkrijgh* (Lambs War), which centered on followers of Galeneus Abrahamsz and Samuel Apostool, beginning in 1664, the latter being more conservative. "The division extended to almost all the Mennonites in Holland. . . . Even today one can see on the weather vane of many a Dutch Mennonite church a sketch of a lamb" (van der Zijpp 1957b). But a host of other factors, such as the ethnic distinctions of Frisian and Flemish, also entered into the conflict. Contention, conflict, schism, and even mutual excommunication have therefore colored the history of Mennonitism from its inception. We begin the quest to understand Mennonite schism, especially as it expresses itself in North America, by a brief historical survey.

Schism among Mennonites: A Brief Review

The infinite variety of Mennonites have confused outsiders and scandalized Christians, especially the Mennonites themselves. But Mennonites are not the only Christians who have split. Christianity has been in a process of fission from the beginning. Joachim Wach, a student of world religions, points out that "the more advanced the process of social and cultural differentiation, the more diversified are the forms of religious expression" and that a major phase in the history of Christianity is the "breakdown of Christian unity" (1951, 268, 274).

Differentiation, a sociological concept, is actually the term used to identify the evolution of new forms, while *schism* is the normative theological term for religious differentiation. But no purpose is served by wringing hands over schism among Mennonites. In fact, as indicated earlier, it is possible to reconceptualize schism and suggest that it is often basically the adaptation of the basic ethos and faith to new situations and conditions. But schisms which involve differences in doctrine and belief are of a different nature. They are much more significant, since they create the conditions which limit or encourage the interactions of the various groups for a long time, including intercongregational relationships and migrations.

The major schisms of the Mennonites were briefly described in Chapter 3. Most of the schisms were very complex and were the result of many different factors. The description and analyses I shall present here reflect only the *major* factors; the subtle nuances and the dynamics of the divisions cannot be listed. Each division was long in coming and was fraught with tension, hostility, conflict, and pain.

Of course, not all the varieties of shadings of belief have been presented; each of these shadings could themselves also be designated as divisions in terms of their consequences. For example, the simple act of migration of the Old Colony Mennonites from Manitoba to Saskatchewan and Alberta has produced differences and created regional identities. These new regional identities have had the effect of producing new self-conscious groupings. Another closely related phenomenon is the creation of conferences or smaller groupings within the affiliation of larger conferences; for all practical purposes, these constitute new groups. For example, the Mennonite Church (MC or Old Mennonite Church) has spawned many new conferences which reflect divisions over differences in lifestyle, evangelism, and the like. The Northern Light Gospel Mission Conference, founded in 1965, is an illustration, as are the older district conferences or, to a lesser degree, the more recent regional structures.

There is at present an increasing unrest within the various Mennonite groups, and separating fellowships are emerging with increasing tempo. Empirical evidence is difficult to obtain because the definition of when a group is officially "independent" is so vague and imprecise. It is probably fair to say that the greatest amount of schism, proportionately, is taking place in the more conservative Mennonite branches. The Old Order Mennonites and Old Order Amish are probably most productive in dividing into new groups. A case study of Ontario Mennonites indicates that three groups existing in 1889 produced ten subgroups still existing today (C. Redekop, unpublished).

The Russian Mennonites have differentiated as much as the Swiss, and add considerable elaboration to the rainbow. A similar study of Manitoba Mennonites indicated that the Bergthal group (1874) produced thirteen identifiable groups (C. Redekop, unpublished). Each division is unique and specific, so generalization is hazardous. It is clear that the conditions and issues involved in the schisms referred to here could be identified among Mennonites in the rest of North America, even though schism has not resulted.

There is thus no easy way at the moment to present a coherent and comprehensive description of the divisions among North American Mennonites. Only the more progressive groups keep extensive records of ecclesiastical activities, and even many of the groups that are seceding from these groups do not wish to be enumerated. It is even more difficult to decide whether to include groups who want nothing to do with anything "Mennonite," such as the Evangelical Mennonite Brethren groups, which in 1987 rejected the name "Mennonite" and all associations within the Mennonite family.

Apart from the special impetus for division on the part of the conservative groups alluded to above, there are other orientations tending to draw Mennonites from the mainstream—for example, the charismatic infiltration and the anti-intellectual reaction of many conservative Mennonites, especially in the eastern United States. The Mennonite Renewal Service, an organization headquartered in Goshen, Indiana, is a group which has maintained that the Mennonite church is not "spiritual" enough, and though it is not forming a new conference, it tends to help congregations align for or against the charismatic emphasis in many areas of the Mennonite church. The "non-conference" movement and the Mennonite Messianic Mission in eastern Pennsylvania are incipient secessionist groups, although it is not clear whether they will separate from the main body. These groups are basically opposed to intellectual and educational emphases.

Analysis of Schism

How can this plethora of differentiation, division, and schism be comprehended and systematized if it cannot be described? First, a general observation: the differentiation of the Mennonite tradition is not unnatural, even though it may represent an extreme example. The reasons for schism must be derived from general sociological processes and could be considered a natural phenomenon.[1] It can be observed that most of the divisions did not take place exclusively over specific points of doctrine and theology, but rather, over disagreements about lifestyle and practice. That is, the difference in perception of what was faithful biblical discipleship constituted the center of conflict, not the beliefs themselves.

From a theological and ecclesiastical perspective, it is obvious why schism could be considered an undesirable and even a moral problem. When fellowship and friendly relationships are cut off, schism is bad, and this has certainly been characteristic of many schisms, including those in the Mennonite community. But when schism is described as the differentiation of social groupings, it loses its edge and can be considered the normal situation, while the lack of division can be defined as abnormal or due to some unusual circumstance. From a sociological point of view, social groups can experience only a limited amount of growth and complexity before the nature of the relationship changes so drastically that a separation is needed. Thus, it is sociologically normal for families to set up separate households, for Sunday School classes to divide after they have grown too large, and for congregations to split off when they have exceeded reasonable proportions.

The Hutterite system of setting up a new colony when the mother colony has grown to around 150 persons is such an example in the Mennonite community, and it has taken place there with relatively little acrimony (J. A. Hostetler 1974, 185ff.). The acrid debate and hostility accompanying many Mennonite schisms may result from an unawareness of the natural need for subdividing into smaller groups to preserve the *Gemeinschaft* conditions. This explanation seems convincing in light of the general agreement among Mennonites that it is not the beliefs and principles that are the cause of the differences but the application in specific situations.

Third, and most importantly, Mennonite schisms must be seen in large part as an adaptation of the traditional practices of groups adjusting to new areas. A German proverb states "Andere Staetten, andere Sitten" (Other places, other folkways). As was indicated in Chapter 4, the migrations in a sense were benign schisms—in that they guaranteed a different set of experiences, a different host society with which to relate, and a new configuration of relationships internally. Furthermore, by its very departure the migrating group extracted itself from original settings and long-standing relationships—never again to interact on a concerted basis. From this point on, interrelationships that were shaped between the migrating group and the mother colony became subtly different.

Adapting the traditional culture and social system to a new environment has an overwhelming impact on the migrating group. Not only do these adaptations create a shock for the migrating group, vis-à-vis the host society, but they also create a notable strain between the migrating group and the mother settlement. For example, the very conservative group which left the Chihuahua Old Colony for Belize has become a separate group even though the family connections are still strong and the overall Mennonite identification is as clear as before (C. Redekop 1969, 22–23, 259–60).

This latter point, however, presents one of the most interesting paradoxes about Mennonite society. In spite of the many migrations and the resulting differentiations—as well as the specific schisms—the historical identity of Mennonite groups with the original and overall Mennonite tradition remains as strong as ever, or even intensifies. Thus, even though there is a greater heterogeneity in lifestyle, there is a continuing or even strengthening commitment to an identification with the *Mennonite heritage*. The contemporary church communities and the associations of small groups of Mennonites who are experimenting with new lifestyles illustrate this very well; they are fiercely loyal to the Mennonite heritage (V. Vogt 1983).

The fact that the Hutterites have not experienced differentiation of major proportions provides a test for the theory of migration and adaptation. Except for one group that defected to the Society of Brothers (the Forest River Colony) and several small groups of families that have defected, the Hutterites have not experienced structural division. The best explanation for this lack of schism and division would appear to be the tight authoritarian structure of the Hutterite system, its extreme isolation in any host society, and the close control it exercises over migrations. When the group migrated to the United States and to Canada, several subgroupings were already distinguishable. These were the Schmiedenleut and the Dariusleut groups, named after their respective leaders. The Lehrerleut emerged in South Dakota after the migration. However, these three ethnic Hutterite groups have remained in close harmony with each other and have retained relative homogeneity in faith and practice (Peter 1976a). It is of great interest to observe the "branching" process by which a Hutterite colony divides to form a new settlement. This process is worked out very carefully so that no ill feeling persists; communication between the dividing group and the mother colony is kept up as much as is deemed necessary. Therefore, even though there are now 203 colonies in Manitoba, Saskatchewan, Alberta, British Columbia, South Dakota, and Washington State, the Hutterite society still maintains one overall pattern of unity, harmony, and uniformity (J. A. Hostetler 1974).

This is not to indicate that there is no disaffection, disharmony, or tension. These are present to some degree, but in the main, the Hutterites have preserved an amazingly effective, economically viable social and religious system. The identity with the Hutterite tradition is just as strong as that obtaining among the Amish and Mennonites, although it is more authoritarian and centralized than among these latter groups.

Among the rest of the Mennonites, however, differentiation and schism have been more extensive and continuous. Nor does the process appear to be at an end or lessening. A careful analysis of the sociological significance of Mennonite schisms is now beginning; several studies have recently appeared, and some generalizations seem to be forthcoming.[2]

All studies of schism among Mennonites reject one of the classic reasons proposed for sectarian separation: economic disparities between members of the religious body. Rather, schism and division among Mennonites have a complex basis; some reasons can be classified as external—that is, resulting from pressures in the interaction with the secular environment—while some are internal—that is, resulting from forces within the group itself. An obvious third factor is some combination of internal and external forces. It is quite likely the best format for explaining most, if not all, Mennonite divisions and schisms. Such an approach, proposed by Beals and Siegel (1966), has been termed *factionalism*.

Schisms involve cause and effect and "looping," or feedback—a situation where an earlier factor feeds back into the system. A simple illustration may help us focus the factors. Let us assume that a conservative Mennonite group secedes from a larger Mennonite group over the issue of worldliness. Specifically, the division represents a termination of fellowship with those who are "modernizing," in this case by allowing their children to go to college. (Of course, this is an oversimplification but it clearly makes the point.)

The first stage leading to schism would be the minority-host society dynamics in which the assimilation forces of the larger society were not fully or successfully avoided or managed—somehow, members of the group allowed the secular values to infiltrate their own value system and thus produce change. That is, some of those going to college would return, for example, and propound liberal or even "heretical" ideas. Those who were less susceptible to assimilation might gravitate toward the schismatic or conservative groups, while the "modernizers" remained in the majority (see Chart 15.1) and began to support college education more strongly.

The second stage of the process would be the internal dynamics of adjusting to the "changing times"; within this frame the congregation and its leaders would be involved in the difficult process of discerning what was "eternal truth" and which things could change. On this level attitudes toward the Bible and the authority of the leadership, along with many other factors, would be implicated. Members of the group would discuss the fact that several of the more "progressive" members

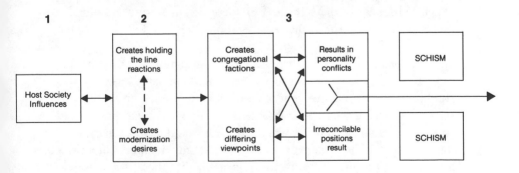

CHART 15.1 A Model of Schism
1. The influences, of course, go both ways, but in this context, the internal dynamics are the focus.
2. Mennonite schisms are socially derived in part, but ideology is central.
3. The reciprocal nature of these four factors hardly allows for positing priority.

had been to a Mennonite college and were now sincerely trying to help modernize the church.

In the third stage sociological factions would be formed in the congregation; these factions would be associated particularly with family structures and politics. Often the leadership of a congregation is centered in a family or in interrelated groups of families who have acculturated; this tends to create resentment among others and unconscious resistances and reactions. Thus, the issue itself—in this case, "modernization" through education—may not be as important a factor as it appears to be from the rhetoric or the theological controversies; rather, the disagreement has to do with families' accepting host society values.

We have discussed the formal contexts in which schism will develop (i.e., the conflict with the host society, the inner tensions and disagreements, and a combination of the two). Now we need to look at the specific precipitating factors that cause schisms:

1. *Migration.* I have already indicated that migrations are a force which contributes to schisms and divisions. There is great power to this process. Usually, there is little that a group can do about this factor, since migrations tend to be either involuntary, or voluntary for reasons not motivated by the desire to break fellowship, for most Mennonites abhor schism.

2. *Disputes over power.* The disruptive influences of differences in the possession of power—in the congregation and community—have operated in many schisms. This factor emerged as one of the most important in Felstead's studies of a number of important schisms in Ontario. Usually, the possessors of power were at the center of the disputes which led finally to the schism. But these disputes were usually also related to factions within the congregation (Felstead 1978; Cressman 1980).

3. *Personality conflicts.* The personality consideration is a factor that cannot be overlooked. Felstead confirms that, in some cases, it was stubbornness or obsessive concern with a certain issue or problem as opposed to seeing the issue or problem in a larger context that created an irreconcilable situation in which the only solution was a parting of the ways. Often the principals or one of the family members of a principal group were guilty of some misdemeanors, but there was no way to save face, so the momentum of divisiveness was allowed to continue toward its inevitable end.

4. *Conservatism versus progressivism.* The process of members becom-

ing conservative with age has also been discussed in the literature; Felstead discovered that aging of the principals in schisms was correlated with divisive factors. As members of a sect become older, they tend to be more concerned with preserving "age-old truths" and hence cannot brook change as well as other people. Of course, this sense of or need to change feeds into the system from the larger society; the existence of a surrounding host society which presents alternatives can contribute to the schismatic tendencies (Cressman 1980).

5. *Loss of uniform beliefs.* Another major factor which has contributed to division is what might be termed disorganization or loss of cohesion because of a loss of solidarity in beliefs and values. The Mennonite attempt to achieve uniformity and conformity to traditional practices and beliefs is written large in almost every Mennonite memory as well as in the official documents, such as conference decisions. Pronouncements on the wearing of hats for women, the use of tobacco, or the use of radios, for example, have confronted almost every Mennonite member in the twentieth century; each locality has had its own specific problem with the plague of "worldliness"—almost always as a consequence of the church's effort to constrain the tendency to "follow after strange gods" (C. Redekop 1970). There was often a very simple reason for the introduction of "worldly" elements: as Mennonite groups settled in and became established in their religious, economic, and community life, they also became wealthy and began to relax the boundaries between themselves and the outside world. Thus, the uniformity of beliefs began to weaken through the acceptance of beliefs from the surrounding society. Thus also, tensions began to emerge as the orthodox group—Graber's "perpetuators"—continued to assert the old norms and beliefs (Graber 1983, 60).

6. *Displaced hostility.* Without a doubt, a major reason for both contention and schism is the time-proven dynamic of the turning inward of hatred and hostility. The concept of displaced hostility or self-hatred has achieved widespread acceptance in social psychology. This dynamic operates on the premise that hostility which for some reason cannot be directed toward the legitimate object is often deflected and turned inward. In this case the inward deflection would include accusing fellow Anabaptists of heresy, impurity, laxity, and similar departures from the faith when, in fact, it was the enemy outside which was causing the tension and the anxiety. As long as a movement flourishes, there is relative harmony within. But when hard times and oppositions come, inner tensions and accusations begin to multiply.

That this discussion has not focused on the theological factors in schisms is not to imply that theology and beliefs are unimportant. But in the analysis here we are dealing with a group whose basic theology and belief system is relatively unified and integrated as compared with that of other groups. In other words, Anabaptist-Mennonite society already represents a concerted withdrawal motivated by a major theological belief system. This means that a Mennonite schism is the very delicate fine-tuning of perceptions and responses in which, uniformly, the "world" is rejected but the determination of what specifically is to be rejected is constantly changing.[3]

Although appearing relatively similar from the outside, Mennonite groups with their delicate distinctives become a great and variegated family when known from within. Of course, each group is convinced that it is most true to the original heritage. This stance leads to real anxieties about other groups; in fact, sometimes Mennonites are more afraid of each other than they are of non-Mennonites. The greatest point of strain within Mennonite groups develops when one group attempts to missionize or convert other Mennonites.

This has happened and continues to happen. The standard form is for the more "evangelical" groups—that is, those who have begun to move away from traditional Mennonite theology and polity—to see their more traditional Mennonite brothers and sisters as candidates for evangelism and conversion. Hence, the Evangelical Mennonite Conference, the Evangelical Mennonite Mission Conference, the Church of God in Christ, the Holdeman Mennonites, and, in certain locations, the General Conference of Mennonites of North America and the Mennonite Brethren have established mission activities among the Old Colony Mennonites and splinter groups in Mexico, Bolivia, Ontario, Manitoba, and Texas. "Sheep stealing"—a euphemism for this process—is well known and deeply resented in most Mennonite groups (C. Redekop 1969, 195, 221–23; J. A. Hostetler 1954).

The activities of the Church of God in Christ, Mennonite—which itself began as a revival movement among Mennonites—are illustrative. The following passage from Hiebert's survey of the Holdeman church outlines one of the more organized attempts at mission among the "apostate" Mennonite family:

> During the 1950 and 1960 decades, some endeavors which strongly resembled those of John Holdeman a century earlier were undertaken in Ohio, Pennsylvania and Oklahoma under the direction of the General Mission Board. A number of discontented Amish, conservative Mennonites, and Wisler Mennonites, who had come to view their churches as "decayed" and

"fallen," saw in the Holdeman church the "true church" they were seeking.

In Wayne County, Ohio, the cradle of the Church of God in Christ, Mennonite, an elderly Wisler Mennonite, Daniel Martin,

> found himself admiring men who wore beards. An inner voice spoke to him that this was right. . . . He did not follow his convictions for a number of years. Finally the voice spoke so loud that he became fully convinced that it was the Lord's will that men should wear beards. . . . He became willing and found grace to take up that cross to honor the Lord in keeping His natural-likeness.

Six Holdeman persons from Michigan visited him. He was convinced that the Holdeman church was the "true church" and was baptized, joining the Pettisville congregation at some distance from where he lived. In his zeal to share his new-found faith, he invited Harry Wenger and a number of other Holdeman ministers to conduct meetings in that area in the winter of 1951–52. As a result, a small congregation was formed of the converts, largely of Amish background, who were baptized. Because there was considerable discontent in Amish and Wisler Mennonite churches in the area, the ferment grew. Others joined their ranks. By 1959 they had built a meeting house two miles west of Kidron and another congregation had been formed at Hartville, Ohio. (Hiebert 1973, 354–55)

Such activities as these are a relatively new phenomenon and reflect the missionary emphasis of contemporary individualism in America. The tendency to different interpretations and the increase in kinds of Mennonite groups, however, is exacerbated in manifold ways when the focus becomes worldwide, when the Mennonite groups resulting from missionary work are included in our total frame of reference. The new Mennonite congregations and conferences in most parts of the world— over and above the vast complexities present in the European–North American Anabaptist-Mennonite stream—also reflect the varied cultural milieus of those regions. Consequently, there are literally hundreds of Mennonite groups today. The total "Mennonite body" goes far beyond the original ethnic identity which has been the focus here. And it is in this world setting that we can shape the only viable definition of the inclusive Mennonite society, a definition that needs to be stated in theological terms: Mennonites are those people who adhere to a historical Anabaptist system of theology and practice, which uniformly is taken to mean the belief *and* practice systems.

The Future

The "Mennonite disease" is a variant of a universal religious phenomenon. As was indicated above, social differentiation is characteristic of modernizing societies (Wach 1951, 205ff.). Social differentiation historically has been partly the differentiation of religion from society—that is, the way in which societal beliefs, values, and institutions have increasingly identified religion as being a separate factor, influenced by and influencing society.

But the differentiation of religion itself is equally predictable and pre-determined. As was indicated above, Mennonite schisms have not concerned so much the propositional aspects (theology and beliefs) as the social applications of those beliefs. That is, the divisions have not concerned the central issues of faith, but how they are to be incarnated in real life. This corresponds to Wach's thesis: "We must re-emphasize the fact that it is objective religion which is influenced by social differences such as occupation, rank, and property. These differences do not immediately affect subjective religion" (234). Wach proposes that religious experience, "being fundamental," allows religious communion on an intimate level, but it is the "objectification and formulation of this experience [which] will lead to division and separation" (234). The Anabaptist-Mennonite tradition's extreme emphasis on the "objectification and formulation of this experience" has created the tendency to division and schism. Empirical proof of this thesis is readily apparent within the Mennonite brotherhood, but needs further cross-religious-group comparisons.

There is in Mennonitism no central nervous system or brain that presides over the body. Mennonite society is more like a single-celled paramecium which moves as a coherent entity but, lacking a central brain to tell it where it ought to go, is hence a very fluid mass. There have been attempts here and there by individuals to challenge and to lead, but Mennonite society in general is like an acephalous body in which each sector affirms that it is led by Christ himself. At times, of course, this creates a condition that is very ambiguous indeed.

In our attempts to understand Mennonite society's tendency toward schism, an "ideological conflict model" may be most helpful in putting the pieces together. This model assumes conflict between an ideologically constituted religio-ethnic group attempting to retain its identity while at the same time being bombarded by competing systems of ideas which purport to explain or interpret the beliefs better than did the old interpretations. This conflict can be seen as an attempt to conceptualize or verbalize the poorly articulated belief system which obtained earlier in the face of new options. (Appendix A provides further analysis of this model.)

Thus the fundamentalist-modernist debate in Mennonite society could be interpreted as the controversy between the retention of an old or traditional articulation of a world view and the adoption of a new one, seemingly more adequate and relevant. Although the actors would not see it in these terms—being rather convinced that truth and error or heresy and orthodoxy were at stake—from a more disinterested position, the exchange of "plausibility structures" would appear to be the real nature of the struggle (B. Hostetler 1987, 201ff.).

The *internal* causes for change, discussed as "dilemmas of institutionalization" by O'Dea and Aviad (1983), can be seen as structurally fixed: that is, already inherent in all social structures are the causes for their modification. Even though Parsons maintains that a theory of social change cannot be constructed at this stage of social science development, he suggests that "structured strain" is a distinct possibility in social structures and a potent instigator of social change (Parsons 1951, 480–531). "Another very important possibility lies in the progressive increase in strains in one strategic area of the social structure which are finally resolved by a structural reorganization of the system" (ibid., 493).

This approach to social change has been called the "structural disequilibrium" theory, a concept which has been promoted especially by Godfrey and Monica Wilson (L. Harder 1962, 28). According to this theory, structural disequilibrium emerges "when the existing social structure is inconsistent with itself, and pressures within the group operate in contrary directions" (ibid.). Harder, taking this theory as the central focus of an analysis of the Mennonites as a sectarian group, states, "It is precisely those sects which show most concern for maintenance of the two decisive criteria for their existence in their most pristine form—voluntarism and separatism—that wrestle most with the problem of disequilibrium" (31).

In the discussion of the "dilemmas of institutionalization" in Chapter 17, I deal with eight conflicting or contradictory processes which have operated in Mennonite society. The conclusion, seemingly already thrust upon us here, is that numerous factors will continue to contribute to social change and schism. Some factors will originate in the larger society—but these external factors cannot provide the full explanation. We are forced to consider both the "structural disequilibrium" theory and the "ideological conflict" theory in order to arrive at a full understanding of social change, especially schism, in Mennonite society. Finally, of course, these theories themselves must be placed in the context of the minority-majority context elaborated upon throughout this work.

The Mennonite sojourn with schism has not gone unlamented.

Through the centuries many sensitive and faithful believers have called for a unity in the spirit if not in organization. The General Conference Mennonite Church, which emerged in 1847–50 to unite all Mennonites, is a case in point. Mennonites usually assume informally that any movement to unite Mennonites will result in another split! Nevertheless, the ecumenical spirit among Mennonites has been growing. Since this phenomenon is so protean and relatively recent, it is not possible to provide substantive discussion and analysis. But it is clear that increasing cooperation in program organizations like the Mennonite Central Committee, Mennonite Mutual Aid, Mennonite Disaster Service, and Mennonite Colleges and Seminaries, to name just a few, shows that Mennonites can work together even if they cannot fully agree on how faith is expressed in religious experience and lifestyle.[4]

The most important area of unification is in the conference structures. Unification here has been slow in coming because of the symbolism involved in joining church structures. Church organizations tend to have imbedded in them the "sacred canopy of truth," and it is difficult to relinquish them. However, this area is also undergoing change; February 1, 1988, was a significant day because it designated the official coming-together of the Old Mennonite and the General Conference Mennonite conferences of Ontario and Quebec into the Mennonite Conference of Eastern Canada. This process took at least ten years of effort and premature starts, but its time had come, according to most members. There are plans and actions underway for the unification of other conferences of Old Mennonites and General Conference Mennonites in areas of the United States where there are considerable pockets of both groups in juxtaposition.

Although there is little empirical evidence to substantiate it, it appears that it is the Mennonite practicality and pragmatism which has caused members to work together. That is, the commitment to stewardship and effectiveness has caused many Mennonites to merge their various organizations and thus avoid duplication, competition, and antagonism. Some agencies, such as the Mennonite Mutual Aid program, have merged, while others, like publishing, are still separate.

But there is an even simpler sociological explanation for the unification movement, and that is the "circulation of membership" in church organizations. The Civilian Public Service program of World War II, Mennonite Central Committee relief and service programs since 1920, attendance at various Mennonite and BIC colleges, service in Mennonite Disaster Service, and many other structures have brought Mennonites of the many groups together. These contacts cause them to recognize each other as "cousins" and discover that it was inertia and isolation that had contributed to the suspicion and avoidance of each other (C. Dyck 1967, 304–6). In fact, an "MCC" church idea is emerging as a strong force for a final unification. Most "ecumaniacs" of Mennonite persuasion know that probably the most effective mechanism resulting from this circulation of membership was intermarriage. No major study of this phenomenon has been carried out, but it is commonly accepted as having been one of the most powerful leavens in the lump of unity.

At present Mennonite society is composed of those who have come into the society by way of birth and marriage, the missionary outreach, and individual volition. But the distinction between these three avenues is not as clear as most Mennonites and others would like to believe. There have been many persons who have joined the Germanic Mennonite congregations because of individual and group evangelistic efforts. On the other hand, in mission churches that have been in existence for more than one generation there are many birthright Mennonites. The population table of the contemporary Mennonite family enhances our perspective on the worldwide family, but it obscures the bewildering variety and heterogeneity of this world-girdling fraternity of Mennonites. It is in this confusing and bewildering cauldron of crosscurrents that the Mennonite movement is attempting to develop a coherence, but it is creating numerous "spin-offs" and unifying movements in the process. Many schisms, changes, and influences continue to create stresses and strains in Mennonite society and on its unity. These internal and external forces are discussed in the following chapters.

Chapter Sixteen

External Threats to Mennonite Identity

Increasingly, Mennonite scholars are talking about a crisis in Mennonite identity. As early as 1968, Paul Peachey stated: "American Mennonites today are undergoing a deep crisis of identity. Thanks to the runaway pace of change in American life, the cultural and psychic substance of Mennonite solidarity is rapidly dissolving" (1968, 243). As evidence of a continuing concern with the threat of identity loss, a conference held in 1986 focused directly and candidly on the subject; the conclusion of this convocation of scholars was that the Mennonite experiment may indeed be at a critical crossroads (Redekop and Steiner 1988).

That Mennonite society has changed from its first century is perfectly obvious, but the reasons for the change are so complex that it is very difficult to identify them. This is especially true because, as has been maintained from the first page of this book, the dialectical interaction between the various host societies and the Mennonites has been at the heart of the developing Mennonite organism (see Chart A.1).

Another factor which makes this analysis so precarious is the fact that the Mennonite project has such diverse parameters: (1) Mennonite groups have continued to immigrate to North America from 1683 to the present; thus, new groups have continually joined the mainstream, each with a different set of understandings of who they are. (2) These immigrant groups have settled in different parts of the continent, in differing rural-urban contexts and situations, increasing the differences they experience once they have arrived. (3) The cultural and social differences of each of these groups have meant a different dynamic in relationship to the host society, as, for example, the temperance movement. Thus, the more recent immigrant groups, who consume alcohol because doing so was a practice in the European or Russian context, have reacted differently from those groups who have been in North America for several centuries. (4) The differential rate at which the various groups have entered into the broader institutional structure of the Mennonite world and even beyond, such as education, has exacerbated even further the great amount of variation in the way external forces have moved into the Mennonite psyche. (5) The spectrum of Mennonite groups representing varying degrees of conservatism or progressivism, from the Old Orders to the most "cosmopolitan" Mennonite groups, makes an inclusive analysis of the influences from the host society very difficult to describe. Nevertheless, it is obvious to the careful observer that the influences are not different in degree, but only in kind and in time.

Another reason for the lack of understanding of the causes of change has been the paucity of studies that have attempted to document the epochal struggle. The Mennonite Experience in America series, just now coming off the press, is for the first time providing unified information and perspectives on this process.[1]

It is presumptuous, for the above and other reasons, to attempt to document and discuss the ways in which the larger society has impinged on the Mennonite community. But it is equally improper not to discuss these forces. So we must leave to the side more specific social events like Puritanism, the temperance movement, the first and second Great Awakenings, the Moral Rearmament movement, the National Council of Churches, and many other factors which undoubtedly affected individuals and congregations at various times and places. The reader is referred to the Mennonite Experience in America series, as well as to specific topical references in the *Mennonite Encyclopedia* and other sources, for more specific discussions.

The extreme difficulty of speaking in a systematic fashion about environmental forces on the Mennonite society is illustrated by the multitude of voices from within the community regarding the outside influences and their significance. These voices are often sharply delineated and aggressively promoted, thus increasing the turbulence and undoubtedly helping to shape the change. An excerpt of one such view will introduce us to the awareness of a fundamental crisis in contemporary Mennonite society; George R. Brunk II, one of the leaders in the Mennonite tent revival movement of the 1950s, wrote recently in *A Crisis among Mennonites:* "The historic practices of the Mennonite church are seriously threatened from two directions—education and publication. In our schools there is doctrinal erosion. In our literature truth is mixed with error" (1983, 1).

Prophets of doom are not new to the Mennonite experience. In fact, this form of pronouncement regarding change has been almost generic to Mennonites—they have always spoken out on many sides of an issue. However, in recent years, the tempo and shrillness of these pronouncements have increased, and often they predict the early demise of Mennonite society.[2]

Although Anabaptist-Mennonite history is replete with illustrations of strong-minded differences of opinion and confrontations between proponents of opposing views, the particular anxiety giving rise to these predictions of disintegration is less than a hundred years old. It is rooted largely in the emergence of what has come to be known as the modern individualistic period. Some historians and sociologists would maintain that the reasons for the crisis is the loss of spiritual vitality through the transformation of the Mennonite group from a religious movement to an ethnic society (Francis 1948; D. Kraybill 1988). Still others assert the exact opposite, that the Mennonite "peoplehood" tradition has been lost and/or exchanged for a watered-down middle-of-the-road American Christendom, of either a middle-class denominational or a neo-evangelical fundamentalist variety (F. Epp 1977; Sawatsky 1973; Schlabach 1980). Another group suggests that Mennonite society is simply a late entrant into the "civil religion" scene of America, in which *religiosity,* of whatever brand, is more important than the substance (Herberg 1960; P. Toews 1983). In any case, many Mennonites believe that the Mennonite church is "falling away from the faith" and is in need of revival, while other Mennonites conclude that something more than revival is needed. These latter tend to approach Mennonite society from, and promote, a more analytical and scientific view of its faith and theology (Goertz 1988).

A "spiritual" view of the Mennonite predicament need not exclude or negate a sociological analysis of the faith and belief of the group. Therefore, in this chapter, we will look briefly at the major external belief systems or ideologies that have made inroads and changed the complexion of the Mennonite faith.

Major Emphases in Orthodox Anabaptist Practice

In earlier chapters, the Mennonite *belief system* and *institutions* were presented and analyzed. Here, I shall begin with a baseline of general orientations and values that constitute the Mennonite system in order to show how these have changed and been eroded by external forces.

As we have seen, it has been proposed that the early Anabaptist-Mennonite movement was a unified and coherent religious system. This view was articulated and perpetuated by a justly famous article entitled "The Anabaptist Vision." In it, H. S. Bender stated, "Anabaptism had not only clearly defined goals, but also an action program of definiteness and power" (1957a, 31). Bender then delineated succinctly the elements of this Anabaptist vision: (1) discipleship, (2) a new concept of the church, and (3) an ethic of love and nonresistance. Others, such as Horsch, Friedmann, Hershberger, and Littell, have supported this position that a coherent system of belief and doctrine has characterized and defined Mennonites throughout their history. Recently, this rather neat and categorical position has been sharply challenged by the polygenetic-origin view of Anabaptism, a view which suggests that there was no central or coherent system of faith and beliefs (Stayer, Packull, and Depperman 1975). An increasing amount of evidence suggests that the polygenetic thesis is much more accurate. In any case, the Anabaptist-Mennonite belief system certainly includes the elements Bender listed, as well as elements elaborated by others. Only some of the most important patterns of behavior relevant for the analysis in this chapter can be noted here:

1. *Rejection of a state church.* The extensive scholarship that has retrieved the early dynamics of Anabaptism strongly affirms that the original Anabaptists rejected the idea of a church that was supported by the state. Fritz Blanke, a careful student, says that "Anabaptists sought a free church in the double sense: a congregation free from the state and based upon voluntary membership" (1957, 60). Grebel and his colleagues simply refused to recognize the *Volkskirche* as the authentic church of Jesus Christ. This has been a central position and teaching of Anabaptism ever since, as we saw in Chapter 4.

2. *Rejection of participation in state activities.* Again it is Blanke who states: "Grebel did not only demand withdrawal from the *Volkskirche;* in the same letter to Müntzer he rejected the participation of the Christian in the life of the state. In the opinion of his group the Christian should accept no civil office or military service" (61). Although since that time there has been some variation, Anabaptists have generally avoided par-

ticipation in the affairs of the state, although they have recognized it, accepted its protections, and prayed for it (see Chapter 13).

3. *A separated life*. The Anabaptists' concept of the kingdom of God and of the church—which they conceived as the means of establishing the kingdom—demanded an absolutist ethic for life; this meant the "rejection of all historical relativities. Anabaptism tried to cast aside all historical adaptations to the institutions of society which were regarded as compromise of the pure gospel. Historically this radical criticism placed them against the very structure of the society of the day" (J. L. Burkholder 1957, 137). This separated life called for an absolute and literalistic following of the commands of Christ, which included mutual love, mutual aid, honesty and integrity, sacrificial and simple living, frugality, and responsibility.

4. *A disciplined community*. As indicated above, the Anabaptists stressed absolute obedience. However, because this could not occur in a vacuum, to maintain the attitude and reality of obedience necessitated a strong binding-loosing process. In fact, it has been proposed by some that binding and loosing was the central dynamic of Anabaptism (J. Yoder 1967); here, however, it is assumed rather to be a means to achieve the end of absolute radical obedience described above. The strict discipline which culminated in both excommunication and the ban in its extreme form is almost unique with the Mennonite church and, at least in part, explains the schisms that have plagued it (C. Redekop 1970).

5. *Mutuality and mutual aid*. As has already been proposed in so many ways, the mutuality of economic, social, and personal life is a hallmark of Mennonite society (Fretz 1947). The range of mutual assistance which has informed Mennonite congregations and communities for centuries continues to amaze non-Mennonites, and to be taken for granted by Mennonites. The structural and behavioral evidences of this impulse continue to change and develop, but they spring from the same source—the communal ethic which Mennonites claim came from the fledgling Christian community at Antioch (Hernley 1970).

With these baselines of Mennonite behaviors as axiomatic, we turn to some of the major external social and cultural influences on Mennonite life.

The Influence of Pietism

Pietism is a "quiet conventicle-Christianity which is primarily concerned with the inner-experience of salvation and only secondarily with the expression of love toward the brotherhood and not at all in a radical world of transformation" (Friedmann 1949, 11). Pietism emerged in the late 1600s in response to what was called the "cold" Reformed and Lutheran orthodoxy; it emphasized a "heartfelt" religion (Krahn 1959, 176).

Although the relation between Anabaptist-Mennonites and Pietism is still not fully documented, Krahn's pronouncement may be taken as authoritative: "No other single religious movement has had such an impact on the Mennonites in all countries with the exception of the Netherlands as Pietism" (ibid.). Though the theologies of Pietism and Anabaptism were different, they did influence each other. The various forms of early Pietism spread over Europe and thus almost always touched Mennonite communities. Friedmann believes that the inroads of Pietism among Mennonites began to develop because the pietistic stance made the Anabaptists' "course easier under the pressure of state and of church, which became unbearable and which took place after the great inner power of the sixteenth century had declined" (Friedmann 1949, 13).

In general, Krahn notes, "the pietist impact upon Mennonites emphasized self-analysis, stressed a personal emotional experience to conversion, and resulted in a non-confirmed daily life with strong emphasis on personal devotion and awaiting the return of Christ" (176). These elements became incorporated into Mennonite family and congregational life in many areas of Europe and spread to Russia, where their emergence contributed to the schism of the Mennonite Brethren from the Kirchliche church in the 1850s (J. B. Toews 1977, 134).

The Pietist influence in America evolved partly through the earlier Mennonite exposure to the movement in Europe, but there was also a Pietist influence already established in America which infiltrated the Mennonite community (Krahn 1959, 179; MacMaster 1985, 157–82). One of the most thorough studies of the influence of Pietism on Mennonites focuses on the Pennsylvania Old Mennonites. Beulah Hostetler documents the proximity and openness to Pietism of the Pennsylvania Mennonites, an influence which expressed itself for many decades (1987, 32ff.).

Before long, Pietism became an important factor in many of the schisms among American Mennonites. One of the earlier divisions, known as the River Brethren, split in 1770 (MacMaster 1985). Later, in 1847, the Oberholtzer faction broke from the main body of Mennonites and—following the arrival of a major segment of that group in the Mennonite migrations from Russia after 1874—became one of the three largest North American Mennonite streams (B. Hostetler 1987).

Although a definitive analysis has not yet been done, it is generally agreed that Pietism had both positive and negative effects. Positively, it helped to awaken and revitalize dead and traditional Mennonite orthodoxy (Krahn 1959, 178). The emphasis on spreading the gospel and sharing the "joy of salvation" was also productive and useful, since Mennonites tended not to be very expressive in their faith. Furthermore, Pietism often gave Mennonites the zeal to live as well as to share their beliefs and ideals (P. Friesen 1978, 212ff.). On the negative side, the Pietist movement tended to deemphasize the importance of the covenanted community and the stress on discipleship or "following Christ," which Pietists understood somewhat more subjectively.

The stress on the conversion experience tended to direct the Christian life away from pervasive ethical concerns and forced it toward a more verbal orthodoxy as well as toward an enjoyment and analysis of the resultant emotional experiences (Friedmann 1949, 86ff.). It is probable that Pietism's most lasting influence was in helping provide the milieu in which revivalism and fundamentalism were able to enter the Mennonite tradition (Friedmann 1949, 87–88; Kraus 1979, 175). Eberhard Arnold, the founder of the Society of Brothers, described the very essence of Pietism when he said, "The pietist feels satisfied when he experiences the personal sense of salvation and the presence of the personal God" (Friedmann 1949, 88). A major conflict has existed between the Anabaptist tradition and Pietism on this very point: Is Christianity primarily a matter of personal and subjective experience, or does it also include the vital and relevant experience of living an ethical life?

Pietism in some form has infiltrated all Mennonite conferences in North America; it continues to inform the religious ritual and religious lifestyle. Singing and prayer, including the freer expression of emotion and joy, reflect the Pietistic emphasis. The increasing Mennonite openness in relating to people of other denominations where religious expression is more free derives in large part from the attraction to this mode of worship (Friedmann 1949; J. B. Toews 1977).

The Impact of Liberalism and Modernism

The role that liberalism and modernism have played and still play within Mennonite society, especially in America, is not clearly understood, nor has any definitive analysis of their inroads been done. Before we take a brief look at their influence, a review of the definitions of these terms is in order. Liberalism and modernism emerged in the larger context of rationalism, which can be designated as that philosophical orientation stressing the ability of reason to comprehend reality independent of outside forces. Kant and Hegel capture many of the central elements of this movement. Liberalism has at least two wings—the political and the theological. Theological liberalism, which concerns us here, "always asserted the claims of reason against a petrified orthodoxy . . . [and] sought freedom for diversity in belief in the church. In the modern period . . . [it] declared the need for theology to incorporate the basic values, aspirations, and attitudes which are associated with modern democratic culture" (Halverson and Cohen 1958, 207). Liberalism rejected some of the traditional orthodoxies of Christianity, such as total depravity and predestination. Modernism—also as applied to theology—was concerned with "reinterpreting traditional Christian beliefs so as to make them intelligible in the light of the scientific understanding of the world and of historical knowledge" (ibid., 233). Modernism has been defined as an attempt to interpret the Christian faith to modern man, a "movement or tendency in Christianity towards the reinterpretation and restatement of the traditional beliefs and doctrines in accordance with the findings of recent criticism and historical research" (258).

The casual observer of Mennonite society could be tempted to reach a quick and superficial conclusion—that almost no possibility exists for liberalism and modernism to have affected the Mennonites in any way. And indeed, one could with some justification reach such a conclusion. These movements have had very little opportunity to bring their influence to bear upon Mennonitism, for two reasons. First, there was practically no intercourse between Mennonites and theologians who were a part of prevailing Christendom. Secondly, there was harsh and drastic opposition to the ethos of rationalism in Mennonite thought. In spite of these barriers, however, there have been some inroads, basically by way of the institutions of higher learning.[3]

Most of the evidence pertaining to the infiltration of liberalism and modernism into Mennonite society centers on the two colleges that existed at the turn of the century—Bethel College and Goshen College—and the professors and administrators who operated them. Bethel College, almost from its founding, was under fire from its more conservative detractors.[4] The same was true of Goshen College, which was closed during the 1923–24 school year because many of the faculty had either voluntarily resigned or were forced to resign because of accusations of modernism. To a large extent Bluffton College was the beneficiary of this fallout of liberal and modernist professors who were forced to leave Goshen College.

Has there been liberalism or modernism in the Mennonite church? One of the most ardent crusaders for fundamentalism clearly thought so. In the foreword to his *Mennonite Church and Modernism* (1924), John Horsch stated: "The Mennonite Church of today finds itself face to face with the most insidious foe of the Old Bible faith. Modernism is a perversion and denial of the fundamentals of the faith yet, by an obvious distortion of church history, it claims to be true Mennonitism, the faith of the Fathers" (1). This book, along with many other of Horsch's writings, was directed at a small coterie of college professors who were accused of being the infiltrators. Persons are named specifically in the polemic—and those accused responded in kind. For example, J. E. Hartzler responded by stating, "I am quite in agreement with the common opinion that the booklet . . . is decidedly unscientific, inaccurate, unfair, unreasonable and uncalled for" (quoted in Horsch 1926, 28).

Other voices joined Horsch in opposing the influence of modernism and liberalism. One of these was *The Sword and Trumpet*. This journal emerged to carry the banner against modernism wherever, among Mennonites, it could find subscribers. The first issue carried an extensive series of introductory articles on the controversy. The first editorial concluded: "There is grave danger that the devil will cut our flock of sheep in two, and chase the one part into the desert of Modernism, and the other into the wolf-infested hills of Calvinism" (Brunk 1928, 3). The journal appeared for ten years until the death of the first editor, George R. Brunk. After five years of silence it appeared again, with its intention stated as "specializing in the defense of our distinctive doctrines" (Brunk 1943).

The General Conference Mennonite Church of North America, especially in the Midwest, also became increasingly influenced by liberal theology and mainline Christian groups. From 1908 to 1917, the conference affiliated with the Federal Council of Churches. In 1917, after considerable controversy, the conference finally withdrew, concluding that the Federal Council was maintaining too positive a stance toward "higher criticism, secret societies and modernism in theology" (C. Smith 1950, 689). But, as became clear later, the controversy had only begun. The attractions of higher criticism and liberal theology continued and seemed to center around the Bethel College faculty at North Newton, Kansas (Haury 1981, 225–53).

The modernism versus traditional faith controversy smoldered for years before it created a polarization throughout the General Conference, as congregations, conferences and even families aligned themselves with modernism or fundamentalism, which was emerging as a response to modernism (ibid., 247ff.). The irony of this condition was that fundamentalism was no more in harmony with historic Anabaptism than was modernism. So, in many ways, the emphasis was misplaced and the battle was spurious. In any case, the conflict came to a head through a withdrawal, from the Bethel College supporting constituency, of a conservative segment in the General Conference Mennonite Church. These dissidents, along with several related smaller groups— especially the Evangelical Mennonite Brethren, which had no school of its own—joined forces to establish Grace Bible Institute (1945), a fundamentalist school, which now calls itself Grace College of the Bible.[5]

Modernism, very loosely defined, did attract some of the ablest and most educated members of the Mennonite family; this becomes clearer as more material on the Bethel College controversy is published. One example was C. C. Regier, a historian on the faculty of Bethel College from 1912 to 1919, who was forced to resign amid bitter and acrid attacks and counterattacks in 1919. Regier, imbibing the optimistic spirit of the pre-World War I period, felt that "the world was improving and progressing, and that mankind was learning wisdom" (Sprunger 1984, 11). Liberally educated and confident in the rational power of the human mind, Regier increasingly alienated himself from the wider conservative Mennonite community and finally became a casualty of what he termed "the conflict between conservatism and liberalism" at Bethel, although he was an excellent teacher and was strongly supported by many of the students.[6]

The modernism-conservatism debate lasted from about 1900 to 1940, although there were lingering vestiges into the 1940s with the coming of the Revised Standard Version of the Bible in 1946. During that decade, *modernism* was still a catchword; it is still possible to encounter its use today.

Inroads by Fundamentalism and Evangelicalism

The modernist debate was one of several that were taking place in the Mennonite community, for fundamentalism was coming on strong in the 1920s and 1930s. Although admitting the power of fundamentalism and evangelicalism, Harold S. Bender states, "Mennonites . . . see more clearly than before that they belong neither in the Modernist nor Fundamentalist camps, but have a satisfactory Biblicism and evangelicalism of their own with its unique Anabaptist heritage" (1956a, 419). This seems to be a bit optimistic.

The fundamentalist and evangelical movement has had many variations and hence cannot be described easily or succinctly; at the same time it is relatively easy to point to its origin and theological heritage.[7] Although in some circles a sharp distinction may be made between fundamentalism and neo-evangelicalism, from the perspective here the latter is largely a more recent version of the former, so I shall discuss both. Fundamentalism derived at least in part from Puritan Protestantism, which included the Great Awakening, and from Wesleyanism, and these two movements worked together to create the phenomenon of American revivalism, symbolized by C. G. Finney. Revivalism stressed individual salvation, evangelism as the mission of the church, nondenominational Christianity, lay-oriented theology, and a conservative biblical position (Kraus 1979, 44ff.). This revivalistic tradition in varying forms contributed to fundamentalism, which was expressed by persons like D. L. Moody, R. A. Torrie, and Billy Sunday (Kraus 1979; Marsden 1980; Sandeen 1970).

Having grown out of revivalism, fundamentalism has many traits in common with it. At the same time, fundamentalism is almost universally recognized as having certain distinctive characteristics: an emphasis on simplified formulations of essential or fundamental doctrines, an emphasis upon the Bible as the source book for theological data which is then used to create theological formulations, an insistence on the infallibility and inerrancy of the Bible, and an emphasis on conversion as a private and spiritual experience. Although these elements are basic to a description of fundamentalism, they have been expanded in a variety of formats and settings (Marsden; Sandeen; and Kraus 1979, 54–59). One fundamentalist creed, that of the World Christian Fundamentals Association (1919), listed the following beliefs:

1. The inerrancy of the Bible, verbally inspired of God and final infallible authority in faith and life.
2. The Virgin birth of Christ.

3. The substitutionary atonement of Christ.

4. The bodily resurrection of Christ.

5. The imminent, personal, and premillennial return of Christ.

6. The creation of the universe by God in six days according to the Scriptures.

7. The bodily resurrection of the just to everlasting blessing and unjust to everlasting conscious punishment. (Kauffman and Harder 1975, 110)

One must also recognize that fundamentalism tended to be a rationalist system with an emphasis on correct and personal experience, traits which were readily found in the emerging North American society (Kraus 1979, 55ff.).

There seems to be general agreement that fundamentalism was a major influence on the Mennonite society:

> By 1937 Fundamentalism had become a solid force within the "Old" Mennonite church—the largest Mennonite group in America. That year the editor of the *Mennonite Cyclopedic Dictionary,* Daniel Kauffman, declared in the article on "Fundamentalism" that the Mennonite Church was "firmly committed to the Fundamentalist faith, including some unpopular tenets of faith which many so-called Fundamentalists reject." The conservative *Sword and Trumpet* magazine added that by their adherence to Biblical literalism in "all things" Mennonites were the true Fundamentalists whereas periodicals such as *Moody Monthly,* the *King's Business* and the *Sunday School Times* neglected "the two central pillars of Gospel fundamentalism, Nonresistance and Nonconformity to the world." (Sawatsky 1973, 72)

As this passage implies, it was not an uncritical acceptance. But because fundamentalism followed the revival movements, it had some foothold already in the Mennonite church, especially in the eastern, more conservative groups (B. Hostetler 1987; Sawatsky 1973, 1977; Schlabach 1980).[8]

It should be noted, however, that fundamentalism was as concerned about combating liberalism and heresy in the church as it was in stressing conversion. Because of this, it tended to polarize Mennonite congregations and conferences along the lines raised by these issues. It is still not clear exactly how fundamentalism and Mennonitism interacted. Paul Toews offers the provocative thesis that fundamentalism was not really accepted wholesale by Mennonites, and that it was really a misplaced controversy in which the real issue was modernization, including the change of language from German to English (P. Toews 1983).

Although it is not possible in this context to evaluate the consequences of fundamentalism on the Mennonite tradition, Sawatsky makes the plausible point that fundamentalism's critique of pacifism forced the Mennonites to part company with the liberal view of pacifism and to develop their own interpretation which was compatible with fundamentalist teachings (1973, 173 passim). Although liberalism was never a strong factor in Mennonite circles, it still served as a foil for the introduction of fundamentalism into many Mennonite communities. That Mennonites were ever susceptible to the inroads of fundamentalism seems almost ironic since the scientific world view was never fully adopted by even a minority of the Mennonite community. Thus the very core of fundamentalism—a reaction against the increasing threat of the modern scientific ethos and world view—had little real claim on Mennonites in general. In spite of this, the influence was strong (H. Bender 1956a).

One reason for this influence were the itinerant evangelists and preachers of the fundamentalist gospel from other denominations actively wooing Mennonite congregations, a great ferment of reconversion the Mennonite congregations as mission fields to be harvested. With preachers of the fundamentalist gospel from other denominations actively wooing Mennonite congregations, a great foment of reconversion and repudiation of heresy followed. Congregations split as the "orthodox" pulled away from the "liberal" or "worldly." Bible schools emerged as a protest to the liberal colleges in the church, while some of the colleges were even shut down for short periods as the struggle between the two camps evolved (Schlabach 1980).

Although fundamentalism spread through every Mennonite conference in North America (of course, not all at the same time or at the same speed), it infiltrated most powerfully those groups which were small, such as the Holdeman, the Evangelical Mennonite Brethren, and the Evangelical Mennonite Church, and among those members who were isolated or marginal in terms of their relationship to a Mennonite church. Kauffman and Harder note: "Fundamentalist infiltration has been greatest in the MBC [Mennonite Brethren Church] and EMC [Evangelical Mennonite Church]. Elmer Martens predicts that the membership of the MBC is on a collision course because of it, and the EMC appears to have become so thoroughly committed to this form of orthodoxy that it has long ceased to be an issue among them" (109). The larger groups were able to withstand the pressures because of the in-group interaction of a larger mass of people. That is to say, the influence of an outside force is not as great in a larger group because the typical member has a far greater opportunity to relate to other Mennonites than is possible in a small group.

The more conservative groups—because of their intentional "separation from the world" and because of their conserving orientation regarding their heritage—did not move as quickly into the fundamentalist orbit. This resistance was also enhanced because of the geographical isolation in which they nurtured their faith. But even they slowly began to yield; now, in conservative circles, there are many small splinter groups who are adopting the fundamentalist orientation, stressing biblical truths and engaging in supporting evangelism and missions at home and abroad (B. Hostetler 1987; Kraus 1979; Sawatsky 1973).

In recent years neo-evangelicalism has emerged. Although in some ways it is different from fundamentalism, from a sociological perspective it can be considered an updated and modernized version of fundamentalism (Kraus 1979, 177–78). The issues addressed by both are much the same. Particularly as the two influence the Mennonite picture, it is difficult to determine much difference between them; and if there is a difference, it is not clear what difference that makes in the way either one affects the Mennonite church (ibid., 167ff.).

In any case, fundamentalism and neo-evangelicalism have made major inroads into the Mennonite tradition; in fact, they have been influential factors in the major divisions and conflicts found today in the Mennonite congregation. Almost every Mennonite congregation in every conference is confronted in some manner with their impact. Members are influenced by television and radio preaching which emphasize the experience of conversion to the neglect of the ethical implications of Christian faith; some are even led to question the traditional Mennonite emphasis on social service and concern. Since fundamentalism encourages a pronationalism position, capitalism and militarism are often the consequence. Congregations who promote these views are thus seeking pastors trained in the fundamentalism–neo-evangelical mode. Mennonite congregations are increasingly supporting the prophets of commercialized religion appearing in the mass media; they also send their dollars increasingly to interdenominational and nondenominational activities. Some congregations have moved so deeply into this general orbit that they have found the designation Mennonite embarrassing and have purged themselves of any outward signs of their heritage.

Some thoughtful Mennonite leaders see fundamentalism and neo-evangelicalism as the major threats to the survival of the Mennonite belief system. Yet the voices of protest dare not be raised too loudly for fear of creating even greater opposition and dissension in the congregations and of charges of departing from the evangelical faith. At this time, this issue represents one of the most explosive conflicts in Mennonite society in North America, for any attack on fundamentalism or evangelicalism is perceived by their defenders as blatant proof of apostasy (B. Hostetler 1987; Sawatsky 1977; Schlabach 1980).

It has often been argued that fundamentalism and evangelicalism are only the religious aspects of a larger socioreligious process of acculturation to cultural and social change—a position which I have assumed in this analysis. Yet, such a stance does not deny the validity of the significance of the religious reality which was expressed in these movements and the controversies which attended them.

It will be apparent from the above discussion that modernism and fundamentalism are interrelated phenomena, twins as it were, the one needing the other to develop a self-identity. As has been stated and implied in the above discussion, the modernist-fundamentalist struggle within Mennonite society may have been a confused, or even misplaced, one. What seems, rather, to be at the heart of the issue is a concern about keeping the traditional Mennonite practices of simplicity and nonconformity in the face of acculturating tendencies in American society and culture. And consequently the Old Order groups and the Hutterites have been barely affected by, if even aware of, this major threat and conflict.

That is to say, the theological principles and teachings of Mennonitism have never been seriously questioned by most Mennonite groups, although much of the rhetoric and pamphleteering seemed to use the language of the modernist-fundamentalist debate. The real questions have related much more to how Anabaptist-Mennonite congregational polity and lifestyle can be maintained in the midst of an urbanizing and increasingly educated membership. The rural community ethos no longer obtained, especially in the sector which was becoming increasingly educated (P. Toews 1983).

After reviewing the fundamentalist controversy at Goshen, Bethel, and Tabor, the colleges of the leading three conferences, Paul Toews states:

> The theology that had crept into the church was clearly not modernism. . . .
> Fundamentalism had come not in response to theological modernism but as part of the larger cultural transition. The loosening of traditional forms of authority, the shift from the lay to the professional ministry and the greater participation in the social order brought uncertainty—even anxiety—and also theological fundamentalism. . . .
>
> All of these episodes of fundamentalist controversy at Goshen, Bethel and Tabor and in their supporting denominations suggests that fundamentalism can be understood at least partly as a transitional response that emerged

during or immediately following alterations in the relationship between Mennonites and American culture. Theologically and culturally it was an antidote to rapid cultural change. For those who grasped fundamentalism in either form, it was a response of sureness to an unsettled condition. (1983, 256)

Fundamentalist-modernist language seemed to fit what the Mennonite church was experiencing, but the winds of social and cultural change soon swept the modernist-fundamentalist issues aside as Mennonites discovered that the real issue was more a maintenance of identity than a theological hair-splitting. Another historian has suggested that "the social or cultural implications of liberalism [and fundamentalism] were probably more important for most MC Mennonites in this context than were theological questions. . . . For good and for ill, Mennonite theology and Mennonite styles of life and institutional development were inextricably interwoven" (Juhnke 1983, 18, 23).

Secularization

Even though the topic of secularization is laced with unclarity and ambiguity, it is one that needs to be discussed. There are numerous other ways of referring to the focus, but for our purposes, we will retain the word *secularization* and use it to mean the process whereby Mennonites forsake the world view of the Anabaptist *Weltanschauung* and biblical beliefs, and adopt instead the prevailing world view of members of the larger society. It is tantamount to discussing the ways in which Mennonites have become "like the nations around them," to use Old Testament imagery.

It is difficult to define exactly the world view of the people in the larger secular society, but Robin M. Williams, an outstanding social scientist, suggested that the following "value-belief clusterings" define contemporary American society (1955, 179):

(1) activity and work;
(2) achievement and success;
(3) moral orientation;
(4) humanitarianism;
(5) efficiency and practicality;
(6) science and secular rationality;
(7) material comfort;
(8) progress;
(9) equality;
(10) freedom;

(11) democracy;

(12) external conformity;

(13) nationalism and patriotism;

(14) individual personality;

(15) racism and related group superiority.

If some system such as this is accepted, then it is possible to discuss the secularization process as it affects Mennonites.

E. K. Francis, a perceptive student of Mennonites, is one of the few scholars who has discussed secularization and Mennonites. He states at the conclusion of his major work on Mennonites, "As long as a Mennonite remains part of a local community in which [Mennonite traditional] values are still dominant, neither secularization or even apostasy are able to destroy his religious heritage entirely, or to eliminate altogether the social controls exercised by the church" (1955, 277). This statement proposes that secularization is a threat, and also suggests the mechanisms that will resist or attenuate its effects. In a sense, this is a tautological statement, but it is nevertheless true—Mennonites will retain their world view to the degree that they retain their community. Thus, to talk about secularization is to talk about the decay or the dissolution of the community. This process or possibility has already been discussed at great length in this volume, and it is probably redundant to discuss secularization separately, but it is appropriate to discuss what evidence there is that Mennonites have adopted the values Williams lists.

Ironically, Mennonites have not spent much effort in mapping and measuring secularization of values. Doing so is particularly difficult because a shift in values involves a chronological time span long enough to measure changes. But some parts and pieces are available and can be utilized. The Kauffman-Harder study, often referred to in this volume, contains the most extensive empirical research on secularization among Mennonites. If Kauffman and Harder's criteria are accepted as defining Anabaptism, then their conclusions can be considered valid. "With a few noted exceptions, doctrinal adherence to the Anabaptist vision has moved 12th-generation Anabaptists to a position that stands against the stream of society on most of the indicators employed in the study and hence may properly be called an autonomous variable of considerable importance" (330). The variables Kauffman and Harder used included associationalism, communalism, conversion, sanctification, devotionalism, general orthodoxy, and Anabaptist vision.

No other broad empirical research exists which tests the degree to which Mennonites have adopted secular values in contrast to their Mennonite beliefs. Community studies that have been made, however, tend to suggest that secularization has taken place (Baehr 1942; C. Redekop 1957). We can agree with these historians that Mennonites became involved in these larger theological and ecclesiological issues, but that they infused them with their own agenda. It is more difficult to prove the conclusion than it is to arrive at it, but the logic of the conclusion seems thoroughly warranted.

The problem, however, of analytically separating acculturation from loss of faith in Christian fundamental doctrines and Anabaptist principles still persists. The Kauffman-Harder research proposes that Mennonites have "modernized" and yet have not lost their orthodox commitments (328ff.). Secularization to the values of the dominant society, as defined by Williams's variables, would have taken place most in the areas of his numbers 2, 5, 7, 12, 13, and 14. These are at once among the most dangerous or threatening to the Mennonite way of life. Acceptance of even a few of Williams's values would spell trouble for the Mennonite community. Number 7, material comfort, has been a threat to Mennonites since World War II, when prosperity and affluence suddenly erupted in most Mennonite congregations. Many are predicting that affluence will destroy the church. But this is just one of the many serious secular threats to Mennonite identity. Some take comfort in the axiom that though there is attrition on the fringes, there is renewal and rebirth at the center of the movement (see Chart A.1).

Conclusions

At the beginning of this chapter, I delineated the key emphases of the Anabaptist movement as a baseline against which the threats to Mennonite identity could be measured. As has already been indicated, it is difficult to present a very convincing argument about what has really happened. On the one hand, as Kauffman and Harder say, the contemporary Anabaptists, the Mennonites, still adhere strongly to some basic Mennonite principles. But since the research methodologies and measures are not standardized and accepted by everyone, it is difficult to reach a definitive conclusion. Further, the factors or measures presented in this book do not correspond closely with the measures Kauffman and Harder used.

This points to the problem of finding solid empirical evidence for the arguments discussed by them, and by this book. A more difficult and confounding problem is the conceptualization of the issue in the first place. I have shied away from focusing on specific beliefs as the baseline for discussing external threats and have emphasized much more general systems of ideas and related behaviors, such as separation. Thus, the problem can be focused depending on which perspective is taken. From a church history perspective, the issue could be described as the denominationalization of the Mennonites, meaning by this the way Mennonite society is adopting the beliefs, ecclesiology, and practices of the predominant religious groups in North America. There is considerable support of this orientation.

From a theological perspective, the issue could be defined as the modernization of Mennonites, by which is meant the way in which the basic *Weltanschauung* of the Mennonites has been influenced by the increasing scientific-rational and relativistic milieu of the West. Another perspective is the psychological, by which is meant the degree to which Mennonites are increasingly becoming subjective and inner-oriented, deriving goals and norms from subjective consciousness and experience. There is, of course, also the sociological point of view, which conceives of the Mennonite movement as a social structure with values, beliefs, norms, institutions, and subjective states constituting the whole. The Mennonites must also be understood from this last point of view.

With these provisos, let us attempt some evaluation of how the baseline behavior systems introduced at the beginning of this chapter have been affected:

1. *Separation from the state church.* The rejection of a church aligned with the state has been largely unaffected by the factors discussed above. This is due not only to the Mennonite belief system itself, but also to the way American separation of church-state structures operates on all religious groups. Fundamentalism has posed a threat, in the way it has promoted support of identification with national purposes, but this tendency seems to have been stemmed by the "renewal" of the Anabaptist vision.

2. *Rejection of participation in the activities of the state.* Rejection of state-related activities may have suffered a bit more, owing basically to modernism, liberalism, and secularism. Mennonites increasingly are becoming enticed to become active in the affairs of the state and federal government because of the belief that the "Kingdom" can be assisted by the state and the nation. The increased witness to government discussed in Chapter 13 speaks to this point.

3. *A separated life.* The separated life has undergone a tremendous shift in the last few decades. Although the religious factors discussed in

this chapter, such as fundamentalism and liberalism, have caused a shift in values, a much more important factor has been economic adaptation made by Mennonites as they have moved from the agrarian to the urban way of life. Across the entire Mennonite spectrum, no issue is creating greater stresses and strains than the changes in lifestyle and practices.

4. *The disciplined life.* An evaluation of the change in the fourth baseline factor is most difficult to make. Most Mennonites would concur that there has been a tragic loss in the authority of the community of believers to achieve commitment to the central faith and behavior of the Mennonite ideal. A measure which was until recently cited as indicative of orthodoxy was the practice of excommunication and the ban; this practice is now almost completely discarded (H. Bender 1956b). Individualism, it is claimed, has eaten at the vital organs of Mennonitism so that there is no longer any vitality left. Although each person has his or her own measuring stick, it is generally assumed that the loss of discipline in the Mennonite church is a sign of the demise of the movement.

5. *Mutuality and mutual aid.* There is no doubt that there is a major renaissance taking place in the service area. There are institutional systems emerging to support the mutual aid practices in the Mennonite community, in health, retirement, education, social and liability insurance, financial foundations and credit unions, and professional organizations, such as the Mennonite Medical Association and the Mennonite Economic Development Association. Moreover, there is increasing emphasis in the theological teaching and congregational activities that the "Body of Christ" is a caring body, which suffers when any member suffers.

In conclusion, Mennonites have adopted external values, beliefs, norms, behaviors, lifestyles, and subjective awareness. The Mennonite story has been a saga of action and reaction, a dialectical relationship with the host societies from the inception of the movement. The Mennonite project is at any moment the sum total of the history of its ongoing inner dialogue influenced and limited by external forces.

Chapter Seventeen

Internal Threats to Mennonite Identity

Mennonite dualistic theology, producing a pervasive emphasis on nonconformity to the world and separation from it, has resulted in a congenital paranoia about "the world," which has fed on itself to produce a host of blind spots about how Mennonites relate to the larger world picture. Mennonites have tended to act as though there was only the inner world of Mennonites. The story is told of a news reporter in Ohio who interviewed an Amish farmer, asking him what he had to say about all this talk about environmental pollution. To this the Amish farmer replied, "Sir, that is a problem for you who live on the other side of this fence and is no concern of ours."

This story may be apocryphal, and unfair to the Amish, but it illustrates the Mennonite stance—an ostrichlike avoidance of the larger world. This dichotomizing practice, of assuming that the problems and threats come from the "outside" and that there are few, if any, problems within, has resulted in ignoring the internal processes and structures which are contributing to increasing difficulties. Of course, Mennonites have always been aware of internal conflicts—the continuing differences of belief and practice which result in increasing schism, as indicated throughout this book, reminds them of inner difficulties—but almost always such inner conflicts have been rationalized as a function of becoming "worldly" or secularized, to use modern terminology.[1] In this chapter we focus on some of the internal dynamics which are creating increasing changes and disequilibriums in the society.

The Dilemmas of Institutional Development

In its internal dimensions, Mennonite society faces all the dilemmas that any religious group confronts. Basic to these is the institutionalization problem by which the aesthetic, subjective, and ideological aspects of religious life become stabilized and standardized. O'Dea and Aviad suggest that religions, in order to survive and be functional, must become institutionalized in worship, theology, and organization. According to O'Dea and Aviad this takes place in the following steps: (1) feelings and attitudes must be stabilized by developing a cult (worship); (2) beliefs and theology must be preserved by developing a system of myths which relates power to experience (theology); and (3) the management of religious expression in the context of social differentiation and of labor and function must be structured (organization). Mennonite-Anabaptist society has responded to these specific institutionalization requirements all along the way.

But the institutionalization process creates dilemmas or problems for all religious communities. O'Dea and Aviad (57–64) list five dilemmas that confront every religious group in its process of institutionalization:

1. Mixed motivation, by which the single-minded charismatic direction becomes contaminated by structures and offices which secularize the original objectives.
2. The corruption of symbols, by which the originally holy and inspiring objects become—through repetition—prosaic and common.
3. The elaboration of charismatic "office" into bureaucratic structures, which results in the alienation of the rank-and-file membership from the religious officeholders. The inability of institutional structures to adapt to new circumstances and the tendency of incumbents to entrench themselves in their positions of power are two of the basic elements in this process.
4. The necessity to make religion relevant; by interpreting beliefs "in a concrete form under particular circumstances, they come to be accepted in a literalistic manner in which the original scope of the implication of the religious message may be lost" (61).

5. The need to control freedom of faith and voluntarism lest heresy and deviance make the religious system completely anarchistic; the power used for these ends contradicts the freedom.

These dilemmas have clearly been operative in the Anabaptist-Mennonite tradition, but, as has been indicated, Mennonites have not experienced these dilemmas in a unique way.[2] A specifically Anabaptist-Mennonite application of the "dilemma typology" would need to deal with the dilemmas O'Dea and Aviad present but also deal with some specific Mennonite problems. In the section following, this additional typology is adapted to the Mennonites.

1. *Separation versus stagnation.* Mennonites have taken very seriously the biblical motif "And be not conformed to this world" (Rom. 12:2). They have separated themselves from the secular and pagan values of society, a stance which most Christians would probably try to emulate, for few can affirm what is being piped into their homes via TV. But the paradox is that separation can breed stagnation. Mennonites would maintain that Christians must separate from the world; but perceptive Mennonites also remain in dialogue with it lest they become self-affirming, self-oriented, rigid, and stalemated. There is almost universal agreement among Mennonites that they have become increasingly ingrown, involuted, and static in their understanding of faith and life. There is of course considerable variation among both the liberal and the conservative groups, but many who are alienated or leave the Mennonite tradition cite this factor as the most destructive of Mennonite health and prosperity.

2. *Worldliness versus purity.* Mennonites have traditionally stressed separation from the world as a means to purity and holiness. "Love not the world" has been taken seriously; the tremendous irony is that the world is not necessarily "out there" but can just as easily exist in their own hearts, families, communities, and settlements. For example, the separated Old Colony Mennonite village may well have been as worldly as the most secular village in Mexico from which the Old Colony members separated. Secularism (paganism) can just as easily crop up in conservative fellowships as in New York's Bowery or on Chicago's Skid Row. The Mennonite subculture which has emerged in many Mennonite conferences and localities has tended to invert the faith-culture issue and has assumed that the Mennonite way of life was the essence of the Christian faith.

3. *Discipleship versus legalism.* The biblical emphasis on discipleship demands a discipline and conformity to Jesus' authority. In practice this

means that the church that wants to take Jesus' teaching seriously will need to lay down certain guidelines and announce certain expectations. Mennonites have identified specifically what were considered marks of following Christ. Again, the irony is that discipline can easily and surreptitiously lead to an arbitrary and authoritarian legalism, one which derives directly out of the gospel message. It seems that one cannot be achieved without the other. Most old order Mennonite groups have been defined as extremely legalistic, especially by those who have broken away to join the more evangelical groups.

4. *Biblicism versus obscurantism.* Anabaptist-derived groups have stressed Scripture as the only guide for life—"the Bible alone." This was the original cornerstone when Anabaptism was founded. In that early setting, however, the Bible was interpreted by the brotherhood and not by an arbitrary hierarchy. Since the Bible is relatively clear on most matters, especially if the secular value system is rejected as the norm, a narrow, doctrinaire, even heretical perspective can emerge. This is even more of a danger when one or a few leaders do all the interpreting. But simple biblicism has the other danger of not allowing the biblical message to permeate and energize the lives of the members. The Holy Spirit is hindered from full action. Here again, the dilemma: which is a more desirable end, extensive knowledge of the Scriptures with its inherent dangers of individualist interpretation, futile controversy and even heresy, or a unified, uniform, traditionalized, lukewarm experience?

5. *Traditionalism versus deterioration.* The significance of the "faith of the fathers"—that is, the meaning of the roots of a heritage or the importance of the history of God's dealing with His people—for a people is clear. "He who has no people has no God" is a dictum which the Mennonites have taken very seriously. Many groups have clung to the "faith once delivered" as their own forefathers have interpreted it, and are not now tempted by every new wind of doctrine that comes along. God has revealed Himself; therefore, it is less important to talk about the meaning of faith than to put it into practice.

Since cultural values are irrelevant, especially to conservative groups, that practice does not need to change. But accepting tradition as the norm can actually hasten a deterioration of the faith, since there is no renewal of the spirit or commitment when doubt and testing are absent. The Old Colony, for example, has not had its faith seriously tested; hence, it is not being renewed (C. Redekop 1978a).

6. *The missionary impulse versus self-preservation.* The original Mennonite charter was premised on a universalistic perception of the bibli-

cal message. Because of persecution and rejection, however, Mennonites were diverted from this early universalistic stance; instead, there was created a tendency to "retreat" from society and focus on self-preservation. This tension between an aggressive missionary movement and a self-defensive retreat has resulted in a continual breaking away of more "evangelistic and missionary groups." However, in that process, the peculiarly Mennonite theology as well as lifestyle have usually been sloughed off as departing Mennonites joined the Baptist, Missionary Alliance, or other missionary groups. On the other hand, those who have retreated from missionary work and effort are under attack both from the more mission-minded people as well as from their own subconscious awareness that the biblical message teaches that Christians must "go into all the world."[3]

7. *Relevance versus co-optation.* Anabaptist-Mennonite society has often been lauded and cited as having made significant contributions to the larger world. In reviewing the impact and relevance of the "left wing of the Reformation"—in other words, the Anabaptists—Ernest Payne writes, "It is time . . . [for] a reappraisal and recognition of all that western Christendom owes to the Left Wing of the Reformation" (1957a, 316). But the danger of such recognition and increasing relevance is cooptation or a yoking with unbelievers through which process the unique "salt" loses its savor. Countless Mennonites have believed that they could be leaven in the lump by going into politics, but few of these have retained any semblance of Mennonite piety (Hershberger 1958, 196). The same applies to Mennonites entering the world of business and commerce. Success in business generally tends to undercut the commitment to Anabaptist-Mennonite values in economics. The world of academics is similar. Great academic achievements and successes have tended to alienate the achievers from their own heritage.

The factors which explain this dilemma include the "minority" or "pariah" status of the Mennonites, at least as they perceive themselves. Along with that is the reluctance of those who have adopted the values of the "world" to admit membership in the Mennonite society. This is known as the group self-hatred syndrome. The other side of the coin requires us to note the over-compensating psychology involved—in other words, the willingness and even eagerness to sell out more than is necessary to indicate full acceptance of the values and norms of the dominant society. Of course, this phenomenon is not limited to Mennonites, but it certainly is operative among them (Dueck 1988).[4]

8. *Faith versus culture.* When different cultures or traditions confront each other, there is normally an amalgamation of traits—an amalgama-

tion that is less than rationally and philosophically derived. Thus, when the European nations invaded Africa, the resultant acculturation of the tribes was not accomplished with careful scientific analysis of the consequences for all concerned. The same has been true of Anabaptist experience. Whenever there has been an interaction between the Anabaptist-Mennonites and the host society, the cultural encounter has always been unequal. Hence, in the interaction of Mennonites in the larger socioreligious system, the interpenetration has never been rational and/or deliberate. As Mennonites have confronted accommodation with the surrounding society, the pressures have been so strong that Mennonites have often relinquished some important and central traits without awareness of what was happening. For example, in the desire to become more relevant and helpful to the surrounding society, Mennonites have relinquished the strong mutual aid thrust (Harder 1962). In the same way, nonresistance has been downplayed in many Mennonite groups as being inhibitive of outreach and church growth. In order to be successful in business activities, "old-fashioned" lifestyles have been sloughed off, and the traditional, telltale marks of hayseed Mennonites have been relinquished—"throwing the baby out with the bathwater."

At every point where the "baby" has been thrown out, the action has been justified on the grounds that the discarded trait was not important or was merely ethnic or was even unbiblical. In this manner, individualist Christianity has been largely accepted by Mennonites without their recognition that a central element in Anabaptist-Mennonite theology and life was being lost: "The humanist individualism which underlies the American creed is man-centered. . . . The divine order . . . is love for God and love for the brother and neighbor" (Hershberger 1958, 5; see also C. Redekop 1970, 125).

I began this section with a reference to Mennonite identity. Although it is obviously impossible to articulate a single, satisfying definition of identity, it is clear that the eight dilemmas just listed have created serious conflict and even schism among Mennonite community members. The cross-pressures and ambiguities have induced many members to question their identification with the Mennonite tradition; this process of questioning is almost synonymous with a loss of identity. For some time, many would agree, there has been a "crisis" in Mennonite identity; however, the outline of that crisis is not yet clear. It is probable that the extensive loss of Mennonite membership in the dominant sectors of Mennonitism (less so in the Hutterite and Amish sectors) and the many schisms are related directly to the sense of loss of Mennonite identity and direction.

Some Specific Issues in Internal Threats to Identity

One of the most disconcerting statements for committed Mennonites to hear is that Mennonites are defecting—"Did you hear that the 'Henry Yoder' family left the Mennonite church?" They would much rather learn of retention of members and growth in church membership; that is by far more reassuring. Probably better than any other factor, this syndrome reveals the Mennonite psyche as it is; it graphically reflects the basic insecurity many Mennonites have about being a Mennonite.

On the other hand, Mennonites are also beginning to be able to laugh at themselves and about themselves, as is exemplified by the *Mennonite Distorter*.[5] This is perhaps the best indication of a growing self-confidence as well as a degree of faith in their own future. Yet Mennonite humor still lacks the carefree flavor which is present in other minority-group humor.

So there is evidence of basic insecurity as well as of growth in confidence and selfhood. In light of this ambiguity, let us examine some major challenges to the future of Mennonitism.

Secularization

Secularization was defined above as the loss of belief in the transcendent, and an increasing acceptance of a materialistic world view, especially with respect to scientific parameters. It was proposed that secularization is making substantial inroads into the Mennonite community. For example, most Mennonites accept the parameters of modern science and technology. Herein lies an intriguing anomaly: it appears that these Mennonites have adopted new scientific perceptions while at the same time retaining the traditional world view (A. Reimer 1988). Somehow, and perhaps not uniquely, Mennonites have been able to compartmentalize their knowledge systems so that both evolutionary theory and the biblical faith have been accepted by most. A venerated biology professor at a leading Mennonite college on rare occasions would confide to a few of his friends that if his evolutionary views had been known by the college administration, or constituency, in the early years when science was still suspect—prior to 1940—he would have been relieved quickly of his revered position as a senior and beloved teacher.

Mennonites are aware of the threat of secularism from the "outside," but there is increasing concern that the Anabaptist-Mennonite religious impulse—which most contemporary Mennonites perceived as the "bond" holding together the entire edifice—may weaken or even dis-

solve by secularism from within. If change by itself brings secularization, as some Mennonites aver, then secularization has indeed long ago
overtaken Mennonite society. For some, particularly in earlier years,
any change toward modernity or the use of modern techniques represented a loss of transcendence in the community. Now, however, Mennonites are more prone to say that changes or modernization have little
to do with secularization.

In any case, secularization is more an internal issue; indeed, for
many, if not most, preservation of the core of the Anabaptist-Mennonite
heritage is the central concern. Whether that core can be protected and
nurtured is, of course, the unanswered question. But with the increased
attendance of Mennonite young people at Mennonite colleges, along
with the increasing esteem that the Radical Reformation is receiving in
society at large, it is possible or even probable that the process of
secularization may be lessened or attenuated.

Social Integration

The evidence indicates that integration with non-Mennonites is growing. Intermarriage of Mennonites and non-Mennonites in Canada has
increased between 1921 and 1981 (Driedger, Vogt, and Reimer 1983,
134). The Canadian statistics can easily be generalized to apply to the
United States as well, although U.S. census reports do not provide such
data. But marriage is only one form of integration. Cultural integration,
meaning the adoption of values and beliefs from another culture, is
certainly also present among Mennonites, especially among those who
live in the more urban areas and less protected environments (Goertz
1988). Mennonites' reading material, mass media consumption, and
leisure activities are very much like that of the world around them. So
the integration is continuing at an increasing tempo.

Except for the Old Orders of Mennonites, integration in professional
and business contexts is also moving ahead rapidly as the frontier continues to vanish. *The Perils of Professionalism* (Kraybill and Good 1982),
a competent book in its field, was produced by Mennonite writers. The
fact of its appearance as well as its message is an excellent barometer of
the degree to which Mennonites are immersed in the business and
professional arenas.

The "cosmopolitanization" of Mennonites is also developing with
great vigor. The Mennonite World Conference, held every five or six
years in various places, reveals the world scope of the Mennonites and
provides regular occasion for intercultural involvements. A term of

service with MCC or the various mission boards provides many individuals with new understandings and a worldwide point of view. Business ventures bring people from other cultures and regions of the globe. The increasing educational attainments of Mennonites are thrusting many of them into intellectual circles and affairs which bring world issues into the Mennonite living rooms.

Altogether, these various facets of social integration produce a major challenge to Mennonites as they attempt to modernize their religious faith to be relevant to the world. In fact, in light of the rapid integration, it may be difficult to bring off a synthesis of vibrant faith and relevance in the short time available.

The Institutionalization of Mennonite Religious Life

There is increasing criticism from many quarters that Mennonite religious organizations have gotten too large, that they are self-perpetuating, and that individual members are not being treated as human beings. The impact of this will be discussed further under "loss of community," below. The growth of the size of the various church organizations, and the increasing number of such organizations, attest to the growth of the Mennonite enterprise and its activities and outreach.

One of the first protests against the institutionalization of the Mennonite church (which protest narrowly missed becoming institutionalized itself) was the so-called *Concern movement*, which emerged in Europe during the early 1950s. This group of young American foreign relief workers believed that the American Mennonite church had become overly dependent on secular structure and organizations and was thereby succumbing to the prevailing "established church model." In the introduction to the first volume of a series of writings which continued for some years, the group stated:

> Despite the weaknesses which we sensed acutely [i.e., the failure to live out the Mennonite faith], we felt a deep loyalty and gratitude to the brotherhood which has nourished us and to which we belong by choice. . . . And so the question arose, a question still unanswered: Are the American Mennonites, in spite of their great institutional and even spiritual progress, perhaps after all moving toward "respectable" denominationalism rather than toward a dynamic and prophetic "grass roots" movement? And if so, what responsibility devolves upon us in our generation? (J. Yoder 1954, 6)

The Concern movement persisted for some fifteen years, and appears to have been the only major warning about the dangers of institutionalization. It spawned a series of conferences and consultations on church structure and function, and as a result there was considerable attention given to the reorganization of the many boards so that they would be more sensitive to the membership. For example, the Study Commission on Church Organization, which began in 1955, resulted in a major reshuffling of the entire structure of the Old Mennonite Church. The General Conference Mennonite Church conducted a number of study conferences, one of the first resulting in the book *Studies in Church Discipline* (Waltner 1958).

But apart from this specific thrust, the bureaucratization and institutionalization of Mennonite society has not received much scholarly attention, and research and writing on this issue is almost nonexistent. (Harder's study of the General Conference in 1962 is a significant exception (1962).) The *Mennonite Encyclopedia* and the *Mennonite Quarterly Review*, two major sources of information, do not carry any articles on this subject. Consequently, also, the survey of Mennonite sociology conducted by Driedger and Redekop does not include much bibliography on the subject. A recent Ph.D. dissertation on the organizational changes and developments of the Canadian General Conference Mennonites (Peters 1986) is one of the first studies to have appeared.

Some of the larger organizations within the Mennonite world are the Mennonite Central Committee, the Mennonite Mutual Aid Association, the Mennonite Foundation, the Mennonite Hospital Association, and the Mennonite Mental Health Association. Then of course there are the various conferences and their congregational ministries and missions organizations. These have been alluded to above, and from one perspective, they are the essence of the Mennonite witness. From another, they can be seen as the threat to almost everything the Mennonite tradition stands for. At this point in the Mennonite saga, it is increasingly urgent that we examine the role of such institutions, but thus far little has been done. As I have noted elsewhere, "The basic problem has been that members of [the Free Church] tradition have tended to ignore or deny the reality of institutions and power within its own borders. Thus in their internal life, Free Church groups like the Mennonites have used institutions and power to achieve their ends, but have tended to admit this reality only in hushed whispers in the hallways, while power is being 'brokered' in the assembly" (1976, 149). Mennonites have not been able to confront institutions and power because their theology and lifestyle has mitigated against admitting that they exist.

The Loss of Leadership

As is well known, the Mennonites have eschewed hierarchy; instead, they have organized themselves within the priesthood of all believers concept. At the same time, leadership has been very influential, in fact crucial, in the life and growth of Mennonite society. But leadership has had a very ambiguous position in the tradition because, although existentially necessary, it has never been rationalized or accepted, either theologically or philosophically (Peters 1986), especially recently as a result of the attack on institutionalization initiated by the Concern movement. As Urie Bender's *Four Earthen Vessels* makes clear, Mennonite leaders have, on the one hand, found themselves expected to preserve the historical faithfulness of the Mennonite heritage, while on the other, they have been practically emasculated in terms of the authority and leadership functions which would enable them to carry out their mandate. When this reality is placed in the context of the priesthood of all believers ideal, the dilemma becomes all the more difficult, although understandable.

The degree of rationalization of leadership that does exist does not find an easy path into general acceptance, simply because it is very difficult to change polity whenever such change challenges traditional practices. There have been times when strong leadership has emerged, but that has usually happened when the congregation has been swayed in directions it has not felt were consistent either with its heritage or with the Bible. So the leadership issue continues to be troublesome and creates a dialectic: strong or centralized leadership creates a reaction against it which tends to result in a weakening of congregational direction, which in turn creates a renewed desire for a strong and centralized leadership (I. Kauffman 1981, 52ff; Sawatsky 1987.).

Often the leadership question revolves around specific issues of application of principles. But the real question often is how issues and problems are conceptualized and treated. With the emergence of a new generation of more educated members, it is probable that this issue can be addressed more easily.

The Loss of Community

I have maintained that the religious impulse is the bond holding the Mennonite edifice together. From one perspective this is true; from another, there is more. That additional binding agent is the community. Whether thought of in geographical or in ethnic terms, community has formed a powerful supporting grid for Mennonite society. It has served a central purpose and is still doing so today (Burkholder 1958). But the nature of the cohesion is changing: the rural community is no longer the nurturing sod for all Mennonites. The urban turf is now becoming the nurturing ground for many first-generation Mennonites. The world of the university and commerce is becoming the reference point for increasing numbers of Mennonites.

The question that confronts Mennonites most fundamentally is, What is the functional equivalent of the earlier rural village community that will provide the direction, commitment, and identity for the coming generations as well as the new converts? In an article entitled "Mennonite Community Change: From Ethnic Enclaves to Social Networks," Leo Driedger (1986) presents a provocative analysis of several approaches to the role of community in preserving ethnic identity. He asks, "To what extent do traditional ethnic enclaves still survive?"(374). He proposes that "middlemen"—cultural brokers—will emerge to provide for a saving of the Mennonite community (Driedger 1986).[6] By itself, intellectual or ideological indoctrination will not provide the engine and the fuel to power the Mennonite society into the indefinite future. Religious revivals, however induced, will also not create the sociological base for the society to continue. The back-to-the-land movement, which waxed and waned in the 1940s and 1950s, was a romantic notion as unachievable as it was unrealistic and illogical and can never offer the entire Mennonite society a viable option. The evangelical strand in the Mennonite family advocates the sloughing of all the Mennonite "cultural trappings" and focusing all energies on the central task of Christianity: the preaching of the Gospel. But this, by itself, is destructive, to say nothing of the fact that such attitudes totally ignore the cultural dimension of the Christian faith (Mierau 1983; C. Redekop 1981; J. Redekop 1987).[7]

One concept that has been developed recently is the idea of "the network" or "portable ethnicity" (Kraybill 1988). Of course, this includes the friendship affiliations which are based on biological relationships; but beyond that, a network can refer to the friendships which have developed over centuries, through membership in the congregation and the community, as well as all the informal connections which these have nurtured and reinforced. It is of more than passing interest to note that the congregation—which was the locus of the emergence of the first Anabaptists and now can be seen as a network—is still the basic center of Anabaptist-Mennonite life.

The congregation, with its centering on the religious life, provides the channels or occasions for social bonds of all varieties—friendship, recreation, social and service opportunities, business associations, leisure organizations and activities, and even primary group activities. As the congregation's primary relationship radiates out to intersect with people from other congregations and institutional structures, such as colleges and service organizations, a larger *network* develops which reinforces and supports the understanding of the Anabaptist-Mennonite heritage and provides the mutual reinforcement and encouragement essential to keeping the faith.

The network of the religious "portable ethnic" group is a reality, and it is functioning. However, this means that the vitality of the congregation becomes the crucial issue. In most other church denominations the congregation is monitored and structured by authority figures working within the hierarchical structures. However, in congregationally organized religious groups, like the Mennonites, the health and well-being of the whole body will depend upon the vitality and cohesion of the local group of people, who will band together—as did their ancestors—to implement their view of the Christian life in response to the "pagan world" around them.

Georg Simmel pointed to the role of the network of affiliations in *The Web of Group-Affiliations*. He states:

> It is understandable that the coexistence and the sharing of human interests is not possible with people who do not share one's faith. The deeply justified need for unity was satisfied, a priori so to speak, in all of ancient civilization, in the Semitic as well as the Graeco-Roman world . . . [but] now religious experience is based upon the soul of the individual and it is his responsibility; on that basis the individual seeks to establish a bond with others who are similarly qualified in terms of their religious experience, but perhaps in no other respect. (1955, 157–58)

A complex matrix of forces brings persons together to form groups. This "bonding" may never be fully understood. But a religious factor is involved for Mennonite society. Simmel proposes that "the success of rational over superficial and schematic principles of group-formation accompanies the general progress of civilization" (191). He continues by saying that while the family is a "natural" expression of solidarity, it does not meet all the needs of the larger society. Religion, he avers, provides one basic force of bonding individuals together: "The disavowal of all social ties, which is evidence of a deep religiosity, allows the individual and his religious group to come in contact with any number of other groups with whose members they do not share any common interests. And the relationships again serve to distinguish and to determine the individuals concerned as well as the religious groups" (158). The social bond involves the cleaving to some people, and the separation from others. The actual factors are revealed as we look at a specific group, such as the Mennonites.

The experience and reality *network* is nurtured today by both a common religious history and ideology (the social bond) *and* by the unusual human need for affiliation. If these two factors can be fruitfully synchronized, the future of Mennonite society is secure. The utopian vision has held for four and a half centuries. This continuity is an example of the power of human hope and faith. But that hope and faith also represent more than inherent human capability and more than historical tradition; together they reflect the spiritual dynamic that has energized and maintained the Anabaptist-Mennonite vision against tremendous odds. Perhaps naively, but certainly with rare commitment and persistence, this community of Christian believers has tried to express in life the great vision of John the Apostle: "Then I saw a new heaven and a new earth, for the first earth had passed away" (Rev. 21:1).

Chapter Eighteen

The Utopian Basis of Mennonite Identity

The preceding chapters have attempted to provide an inclusive description and analysis of the Mennonite phenomenon in North America, an ambitious task indeed. A seemingly simple society becomes, upon closer analysis, a microcosm; for those inside, it is literally the macrocosm—the entire world. How well the attempt to be fair yet critical and comprehensive has succeeded is for the reader to judge. In this final chapter, I present my personal understanding of the "soul" of the Anabaptist-Mennonite experience in North America, derived, naturally, from my experience in it and my training in the social sciences.

My central thesis, as indicated especially in Chapters 2, 5, and 6, is that the Anabaptist-Mennonite phenomenon is and was a religiously motivated utopian movement, emerging during the great social upheaval of the sixteenth century (Troeltsch 1960, 697). And as a religious movement, because of its utopian goals and cultural and social opposition, it was constantly faced with "ethnicizing" tendencies, but never accepted, or capitulated to, becoming a sociological ethnic group because of the religious ideology which was at the heart of its origins. It is my contention that Mennonites have faced a continuing "crisis" be-

310

cause the utopian ideology of becoming "true people of God" has constantly been corrupted by the natural tendency to turn inward, to become an ethnic group, identifiable by a "subculture." By trying constantly to become a "people of God," Mennonites could resolve this inherent contradiction; this effort thus became the guiding light of the group (C. Redekop 1984a). In this concluding chapter, I attempt to present an interpretive summary of the Mennonite story.[1]

The Utopian Milieu

The Renaissance and Reformation were periods of change, of turmoil, confusion, division, invention, and violence, of a search for a new age. There seems to be general agreement that there have been in Christian history many "historical movements and ideologies that yearned for the radical renewal and transformation of society" (Ruether 1970, 3). Ruether suggests three different responses to the need for renewal and transformation: the apocalyptic crisis, the inward journey, and the Great Master Plan (4). She claims that the Anabaptists were of the first type: "Any left-wing view of the church, by its very nature, is inaugurated in a crisis relationship with present history and society. It is born in a movement of rejection of the present order and an anticipatory leap into a radically new age to come. In its original form, such a view is necessarily short-lived. It has no principle of institutionalization and historical perpetuation" (29). These remarks will be of particular use later, but here it is important to suggest that the Anabaptists have been generally classed in the tradition of religious social change, even the revolutionary tradition (e.g., Cohn 1957; Kautsky 1966; Mannheim 1936; Seibt 1972). The desire for renewal and transformation was practically universal, and Anabaptists participated in this renewal in a form now discussed as utopianism. This is to say, utopian thought was everywhere, and the Anabaptists were influenced by this movement (ibid.; also, Troeltsch 1960; Zschäbitz 1958).[2] Several novels about Mennonites—for example, by Voltaire and Gottfried Keller—even take on this theme (Loewen 1980, 209).

The emerging class consciousness and the consequent demands for leveling, as well as access to social and economic institutions, were without a doubt operative in almost all corners of Europe. It is not possible here to evaluate the relative power of the emerging class consciousness (the common man).[3] Scholars as diverse as Kautsky, Clasen, Goertz, Packull, and Stayer, to name a few, claim that Mennonites were to a considerable extent influenced by the increasing unrest among the lower social groups in European society. Further, they were motivated to make some changes in the existing system, especially in the area of communal property (Stayer 1984).[4] This massive upheaval concurred with the development of towns, and the emergence of capitalism also played a part.

Other aspects of the utopian ideology include the response to corruption of the Roman church. The papacy was held in low esteem and often despised. Again, it would be pure redundancy to specify the myriad ways in which there was a general revulsion against the Roman Catholic church. The Hussite rebellion in Bohemia is but one example of the consequences. The Anabaptists reflected and championed the same objections, focusing especially on the corruption of the local clergy and the oppression of the tithe. Indeed, some historians, such as Martin Haas, suggest that the misuse of the tithe was basic for the Swiss Anabaptist revolt.

A development which is more difficult to specify is the revolt against social, political, and religious authority. The rapidly changing political situations in which the Holy Roman Empire was having to give way to regional national interests, and the emergence of "rival" authorities to the Roman church, point to very protean institutional changes. In a word, a unitary European church, at least in idea if not in fact, was being seriously fractured, and authority was being challenged at every point (Mannheim 1936).

The most significant utopian dynamic of all, of course, was the philosophical and theological revolt. Luther's challenge had been predated by (among others) Wycliffe in England and Huss in Bohemia, and although historians may ascribe the causes of this movement to socioeconomic conditions, it cannot be denied, if the sociology of knowledge axiom is at all useful, that the ideas resulting from the interaction of thinkers and social conditions were also operative. The question of communion (lay or clerical), the question of baptism (child or voluntary adult), the question of religious freedom (whether congregation or political authorities have power), and the question of congregational discipline (based on confession or lifestyle) were among those that concerned the various religious revolts. From the twenty-six points of the professors at Prague against the Hussites, to Luther's Ninety-five Theses, to the Anabaptist Schleitheim Confession, basic theological and practical issues were lifted up as lines of battle. John Huss, for example, "denounced the evils of the Church, from parish priest to Pope, held that Christ and not Peter was the foundation on which God had founded the Church, and that far from being inerrant, many popes had been heretics" (Latourette 1953, 667). The interlacing of religious and economic is expressed by the Taborite teaching that, "as in the town of Tabor there is no mine or thine, but all is held in common, so shall everything be common to all, and no one own anything for himself alone. Whoever does so commits a deadly sin" (Kautsky 1966, 59).

The Utopian Dynamic

Anabaptists did not promote utopianism as such; rather, they responded in a simple way which eventually emerged as the "radical Reformation," or "free church" movement, and that turned out to be utopian. Anabaptists did not follow a "grand master plan," though Münster may be misconstrued to be that. Nor did they turn inward, as many other religious movements did. The Anabaptists fully expected that the church could be renewed and restored, if only people, especially those in authority, would take the biblical teachings seriously (Ruether 1970). Failing that, they had no other options ready. The Anabaptist movement, emerging as it did in numerous places within a very short time, by definition could not have envisioned the signing of a petition by young radicals in Zurich, as though thousands all over Europe were waiting for this one event to occur so they could join. Polygenesis by definition argues for local conditions spawning local actions, resulting in variations on a general movement (Stayer, Packull, and Depperman 1975).

A cross-regional comparison of the various Anabaptist groups would provide us with an understanding of their specific underlying concerns, and the expected responses.[5] Small wonder that there have been so many different interpretations of the basic teachings and positions among Anabaptist scholars. It could be said that they are *all* right because the interpretation depended upon the area or the perspective the scholar brought to the material.[6] Thus, it is not mere obscurantism to suggest that the restitution of the church suggested by Littell and Blanke, the recovery of congregational authority outlined by Krahn, the recovery of early Christian communism prepared by Kautsky, the rejection of the authority of the state noted by Yoder and Williams, the reassertion of New Testament existential dualism introduced by Friedmann, the emphasis on personal and congregational ethics associated with Bender, the New Testament biblicism promoted by Wenger, and the love and nonresistance long-championed by Hershberger, are all valid interpretations of the central foci of Anabaptism. But as recent scholars caution, not all of these, and others that could be mentioned, were held uniformly by any or all of the groups who have later been termed Anabaptist-Mennonites. Thus, the *Schwertler* ("bearer of the sword") among the Hutterite Anabaptist groups cannot be automatically excluded from the movement (Stayer 1972).

The central point, however, is that the general conditions were such that all the issues mentioned above plus many others were fomenting serious objections and debates and an increasing protestation. But what is more interesting and central for our analysis of the Anabaptist movement is the kind of thought and protest that emerged, and any differences these might have from the rest. To address this issue, we must embark upon an excursis into ideology and utopia.

According to Mannheim, ideology is the result of the awareness that one's opponent's life ideas and purposes are a "function of the life situation of the one who expresses them" (1936, 56). It is but a short step to suspecting the person or antagonist of expressing false intentions (either consciously or unconsciously). This false consciousness can be either particular or total, the latter being a case in which the antagonist is guilty of total misperception of "reality," at least from the perspective of ego. As Mannheim points out, however, this is a two-edged sword and can be used on the accuser as well as the accused. Hence, the Radical Reformers' accusation that the established church or Reformers were guilty of corruption based on the "ideology of self-interest" could be turned on the Radical Reformers, to charge them of the ideology of resentment or youthful arrogance.

Critical to the emergence of the concept of ideology, however, is the effectiveness of the traditional unitary authority. The various reform groups of Roman Catholicism, as long as they were sporadic and isolated, did not challenge the idea of an authority and truth beyond the breaking point. But with the escalating number of "Protestant" groups emerging here and there, the overarching unity of faith, authority, and social hierarchy was broken. As Mannheim notes, "This profound disintegration of intellectual and social unity is possible only when the basic values of the contending groups are worlds apart" (1936, 65).

With the development of the suspicion of false consciousness, resulting from the increasing number of divergences, the next step in the emergence of ideology is the awareness that all positions are relative and that all "truths" are functions of one's social position. This step is not very tenable, however, when it comes to religious matters, for every religion assumes there are absolutes. The Anabaptists dogmatically maintained they were correct, while the "Reformers" and the Popish church were wrong, and rigidly insisted that they were adhering to the

Bible, thus avoiding the final relativizing step in ideology, namely, the acceptance that all positions are relative and functions of the social conditions (Troeltsch 1960, 699).

The utopian movement emerges precisely at the point where the authority which is being challenged defines the appeals for any reform as "utopian"—that is as unrealizable or unrealistic (Mannheim 1936, 192ff.). But the "utopian" ideas are not unreal or unrealistic, since they are imbedded in the cultural context, but have been suppressed or denied for ideological—that is, self-serving—motives. "In this sense, the relationship between utopia and the existing order turns out to be a 'dialectical' one. By this is meant that every age allows to arise (in differently located social groups) those ideas and values in which are contained in condensed form the unrealized and the unfulfilled tendencies which represent the needs of each age. . . . The existing order gives birth to utopias which in turn break the bonds of the existing order, leaving it free to develop in the direction of the next order of existence" (ibid., 199). The psychological energy needed for the protest to emerge is the presence of diversity and the increasing mistrust of the motives of others, as they are presumed to be victims of "total ideology." This also provides the social structural supports for individuals to act. "The distrust and suspicion which men everywhere evidence toward their adversaries . . . may be regarded as the immediate precursor of the notion of ideology. . . . We begin to treat our adversary's views as ideologies only when we no longer consider them as calculated lies and when we sense in his total behavior an unreliability which we regard as the function of the social situation in which he finds himself" (ibid., 60).

Thus, labeled and rejected as "utopian," the Anabaptist-Mennonite protest ran into opposition, hostility, rejection, and ultimately annihilation. Mannheim states the case for the significance of utopian Anabaptism as follows: "The decisive turning-point in modern history was, from the point of view of our problem, the moment in which 'Chiliasm' (Anabaptism related to Müntzer) joined forces with the active demands of the oppressed state of society" (211). Mannheim defines Anabaptism too widely, but the overarching picture of the Anabaptist response to the rejection of its reform includes the chiliastic, communal, and withdrawal tendencies, no matter how narrowly the definition of Anabaptism is drawn.[7]

The Utopian Movement Becomes "A Story"

More and more, it is being affirmed that the Anabaptists did not want to separate from the orthodox Christian tradition, but, on the contrary, wanted to "achieve power" so they could realize their utopian dream. Troeltsch affirms that "they had renounced the Catholic system of stages, and had given up the hierarchial authoritative direction of souls, but their great desire was to penetrate the whole mass of the population equally with the miracle of the strict Christian ethic of love" (697). Haas states: "A certain openness to compromise was apparent in the Anabaptist willingness to join the collective movement of anticlericalism. . . . This is a mode of behavior that openly announces the willingness to become a mass movement, and to relinquish strict control over members of the *Gemeinde*. From the point of view of the sociology of religion this was not a case of separation, much less of sectarianism" (1980, 79). Utopianism does not ipso facto imply sectarianism—often, rather, the opposite—and the subsequent missionary expansion of the Anabaptist movement, itself a phenomenal event, proves the universality of the "utopian" dynamic (*Schäufele*). But the "radical" challenge *was* too unrealistic in the eyes of others: it was unrealistic because it threatened and challenged almost every traditional and hallowed institution on the Continent, and unrealistic in the sense that it had little, if any, chance of succeeding, any more than did the movements of the Waldensians, Lollards, or Hussites, all of which, along with many other movements, were ruthlessly suppressed. The inability to initiate reforms by way of the "legitimate" route was quickly impressed upon the members of the new movement by way of repression, and the Münster debacle quickly sealed off any utopian hope, as Menno himself indicates.

The Anabaptist "diaspora," which at first was motivated partly by the mission of urgency and universality, was soon transformed into a diaspora of survival. The fugitive movements along the Tyrol into Bohemia, northward down the Rhine, eastward from the coastal area in Holland into North Germany and Prussia, and elsewhere was changing Anabaptism's character from an attempt to propagate the reform of Christendom to a self-preserving retreat.

From the day of its birth, Mennonitism was nurtured on the biblical story of God's suffering remnant. Many recent scholars have remarked that *The Martyrs' Mirror* is one of the major "markers" of Anabaptist-Mennonite identity (e.g., Miller 1985; Sawatsky 1977). A recent corroboration of this is *Edward: The Pilgrimage of a Mind*, in which Edward Yoder (1893–1945) states that three books were present in his home—the Bible, *The Martyrs' Mirror,* and a devotional book whose name he did not remember. *The Martyrs' Mirror* presents its own best case for why it was published and compiled. Among the main reasons for compiling the volume, Van Braght states, were the "sad times, in which we live; nay, truly, there is more danger now than in the time of our fathers, who suffered death for the testimony of the Lord" (Sauder 1945, 8). He continues toward the end of his introduction: "Let us be patient together, then most beloved in the Lord, till the day come, which, if we remain faithful unto the end, will assuredly bring us that which we here wait for and hope" (ibid., 11). Almost three hundred years later, a popularized version of *The Martyrs' Mirror* that has gone through at least three editions states in the introduction: "[This book provides] glimpses of how the early Christians and especially those of the Middle Ages, generally known as Anabaptists or Mennonites, have earnestly contended for the Faith which was once delivered to the saints, Jude 3. . . . they were, in a sense, eternity people, that is, they were looking for and aiming for the things that are eternal" (ibid., v). This edition has been circulating especially among the more conservative groups in recent years.

The above examples illustrate the principle: Anabaptists soon began to tell the story of rejection, suffering, and persecution, which included the idea of faithfulness to the heavenly vision, of the "unspotted and unblemished" people. Van Braght even identifies them with "classic tradition": "Of old, among the heathen, the greatest and highest honors were accorded to the brave and triumphant warriors, who, risking their lives in the land of the enemy, conquered, and carried off the enemy" (ibid., 11).

As the utopian vision of becoming a mass "people-of-God" movement became less and less possible and significant, the need for reform of the corrupt "harlot" was forgotten, and the basic theological and ecclesiological issues were turned inward toward survival. That is, principles such as adult baptism, church discipline, and the nurturing of the flock became central to achieving utopia. This emphasis tended more and more in the direction of a "faithful remnant" motif, which focused on retaining the heritage and transmitting it to the coming generations in the most intense fashion possible.

The gradual change from being at the center of the general protest and utopian reform to the periphery through rejection, migration, and isolation had the profoundest implications for the Anabaptist movement. The public and scholarly designation of "Die Stille im Lande" best describes what happened. In fact, for many it meant an attempt to cover up any identification with the unsavory past. Friedmann, in describing a Mennonite leader, states: "Roosen wanted to cover up anything (in the Catechism) that might have been shocking to his non-Mennonite fellow-citizens of Hamburg-Altona and to make his faith as like as possible to that of general Protestantism. Mennonites have (had) become the Stillen im Lande" (1949, 146). There was a dramatic though gradual transformation from an aggressive religious protest and reform movement to a quietistic group perpetuating as best it could the original vision. What seemed to be the cohesive cement holding the movement together was the knowledge, propagated through oral tradition, experience, and nonconformist practice, that the ancestors had struggled and suffered and died, and that though they had been quashed, the ideals had to be preserved because they were true. The "story" was as real as though the vision had succeeded.

The Emergence of Self-conscious Peoplehood, not an Ethnic Group

The Mennonites are one of many groups which emerged as religious movements but which have become transformed in subsequent years into groups with ethnic characteristics, but Mennonites reflect a rather unusual example of a religious movement that became only partly an ethnic group, or—to state it differently—has always been more than merely an ethnic group.

If the Anabaptist-Mennonite event is defined as a movement, we cannot speak of an ethnic group in any form in the early period. But the authorities' rejection of their calls for restitution became increasingly hostile and finally so brutal that Anabaptists were hunted and martyred. This was the beginning of an awareness of being "on the other side" or being in opposition. This opposition resulted in physical, social, cultural, and ideological separation, or "enclavement." All over Europe, the Anabaptist-like groups found themselves in isolated and obscure places, protected by the most curious mixtures of Roman Catholic and Protestant princes, sympathizers, craft guilds, and city fathers. Attempts to continue the dialogue, however, became less and less prevalent, so that a spirit of resignation emerged. The publication of *The Martyrs' Mirror* was one signal of the process of enclavement.

With the development of enclaves, never very secure, self-preserving actions, norms, and beliefs naturally emerged. The symbols, language, art, stories, and memories began to produce an image of a people rejected and unwanted, but energized by the dogged conviction that the

Word of God was with them. The Münster episode especially served to cast a pall over the Anabaptist movement, and the very pejorative "sectarian" badge of Anabaptism probably held sway longer in the public and academic mind than any other movement in the fifteenth and sixteenth centuries (Kautsky 1966).

Separation from the world, which has figured so largely in subsequent Anabaptist-Mennonite life, was not originally the animus, as some interpretations would have us believe (Wenger and Bender 1957; Miller 1985); rather, it was the consequence of actual experience. Granted, the early Anabaptists stressed a dualism of the faithful from the world, the kingdom of God and the kingdom of the world, but the original intent was not to set apart a remnant, but to call all persons to become a part of the heavenly kingdom. Certainly the mission emphasis of the early Anabaptist-Mennonite movement attests to this (Haas 1980; Littell 1947; Schäufele 1962).

The emergence of what could be confused as ethnic Mennonitism needs some analysis at this point. In a study of the Russian Mennonites, E. K. Francis, came to the conclusion that the Mennonites went from religious to ethnic group: "In the particular case of the Russian Mennonites, a religious group [movement?] was transformed within a comparatively short time into a distinct ethnic and folk group. While the specific religious system, which afforded orientations in the formative states, changed and even lost much of its appeal, the identity and cohesion of the group did not suffer materially" (1948, 101). Other scholars, both outside the tradition and inside, have characterized the Mennonites as having religious distinctions early, but increasingly constituting an ethnic culture (e.g., Anderson 1972; Bennett 1967; Dawson 1936; Driedger 1975, 1986; Kraybill 1988; Thielman 1955; Urry 1978). The increasing debate about the "Mennonite identity" is focusing more and more on the confusion of ethnic and religious factors (Peachey 1968; C. Redekop 1988; J. Redekop 1987). This I call the "ethnic trap." An analysis of the forces that create this "trap" is appropriate at this point.

The concept of adult baptism and voluntarism. Baptism of mature adults, who are consciously joining the body of Christ, was a central tenet of all strands of Anabaptism. Sociological analysis of the sect type, of which the Mennonites were a prime example, has stressed this central factor (Troeltsch 1960; Weber 1946). This central dogma would probably have been impracticable, and even contradictory, if it had become the universal norm, however, for if everybody were to join as an adult on a voluntary basis, this would become the practice and hence lose its voluntariness (as, in fact, has happened in those Mennonite "states within a church"; Redekop 1980). But in the context of rejection and enclavement, voluntary church membership became restricted and turned inward, and hence became a self-fulfilling prophecy: that is, so long as the fact and teaching (or myth) is kept alive that voluntary membership is being practiced, the proof of exclusive authenticity and genetic heritage is maintained. The continuing concern among Mennonite critics that adult baptism is only "form" points to the awareness of the loss of the belief as a guiding force and proves the ambiguity of voluntarism as a defining characteristic.

Congregationalism. The early stress on the centrality of the congregation, the body of believers, which was at the heart of the Anabaptist revolt as proposed by Blanke and others, could have one meaning or impact in an expanding missionary mode, but quite another in an enclavic or contracting one. Thus, the congregational idea latterly served to create a "closed," or ethnocentric, orientation rather than an engaging, or open, stance. The beliefs, norms, and practices developed by the local congregations became increasingly involuted and restrictive. There was more and more conformity to traditional behavior and precedent; leadership became increasingly intent upon reflecting the wishes of the group, rather than following or promulgating a renewed vision.

Congregationalism, a profound and central truth of Christian living, could thus become an end in itself, encouraging narrow-mindedness and conformity, with extreme stress on mutual submission and self-abnegation. The tyranny of the misuse of excommunication and the ban has been generously documented, and the degree of loss of membership in many congregations in recent centuries suggests that the noble idea of democratic Christianity can be misdirected or become corroded when it is not allowed to retain a tension with other aspects of truth. The Anabaptist-Mennonite teaching of congregationalism had a direct contribution to make to the formation of a self-conscious people, which in its more problematic modes, became an undergirding force in the exclusive nature of Mennonites (C. Redekop 1984a).

The stress on Christian ethics. It is generally agreed that Anabaptism was based less on abstract visions of how the new society might look than on a vision which demanded that the Christian disciple bring his life into alignment with the Christian confession that he had already made (Burkholder 1959a). Even the most hostile detractors of Anabaptists admitted that they attempted to live "blameless" lives. A high ethical practice was often achieved among the early Anabaptists, by the testimony of many critics.

But this "utopian" ethical emphasis could also contribute to the development of an exclusive, self-conscious people through the development of very specific views of how the Christian life and ethics should be understood. Congregational discipline of the voluntary member could develop into a highly codified system of norms and values which became ever more imprinted in the individual member as the truth or the way things really were (C. Redekop 1984a). In other words, the mutual communication of ideas and sentiments based upon a common experience and oriented toward the same objectives tended to develop an involuted "plausibility structure" in a subcultural context, a process which is universal in operation. Without intervening objections or counterperspectives, the Mennonite congregation could continue to go in a direction which it assumed was right.

The catch in this process, of course, is the theological truism that the Christian life demands a regenerated life, a life that is different from the "fallen world." Both the definition of what the "fallen world" is and of what the Christian life is need some consensus among a group; otherwise, the understanding of Christian faith remains an unformed individualistic subjective attitude. Jesus' teaching that his disciples should take up their crosses and follow him involved a drastic change in lifestyle. Yet, the concept of a change in lifestyle, or conversion, needs to be defined and supported to have any meaning or context. The Anabaptists were singularly encumbered by this process, for they were among the most extreme in their stress on the "new life." But the new life had to be named, identified, and agreed upon. And in this process the structural factors were present for the creation of a strong exclusivity, for only those who conformed to the Anabaptists' interpretation were a part of the people (not ethnic) and submitted themselves to it; those who objected were sloughed off (C. Redekop 1984a).

The stress on mutual aid. It is generally assumed that the Hutterite wing of Anabaptism was formed in the struggle to survive, but the rest of the Anabaptist groups also emerged in periods of great economic and occupational stress as the faithful were dispossessed and dislocated and moved. The degree of help the Dutch Mennonites offered to the Swiss at Berne as early as 1711, to help them escape to America, was of great meaning and set in motion reciprocal mutual aid from that time forward for many centuries. "Helping brothers in need" thus early became a structural factor of survival and continued to operate through many famines, expulsions, and persecutions.

The idea of "having been helped" undoubtedly contributed in keeping Mennonites in communication with each other, and perpetuated the exchange of physical, psychological, and spiritual help. This attitude and emotion—most recently, the assistance given to the Mennonites of Russian extraction after World War II—can still be felt today among Mennonites. The idea of mutual aid (love of brethren) was originally stressed and taught as incumbent upon the Christian community, and what was an early biblical teaching, although certainly the result of existential need, served to develop a normative structure which interacted with continuing experiences of need and the responses to that need, as various people were able. Anabaptist-Mennonite communalism, while clearly there from the beginning, became entrenched as a practice, almost independent of its original ideological source, and became a "marker" of Anabaptist-Mennonite self-consciousness as a "people of God."

THESE FOUR STRUCTURAL factors, originally religious principles which emerged as part of the utopian vision, served to create a conscious peoplehood, unique to Mennonitism and often termed "ethnic Mennonitism." The conclusion of this argument is therefore to propose that Anabaptism did not move from a religious movement to an ethnic group. Rather, it developed into a religious people—*one that maintained it was keeping the truth and the vision of Christianity alive.* The recognition by outsiders, laymen, and scholars alike that the "Radical Reformation" was indeed a legitimate and central renewal movement of Christianity has given some credence to the ideas held by many Anabaptist martyrs and others of themselves. A comment by Rosemary Ruether, while not totally correct, expresses the general view:

> One way [the belief in the coming Kingdom is kept alive] is for the revolutionary community to overcome the world not by direct attack, but by separation and the creation of a provisional alternative. . . . Migrating to rural areas, Mennonites and Hutterites set up agrarian utopias. Here and now they have already passed over to the new principle of existence of the Kingdom of God and are living separated from the "world and from the Kingdom of Satan and from all that is of the Old Adam." . . . They [however] must keep up a constant effort to maintain the new moral style of life. (1970, 32–33)

The Anabaptist-Mennonite protest movement has indeed evolved into a people with a self-conscious awareness of its past, present, and future

(Gordon 1964), but the awareness has been continually informed by, or critiqued by, a religiously based conflict with the secular environment—in other words, a utopian ideology. This very point has been denied by many latter-day Mennonites, especially those who have been influenced by fundamentalism and evangelicalism, who have dismissed as "ethnic" anything that was not like "civic religion." Mennonites are not a pure ethnic group, meaning by that a society (or subsociety) identified by subcultural traits as such without a central ideological animus.

A recent study of a concentrated Mennonite settlement area which focused on the relationship of ethnic identity and religious belief provides strong evidence for the position taken here. Baar states:

> Urbanization challenges [Mennonites] to organize themselves in ways that will reinforce religious beliefs so as to prevent a hostile environment from undermining their distinctiveness. . . . Eighty percent of respondents report that Mennonites continue to remain separate. The prime reason for this is reported to be the centrality of religion in the lives of Mennonites.
>
> "We are separate from others because church is the focal point of our life."
> "The relevance of our church encourages separateness."
>
> Differences which had appeared to be ethnic when contact between the populations was limited were now seen as religious rather than ethnic. . . . Their Christian tradition, not Anabaptism or cultural distinctiveness, are seen as differentiating Mennonites from non-Mennonites. (1983, 81, 83)

The religious origins, and the essence of the "story" which has permeated the Mennonite society, continue to highlight the spiritual and visionary. The consciousness of a "faithful original Christianity" has lurked in the back of the mind of every Mennonite, regardless of how nominal or secularized or "ethnic" he or she has become. When members have relinquished their religious interests and motivations in the Mennonite community, there has been community discomfort and even ostracism. The fact and memory of a religious schism and ostracism based on an attempt to be faithful exists in the very center of the Mennonite genius. Baar states: "Of all the variables used to account for the strength of ethnic identification, the importance of Anabaptism proved the most useful. Ethnic identification is thus strongest when non-resistance, collective responsibility and the voluntary nature of religious commitment are emphasized" (86).

What makes Mennonites unlike an ethnic group is the attempt to do what Ruether suggests they could not do—keep their original vision clear without "reformulating its original view" (1970, 29). The revolutionary nature was not totally lost, but it was turned inward and expressed in the inner life of the society in an institutionalized form. Thus, what the rest of "fallen Christendom" would not accept became an ethic for the remnant, the "provisional paradise" (32).

The Mennonite consciousness of a peoplehood—ethnicity according to many, a utopian ideology in my view—has been so marked that strong countercurrents of resistance have emerged. These dissenters object that the strong religious-group consciousness makes it almost impossible for Mennonites to carry on missions and to proselytize new converts, since converts find it so difficult to gain admittance and achieve a sense of belonging and acceptance. My argument is the precise opposite of the traditional "ethnic" argument—it is the stringency of the religious demands rather than the "culture" which makes the outreach so difficult. In fact, recent scholars maintain that the only viable definition of an ethnic group is one which holds that ethnicity emerges and perpetuates itself from a particular set of events cohering around an ideological commitment (Aronson 1976, 12ff.). If this argument is true, then ideology can be the only basis for any group identity and hence boundary creation.

This ambivalence about the Mennonite identity has become the engine of serious divisions and conflicts, including conscious efforts by some to delete all things "Mennonite" in order to be able to recover the original Christian mission. Some of the most vociferous of these people are not necessarily antagonistic to the original Anabaptist tenets; in fact, they would probably accept most of them, except for the peace and nonresistance issue. But they object vehemently to the intermeshing of cultural factors (e.g., language, lifestyles, family networks—all the marks of ethnicity) with religious principles.

Baar comes to the conclusion that Mennonites are taking two approaches to solve this question: either they drop the ethnic identity and adopt predominantly (strict) Christian identification, or they retain the Anabaptist orientation and thereby also retain the traditional subcultural identity: "Increasing emphasis on religious commitment and the Christian component together with decreasing emphasis on ethnicity and the Anabaptist component among Niagara Mennonites, is, at least in part, a result of a change in the priority to subsets of core Mennonite values and beliefs." Change in this orientation will create a new threat "that Niagara Mennonites will be absorbed into a new social system, thus becoming an indistinguishable segment of the strict Christian community" (87). This poses the dilemma for Mennonites rather clearly. The causes of the identity crisis in the Mennonite community need to be understood if the Mennonite society in all its richness is to believe in itself and continue to witness to the world.

What of the Future?

The religious rejection of Anabaptism has mellowed through the centuries and decades, especially in recent decades. "Mainline" Protestantism has, however, ignored Anabaptism; Mennonites have thus mistakenly assumed that the issues of rejection and apostasy are still viable. This thesis abounds, particularly in the Swiss Mennonite but also in the Russian Mennonite tradition. Wenger and Bender say, for example: "The struggle to maintain true Scriptural conformity continues to be a major problem for the Mennonite church (MC). The moving line of demarcation between the church and the world is increasingly hard to define" (1957, 896). The world's rejection has been more by way of evasion and ignoring Mennonites than it has been active rejection. The dynamic changed dramatically with the "denominationalizing" of America, which has given respectable status to all "sects." Hence, especially in the United States and Canada, Mennonite groups have a recognized status as religious organizations, but Mennonites have continued to feel as if they were struggling with the religious protest of the sixteenth century (Wenger and Bender 1957).

The social and political relation has changed as well, but again the withholding of special privileges or status in numerous contexts in Mennonite history has kept alive the idea that the state or society at large was not very friendly and accommodating. A particular illustration of the point is the wish of the more conservative groups such as the Hutterite, Amish, and Old Colony to be allowed to practice their own ways of life. The issue of the privileges (*Privilegien*) has played a large part in many Mennonite migrations up to the present day and continues to create considerable tension (Crous 1959, 220; Franz and Hiedebrecht 1984; M. Friesen 1977; J. A. Hostetler 1974; C. Redekop 1969, 1982). For more progressive groups, the tension with the state and society has not involved rejection of Social Security and setting up their own school systems, but more subtle conflict, such as the refusal to bear arms and to become involved in national programs requiring paying of taxes that support the military. But the tension has persisted and is escalating in recent times at the behest of more radical elements, especially youth, who believe that Mennonites have been co-opted by the state.

The net effect of the external and internal dynamics over the span of four and a half centuries has resulted in the following consequences: (1) The memory of suppression and exile is lessening with each generation; hence, there is an increasing need to "hype" the story of rejection in order to maintain the power of the original rejection. (2) The powerful impact of "mundane existence" which has existed from earliest persecution has tended to transform the nature of the earlier relationship with the outside world from one of objective enmity to psychological and social isolation. The "enemy" thus is not the church or the state, but "the world," however vaguely and ephemerally defined. Hence the continuing "drawing of lines" which are constantly yielding to "modernizing," such as the retreat from refusing telephones, to refusing radios and television, and finally accepting them all in succession. Maintaining a religiously informed way of life when external opposition and oppression is being weakened or transformed puts an enormous load on "mundane" (i.e., normal) living to continue to provide the ideology of protest and survival.

The maintenance of a "peoplehood tradition" has thus become the bottom line; for a self-conscious history, once created, tends to nurture itself and want to survive (C. Redekop 1984a). An example today would be the public trauma experienced at the demise of the invincible International Harvester "empire" and image. Death comes hard to a utopian ideal, an image, and a symbol system. "Mennonitism cannot and must not die" is the powerful self-consciousness which has emerged in the collective memory of the biological and proselytized descendants, fed by the increasing body of autobiography, biography, family genealogies, history, research, and institutional histories, retelling the incredible story of the many ancestors who willingly marched to the stake for their beliefs.

IT HAS OFTEN been said that the ability to laugh at oneself is a sign of maturity. Throughout this book, I have attempted to look at the Mennonite story with a touch of irony and sardonic wit when that was appropriate. Mennonites are beginning to tell stories about themselves, indicating an ability to take themselves less seriously, and with a bit more perspective. The following story, full of symbolism, may be an appropriate way to end our excursion in Mennonite country.

A plain Mennonite farmer and his son were driving a team of horses and wagon to Lancaster one spring morning. The snows had just melted, and the ruts on the road were muddy and very deep—so deep that once the wagon wheels were in the ruts, it was impossible to get out until you got to Lancaster. About halfway to town, the Mennonite farmer noticed a Lutheran farmer approaching him, faced with the same situation. As they approached each other, they both stopped. The Lutheran called out, "You had better back up, because I have a load and can't get out of the ruts." To which the Mennonite farmer replied, "I have farther to back than you, and I am not going to give in to threats." After more threats and counterthreats, with neither giving in, the Mennonite farmer, in a very firm voice, finally said, "If you don't back up, I am going to have to do something I would very much rather not do," and he flexed his muscles. Reluctantly, the Lutheran backed up, and the Mennonite and his son drove on. After he was sure the disgruntled Lutheran could no longer hear him, the son asked, "Dad, what would you have done?" The father replied, "I would have backed up."

Appendix A

The Mennonites: A Typological Analysis

Can the observation that the Germanic Mennonites in North America constitute a subcultural system be harmonized with the position the Mennonites are the descendants of a religious-social movement which set out to change the world? Is it possible to integrate the religious impulses with the sociological facts? That question has been a major question of this book. I am not alone in posing this question, for some of the foremost scholars in religion and society have used the Mennonites to try to understand the relationships between religious factors and social structure. Here, I shall attempt to deal with the issues regarding religion and society which invariably come up when Mennonite society is discussed.

Mennonites as a Sect

Max Weber and Ernst Troeltsch were two leading early scholars who studied how religious forces express themselves in social form. Focusing on the Reformation and its aftermath, Weber first developed the sect-church idea and suggested that the Anabaptist-Mennonites were a good example of the sect: "A sect . . . is a voluntary association of only those who, according to the principle, are religiously and morally qualified" (Weber 1946, 306). The church is a "compulsory association for the administration of grace, and . . . the 'sect' [is] a voluntary association of religiously qualified persons" (314). Beyond voluntary association, Weber listed three other characteristics of the sect: (2) the sovereignty of the local sacramental community, (3) strict moral discipline, and (4) a spirit of early Christian brotherhood (328).

Building on Weber's idea, Troeltsch described the sect type further using the Mennonites in his prime exhibit: in his section dealing with the sect, he begins by saying, "The first question with which we have to deal is that of the Protestant sect or the Anabaptist movement" (1960, 694). He defines the church as being the opposite of the traits that Weber outlined for the sect. Troeltsch, a colleague of Weber, expanded Weber's typology by defining the church type and then introducing a third type, namely, mystics. Since I have already described Troeltsch's characterization of Mennonites in Chapter 4, here I shall expand a bit on the church typology.

Troeltsch's starting point was the positing of a fundamental difference between the way grace came to man. For the church type, the "main question was this: How could they gain influence over the masses? Salvation and grace are independent of the measure of subjective realization of strict ethical standards" (702). Of course, there had developed the "great historic powers." But the way in which these powers were used actually helped to plant the seeds of protest by persons who "were entirely opposed to the ecclesiastical system, with its inclusive character and its claim to be the sole depository of grace" (702). An object of this protest was the domination or control of a person or persons by another. In fact this idea of domination of one person or set of persons over others is the central truth of the churchly stance as defined by Weber and Troeltsch. A recent elaboration of this idea seems to substantiate the view. William Swatos (1979) proposes that the church type of religious organization is identified by the desire to monopolize grace, to be the only institution which dispenses grace and to be able to impose it on everyone in the society.

Sect members, on the other hand, maintain that religious faith and grace can be mediated only by freedom of belief and that there must be freedom from hierarchy in the way the religious sacraments are mediated. In the context of this definition the Mennonites are definitely sectarians. The biblical constraints to be humble, submissive, and passive, and even to suffer if need be for the sake of the church, further confirm the presence of the sectarian stance. The separation of sects from Catholicism and Protestantism expresses "itself in an individualistic and subjective method of interpreting the Scriptures and [in] its emphasis upon the attainment of salvation without priesthood or hierarchy" (Troeltsch 1960, 702).

According to Troeltsch, the central characteristic of the sect type is that the sectarians work from the bottom up (from the position of the "common man" or common humanity), while the church works from the top down (703). This refusal of a hierarchy to dominate or control religious life is a very helpful concept in explaining Anabaptist-Mennonite social structure. The lay ministry, the locus of authority in the congregation, the refusal to participate in service to the state which exercises power over others, the simple lifestyle, the mutual-aid practices, the strict rules regarding ethical practices, the expulsion of deviants— these and many other practices are understood in the idea of the sect, that is, the refusal to assume the monopoly of grace.[1]

A problem with this typology was that a sect was assumed to remain a sect until it was eradicated or disappeared in some other fashion. Scholars soon solved the problems with this conceptualization and began to suggest that the sect type could move toward the church type. Among the numerous elaborations the most celebrated was the "social disinheritance" theory of H. Richard Niebuhr, which stated that as a sect became freed from its economic deprivation, it moved up the socioeconomic ladder and became a denomination or a church. This elaboration has been debated for a long time.

It is important to note, however, that Weber never assumed that the sect would always remain a sect; he said, rather, that it would succumb to the process of secularization (Weber 1946, 307). Through his experience in America, Weber observed that "otherworldly sects" became middle class through the emergence of voluntary organizations which became substitutes for the exclusive brotherhood (306–11).

The church-sect idea has considerable cogency in helping to explain the origin of the Anabaptist-Mennonite movement; indeed, it still offers considerable insight to the process of defining and analyzing the Mennonites, and has been more widely used than any other perspective (see Driedger and Redekop 1983). The sect-church-mysticism typology which Troeltsch developed around the turn of the century (his great work was published in 1911) subsequently became the accepted definition of Mennonites. In fact, the church-sect typology has probably been more widely used by both Mennonite and non-Mennonite scholars to study and define the Mennonite society than any other typology. At the same time, it should be noted that most Mennonites, including the most conservative, would stoutly deny the designation of "sectarian" because of its derogatory connotation.

The loss of the original sectarian purity was, however, a fact of life for the members of the Mennonite society. One celebrated schism in the Mennonite family which expressed very well the reluctance to relinquish the sectarian stance was the Holdeman schism of Ohio in the mid-1850s. John Holdeman had begun to realize that "the church had strayed from the 'right and true ground,' and had accepted many unconverted members. The decay of the church troubled him, and he admonished the members for worldly and flippant conversations" (Hiebert 1973, 176). The acrimonious debate which developed contributed to the formation of a group which wanted to return to the "basics," as Menno Simons and others had commanded. "When a church lapses so far from the Word of God that one becomes a transgressor by remaining in it, because the members refuse to reform, one can only be obedient by going out," Holdeman said (183). The Church of God in Christ, Mennonite, was the result; it reasserted a strict application of nonconformity, especially in areas of dress and lifestyle.

It is clear that the Mennonite movement today is different from what it was in the beginning and cannot uncritically be called sectarian. My designation of three models of Mennonite structure in Chapter 6 is premised on the great changes and differentiation which have come into the Mennonite heritage. Even though the general parlance still refers to the Mennonites as sectarian, the predominant view now is that sectarianism was a useful concept historically but has less utility as the original Reformation influences fade. It is thus both important and relevant to bring another dimension into the discussion of the Mennonites, namely, the concept of ethnic group.

Mennonites as an Ethnic Group

As indicated earlier, E. K. Francis, a Roman Catholic sociologist, came to the conclusion that Mennonites had changed "from religious movement to ethnic group" (1955, 9). He states: "In the period between 1790 and 1870 the Mennonite sectarians in Russia had become a people (an ethnic group) whose conspicuous secular successes were bought at the price of institutionalization of religion and secularization of the inner life of the group" (27). Francis has spelled out the mechanisms by which this took place.

Although Francis focused on the Mennonites of Russia, his general theory and interpretations apply to all Mennonite groups. According to Francis, Mennonites, being a voluntary brotherhood, form their own communities of the faithful "under the guidance of the self-chosen lay ministers" (1976, 173). At this stage, however, they were not required to be concerned about the management of secular institutions and processes. With the coming of the second generation and with subsequent migrations, Francis maintains, "anyone born of Mennonite parents now had to be admitted to church membership, for he could otherwise not logically live in a Mennonite community." Further, as the Mennonite congregations began to settle in regions where they were given asylum, they were increasingly given the responsibility "to take care of all their worldly affairs within their settlements."

This was very tricky, Francis maintains, "since Anabaptist doctrine insisted upon the strict separation of church and state" (173). The Mennonite religious community was thus forced to become a self-governing unit. Along with the increasing number of new people joining the group, a self-conscious society began to emerge. The shaping of this self-conscious identity was exacerbated when the groups were continually forced to migrate. This tended to increase even further the self-limiting boundaries and self-delineation of the Mennonites from others, "a commonwealth."

The formation of separate communities through the religious sanctions of separation from the world contributed further to the emergence of endogamy— that is, marriage inside the group—for both religious reasons (separation) as well as for practical reasons (outsiders were not available). The process of interaction also became restricted, so that relations with outsiders became fewer; in fact, the separations became so complete that language differences began to appear quite early.[2]

So distinct cultural practices, including language, developed within the segregated communities where groups were forced to manage their own affairs. The emergence of dress codes and of norms for the relationship between the sexes, parents, children, and others expressed the peculiar and unique elements in the religious system. With the passage of time, these norms began to receive the status of moral laws, and in time, deviance became identified as an abhorrent infringement of sacred traditional practices.

In summary, Francis contends "the principal condition" for the formation of a Mennonite ethnic group "was apparently the effective segregation of a relatively large population from its societal environment" (1976, 183). The separation was caused by religious factors, but once it was in operation, the strength of the ethnic principle was determined "in proportion to the contrast between the segregated group and its societal environment" (184).

Francis believes that the most important variable in the process of ethnic formation is symbolic. "The more readily the differences can be perceived and the greater their discriminatory power is, the better they can serve as symbols for the distinctiveness and unity of the group" (184). The basic foundation of the Mennonite community derived from the religious congregational base, which, from its earliest days to the present, has been the symbol system that has expressed the basic beliefs, meanings, and commitments of Mennonite society. The consolidation of this orientation has been strengthened in a degree directly related to how much the group experiences opposition or persecution. *The Martyrs' Mirror*, written to encourage steadfastness in the light of persecution, has served more powerfully than probably any other symbol to identify the sense of peoplehood which the Mennonites have developed.[3]

Persecution and opposition alone, however, have not formed a Mennonite ethnic identity. The fact of ecological concentration serves several functions in the maintenance of an ethnic group. Its territory becomes identified with the group and thus an added symbol of it. "If commensalitas can be confined to the members of the group, connubiam, that is marriage, follows" (Francis 1976, 183). The ethnic factor which thus emerges, Francis maintains, has been variously defined to include common nationality, religion, and language.

But these ethnic elements alone are inadequate in defining the Mennonites. Milton Gordon comes much closer when he defines ethnic groups as containing "the socio-psychological elements of a special sense of both ancestral and future-oriented identification with the group" (1964, 29). But even this definition is inadequate because it does not indicate what the underlying substance of the sociopsychology is. A full definition of Mennonite society would need to include the basic religious and social conceptions of reality which the belief and symbol system has created for members of the group.

In Chapter 18 I defined Mennonite identity as a cognitive, social, and psychological sense of both ancestral and future identity with the group, based on identification with the symbols, beliefs, and meaning systems which the group has developed and elaborated. The ethnic dimension of Mennonite identity therefore must derive from an "ideology" which outlines a total explanation of how the group emerged, why it is experiencing reality as it is, and why it should continue. Within this setting, concepts like "the world," "the fall of the church," "the pure church," "*Gelassenheit*," and "humility" articulate the amazingly intense "world view" that is a part of the Mennonite identity (Aronson 1976, 12).

In the final analysis, the question of religious *or* ethnic group is spurious, for Christian theology assumes that the religious impulse can be understood only as it expresses itself in social form. The religious versus cultural issue, therefore, needs to be changed to "religious expression in culture or through culture." In other words, the Mennonite religion has tended to develop specific cultural expressions. The religious philosophical issue for Mennonites is therefore not "Is ethnicity wrong?" but, rather, "How is the religion created by, and expressed, in culture?" The ethnic form may not be accepted by Mennonites, but the realistic and functional alternative can never be the rejection of social and cultural forms in the hope of being freed from culture; that hope can only lead to a futile search (C. Redekop 1984a).

Mennonites as Cult or Denomination

Can the Mennonites be defined as a denomination, as Kauffman and Harder do in Chapter 2 of *Anabaptists Four Centuries Later?* What about the Mennonites as a cult? Or what about viewing the Mennonites as a minority group (Redekop and Hostetler 1977)?

First, the issue of cult: Mennonites have rarely been defined as a cult. Insofar as a cult is defined as a subjective individualism, rather emphemeral in character, deviant in theology, and led by a charismatic figure, Mennonites clearly do not qualify (Martin 1983).

In a way, the Mennonites are a minority group, but this term, if used at all, must be used in an adjectival, not substantive, sense. Mennonites do have a *minority status*, and have had for many years, if one uses the classic definition by Louis Wirth: "We may define a minority as a group of people, who because of their physical or cultural characteristics, are singled out from the others in the society in which they live for differential and unequal treatment, and who therefore regard themselves as objects of collective discrimination. The existence of a minority in a society implies the existence of a corresponding dominant group with higher social status and greater privileges. Minority status therefore carries with it exclusion from full participation in the life of society" (1945, 374). Of course, the physical or racial factor can be dismissed out of hand. Nor have cultural aspects such as language or dress been the basis for the rejection. Rather, it has been the ideology of separation and nonconformity, and this is not normally included in the definition of a minority. Typically, social scientists would say that any minority which can, by changing its *negative stance* toward the host society, dispose of discrimination, is not a true minority (C. Redekop 1969, 233–236). And the Mennonites could have avoided discrimination if they had chosen to give up their separation.

Today many Mennonites themselves consider their tradition a denomination, parallel to other religious groups in North America. But this conclusion reflects a serious misunderstanding of the nature of denominationalism. On this subject, the greatest advance in recent years has been made by William Swatos (1979), who proposes that there are two axes that can be used to understand religious organization in society. The first axis is the monopolism-pluralism axis, which pertains to whether the religion is a unified and coercive system in a society (e.g., the Roman Catholic church in the medieval period)—called the monopolistic condition—or whether it is one of a number of differentiated and splintered religious institutions (e.g., the many denominations in America)— called the pluralistic condition. The other axis is the acceptance or rejection of societal values and environment. Swatos maintains that those groups that accept the pluralistic structure as normative (that is, that believe religion cannot be established) but who at the same time accept the dominant culture are denominations. On the other hand, those groups that recognize the pluralistic structure but do not accept the prevailing societal structure are sect-type groups. Mennonites have traditionally been on the rejection-of-social-values end of the scale and are clearly not a denomination by Swatos's definition. They do not consider themselves to be another religious grouping competing for membership in the religious marketplace. The Mennonites in fact consider most other denominations as part of the establishment because they support *both* the pluralism of religious freedom *and* the acceptance of the dominant culture (Swatos, 10).

Just as ludicrous is the tendency among Mennonites to designate the various divisions among themselves as denominations. Thus, for example, the Mennonite church is often designated as a denomination in a double sense—Mennonites as one group among other American groups, and Mennonites of a particular type among Mennonites! Denominationalism is an American designation emerging out of the pluralism of religious groups which found themselves competing on the new American frontier for membership, status, and legitimacy (Richey 1977). Mennonites are simply not part of mainstream Protestantism from either a sociological or theological perspective.[4]

To the degree that Mennonites use the denominational category to define themselves, they reflect the integration of prevailing values into their own system (Sawatsky 1978). Mennonites cannot be called a denomination, for that is almost a contradiction in terms.

In an article entitled "Who are the Mennonites?" James Urry—an anthropologist who has devoted a large amount of intellectual energy to understanding the Mennonites—states:

> The search for "Anabaptist" origins was both historical research and theological revelation. . . . It is a search back to origins, to a safe foundation not unlike the claims of many of the Reformation figures who themselves looked back to the early Christian church for models of religious behavior and community organization. The appeal of both ethnicity and "Anabaptism" is that they are distinctly Mennonite and the distinctiveness is derived from historical experiences. Through "Anabaptism" Mennonites discovered a "theological" origin and putative kinship connections with early Anabaptist individuals. . . . Later history explains their distinctive ethnic identity. . . . In recent years, through the concepts of ethnicity and Anabaptism, they have begun to reinvent a distinctly "Mennonite identity"; whether it succeeds or not, only time will tell. (1978, 257, 260)

Even though few Mennonites themselves would draw the issues as sharply, or "simplify" the history so drastically, by and large they will need to admit that the basic tension Urry presents is there, in fact, and that his analysis points to a basic dilemma for Mennonites. Are they sectarian? No, not really, for they do not claim to have a "peculiar" theology or doctrine; rather, it is "for all men." Are they an ethnic group? No, for that is seen as downgrading the essence of faith. If neither, then what? Most would answer "denomination," but that designation is quickly betrayed by the internal evidence as well as by the way the rest of society treats the Mennonites. *Religious-utopian movement* seems to be the best definition—and it is one which Urry proposes—but this concept may be as difficult to understand and assimilate as any of the others.[5]

A Paradigm of Mennonite Society

Attempting to present a simple typology of Mennonite society may well be an exercise in presumption. Students who know Mennonites are fully aware of the difficulty of arriving at a neat descriptive or analytical synthesis. However, scholars have attempted even more formidable tasks—for example, analyses of the Roman Empire or of the "Third Reich." So we turn to our task with some noble precedents. Although in a very terse form, here I will try to utilize the analysis of the Anabaptist-Mennonites as presented in this volume to suggest ways of looking at the Mennonite phenomenon in historical and cross-sectional perspective.

Any attempt at analysis must necessarily take into consideration the various historical, national, and dynamic factors that have produced Mennonite society. That is to say, both the Mennonite inner logic *as well as* the interaction with societies with which Mennonites have come into contact have produced the Mennonite phenomenon. Furthermore, a full understanding involves a breakdown of the major or comprehensive movements into understandable and manageable units.

Table A.1 presents in brief form the essence of my effort to provide a synthesis. It will be observed that the Anabaptist-Mennonite history has been broken into three frames which are easily discernible in the Mennonite saga. These three periods seem to have notable counterparts in the society at large. The first thirty years of Anabaptist-Mennonite history can be considered as an identifiable period. The second period, from 1555 to 1850, has striking applicability for the Mennonite scene as a whole, even though Mennonite society proliferated and dispersed over much of the globe. The final period, from 1850 to the present, presents the most complex and dynamic era, especially in North America, which has been the major focus of this book.

In order to gain a more holistic picture of Mennonites, we have had to consider the various aspects of the social life of the Mennonites. Beliefs, community, ethnicity, politics, economics, intellectual life, and mission—noted in the table—are probably not the only elements, but they do all pertain to the creation and maintenance of Mennonite characteristics. Of course, the belief system is central, but, as I have emphasized many times in the text, the belief system should not be considered to be the independent cause of all the other elements.

The interaction of the elements in the time context has produced some general configurations, which I have defined in Table A.1 as (1) the period of the utopian (sectarian) movement, (2) the institutional religious protest, and (3) the pluralistic society period. The *utopian-sectarian movement* characterization, however, has not completely disappeared. It is quite correct to say that many Mennonite individuals and groups could still be described as sectarian—for

TABLE A.1 A Typology of Anabaptist-Mennonite Life and History

Element	1525–1555	1555–1850	1850–present
Ideology/belief	Utopian protest; kingdom-building	Retreat; survival; community-building	Separation; assimilation; recovery of utopian vision
Community structure	Mobile; itinerating movement	Based on family, land, congregation	Individualizing; urbanizing; communal recovery
Cultural content	Heterogeneous; fluid; incidental	Germanic; rural folk	Disparagement of ethnic debate; rediscovery
Intellect/education	Open; aware; wary of intellectualism	Utilitarian; traditional; transmission of values	Anti-intellectual; emphasis on enlightenment; return to sectarianism
Economic sphere	Subordinate to religious goals	Subsistence; rural way of life	Traditional; capitalist; communal
Political sphere	Opposition; conflict; challenge of authority	Retreat; dependence on state; compliance	Participation; compliance; opposition
Mission stance	Universalistic; aggressive	Separatist; community as mission	Institutionalized; evangelical; service-oriented

General type	Ideological/utopian movement	Institutionalizing peoplehood	Pluralistic family:
			(1) Traditionalists
			  a) plain peoples
			  b) rural people
			  c) the traditionally religious
			(2) Acculturationists
			  a) pietists/fundamentalists
			  b) advocates of civil religion
			  c) advocates of secularism/capitalism
			(3) Utopian restitutionists
			  a) Anabaptist "recovery" advocates
			  b) Neo-Anabaptists
			  c) the radical left wing

example, the Old Order groups. As a study of the descriptions in column 1 will make clear, for the main body of Mennonites, at least, the sect designation does not imply retreat and separation, but rather engagement and active interaction.

To acknowledge the *institutionalized religious protest* phase also does not imply that all of the sectarian traits have evaporated. Rather, one can suggest that the sectarian impulse was suspended or made less visible and relevant as a result of the consequences of the "flight to the hills" in order to survive and to achieve stability. The "commonwealth" period therefore became another layer in the Mennonite psyche, but was not as visible as were the first years—the sectarian movement period.

The *pluralistic society* epoch from 1850 to the present is the most complex because of the variety of directions that exist; it is therefore exceedingly difficult to synthesize. What is more important than synthesis, however, is the fact that both the sectarian and institutionalized protest experiences have been superseded by another mode of experience—the pluralistic society, which is considerably more ambiguous. In consequence, since the 1950s, there has emerged an increasing ambivalence and doubt as to whether Mennonitism can really any longer be defined.

So we are forced today into viewing a strangely variegated milieu, a multifaceted Mennonite present and future; the serious scholar cannot escape this perspective. There are also Mennonites who operate according to none of the epochs of Mennonitism described above. There are Mennonite traditionalists (those who affirm the validity of the sectarian-ethnic past), assimilationists (those who want to forsake the Mennonite tradition), and restitutionists (those who affirm the Anabaptist-Mennonite heritage but believe it needs to be updated and made relevant to today's society). The last group takes the position that Anabaptist-Mennonite tradition has to evolve from the trajectory established earlier and that is not fully evolved at present. It will be obvious immediately that these categories are similar in many ways to the three sects of Judaism: the Orthodox (similar to the traditionalist Mennonites), the Reformed (the assimilationists), and the Conservative (the restitutionists).

It would be easy to suggest that the above typology simply reflects the degree of conservatism or liberalism of the Mennonite group in question, but this would be an oversimplification. Such an approach tends to focus on the theological elements alone—that is, on ideology and beliefs (see row 1 of Table A.1)—and does not consider carefully enough the fact that Mennonite society is a configuration or concatenation of cultural, social, economic, and other factors as well. There is simply no easy way in which to classify all Mennonites over time. For example, some Mennonites who might be called theological liberals according to prevailing definitions might be traditionalists or restitutionists, and in fact often are. Some Mennonites who are theologically conservative could be and often are assimilationist in orientation. Or Mennonites with evangelical leanings may still be conservative regarding Mennonite stress on missions or political activity. So it becomes clear that Mennonites—unlike Jews, who can be identified easily as orthodox, reform, or conservative—cannot be segmented into easily discernible types. Actually, the typology I have discussed best serves to describe the contemporary orientations if the image of a "pluralistic society" is used where a great latitude of behavior is present and allowed, but where acceptance of the "common ancestry"—the original utopian protest—still transcends the obvious differences in economic, political, educational, or other dimensions of life.

A Paradigm of Mennonite Conflict with Society

We have seen how the Mennonites differentiated themselves (separated) from the larger host society. This took the form of conflict over cultural factors such as beliefs, values, norms, and behaviors (stage I in Chart A.1). The other side of the differentiation was structural—involving endogamy, spatial separation, and educational, social, and religious "partings." The period 1525–55 in Table A.1 conforms to stage I in Chart A.1. The reasons for this differentiation were expanded on in the earlier chapters.

In actuality, stage II in Chart A.1 is not as clean as the diagram indicates; nevertheless, it was conceptually always present. That is to say, two distinct entities existed—the dominant, or host, society and the Mennonites who separated themselves from the larger society, defined as the 1555–1850 period in Table A.1. This does not mean that the schismatic group is totally set apart, but it does mean, minimally, that there is a clearly marked boundary system between *them* and *us*. Of course, there are still economic, political, and social interrelationships as well as interdependency, but these interactions are limited by a new internal "charter."

Stage II, which is in reality an interactional process, extends on through stage III. In chart A.1, *A* is the force of the major society trying to impose its rules and structures on the minority group; *B* and *C* are the forces attempting to reject that influence (*B*) and/or to witness to it (*C*). Stage III is a conflict type almost unique for separatist religious groups—for not only is there a mandate

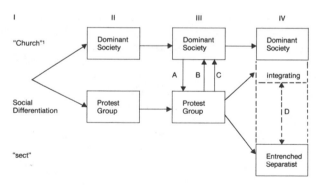

CHART A.1   A Sociological Model of Mennonite Conflict
 [1]The Troeltschian definition of the basic division in orientation.
A. Societal influences for integration and conformity
B. Protest-group rejection of dominance and conformity
C. Protest-group intention to "evangelize" dominant society
D. Context of great conflict between integrating and entrenching factors

(goal) to separate from the "bad" world, but there is also a mandate to witness and preach to that world, described by the 1850–present period in Table A.1. So the separatist religious group will have a basic internal conflict: a desire to remain separate and preserve autonomy, and yet a desire to be relevant and to make an impact on the larger society. Leland Harder has described the problem as follows:

> If the sect type of structure is defined both in terms of a distinctly voluntary religious membership and in terms of separation from society, it is involved in a structural disequilibrium that must inevitably lead in one direction or the other. The voluntary aspect of its constitutive basis tends to give the sect a conversionist character as it seeks to propagate its principles in society, thereby recruiting men and women for membership in the body of believers. The separatist aspect tends to give the sect an avoidance character as it seeks to divorce itself from societal evils. (1962, 31)

This uneasy equilibrium or tension within the group will pull the members of the separating groups in two directions, and actually cause some individuals or groups to move toward integration with the large society in order to be relevant (that is, to witness) to it. Others, very aware of the seductive lures of integration, will want to continue to remain separate and will work hard to entrench the boundary maintenance elements even more. Thus, stage IV becomes the end product, in which the segment that has taken the direction of relevance becomes accommodated to and legitimates the existing order; in turn, this segment receives legitimation by the host or dominant society.

However, Harder takes the position that it is basically the internal contradictions of the religious beliefs of the group that cause it to change, so—against the perspective outlined in Chapter 16—his basic thesis must be considered only partially adequate. But the internal conflict between relevance and separation is consistent with minority-majority conflict theory and forms a part of the larger explanation.

The interactional approach to conflict taken in this book thus maintains that the emergence of the differentiated group came about through *cultural* and *structural* conflicts. Furthermore, the persistence of the separated group will continue to produce tensions as the host society influences and attempts to integrate the deviant group, while the minority group tries to remain autonomous and/or influence the larger society. This latter process—itself in part the consequence of outside forces—continues to exacerbate the conflict by producing new dimensions or expressions of belief, values, and norms.

That is, the tendency to divide again at stage IV (Chart A.1) is the result not only of the internal conflict of values over the original separation and subsequent efforts at evangelization, but also of conflict with the larger society, including the religious structures of the larger society, which places great stress on the original self-understanding. Put concretely in the contemporary context, the emphasis of mainline evangelical Christianity on church growth, evangelism, and outreach—as well as the great value placed on growth and progress by the secular society—contributes to the internal conflict of the group and to the basic relevance-versus-autonomy tension indicated earlier, but without being directly derivative from the original vision. In fact, it is not related.

But for various reasons, including past rejection, the subsystem may not wish either to cater to the needs of the larger system or to assimilate into the larger system. Such reluctance or refusal then becomes the agenda for the ongoing relationship. Viewed as a historical phenomenon that is developing and growing, Anabaptist-Mennonitism has developed by now a "life of its own" which includes an autonomous, institutionalized, integrated, and dynamic ideology. Of course, there are constant defections of members as well as loss of ideals and convictions, but the "Mennonite peoplehood" will continue because many persons born into the society of Mennonite parents internalize the ideological and emotional past and identify it as their own. Simultaneously, persons who are not "birthright" Mennonites join the movement and internalize its history as their own. That the Mennonites are no longer purely a movement does not change their commitment to it; often these new converts become the strongest voices calling for the Mennonites to return to the first stage.

Appendix B

A Bibliographic Survey of Mennonite Sources

The range of interests and perspectives of readers of this book may be so wide as to make a useful commentary on further sources impossible. Nevertheless a general review of sources may still be useful. The bibliography presented in this volume is already a substantial start. The following review is classified into sociological, historical, and theological studies. Full citations for the books discussed appear in the bibliography.

Sociological Sources

Bibliographies. Fortunately, there is a bibliography of sociological and anthropological research, edited by Donovan Smucker and entitled *The Sociology of Canadian Mennonites, Hutterites, and Amish* (1977). Although the title indicates a Canadian content, it deals with North American Mennonites. An updated version, with critical annotations of works published since 1977, is forthcoming. This is without a doubt the most useful tool for sociological and anthropological research on Mennonites, Hutterites, and Amish available.

State-of-the-Art Reviews. "Mennonite Sociology: State of the Art and Science," published in 1983 by Driedger and Redekop, presents the most comprehensive survey of leading research on Mennonites. Earlier, J. Howard Kauffman published an article entitled "Toward a Sociology of Mennonites" (1956a). This article reviews areas which have been studied and presents suggestions for further research and attention; it also includes a bibliography of material published up to that date.

Journals and Series Publications.   Even though it ceased publication in 1967, the *Proceedings of the Mennonite Educational and Cultural Conference* is the most specifically social-science-oriented series of publications available on Mennonite economics, psychology, history, sociology, philosophy, and education. The *Mennonite Quarterly Review* contains a considerable amount of sociological and social science material, even though it is normally perceived as a historical Anabaptist-Mennonite journal; the policy of its editors is to publish relevant and quality materials in all the social sciences. The book reviews and citations also provide very useful bibliography. *Mennonite Life,* while written in a more popular style, has consistently published high-quality social and cultural studies on a variety of topics and provides specific material on a vast number of local Mennonite communities and institutions. Unfortunately, its good bibliography is not consistently published. *The Journal of Mennonite Studies* (1983–) is rapidly becoming an important source of materials in sociology, history, theology, and the arts.

As readers of this volume already know, the *Mennonite Encyclopedia* is an invaluable source for information on the entire gamut of Mennonite institutions, organizations, and history. Written by experts in various areas, it is indispensable for general orientation and specifics on almost any topic. The bibliographies are very useful, though quite dated. An updated supplemental Volume 5 slated for publication by 1991 will provide a number of articles written by the growing number of social scientists doing research on Mennonites. *Direction,* published by the Mennonite Brethren colleges and the seminary, contains very useful material, although it is oriented more toward theological and church-building matters.

Major Books.   Monographs on Mennonite communities and groups are few, but their number is increasing. Certainly the books by John A. Hostetler on the Amish and Hutterites, cited so copiously in this book, are foremost. The bibliographies on the Hutterites and Amish in these books are extensive, though not fully up to date. *The Holdeman People* by Clarence Hiebert, Sawatzky's *They Sought a Country,* and my *The Old Colony Mennonites* provide material on Russian Mennonite conservatism. These books also provide bibliographies. *Mennonite Identity: Historical and Contemporary Perspectives* by Redekop and Steiner, often cited in this book, is an important bibliographical source for sociology, psychology, theology, history, and the arts. *Mennonite Identity in Conflict* by Leo Driedger presents research on Mennonite themes, including community, urbanism, kinship, and ethnicity. Finally, a specifically empirical monograph on Mennonite beliefs and practice, *Anabaptists Four Centuries Later* by Kauffman and Harder, provides some useful information on a wide range of topics and has some references; an update is in progress. J. Winfield Fretz has written a significant Mennonite community study, *The Waterloo Mennonites* published in 1989 (Wilfrid Laurier Press). Leading sociology and anthropology journals also carry articles on Mennonite themes; such articles are listed in Smucker's book.

Historical Sources

Bibliographies. The most extensive bibliography on Anabaptist-Mennonite history is the two-volume *Mennonite Bibliography, 1631–1961* by Nelson P. Springer and A. J. Klassen. It purports to list all published Mennonite materials and contains a complete author index. The more than twenty-six monographs published in the Studies in Anabaptist and Mennonite History series of the Mennonite Historical Society list a wide variety of sources on Mennonite history and thought. Volumes in the Institute of Mennonite Studies (IMS) series Classics of the Radical Reformation, published by Herald Press, also provide important early history. These all contain very useful sources and bibliographies.

State-of-the-Art Reviews. Up-to-date reviews of work on the early Anabaptists have been produced from time to time, the most recent being "Problems of Anabaptist History: A Symposium" (1979) appearing in the *Mennonite Quarterly Review*. More recently the Mennonite Experience in America commission, which is supporting the publication of four volumes of history of the North American Mennonites, has held symposia bringing research issues to focus, the most recent reported in the January 1986 *Mennonite Quarterly Review*. The first issue of the *Journal of Mennonite Studies* (1983) reviews politics, education, history, sociology, psychology, and other topics.

Journals and Series. Again, the *Mennonite Quarterly Review* is undoubtedly the best source for historical studies and research. Recent volumes contain increasingly significant materials on Mennonite experience and life in North America. The *Mennonite Quarterly Review* publishes periodic bibliographies and indexes, which make it a very useful research tool. *Mennonite Life* also provides some significant, although shorter articles and research reports on a large variety of topics, from missionary activities to frontier settlements and economic life. The *Mennonite Encyclopedia* provides considerable historical material; though its articles are necessarily brief, the citations in the articles provide leads for further research.

Monographs and Books. General histories of Mennonites in America are limited. The standard work is C. Henry Smith's *The Story of the Mennonites*. Updated several times, it is still the single most comprehensive account of Mennonites in North America although many issues are in need of reinterpretation. C. J. Dyck's *Introduction to Mennonite History* brings more modern scholarship to bear on the topic, although only a part of the book deals with the North American experience. Frank Epp's *Mennonites in Canada, 1786–1920* presents the first comprehensive history of Canadian Mennonites. His second volume, *Mennonites in Canada, 1920–1940*, continues the history. A third volume is in preparation, bringing the history into the 1960s. As noted above, in the United States, the Mennonite Experience in America project plans four volumes covering the years from 1683 to the present, the first of which, Richard MacMaster's *Land, Piety, and People*, was published in 1985. Theron Schlabach's *Peace, Faith, Nation* was published in 1988. The remaining two are in the final stages of preparation. There is a bevy of conference and regional histories, among them accounts of the Old Mennonites (Wenger 1966), the General Conference (Pannabecker 1977), and the Mennonite Brethren (J. A. Toews 1975). These are clearly in-group oriented and provide helpful materials to gain a pan-Mennonite perspective.

Theological Sources

It should come as no surprise to learn that there are few writings on Mennonite theology and faith. As has been indicated, this is because Mennonites have accepted the general beliefs of Christendom while differing enormously in their application.

Bibliographies. No bibliography on Mennonite theology, belief, or doctrine exists. However, the bibliographies in history noted above contain many references and should be consulted. Neff's article "Confessions of Faith" provides the major sources on Mennonite faith (1955b).

State-of-the-Art Reviews. A movement toward identifying a Mennonite theology is discernable. Two publications edited by Willard Swartley, *Explorations of Systematic Theology from Mennonite Perspectives* and *Essays on Biblical Interpretation: Anabaptist-Mennonite Perspectives* present such evidence. The section on theology in Redekop and Steiner's *Mennonite Identity: Historical and Contemporary Perspectives* provides a very recent survey of the state of Mennonite theology. A spate of articles in the *Conrad Grebel Review*, especially A. James Reimer's "The Nature and Possibility of a Mennonite Theology" (Winter 1983) and Denny Weaver's "Perspectives on a Mennonite Theology" (Fall 1984), are very useful.

Journals and Series. As already indicated, the *Conrad Grebel Review* and the *Mennonite Quarterly Review* provide the most extended channels for theological reflections. A content analysis of these and other Mennonite journals and periodicals would reveal how little theological reflection has occupied Mennonitism.

Monographs. The earliest specifically Mennonite monograph on Mennonite theology was J. C. Wenger's *Introduction to Theology* (1954), which was followed by Friedmann's *The Theology of Anabaptism* (1973), the latter being more thematic, focusing on dualism as the essence of Anabaptist faith. Three very recent books indicate the emergence of interest in Mennonite theology: Howard Loewen, *One Lord, One Church, One Hope and One God: Mennonite Confessions of Faith* (1985), Thomas N. Finger, *Christian Theology: An Eschatological Approach* (Vol. 1, 1985); and C. Norman Kraus, *Jesus Christ Our Lord: Christology from a Disciple's Perspective* (1987). The forthcoming Volume 5 of the *Mennonite Encyclopedia* contains an extensive series of articles on Mennonite theology.

Document and Research Centers

Most of the major Mennonite conferences have established research and document collection centers. These centers provide numerous services and house the most complete collections of materials pertaining to the conferences they represent. Only the three major conferences and their centers are listed. Other conference centers can be obtained by writing one of these:

1. The Institute of Mennonite Studies, 3003 Benham Ave., Elkhart, Indiana 46517. This center is the research agency for the Mennonite church and the General Conference of Mennonites in North America. It promotes research and writing in the areas of theology, peace, missions, faith, and other areas. It has also produced numerous bibliographies.

2. Mennonite Historical Library, Goshen College, Goshen, Indiana 46526. Founded in 1906, this library contains over 35,000 books and documents pertaining to Anabaptists and Mennonites.

3. Archives of the Mennonite Church, 1700 South Main, Goshen, Indiana 46526. This is the main research and collection agency for the Mennonite church.

4. Center for Mennonite Brethren Studies, 4824 East Butler Ave., Fresno, California 93727-5097. The Fresno Center is affiliated with the Mennonite Brethren Seminary at Fresno. There are also centers for the Mennonite Brethren in Winnipeg and Hillsboro, Kansas.

5. Mennonite Library and Archives, Bethel College, North Newton, Kansas 67117. With about 30,000 books and papers, this library is the main repository for General Conference Mennonite materials. The Mennonite Heritage Center Archives, 600 Shaftesbury Blvd., Winnipeg, Manitoba R3P OM4, provides special services to Canadian General Conference Mennonites.

Notes

Chapter 1 The Origins of the Mennonite Movement

1. This volume does not purport to be an exhaustive history of the Mennonite movement. Sources for the general reader include Dyck 1967; F. Epp 1974; Horsch 1950; Wenger 1947. More specific materials, for the general reader as well as for the scholar, can be found in the *Mennonite Encyclopedia* and the *Mennonite Quarterly Review*. A more popular source for the life and culture of the Mennonites can be found in *Mennonite Life*. Appendix B, "A Bibliographic Survey of Mennonite Sources," discusses the most relevant sources for further study and investigation.

2. The interpretation of the origins of the Anabaptist movement has undergone a number of "revisions" which will be noted in the ensuing chapters. Briefly stated, the interpretations of Anabaptism can be classified as follows: (1) The view of the established religious institutions (Catholicism and Protestantism) considered the Anabaptists a sect and even practitioners of a false religion. (2) A revision conceded that Anabaptism had some legitimate concerns, as evidenced by religious historians such as Ludwig, Keller, and Kohler, and should not be seen as a heretical group. (3) The Mennonite self-interpretation, centered on the "Goshen School," placed Anabaptism at the center of the Reformation. Anabaptism was then labeled the "radical wing of the Reformation" (George Williams 1962); Anabaptism was seen as having a monogenetic origin in the "Zwinglian Circle" and as having then fanned out from there to

the rest of Europe (H. Bender, Blanke, and others). (4) The revisionist school claimed with increasing support that Anabaptism emerged in various parts of Europe and that it cannot be "normatively" defined on the basis of original theology and/or ecclesiology. The classic formulation of the "revision" school is contained in Stayer, Packull, and Depperman 1975. A major bibliographical source is Ozment 1982.

3. No intensive research has been done on the sociological aspects of the movement and its founders. Clasen's work (1972) is a social history and deals with the sociological characteristics of the South German Anabaptists, but he does not address the youthfulness issue. Clearly, because of the youthfulness of its founders, the movement must be recognized as strongly idealistic.

4. The general socio-religio-economic conditions of middle Europe during the time of the Reformation have been extensively described. Recent research has provided much more adequate analysis of the conditions. The neo-Marxist attempt to place the Radical Reformation into a pre-socialist revolution has contributed to this analysis. Clasen, Friesen, Mullet, Kautzky, Zschäbitz, Goertz, and others listed in the bibliography provide information on this subject. For a very recent review of the social history of the Reformation period and a bibliography, see Brody 1982.

5. For an extensive treatment of martyrdom among the Anabaptists, see van Braght 1950. There is continuing insistence that the Anabaptists were not Protestants, but a "third way," since the protest and separation was originally from the Reformed church in Switzerland; see Klaassen 1981b. Van Braght agrees with this position, arguing that Anabaptism cannot be classed with any of the dominant religious systems.

6. "The period of a thousand years during which Christ will reign on earth" (Pike 1958, 254).

7. The belief that "immediately after or before Christ's Second Advent, the saints will live for a thousand years here upon earth in the enjoyment of every kind of innocent pleasure and delight" (Pike, 92). For an extended discussion of millennialism and utopianism, see Olson 1982.

Chapter 2 The Dispersion and Expansion of Mennonite Society

1. Migration is a complex subject and is influenced by many factors, including population pressures, climatic conditions, wars, and cultural conflict. H. P. Fairchild has proposed the following general types: (1) dispersion, (2) nomadism, (3) invasion, (4) conquest, (5) colonization, (6) forced migration, (7) immigration, and (8) internal migration (Berry 1965, 74ff.). Mennonite migrations can probably best be defined as approximating nos. 1, 4 (if by conquest we refer to evangelization), 5, 6, and 8.

For an analysis of Mennonite migrations in terms of causes and consequences for indigenous groups, see C. Redekop 1982. Rose (1982) analyzes the internal migrations of members of a local Mennonite society.

2. The sociology of Mennonite migrations has not been explicitly studied, but evidence has been accumulating. For Mennonites the causes of migration have included (1) religious freedom, (2) social freedoms, such as the freedom to

conduct Mennonite schools, (3) economic pressures, (4) population pressure, (5) missionary impulses, (6) release from internal restrictions, and (7) preservation of a way of life. The corresponding consequences are no less numerous: (1) religious narrowing and traditionalism, (2) development of internal social restrictions and inhibitions, (3) economic differentiation and accommodation, (4) continuing population growth, (5) assimilation of proselytes and consequent changes in Mennonite values, (6) loss of internal norms and controls, and (7) entrenchment of a traditional way or loss of tradition and accommodation to another. These issues are treated at length in succeeding chapters of this book.

3. The defection of Mennonite society members has received only sporadic treatment. During the early decades of Anabaptism, the defection was high, though few statistics are available. Although Clasen does not give figures, he suggests that "most Anabaptist leaders preached only for a short time, a few years at the most" (1975, 123). He gives the impression that a vast majority of Anabaptists defected. Defection of subsequent generations of Anabaptist-Mennonites is even more difficult to ascertain. Hutterite and Amish defection has been relatively low throughout the centuries (J. A. Hostetler 1974, 1980). Defection among the "mainline" Mennonites from around 1600 was probably relatively low until the mid-1800s. With the Awakening in Russia and in America, numerous persons and congregations left the church. The genealogy of one Russian Mennonite family suggests that of a total of 1,544 members, over 65 percent left the Mennonite church for other or no religions. This is not too far from representative, according to some experts on Mennonites generally (C. Redekop 1984d).

4. A recent demographic analysis in Canada (Heaton 1986, 59) shows that for samples of 1,000 women, Mennonite women had an average of 3.308 children over their lifetimes, and Hutterite women, 5.281, as compared with 2.493 for women in the population as a whole.

5. It is doubtful that accurate information on modern defection among Mennonites can be obtained. Since persons join the church as adults, only those who have joined and then left would be recorded as defectors. What happens in many if not most Mennonite communities is that a person who is alienated from Mennonite society simply does not join the church; hence, his or her defection is of a benign sort not subject to ecclesiastical pressure or enumeration. Mennonite literature abounds with allusions to this phenomenon.

6. One of the most productive sources of insight on the cohesion of a group is the type and rate of defection from it. It is unfortunate that little research has been done on defection from Mennonite society, either historically or sociologically. Some estimates indicate that the majority of the Anabaptists defected (see note 3 above) and that at least half of those born into contemporary Mennonite families leave the Mennonite church.

Chapter 3   The Differentiation of the Mennonite Family of Believers

1. *Birthright* is a term used by Quakers to designate the person who has been born of Quaker parents and has joined the church in a natural way. "Convinced Friend" refers to a person of non-Quaker background who joins the Friends by

choice. In Mennonite circles the designation is less forthright. An "outsider" is often called a "convert," which is not always an appropriate term, since the person may have already been a Christian.

2. This issue is discussed in Chapter 16.

3. The issue of Mennonites as a denomination is discussed further in Appendix A.

4. The Society of Brothers deserves more extensive treatment because of its important influences on the Hutterite society, but space prohibits such an effort here. Because the society originated in Germany in the twentieth century, its intellectual level, under the leadership of Eberhard Arnold, and its understanding of the relation of religion and culture has been much more "urbane" than that of the "old" Hutterites. Hence, the group is continuing to challenge and stimulate the historical Hutterite community. The "New" Hutterite *Bruderhofs* are located in England (Darvel), New York (Woodcrest), Pennsylvania (Meadow Run), and Connecticut (Deer Spring). These are quasi-urban communities which have developed flourishing industries (for example, Community Playthings) which employ their own members as well as outsiders. The "Arnold Leut"—as they are designated in the larger Hutterite family—are rapidly becoming the evangelism arm of the entire Hutterite society through their numerous publications on Christian piety and community (Eggers 1985).

5. The Brethren in Christ have adhered to most of the Mennonite principles, although this has varied. Mennonite institutions and organizations have welcomed the BIC to participate in all of their activities as a member of the family, but the response has been casual. This book does not treat the BIC as a significant part of the story, because doing so would add considerably to the complexity of the analysis, especially since it is not clear how strongly the BIC considers itself a member of the Mennonite body. For further readings, see Climenhaga 1942; Hosteter 1955; and Wittlinger 1978.

Chapter 4   The Belief System of Anabaptist-Mennonites

1. John C. Wenger, for example, suggests that "the unique tenets and emphases of the Mennonites theologically can perhaps be subsumed under three heads, related to (*a*) the Bible, (*b*) the Church, and (*c*) the Christian Life and Ethic" (1947, 147). He characterizes Mennonite beliefs as "biblicism" which rejects the traditional separation of form and spirit (149).

2. Many Mennonites disagree with the "biblicism" label and would rather identify the distinction as that of being a "hermeneutical community" in which the members of the local congregation use the Bible as the absolute source of doctrine, but depend upon the fellowship of believers (the committed members of the congregation) to study, discern, and apply the message of the Holy Word. For recent analysis of this interpretation, see Burkholder and Redekop 1976, especially Millard C. Lind, "Reflections on Biblical Hermeneutics," 81–117. See also Littell 1960 and C. Redekop 1970; Mennonite scholars maintain that it is this emphasis upon congregational interpretation of Scripture which distinguishes Anabaptist congregationalism from other types of congregationalism. In other types, it is usually the position of preacher or leader, or the denomina-

tional doctrine, which is accepted as normative for the congregation; further, the main expression of typical congregationalism is the ecclesiological power of employing leadership, or managing the organizational aspects of congregational life. See "Congregationalism" in Halverson 1958, 58–60: "Congregationalism is that type of church government which promotes and protects the spiritual values which lie in regular meetings of Christian groups . . . the theology of the Congregational Christian Churches has always been that of the Christian Church in general. Its ministers keep *au courant* of the thinking of leaders" (59).

3. The congregationalism of Anabaptism has not gone smoothly. The question of authority—whether centered in the Bible, expressed in leaders, or experienced in the life of the congregation—has resulted in enormous conflict, a variety of ecclesiastical structures, and study. Many scholars maintain that because of their congregational theology and pacifistic commitments, Mennonites have avoided or ignored the power and authority issues. Increasingly, latent or covert authority and power conflicts are surfacing in conferences. This question has a number of facets, including the structural life of the congregation and the discipline of members: in other words, "Who leads?" and "How is discipline administered?" One study on the issue is Waltner 1958. A significant reform movement within Mennonitism was the "Concern Movement." Issues no. 2 and 14 of the publication *Concern* deal with this problem on a theological and sociological level. See also Burkholder, Redekop 1976, and Sawatsky 1987.

4. See Jean Séguy (1977) for an outstanding analysis of the Alsatian Mennonites.

5. A beginning in the analysis of diverging emphases is contained in Harry Loewen 1980b.

6. Weber's classic forms of authority—legal, traditional, rational, and charismatic—are relevant here because they are "rolled into one" for Anabaptist-Mennonites. It is probably fair to say that specific Mennonite groups, at certain times in their history, can be described as having been guided by one of the four forms of authority, but it would be more accurate to suggest that if the forms of authority were seen as a rectangle, Mennonite structure has moved between the four poles in a fluid way.

7. *Schwertler*—"those who take the sword"; *Staebler*—"those who refuse to wear the sword."

8. This position reflects the assumption that religious impulses are not entirely socially determined, but are the result of theological or superempirical revelations and insights. If religious factors are merely social factors, then we cannot impute any other meaning to "religious" events. On this topic, see Mehl 1970.

Chapter 5   The Religious Base of the Mennonite Community

1. There have been many attempts to describe this idea. Cultural definitions which describe cultural distinctions as the boundary markers are an example. But the Mennonite network has a much more personal, "in-group" dimension. One of the most intriguing illustrations of this dimension is the "Mennonite Your Way" movement among Mennonites, an idea which has now been institu-

tionalized with the annual publication of 2,300 households which are willing and eager to host fellow Mennonites as they travel. Persons who have utilized this procedure almost uniformly testify to the gratifying experience of learning to know fellow Mennonites, almost invariably discovering in the process that they have friends in common, or are in fact related.

2. Mennonite dialects have not been extensively analyzed, and there is considerable ambiguity as to how distinct they really are. The *Mennonite Encyclopedia* (2:51) lists Low German (Plattdeutsch), Alsatian German, Swiss German, and Galician (basically Carinthian) as the principal dialects. Low German is the most distinctly original Mennonite dialect of them all; considerable literature exists in Plattdeutsch, and in recent years a lexicon and a grammar have appeared. The Hutterite, Volhynian, and Galician dialects are less distinct while contemporary Swiss German is quite similar to an earlier dialect spoken in Switzerland.

3. Biblicism as the distinguishing characteristic of Anabaptists has been a dominant motif in Mennonite theological and doctrinal thinking. J. C. Wenger, a proponent of this position states, "The Anabaptists were above all else men of the Word . . . the Anabaptists made their attitude toward the Bible operate in daily life to a degree which seemed fanatical to many sixteenth-century Christians" (1947, 147). This view has been challenged and is no longer held very strongly. A more prevalent view now is that the Anabaptists approached the Bible in a unique way, using the "hermeneutical community" as the methodology in understanding the biblical message.

4. The understanding that Anabaptist biblicism was a method rather than a literalistic application of holy writ has emerged as a part of the rediscovery of the centrality of the congregation in matters of faith and discipline. A significant statement of this discovery is Millard Lind's "Reflections on Biblical Hermeneutics" (Burkholder and Redekop 1976, 91–102). He suggests, "Viewing the congregation as a hermeneutical community is an important contribution of Anabaptism to biblical hermeneutics" (93). A more recent and extended application of the approach is found in Perry Yoder 1982.

5. The Anabaptist-Mennonite treatment of the congregation-leadership question has been exacerbated because of the lay-minister practice and understanding. As is indicated in the chapters on schism, the question of leadership in the congregation has often been the cause of division. This question has become even more urgent in recent decades, and many study conferences and convocations dealing with theoretical and practical issues have been held. One recent instance of this process produced a document by the Mennonite Church: *Leadership and Authority in the Life of the Church* (1981).

6. Documentation for this phenomenon is not easily obtained, since few people have written about their experiences. But the alienation has been extensive. Recent biographical literature, however, provides a wealth of second-hand information. Rudy Wiebe's *Peace Shall Destroy Many* (1962) was a literary sensation in exposing Mennonite authoritarianism. A recent biography entitled *Stumbling Heavenward*, by Urie Bender (1984), the story of a Peter Rempel, offers an archetype on this issue.

7. Guy F. Hershberger's *Recovery of the Anabaptist Vision* (1957a) is an influential study of this topic, and symbolizes the extent of interest and concern.

There is no more general slogan or cliché in Mennonite circles than "the Anabaptist vision."

8. Women's role in church structure has been receiving greater attention in recent years, and is creating a great strain in terms of church authority. Although the discussion in Mennonite circles is very similar to the discussion of the role of women in the broader Christian context, the entrance of women into all sectors of the Mennonite church will be very difficult because of the extremely masculine polity and because of the extreme biblical literalism regarding women's role in the church.

9. There is a structural basis for this phenomenon. Since the community, the family, and the congregation are parts of the triad composing Mennonite reality, there are built-in correctives or limits to the degree that one family achieves hegemony, for example. Again, the power of tradition in a community is limited and corrected by the congregation, which ideally receives its mandate from biblical norms.

10. This may be an ideological statement, but it is the belief that energizes Mennonites. That is, Mennonites believe that theirs is not a secular society, but a community based on faith, and it is because of the notion of nonconformity to the world that a peculiar subculture emerges.

Chapter 6   Mennonite Social Organization

1. This section benefits greatly from the work of E. K. Francis (especially 1955), Donovan Smucker (1976), and Roy Vogt (1980).

2. The Russian "commonwealth" idea has been described in numerous places. Francis 1955 provides the most explicit analysis. David G. Rempel 1933 provides the best overall description of the origins of the commonwealth. Kreider 1951 and Calvin Redekop 1980 deal with the historical and sociological consequences. The commonwealth is probably best exemplified by the Paraguayan Mennonites in the Chaco. Cf. C. Redekop 1973.

3. For a bibliography of literature on acculturation and assimilation research, see Driedger and Redekop 1983. For a community study, see C. Redekop 1953; the most recent of such studies is a Ph.D. dissertation by Robert Graber, "The Sociocultural Differentiation of a Religious Sect: Schism among the Pennsylvania German Mennonites" (1979).

4. The deeply rooted tension and debate within the Mennonite Brethren regarding that group's identity, which includes its commitment to the Anabaptist-Mennonite tradition has erupted in recent years to become an intensely emotional and extended controversy. The publication of John Redekop's *A People Apart: Ethnicity and the Mennonite Brethren* (1987) has intensified the battle and brought it into the public arena. The attempt to pin the identity problem on ethnicity is a misreading of the deeper issues, according to many of the responses to the issue.

Chapter 7   The Mennonite Personality

1. The discussion of a Mennonite personality derives its justification not from the psychological behaviorist school, but from the social psychology of subcultural socialization. We are concerned about the development of a particular personality type that is the result of the operation of strong normative assertions as well as the sharp and sometimes complete separations from outside societal models. Put very bluntly, is it possible to talk about a Mennonite personality type? Can Mennonites be characterized as behaving in a generally similar way? This line of reasoning is not intended to establish whether all Mennonites are alike: we know there is a great variation among them. Rather, we are attempting to determine whether or not there are similar and predictable behavior patterns among Mennonites. The question of personality types has been debated heatedly in the scientific community, with little agreement. In regard to the Mennonite tradition, some research has been done; the most focused is that by John A. Hostetler in *Hutterite Society* (1974, 244–51), as well as Hostetler, *Amish Society*, (1980, 185–89). I have also studied personality types among the Old Colony Mennonites (1969).

Of course, discussion of Mennonite personality may in reality be partly a study of the value commitments of members of the community. Anabaptist-Mennonites are known by the values they hold, which express themselves in daily life. While this is true to a certain extent, I maintain that the Mennonite social system, and the socializing process, contribute to the creation of a very complex culture, social structure and personality. If it is true that culture and society in interaction create personality structure, then there is full logical justification to assert that subcultures can create at least a subpersonality type.

2. Based on preliminary analysis of 100 Mennonite entrepreneurs interviewed by the author in 1985–86. These entrepreneurs were randomly selected from Mennonite communities in Canada and the United States.

3. The Mennonite commonwealth of Russia was the first Mennonite group to establish mental hospitals. It is obvious that when a society is almost self-sufficient, it is forced to develop services and institutions to take care of its own population. Mennonites in less self-sufficient contexts could let the host society take care of its handicapped. For a review see Fast 1957.

4. For a concise review of the Mennonite Mental Health Movement in North America, see the special issue of the *Mennonite Quarterly Review* 56, no. 1 (January 1982). See also Neufeld 1983 for a more self-congratulatory view of the movement.

Chapter 8   Mennonite Intellect and Aesthetics

1. Although aesthetics and intellect could be discussed separately, they impinge deeply on each other. I am focusing on the creative and conceptualizing functioning of the human mind and how it has affected Mennonite life. The more logical and functional aspects of human reasoning are not as relevant for this discussion, since it is clear that Mennonites very thoroughly understand the practical uses of the mind.

2. It is my conclusion that the Mennonite burden with the life of the mind and beauty is hence the result not of narrow-mindedness and empty tradition, but rather of the difficulty of resisting acculturation to North American civil religion, which preaches a faith closely or totally integrated with Western secularism and consequently disparages a religious group that maintains its own traditions as being adherents of a "culture-religion" or simply of "Mennonitism," as many more evangelical Mennonites phrase it. It is the burden of being considered "ethnic" which has dogged Mennonite self-understanding. Other groups, especially the mainline American denominations, are given the right of their subcultures (fast food and rock music), but Mennonites are not. I have attempted to state this case in "Why I Am Still a Mennonite," in Harry Loewen 1988. This is the issue of identity, discussed below.

3. Identity is expanded upon further in Chapters 16–18, and forms a central factor in my analysis. See also "Aesthetics and Fine Arts in Mennonite Self-Understanding," in Redekop and Steiner 1988.

4. For one of the most articulate but poignant discussions of this dilemma, see Magdalene Redekop 1988. Redekop emphasizes how membership in Mennonite society literally destroyed the "imaginative" life of her mother, and she further describes how she herself very nearly became estranged from Mennonite society because of its restrictiveness. It has been her deep respect for the faith principles of Anabaptist-Mennonitism which has kept her clinging to her Mennonite roots. The theme of pride in the heritage and faith of the Mennonite tradition, but sorrow for its restriction of the life of the imagination is also expressed in Al Reimer's "Coming in out of the Cold" in the same volume (Loewen 1988).

Chapter 9 The Mennonite Community

1. Mennonite subculture is best documented in several magazines, especially *Mennonite Life*, *Festival Quarterly*, and the *Journal of Mennonite Studies*. Mennonite art, folklore, humor, and literature are featured in these in a focused way.

2. This section is adapted from Redekop 1970.

3. Community theory has remained relatively dormant for the last few years. I favor a focus on community which includes the geographical community, the spiritual community, the purposive community, and the intentional community. (Cf. Redekop 1975.)

4. The function of the Mennonite community in the formation of norms has not been treated directly in Mennonite literature, but almost all sociological and historical treatments of Mennonite communities deal with this process indirectly. Donald Kraybill's "Mennonite Women's Veiling: The Rise and Fall of a Sacred Symbol" (1987) is a very helpful example.

5. It is evident that the individualist model can hardly express any focus on community, almost by definition. But even the individualistic Mennonites live with the memories of Mennonitism, which cannot easily be forgotten.

6. "Peoplehood" is a somewhat unusual term in contemporary sociology. In the Mennonite context it refers to the way Mennonites are conscious of each

other and of the presence of other Mennonites in an area, and seek each other out and relate on a "family" basis, even though they may not have previously known each other. The Jewish community experiences this "consciousness of kind" in a very similar way, and the phenomenon has been expressed in a way very applicable to Mennonites by the Jewish sociologist Milton Gordon in his *Assimilation in American Life* (1964).

Chapter 10   The Family in Mennonite Life

1. The Mennonite family is a remarkably understudied aspect of Mennonite life. This is probably because it is such an integral part of Mennonite life; and the lack of attention to it is reasonable, since, as indicated in this volume, Mennonite congregation, community, and family are all closely knit parts of a whole. Nevertheless, the research on the family has been limited basically to community studies, and is normally a bit tangential. Thus, the family is described and discussed in Hostetler's treatment of the Hutterites and Amish. But few if any works have been initiated as studies of the family per se: see Driedger and Redekop 1983, 49. For a good overview, see J. Howard Kauffman's article in the *Mennonite Encyclopedia*, "Family in Mennonite History and Life" (1956). Cornelius Krahn's article on the family in the same volume is also helpful. See also M. Lucille Marr's "Anabaptist Women of the North: Peers in the Faith, Subordinates in Marriage" (1987).

2. Descriptions of this type of Mennonite family are most easily derived from the fiction and biographies which have emerged, especially in the Russian Mennonite tradition. The literature is vast, although not widely circulated: that is, many of these accounts are privately published, or published in limited amounts. The article "Mennonites in Literature," one of the longest in the *Mennonite Encyclopedia*, provides a comprehensive list of writings which provide rich materials for an indirect understanding of the Mennonite family.

3. Women's Concerns, an organization sponsored by the MCC, publishes an occasional *Resource Listing of Mennonite Women*, and this publication is a good source for discovering the "flavor and temper" of Mennonite women's concerns. The 1983 edition states: "The Mennonite and Brethren in Christ women listed herein are eager to use their gifts, talents and expertise in a wide variety of ministries related to the church and to meeting human needs in the local community and around the world. By offering themselves, these women are an encouragement toward greater stewardship of the God-given talents within our churches and church related organizations." The relatively passive and benign tone of this preface indicates the cautiousness with which Mennonite women are approaching the issue. The more strident voices are heard in less public places. For an analysis of the Old Mennonite Church's treatment of women, see Klingelsmith 1980.

Chapter 11   Mennonites and Educational Activities

1. The classic definition of functionalism is as follows: "The function of a particular social usage is the contribution it makes to the total social life as the functioning of the total social system" (Merton 1957, 25). Although there are theoretical difficulties with functionalist theory, it is a helpful way to describe and analyze subsocieties, such as the Mennonites. I am very much aware of the fact that Mennonite institutions can be explained on ideological terms as well, and I do so in other contexts in this book.

2. All the Mennonite colleges and Bible schools in Canada and the United States have experienced almost continual criticism from their constituencies, from opposing factions within the schools, and from individuals. Goshen, Tabor, and Bethel were closed for brief times owing to severe tensions and conflicts. Eastern Mennonite College, Bluffton College, Canadian Mennonite Bible College, and Mennonite Brethren Bible College also have been involved in serious and painful struggles. Adequate social analyses have not been written yet, but a number of studies deal indirectly with these conflicts. Tabor College's existence from 1907 to the present has expressed in bold relief the tension between a conference which expected the college to preserve the best in the tradition and a college with a strong commitment to intellectual integrity. Because of the sensitiveness of interpersonal relations between families who have been protagonists in such conflict, objective analyses have not yet been done. As the generations pass on, the defensiveness will decline, and the research will be done. For a theological analysis of the Goshen closing, see Sawatsky 1977.

3. The overpowering ambivalence that has been experienced by Mennonites who enter higher education, particularly graduate school, has been expressed in the history of the Mennonite Graduate Fellowship, which was initiated by several church conferences in an attempt to pastor young students as they confronted the "dangers" of the secular world. Its turbulent history itself demonstrates students' mixed feelings about being "shepherded" while they are trying their own wings in the "unprotected" environment of the university; see Driedger 1965.

4. It is disconcerting to discover that the *Mennonite Quarterly Review*, the *Proceedings of Mennonite Educational and Cultural Problems*, and the *Mennonite Encyclopedia* do not carry articles on the impact of education on faith and theology. There are a few articles on a Mennonite philosophy of education (e.g., Mininger 1967). This is not to deny that much discussion has taken place in promoting the colleges and seminaries, but there has been little academic research on education, a lack which implies that the power and effectiveness of education are assumed.

Chapter 12   Mennonites and Economics

1. R. H. Tawney begins his famous book, *Religion and the Rise of Capitalism* (1926), with the comment that the connection between religious thought and economic practice was "intimate and vital" (1). Tawney then proceeds to list a

host of scholars who have investigated the relationship, which includes Troeltsch, Choisy, Sombart, Levy, and Weber.

2. The development of economic models in this chapter has utilized especially the contributions of J. L. Burkholder 1959; Smucker 1976; Fretz 1957b; R. Vogt 1972; and Nafziger 1965, 1986.

3. An analysis of the study conferences and organizations that have been formed to deal with the faith and economics issue has not been done, but it would provide a revealing and fascinating process at work in the Mennonite community. The Mennonite Community Association, the Committee on Economic and Social Relations, the Conference on Educational and Cultural Problems (held biennially for a number of years), the Mennonite Central Committee's occasional conferences on economics and disparity, the Laurelville occasional "Businessmen's Week," the Mennonite Economic Development Associates with its annual meetings and its journal (the *Marketplace*), and the conferences conducted by the Mennonite Brethren and reported in the journal *Direction*, indicate the vast amount of interest in, discussion of, and concern about how economic factors are influencing Mennonite faith.

4. A Mennonite theology of work has not yet emerged. Neither the *Mennonite Encyclopedia* nor the *Mennonite Quarterly Review* refer to the topic. A conference on a theology of work took place in June 1988, and a Christian view of work has just been published (Redekop and Bender 1988). Though this latter is not explicitly Mennonite, implicitly it derives from, and presents, a Mennonite theological orientation.

5. A recent attempt in this direction is that reported by John Redekop in "The Interaction of Economics and Religion: The Case of the Mennonite Brethren" (1981). This study is limited, since it was directed to the pastoral leadership of the Mennonite Brethren, who were asked to comment on questions such as whether "Mennonite Brethren theology in Canada has been significantly affected by economic factors." Further, its utility is questionable, since it depended on the respondents' opinions of others' behavior—for example, whether "our church members tend to acquire their economic values more from their church than their place of work."

6. Estel Nafziger's discussion, "The Mennonite Ethic and Weber's Thesis" (Nafziger 1986), is in many ways supportive and helpful for the orientation presented here, but needs some corrections. He overstates the case for the "absolutist economic ethic" (265–66), which is similar to my "confrontational model." The Mennonites were never as totally rural and retreatist in economic activity as he states. He also overstates the "calling" aspect (269–70) of Mennonite economic behavior. His emphasis on the role of Mennonite religious norms in directing and limiting Mennonite activity is clearly correct, but it contradicts his promotion of the "calling" rather directly. John W. Bennett is more direct in his rejection of the Weberian thesis in his analysis of the Hutterites. He states, "The Hutterites exemplify the theory that strong incentive can exist in social systems that suppress individualistic competition and aspiration" (1967, 160).

Chapter 13   Mennonites and the Political Process

1. In this discussion, I cannot treat the theological and ethical aspects of the question. I have restricted my analysis to the institutional dimensions which can be described sociologically.

2. The "two-kingdom" idea is complex and relates to nonconformity, separation, church discipline, discipleship, and a host of other issues. No full and adequate description is easily available. One of the most extensive attempts is Robert Friedmann's idea of "the doctrine of the two worlds," discussed in his *Theology of Anabaptism* (1973). The "rule of Christ" is the central idea for Friedmann (43).

3. The Old Order groups have developed a pervasive tradition of rationalizing their participation in government and in technological developments. The public press exploits this issue more than any other, as it attempts to interpret these groups to the public. Hardly a week or month goes by in which some issue is not presented and discussed.

Chapter 14   Mennonites in Missions and Service

1. The history and theology of the service motif in Mennonite society is strangely moot. Mutual aid has been relatively rationalized in Mennonite thought, and reflects both theological and sociological dimensions. But why Christians should serve others is more difficult to determine. The theological source must be the teachings of Jesus, who stressed giving a cup of cold water and giving the scarf to someone who asked for a coat. But it is my contention that service derives more fundamentally from the "Anabaptist ethic" as it pertains to economic activity and work. As opposed to the "Protestant ethic," which stressed individual effort, the "Anabaptist ethic" emphasized the collectivity in regard to individual effort, downgraded personal accumulation, and emphasized Christian obligations to the world. See Studer 1970, 231: "A mutuality of interest and work between the Father and Son, and between Christ and man, and Christ and the creation is abundantly evident in the life of our Lord."

2. See C. Redekop 1981. The response to that article by an officer in the Evangelical Mennonite Brethren Church illustrates well the problem; see W. Regehr 1982.

3. The debate among Mennonites as to whether Mennonite distinctives such as nonresistance and plain dress (and most pointedly the female costumes) hindered the attractiveness of Mennonitism has been going on for many decades. Most of the controversy has been couched in religious terms in the church periodicals. But some careful analysis has been done. Thus, Donald Kraybill in "Mennonite Women's Veiling: The Rise and Fall of a Sacred Symbol" states, "This symbol that was fashioned in a rural separatist environment is becoming incongruent with the social realities of a subculture that is assimilating its professional and urban society" (1987, 319). Maurice Martin believes, however, that "if our faith is real for a real world it will surely stand up to a close look by seekers" (1983, 36).

4. Functionalism was defined above. A framework for the functions of the

MCC can be derived from reading the sixtieth anniversary records of the MCC, *The Mennonite Central Committee Story* (C. Dyck 1980–85). Many of the functions of the MCC are explicitly stated in the mandates and in the names of the departments themselves, such as the Self-Help Program. For instance, "the Overseas Needlework and Crafts Project attempts to provide needy women in underdeveloped countries with a meaningful way of earning a living. It is a way of people helping themselves" (2:143). The functions for members of the Mennonite church are obvious: "The family-to-family self-help project helping human needs in various parts of the world has been a rewarding experience" (2:145). It has been rewarding for the givers, rewarding in terms of being able to do something for others, and allowing isolated church people to find occasions to be together (2:144).

Chapter 15 Schism among Mennonites

1. Social scientists have provided copious and convincing documentation that human societies have become increasingly complex and, in that process, have become increasingly differentiated. This means that there is a splitting off of various institutional aspects and organizations into specialized orders. It is imperative that we see many religious schisms from this perspective, and hence as a normal and natural phenomenon.

2. The phenomenon of schism has been relatively unresearched by Mennonite scholars; most of the research on schism is indirectly related to that topic. The subject is obviously unsavory or threatening to in-group members, as it is to other religious groups. Indeed, social science literature as a whole has provided very little on the specific nature of denominational schism. One of the first specific discussions of schism in the Mennonite context was Calvin Redekop, *Brotherhood and Schism*, published in 1963.

3. I have proposed elsewhere that there are three approaches to the understanding of schism—conceptual, theological, and sociological. From a theological-religious perspective, Mennonite schism is exacerbated by the differences in doctrinal belief, religious experience, and organizational structure, which can develop in everyday social life. I further argued that the adherence to "sola scriptura" (the scriptures alone), the priesthood of believers, the importance of experience, and voluntary membership were specific beliefs of Anabaptists that contributed to the schismatic tendencies— although this stand is difficult to prove (Redekop 1963).

4. Cooperation and unity, though they may be desired by all Mennonites, are not extensively discussed or researched. Edmund G. Kaufman treats the subject in "Nontheological Cultural Factors in the Origin and Current Relationships of Mennonite Groups" (1957). On a general and hence, some would say, an innocuous level, the Mennonite World Conference has tried to promote unity. Erland Waltner, vice-president of the conference, said, "The Seventh Mennonite World Conference contributed significantly to the realization of the stated purpose 'to bring the Mennonites of the world together. . . thereby to strengthen for them the awareness of the worldwide brotherhood in which they stand'" (1962).

Chapter 16   External Threats to Mennonite Identity

1. Richard MacMaster's *Land, Piety, and Peoplehood* (1985) is the first volume; the second, by Theron Schlabach, appeared in 1988.

2. Gauges of the barometer of change and the temperature regarding the issue are the letters to the editors of Mennonite church periodicals. Numerous surveys conducted among Mennonite official organs consistently show that letters to the editor are the most popular and widely read sections. Among the most prevalent topics in such letters is the reaction to changing practices, · positions, and beliefs.

3. As will become clear in subsequent discussion, modernism and liberalism are indeed implicated in American Mennonite history. The *Mennonite Encyclopedia*, which set itself the task of reporting on all aspects of Mennonite life, does not have a heading "modernism," and under "liberalism" describes only the Dutch Mennonite scene. The best explanation is clearly that these subjects are better left untouched. Many of the protagonists were still alive when the volumes of the encyclopedia were published. The recent furor over Theron Schlabach's *Gospel versus Gospel* (1980) illustrates the controversy on the fundamentalism-modernism motif, since Schlabach defines many Mennonite leaders as having been influenced by fundamentalism rather than modernism.

4. For an interesting and illuminating review of the strenuous conflict, see *Mennonite Life* 42, nos. 1–3, which deals with the formation and history of Bethel College. Almost all the issues and dynamics discussed in this chapter are treated there.

5. Since its inception, Grace Bible College has derived its support and student body from congregations and families who have been convinced by the fundamentalistic and evangelical mass media that modernism liberalism is the great scourge and deduced that it is infesting Mennonitism. The school has rejected the traditional Mennonite tenets of faith and has substituted a generalized brand of fundamentalism-evangelicalism. It is now administered by a staff of persons who either come from non-Mennonite backgrounds or who have totally rejected Mennonite theology. The student body, though still largely from Mennonite families, is being trained to work in a nondenominational context (Haury 1981, 240).

The issue of modernism and fundamentalism and the lack of analysis of it again illustrates the Mennonite aversion to confronting conflict. Thus, in the official and definitive story of the General Conference Mennonites, *Open Doors* (1977), S. F. Pannabecker does not refer to liberalism, modernism, or fundamentalism in the entire book. Nor does he refer to the conflicts and divisions that occurred over this issue and the secession of numerous congregations. Neither does he treat Grace Bible College, which is supported by the Mennonite General Conference.

6. One student who later took a Ph.D. at Stanford recalled that C. C. Regier "was the best history teacher he had ever had" (Sprunger 1984, 13). But a middle ground between liberalism and conservatism could not be found, and Regier, "considered to be the faculty ringleader and an extreme liberal," knew that time was running out for him. He stated that "the conflict between conservatism and liberalism has come to a head" (14). He was finally "relieved" by the

board, which was simply not willing or not able candidly to face the real issue. The board, in its action, as interpreted by H. P. Krehbiel, "did not so much 'fire' [Regier] as fail to reemploy [him]" (15).

7. It is not possible in this condensed discussion to address all the nuances and differences among the various types of fundamentalism and evangelicalism. The reader is encouraged to consult the sources indicated in this chapter. For the significance of fundamentalism and evangelicalism for Mennonites, and vice versa, the best source to date is Kraus 1979.

8. The revivalist movement has had considerable influence on Mennonite society. The Wesleyan revivals, including the camp meetings, were attended by Mennonites and invaded Mennonite society itself in some cases. These meetings are described by B. Hostetler: "The meetings held were such prayer meetings in which much ado was made, loud crying and weeping, howling that could be heard a long distance . . . half a mile . . . sitting or lying on the floor and making a great confusion" (1987, 68). A number of schisms in the latter half of the nineteenth century resulted in part at least from this movement in the Mennonite church. On the one hand, some sectors of the church simply could not reconcile this movement with the tenets of the Mennonite heritage; on the other hand, there were those who maintained that any who rejected these new outworkings of God's spirit were spiritually dead.

Chapter 17   Internal Threats to Mennonite Identity

1. In this discussion, as in most of these chapters, the reader must bear in mind that I am speaking of a tremendously varied religiosocial group, so that some of the issues and observations, as well as generalizations, apply more to one segment of the spectrum than others.

2. For this reason it would be redundant to explicate the dilemmas separately here. As a matter of fact, I discussed the dilemmas O'Dea and Aviad propose in the preceding chapters.

3. As indicated earlier, the dilemma of self-preservation versus outreach has troubled the Anabaptist-Mennonite movement from its inception. Harder (1962) has dealt with this dilemma for the General Conference Mennonites in a very extended fashion. His thesis has not received the attention it deserves, possibly because his analysis is directed specifically at discussing the utility of the dilemma in predicting the preservation of the sect typology, whereas the idea has greater contemporary relevance to the socioreligious aspects of Mennonitism.

4. The ambivalent attitude of Mennonites toward their own group was discussed in Chapter 7. The alienation of individual members from the Mennonite group has not received much analysis, but it has already been termed the "Mennonite psychosis" (Dueck 1988, 217), related "to strong guilt feelings, hostility, ambivalence toward parental and religious values, [and] a need to blame themselves for not being a good Christian in the sense of their church community."

5. The *Mennonite Distorter*, an occasional mimeographed periodical published by a group of Mennonite and non-Mennonite graduates of Mennonite

colleges, especially Conrad Grebel College, is a rather impressive effort at putting the Mennonite enterprise into a human perspective; but it is not universally perceived as a healthful exercise, which in itself indicates an inability among Mennonites to take themselves less seriously. Other attempts at humor, such as *The Mennonite Muppy Manual,* sold out in a few weeks.

6. Driedger suggests that a good balance of opening and closing the Mennonite community to change depends upon cultural brokers, who have an openness to the outside but also preserve the good. He does not discuss the possibility of good and bad brokers, both of which are obviously very possible and prevalent. A more serious issue which he does not analyze is the nature of the Mennonite community itself. He refers to these communities as basically "segregated, rural, ethnic enclaves" (1986, 374); I maintain that the Mennonite phenomenon cannot be understood without considering the ideological/religious "struggle" as central to the form the society takes.

7. An identity crisis is indeed confronting Mennonites, as has been noted in many sections of this book. The decision to delete the word "Mennonite" from some conference names has already been discussed. The topic of crisis is emerging more often in various places. The pertinence of this topic is illustrated by a recent conference on Mennonite identity held at Conrad Grebel College in 1986. For the papers of this conference, which approached the issue in a most comprehensive way, see Redekop and Steiner 1988.

Chapter 18   The Utopian Basis of Mennonite Identity

1. In this chapter, I argue that the "object" of the Anabaptist/Mennonite religious movement is the key to understanding it. In discussing the possibility of a sociology of religion and of Christianity, Roger Mehl contends that "Christian communities [can] be understood only if one takes account of the reality to which they give allegiance, for this reality informs their existence, in their institutions and practices as well as in their reformations, their abortive endeavours, their regrets, and their guilty consciences" (1970, 4). Hence the definition of Mennonites as a religious group, regardless of its "ethnic" nature, is critical in my analysis.

2. As can be inferred, I accept the polygenetic-origins interpretation of early Anabaptism as historically accurate. It is unthinkable that a movement such as the Anabaptist one could emerge and spread over western Europe as rapidly as it did without the presence of similar conditions so that the movement could catch fire. The "precipitating factors" for social movements presuppose the requisite "pre-existing" conditions, and these were quite general in Europe.

3. The idea of the "common man" represents an attempt to look at social conditions during the Reformation period differently from the Marxist, "communistic" perspective, popularized by Kautsky, Zschäbitz, and others. See Packull 1985 and 1986.

4. Although both friends and foes have characterized Anabaptism as communal, Mennonites themselves and Mennonite scholars have tended to downplay, evade, or deny the communalistic nature of their heritage. "Few charges recurred so frequently as the one that Anabaptists wanted to have all things in

common," Klassen says (P. Klassen 1964, 24), but Klassen himself, it seems to me, dismisses too easily the claim that Anabaptism was motivated by a communal ethic.

5. The many confessions of faith which early Mennonites hammered out can be interpreted in several ways, but certainly one dynamic must have been the attempt to come to some common point of view, since there were emerging so many groups who were seemingly claiming similar objectives and who were identified as being similar by their opponents. Although this idea has not been extensively developed, there are inferences: e.g., Neff points out that "the Anabaptists never attached the weight to creeds or confessions" (1955b, 679). He quotes Van der Zijp: "The main concern in the confessions was to learn to know one another. One did not write what had to be believed, but what was believed in the particular group!" (680). This latter statement provides some provocative suggestions for in-depth analysis of the *context* of the confession writing and how this would affect the *content* of the confessions.

6. There is an implicit reason why the Anabaptists have not been seen as aggressive and mission-oriented in their early behavior, and that is their pacifism and their relations with authorities. To challenge authority, but to do it nonviolently, creates a very unstable relationship—i.e., either one in which the challenge is successful so that nonviolence becomes the mode of operation, a totally unlikely situation, or one in which the challenge is unsuccessful because it does not "fight back" with the same measures, in which case the nonviolent tactic becomes defensive and retreatist. Further, because "normative Anabaptism" was nonresistant and nonviolent, its leaders did not know how to handle a positive aggressive relationship with authorities.

7. Although non-Mennonite writers have described Mennonites as utopian, this orientation has been rather emphatically rejected by Mennonites themselves. This rejection, I suggest, is basically because utopianism has always seemed to be almost totally politically motivated or directed, an orientation which Mennonites have rejected. But utopianism can also be motivated by religious factors, as Seibt and others have argued. If utopianism is defined as focusing on the achievement of social harmony by way of equality of social status, communism in property, promotion of peaceful and nonresistant love, and the subordination of work to the good of the community, as I have argued elsewhere (Redekop and Koop 1988), then Anabaptists are at the center of utopian activity.

Appendix A   The Mennonites: A Typological Analysis

1. This emphasis focuses on the central issue of the nature of the kingdom of God. The Radical Reformation, seen from a theological perspective, has interpreted the concept of God's activity on earth as the formation of a community where mutuality and love are the fundamental elements, rather than order and control (power). The latter orientation was the one which the post-Constantine church accepted, but it has been resisted by the many protests which have emerged in subsequent years. Troeltsch, Weber, Wach, and many other social historians or sociologists were the first to define this basic difference, mainly in

sociological terms. The theological analysis has been much slower in emerging (Finger 1985; Williams 1962).

2. The Swiss Mennonites participated in the development of what is now known as the Pennsylvania Dutch dialect, which has subtle variations among the U.S. Amish and other groups. In this dialect designation is included the dialect of the Canadian Amish, based in part on the Pfälzisch regional German but also quite similar to the so-called Pennsylvania Dutch. The Volhynian Mennonites developed a dialect that is not spoken by other Mennonites. The Hutterite dialect has similarities with the language spoken in Carinthia, Austria, but in many ways it is a separate and unique dialect (J. A. Hostetler 1974, 149). The Mennonites of Prussian origin have developed their own extensive dialect, namely, a Mennonite Low German which is probably not spoken by any other group (Epp 1987).

3. Thus, John A. Hostetler says of the Hutterites: "As in all distinctive cultural groups, the sense of belonging is enhanced by signs and symbols that distinguish members from non-members. For Hutterites the whole colony and its pattern of living become symbolic. . . . The signs and symbols distinguish *unser Leut* (our people) from *Weltleut* (worldly people)" (1974, 173). In an earlier study of the Old Colony system, I concluded: "The Old Colony way of life has come to symbolize and even to actually incarnate the will of God. The forms of dress, the patterns of behavior, the artifacts of farming and recreation have taken on religious and moral significance" (1969, 216).

4. The predominating view now seems to be that denominationalism is the unique accommodation of religion in North America. This involves the disestablishment of religion and the consequent norms of religious freedom, the dissolution of geographic or parish concepts, the open competition for members, and the acceptance of civil religion as a definition of the religious quest. For the best treatment of the issue from various perspectives, but reflecting the above ideas, see Richey 1977, especially the chapters by Timothy L. Smith and Sidney Mead. The religious and ethnic pluralism of North America makes the importation of European religious structures and ideas to America impossible, as even the "established" churches discovered.

5. I have repeatedly maintained that the religious impulse was primary, but that Mennonites were not able to avoid totally the ethnic attributes. Many Mennonites have deplored the fact that the Anabaptist tradition has developed into an ethnic group, claiming that the ethnic formation has stunted the growth of the Mennonite heritage, or even worse, that the more a church becomes ethnic, the more likely it is to lose the religious element, perhaps entirely. Writing about a "Mennonite identity crisis" (1968, 243), Peachey suggested that the ethnic character can "overpower the specifically religious impulse in the structure of Mennonite identity" (248). Peachey feels so strongly that the ethnic and religious factors are incompatible that he states, "In the end, Mennonitism itself was seduced by the same ethnic impulses that had constituted, though on a vaster scale, medieval Christendom" (249).

The issue has created great controversies within the Mennonite community, especially in those groups which have embraced the theology known popularly as evangelical (J. Redekop 1987). In numerous instances congregations have dropped the name "Mennonite" because they considered it to be a hindrance to outreach and church growth. The recent turmoil in the Mennonite Brethren Conference, exacerbated partly by John H. Redekop's *A People Apart*, is a contemporary example. Whether the ethnic element has destroyed the vital religious thread, as Peachey maintains, or whether it has served to keep the vision alive, as others maintain, is still not clear (J. Redekop 1984a).

I have proposed that the ethnic tendency is inherent in a utopian movement that attempts to apply literally the biblical message of separation from the world in order to become a faithful people (Redekop 1984a). Yet the group need not become fully ethnic. A third way to understand the Mennonite phenomenon, beyond sect and ethnicity, is to define Mennonitism as a religious-utopian movement, which will continually be tending toward ethnicity as it establishes its ideals, but which always pulls back to its ideology.

Bibliography

Allport, Gordon. 1961. *Pattern and Growth in Personality*. New York: Holt, Rinehart and Winston.

Anderson, Alan B. 1972. "Assimilation in the Bloc Settlements of North-Central Saskatchewan." Ph.D. dissertation, University of Saskatchewan, Saskatoon.

Appavoo, David. 1978. "Religion and Family among the Markham Mennonites." Ph.D. dissertation, York University, Toronto.

Appling, Gregory B. 1975. "Amish Protestantism and the Spirit of Capitalism." *Cornell Journal of Social Relations* 10:239–50.

Apter, David, ed. 1964. *Ideology and Discontent*. New York: Free Press.

Aronson, Dan R. 1976. "Ethnicity as a Cultural System: An Introductory Essay." In Henry 1976.

Augsburger, David. 1974. "The Control and Management of Hostility in a Nonviolent Nonresistant Community." Ph.D. dissertation, Claremont School of Theology, Claremont, Calif.

Baar, Ellen. 1983. "Patterns of Selective Accentuation among Niagara Mennonites." *Canadian Ethnic Studies* 15:77–91.

Baehr, Karl. 1942. "Secularization among the Mennonites of Elkhart County, Indiana." *Mennonite Quarterly Review* 16:131–60.

Bainton, Roland H. 1952. *The Reformation of the Sixteenth Century*. Boston: Beacon.

————. 1957. "The Anabaptists' Contribution to History." In Hershberger 1957a.

Banner, David K. 1979. *Business and Society: Canadian Issues.* Toronto: McGraw-Hill.

Barrett, Lois. 1983. *The Vision and the Reality.* Newton, Kans.: Faith and Life Press.

Beals, Alan R., and Bernard J. Siegel. 1966. *Divisiveness and Social Conflict.* Stanford: Stanford University Press.

Beiler, Joseph. 1977. *Old Order Shop and Directory Service.* Gordonville, Pa.: Published by the author.

Bell, Colin, and Howard Newby. 1973. *Community Studies.* New York: Praeger.

Bender, Harold S. 1944. *Menno Simons: Life and Writings.* Scottdale, Pa.: Mennonite Publishing House.

————. 1945. "The Mennonite Conception of the Church." *Mennonite Quarterly Review* 19:90–100.

————. 1953. "Outside Influences on Mennonite Thought." *Proceedings of the Conference on Mennonite Educational and Cultural Problems* 9:33–41.

————. 1955a. "Amish Mennonites." *Mennonite Encyclopedia,* 1:93–98.

————. 1955b. "Anabaptist." Ibid., 113–16.

————. 1955c. "Art." Ibid., 165–72.

————. 1955d. "Bible." Ibid., 322–32.

————. 1955e. "Bible Translations." Ibid., 333–34.

————. 1955f. "Bishop." Ibid., 347–49.

————. 1955g. "Church." Ibid., 594–97.

————. 1956a. "Fundamentalism." Ibid., 2:418–19.

————. 1956b. "Excommunication." Ibid., 277–79.

————. 1957a. "The Anabaptist Vision." In Hershberger 1957a.

————. 1957b. "Mennonite." *Mennonite Encyclopedia,* 3:611–16.

————. 1957c. "Mennonite Church." Ibid., 611–616.

————. 1957d. "Migrations of Mennonites." Ibid., 684–87.

————. 1957e. "Music." Ibid., 791–92.

————. 1959a. "Anabaptist-Mennonite Attitude toward the State." Ibid., 4:611–18.

————. 1959b. "Mennonite Theological Seminaries." Ibid., 499–500.

————. 1959c. "Old Order Amish." Ibid., 43–47.

————. 1959d. "Secondary Education." Ibid., 490–93.

————. 1959e. "Zuerich." Ibid., 1042–47.

————. 1959f. "Sword and Trumpet." Ibid., 677.

————. 1962. *These Are My People.* Scottdale: Herald Press.

Bender, Mary E. 1957. "Mennonites in Literature." *Mennonite Encyclopedia,* 3:366–69.

Bender, Urie. 1969. *Soldiers of Compassion.* Scottdale: Herald Press.

————. 1982. *Four Earthen Vessels.* Scottdale: Herald Press.

————. 1984. *Stumbling Heavenward.* Winnipeg: Hyperion Press.

Bennett, John W. 1967. *Hutterian Brethren: The Agricultural Economy of Social Organization of a Communal People.* Stanford: Stanford University Press.

Berry, Brewton. 1965. *Race and Ethnic Relations.* Boston: Houghton Mifflin.

Bierstedt, Robert. 1963. *The Social Order*. New York: McGraw-Hill.

Blanke, Fritz. 1957. "Anabaptism and the Reformation." In Hershberger 1957a.

———. 1961. *Brothers in Christ*. Scottdale: Mennonite Publishing House.

Brady, Thomas A. 1982. "Social History." In Ozment 1982, 161–81.

Braun, Abram. 1955. "Conferences in Russia." *Mennonite Quarterly Review* 1:678–79.

Brubacher, J. Lester. 1968. "Philosophy of Christian Education Study for the Mennonite Church." Mimeo. Goshen Historical Library, Goshen College, Goshen, Ind.

Brunk, George R. 1928. "Editorial Message: The Drift." *The Sword and Trumpet*, 1:1.

———. 1943. "The Sword and Trumpet Comes Back!" *The Sword and Trumpet*, 11:5.

Brunk, George R., II. 1983. *A Crisis among Mennonites: In Education, in Publication*. Harrisonburg, Va.: The Sword and Trumpet.

Brunner, Emil. 1953. *The Misunderstanding of the Church*. Philadelphia: Westminster.

Burkholder, J. Lawrence. 1957. "The Anabaptist Vision of Discipleship." In Hershberger 1957a, 135–51.

———. 1958. *The Church and the Community*. Scottdale: Mennonite Publishing House.

———. 1959a. "Ethics." *Mennonite Encyclopedia*, 4:1079–83.

———. 1959b. "Social Implications of Mennonite Doctrine." *Proceedings of the Conference on Mennonite Educational and Cultural Problems* 12:91–112.

———. 1976. "Nonresistance, Nonviolent Resistance, and Power." In Burkholder and Redekop 1976.

Burkholder, J. Richard, and Calvin Redekop, eds. 1976. *Kingdom, Cross, and Community*. Scottdale: Herald Press.

Cadoux, C. J. 1925. *The Early Church and The World*. Edinburgh: T. and T. Clark.

Cavan, Ruth Shonle. 1977. "From Sociological Movement to Organized Society." Unpublished paper. Northern Illinois University, DeKalb.

Cavan, Ruth Shonle, and Man Singh Das, eds. 1979. *Communes: Historical and Contemporary*. New Delhi: Vikas Publishing House.

Centennial Committee. 1986. *Mountain Lake, 1886–1980*. Mountain Lake, Minn.: Centennial Committee.

Chesebro, Scott. 1982. "The Mennonite Urban Commune: A Hermeneutic-Dialectical Understanding of Its Anabaptist Ideology and Practice." Ph.D. dissertation, Notre Dame University, South Bend, Ind.

Clasen, Claus-Peter. 1972. *Anabaptism: A Social History*. Ithaca: Cornell University Press.

———. 1975. "The Anabaptist Leaders, Their Numbers and Background: Switzerland, Austria, South and Central Germany." *Mennonite Quarterly Review* 49:122–64.

Climenhaga, A. W. 1942. *History of the Brethren in Christ Church*. Nappannee, Ind.: Evangel Press.

Cohan, A. S. 1975. *Theories of Revolution*. London: Thomas Nelson.

Cohn, Norman. 1957. *The Pursuit of the Millennium*. New York: Essential Books.

Correll, Ernst. 1942. "Sociological and Economic Significance of the Mennonites as a Cultural Group in History." *Mennonite Quarterly Review* 16:161–66.

———. 1957. "Marriage." *Mennonite Encyclopedia*, 3:502–10.

Cressman, Kenneth. 1980. "The Development of the Conservative Mennonite Church of Ontario." Unpublished paper, Conrad Grebel College, Waterloo, Ont.

Cronk, Sandra. 1981. "*Gelassenheit:* The Rites of the Redemptive Process in Old Order Amish and Old Order Mennonite Communities." *Mennonite Quarterly Review* 55:5–44.

Crous, Ernst. 1959. "Privilegium." *Mennonite Encyclopedia*, 4:220.

Dawson, C. A. 1936. *Group Settlement: Ethnic Communities in Western Canada*. Toronto: Macmillan.

Dodd, C. H. 1920. *The Meaning of Paul for Today*. New York: George H. Doran.

Driedger, Leo. 1965. "Mennonite Graduate Fellowship: Its History, Purpose, and Future." *Mennonite Life* 20:67–72.

———. 1967. "Developments in Higher Education among Mennonites of Manitoba." *Proceedings of the Conference on Mennonite Educational and Cultural Problems* 16:60–72.

———. 1975. "Canadian Mennonite Urbanism: Ethnic Villagers or Metropolitan Remnant?" *Mennonite Quarterly Review* 49:226–41.

———. 1986. "Mennonite Community Change: From Ethnic Enclaves to Social Networks." Ibid. 60:374–86.

———. 1988. *Mennonite Identity in Conflict*. Lewiston, N.Y.: Edwin Mellen Press.

Driedger, Leo; J. Winfield Fretz; and Donovan E. Smucker. 1978. "A Tale of Two Strategies: Mennonites in Chicago and Winnipeg." *Mennonite Quarterly Review* 52:294–311.

Driedger, Leo, and J. Howard Kauffman. 1982. "Urbanization of Mennonites: Canadian and American Comparisons." *Mennonite Quarterly Review* 56:269–90.

Driedger, Leo, and Calvin Redekop. 1983. "Sociology of Mennonites: State of the Art and Science." *Journal of Mennonite Studies* 1:33–63.

Driedger, Leo; Roy Vogt; and Mavis Reimer. 1983. "Mennonite Intermarriage: National, Regional, and Intergenerational Trends." *Mennonite Quarterly Review* 57:132–44.

Driedger, Leo, and Dan Zehr. 1974. "The Church-State Trauma." *Mennonite Quarterly Review* 48:515–26.

Dueck, Al. 1988. "Psychology and Mennonite Understanding." In Redekop and Steiner 1988.

Duerksen, Menno. 1986. *Dear God, I Am Only a Boy*. Memphis: Castle Books.

Durkheim, Emile. 1915. *The Elementary Forms of the Religious Life*. London: Allen and Unwin.

Durnbaugh, Don. 1968. *The Believers' Church*. London: Macmillan.

Dyck, Bill W. 1983. "Psychology and Mennonite Studies." *Journal of Mennonite Studies* 1:149–60.

Dyck, C. J., ed. 1962. *The Lordship of Christ*. Scottdale: Mennonite Publishing House.

———. 1967. *An Introduction to Mennonite History*. Scottdale: Herald Press.

———. 1980–85. *The Mennonite Central Committee Story*. 5 vols. Scottdale: Herald Press.

———. 1980a. *From the MCC Files 1*. Vol. 1 of C. Dyck 1980–85.

———. 1980b. *Responding to Worldwide Needs*. Vol. 2 of C. Dyck 1980–85.

———. 1980c. *Witness and Service in North America*. Vol. 3 of C. Dyck 1980–85.

Eaton, Joseph W., and Albert J. Mayer. 1954. *Man's Capacity to Reproduce*. Glencoe, Ill.: Free Press.

Eaton, Joseph W., and Robert J.Weill. 1953. *Culture and Mental Disorder*. Glencoe, Ill.: Free Press.

Eby, John. 1976. "The Institutionalization of the Church." *Mission Focus* 4:1–3.

———. 1986. "Must Successful Mennonites Leave the Church?" *Festival Quarterly* 13:11–13.

Effrat, Marcia. 1974. *The Community: Approaches and Applications*. Glencoe: Free Press.

Eggers, Ulrich. 1985. *Gemeinschaft-lebenslänglich*. Witten: Bunders.

Ehrenstrom, Nils, and Walter G. Muelder. 1963. *Institutionalism and Church Unity*. New York: Association Press.

Epp, David. 1981. "The Emergence of German Identity in the South Russian Colonies." *Mennonite Quarterly Review* 55:289–371.

Epp, Frank. 1974. *Mennonites in Canada, 1786–1920*. Toronto: Macmillan.

———. 1977. *Mennonite Peoplehood: A Plea for New Initiatives*. Waterloo: Conrad Press.

———. 1978. "The Migrations of Mennonites." In Kraybill 1978.

———. 1982. *Mennonites in Canada, 1920–1940*. Toronto: Macmillan.

Epp, Reuben. 1987. "Plautdietsch: Origins, Development, and State of the Mennonite Low German Language." *Journal of Mennonite Studies* 5:16–72.

Epp-Tiessen, Esther. 1982. *Altona: The Story of a Prairie Town*. Altona, Manitoba: D. W. Friesen and Sons.

Erb, Alta. 1920. *Our Home Missions*. Scottdale: Mennonite Publishing House.

Fast, Henry A. 1957. "Mennonite Mental Hospitals." *Mennonite Encyclopedia* 3:653–54.

Fathauer, George. 1964. "Missionaries: An Anthropologist's View." *Journal of Human Relations* 12, no. 2:189–97.

Felstead, Clair. 1978. "A Socio-Historical Analysis of the Sectarian Divisions in the Mennonite Church of Waterloo County." M.A. thesis, University of Waterloo, Waterloo, Ont.

Fichter, Joseph. 1983. *Alternatives to American Mainline Churches*. Barrytown, N.Y.: Unification Theological Seminary.

Finger, Thomas N. 1985. *Christian Theology: An Eschatological Approach*. Vol. 1. Nashville: Thomas Nelson.

Francis, E. K. 1948. "The Russian Mennonites: From Religious to Ethnic Group." *American Journal of Sociology* 54 (Sept.): 101–7.

———. 1955. *In Search of Utopia.* Glencoe: Free Press.

———. 1976. *Interethnic Relations: An Essay in Sociological Theory.* New York: Elsevier.

Franz, Werner, and Darrell Heidebrecht. 1984. "The Mennonite *Privilegeum* in Paraguay: Some Historical and Theological Considerations." Mimeographed term paper, Associated Mennonite Biblical Seminaries, Elkhart, Ind.

Fretz, J. Winfield. 1941. "Mennonite Mutual Aid: A Contribution towards the Establishment of Christian Community." Ph.D. dissertation, University of Chicago.

———. 1947. *Christian Mutual Aid: A Handbook of Brotherhood Economics.* Akron, Pa.: Mennonite Central Committee.

———. 1953. *Pilgrims in Paraguay.* Scottdale: Herald Press.

———. 1955. "Community." *Mennonite Encyclopedia,* 1:656–58.

———. 1956. "Farming." Ibid., 2:307–9.

———. 1957a. "Brotherhood and the Economic Ethic of the Anabaptists." In Hershberger, 1957a.

———. 1957b. "Mutual Aid." *Mennonite Encyclopedia,* 3:796–801.

———. 1979. "Newly Emerging Communes in Mennonite Communities." In Cavan and Singh Das 1979.

———. 1989. *The Waterloo Mennonites.* Waterloo: WLU Press.

Friedmann, Robert. 1949. *Mennonite Piety through the Ages.* Scottdale: Mennonite Historical Society.

———. 1955. "*Ausbund.*" *Mennonite Encyclopedia,* 1:191–92.

———. 1956. "Denominations." Ibid., 2:37–38.

———. 1973. *The Theology of Anabaptism.* Scottdale: Herald Press.

Friesen, Abram. 1974. *Reformation and Utopia.* Wiesbaden: F. Steiner.

Friesen, Martin W. 1977. *50 Jahre Kolonie Menno.* Chaco, Paraguay: Verwaltung Menno.

———. 1987. *Neue Heimat in der Chaco Wildnis.* Altona, Manitoba: D. W. Friesen and Sons.

Friesen, P. M. 1978. *The Mennonite Brotherhood in Russia.* Fresno, Calif.: Board of Christian Literature.

Gardner, E. Clinton. 1967. *The Church as Prophetic Community.* Philadelphia: Westminster Press.

Geertz, Clifford. 1964. "Ideology as a Cultural System." In Apter 1964.

Geiser, Samuel. 1959. "Switzerland." *Mennonite Encyclopedia,* 4:673–77.

Gingerich, Barbara Nelson. 1985. "Property and the Gospel." *Mennonite Quarterly Review* 59:248–67.

Gingerich, Melvin. 1953. "Mennonite Attitudes toward Wealth, Past and Present." *Proceedings of the Conference on Mennonite Educational and Cultural Problems* 9:89–98.

———. 1955. "Colleges, Mennonite." *Mennonite Encyclopedia,* 1:636–39.

———. 1963. *The Mennonite Family Census of 1963.* Goshen, Ind.: Mennonite Historical and Research Committee.

Goertz, Hans-Jürgen. 1980. *Die Täufer: Geschichte und Deutung*. Munich: C. H. Beck.

———, ed. 1984. *Alles gehört Allen*. Munich: C. H. Beck.

———. 1988. "The Confessional Heritage in Its New Mold: What Is Mennonite Self-Understanding Today?" In Redekop and Steiner 1988.

Gordon, Milton. 1964. *Assimilation in American Life*. New York: Oxford University Press.

Graber, J. D. 1957. "Anabaptism Expressed in Missions and Social Service." In Hershberger 1957a.

Graber, Christine. 1987 *Handbook of Information: General Conference Mennonite Church*. Newton: Faith and Life Press.

Graber, Robert Bates. 1979. "The Sociocultural Differentiation of a Religious Sect: Schism among the Pennsylvania German Mennonites." Ph.D. dissertation, University of Wisconsin, Madison.

———. 1982. "The Sociocultural Differentiation of a Religious Sect: Schisms among the Pennsylvania German Mennonites." *Mennonite Quarterly Review* 56:196–99.

———. 1983. "Archival Data on Pennsylvania German Mennonite Schisms, 1778–1927." Ibid. 57:45–63.

Groenveld, S.; J. P. Jacobszoon; and S. L. Verhew. 1980. *Nederdoper, Menisten, Doopsgezinden*. Zutphen: De Walburg Pers.

Gross, Leonard. 1980. *The Golden Years of the Hutterites*. Scottdale: Herald Press.

———. 1986. "Recasting the Anabaptist Vision: The Longer View." *Mennonite Quarterly Review* 60:352–63.

Gross, Paul. 1978. "Hutterian Brethren." In Kraybill 1978, 352–58.

Haas, Martin. 1980. "The Path of the Anabaptists into Separation: The Interdependence of Theology and Social Behavior." In Stayer and Packull 1980.

Hallowell, A. Irving. 1953. "Culture, Personality, and Society." In Kroeber 1953.

Halverson, Martin, and Arthur Cohen. 1958. *A Handbook of Christian Theology*. New York: Meridian Books.

Hannerz, Ulf. 1976. "Some Comments on the Anthropology of Ethnicity in the United States." In Henry 1976.

Harder, David. 1969. *Schule und Gemeinschaft*. Privately published in Mexico.

Harder, Leland. 1949. "The Origins, Philosophy, and Development of Education among the Mennonites." Ph.D. dissertation, University of Southern California, Los Angeles.

———. 1962. "The Quest for Equilibrium in an Established Sect: A Study of Social Change in the General Conference Church." Ph.D. dissertation, Northwestern University, Evanston Ill.

Harder, Menno S. 1956. "Education, Mennonite." *Mennonite Encyclopedia*, 2:150–53.

Hartzler, J. E. 1925. *Education among the Mennonites of America*. Danners, Ill: Central Mennonite Publishing House.

Haury, Dave. 1981. *Prairie People: A History of the Western District Conference*. Newton: Faith and Life Press.

Heaton, Tim B. 1986. "Sociodemographic Characteristics of Religious Groups in Canada." *Sociological Analysis* 47 (Spring): 54–65.

Hege, Fritz. 1957. "Martyrs' Synod." *Mennonite Encyclopedia,* 3:529–31.

Henry, Francis, ed. 1976. *Ethnicity in the Americas.* The Hague: Mouton.

Herberg, Will. 1960. *Protestant, Catholic, Jew.* New York: Doubleday.

Hernley, Ralph, ed. 1970. *The Compassionate Community.* Scottdale: Association of Mennonite Aid Societies.

Hershberger, Guy F. 1951. *The Mennonite Church in the Second World War.* Scottdale: Mennonite Publishing House.

———. 1955. "Committee on Economic and Social Relations." *Mennonite Encyclopedia,* 1:650–51.

———, ed. 1957a. *The Recovery of the Anabaptist Vision.* Scottdale: Herald Press.

———. 1957b. "The Mennonite Community Association." *Mennonite Encyclopedia,* 3:619.

———. 1958. *The Way of the Cross in Human Relations.* Scottdale: Herald Press.

———. 1959. "Relief Work." *Mennonite Encyclopedia,* 4:284–91.

Herztler, Silas. 1966. "Attendance in Mennonite and Affiliated Colleges." *Mennonite Quarterly Review* 40:212–16.

Hiebert, Clarence. 1973. *The Holdeman People.* S. Pasadena, Calif.: William Carey Library.

Hobhouse, Walter. 1910. *The Church and the World.* London: Macmillan.

Horsch, John. 1924. *The Mennonite Church and Modernism.* Scottdale: Mennonite Publishing House.

———. 1926. *Is the Mennonite Church Free of Modernism?* Scottdale: Mennonite Publishing House.

———. 1950. *Mennonites in Europe.* Scottdale: Herald Press.

Horsch, James. 1988. *Mennonite Yearbook, 1988–1989.* Scottdale: Herald Press.

Hosteter, C. N. 1955. "Brethren in Christ." *Mennonite Encyclopedia* 1:424–25.

Hostetler, Beulah. 1987. *American Mennonite and Protestant Movements.* Scottdale: Herald Press.

Hostetler, J. J. 1978. *Mennonite Business and Professional People's Directory.* Scottdale: Mennonite Industry and Business Associates.

Hostetler, John A. 1954. *The Sociology of Mennonite Evangelism.* Scottdale: Herald Press.

———. 1959. "Old Order Amish." *Mennonite Encyclopedia,* 4:43–47.

———. 1965. *Education and Marginalization in the Communal Society of the Hutterites.* University Park: Pennsylvania State University.

———. 1974. *Hutterite Society.* Baltimore: Johns Hopkins University Press.

———. 1980. *Amish Society.* 3rd ed. Baltimore: Johns Hopkins University Press.

Huntington, Gertrude. 1965. "Freedom and the Hutterite Communal Family Patterns." *Proceedings of the Mennonite Educational and Cultural Conference* 15:88–111.

Ishwaran, K., ed. 1976. *The Canadian Family.* Toronto: Holt, Rinehart, and Winston.

Jeltes, H. F. 1957. "Mennonites in Literature." *Mennonite Encyclopedia,* 3:353–60.

Juhnke, James. 1975. *A People of Two Kingdoms: The Political Acculturation of Kansas Mennonites.* Newton: Faith and Life Press.

———. 1979. *A People of Vision.* Newton: Faith and Life Press.

———. 1983. "Mennonite Church Theological and Social Boundaries, 1920–1930." *Mennonite Life* 38, no. 2:18–24.

———. 1988. "Mennonite History and Self-Understanding: North American Mennonitism as Bi-Polar Mosaic." In Redekop and Steiner 1988.

Kauffman, Ivan, ed. 1981. *Leadership and Authority in the Life of the Church.* Scottdale: Mennonite Publishing House.

Kauffman, J. Howard. 1956a. "Toward a Sociology of Mennonites." *Mennonite Quarterly Review* 30:163–212.

———. 1956b. "Family." *Mennonite Encyclopedia,* 2:295–99.

———. 1960. "A Comparative Study of Traditional and Emergent Family Types among Midwest Mennonites." Ph.D. dissertation, University of Chicago.

———. 1965. "Authority and Freedom in Mennonite Families." *Proceedings of the Conference on Mennonite Educational and Cultural Problems* 15:75–87.

Kauffman, J. Howard, and Leland Harder. 1975. *Anabaptists Four Centuries Later.* Scottdale: Herald Press.

Kaufman, Edmund G. 1931. *The Development of the Missionary and Philanthropic Interest among the Mennonites of North America.* Berne, Ind.: Mennonite Book Concern.

———. 1956. "General Conference Mennonite Church." *Mennonite Encyclopedia* 2:465–71.

———. 1957. "Nontheological Cultural Factors in the Origin and Current Relationships of Mennonite Groups." *Proceedings of the Conference on Mennonite Educational and Cultural Problems* 11:49–57.

Kautsky, Karl. 1966. *Communism in Central Europe in the Time of the Reformation.* New York: Augustus M. Kelly.

Keeney, William E. 1965. "Mennonite Cooperation with Government Agencies and Programs." *Proceedings of the Conference on Mennonite Educational and Cultural Problems* 15:62–74.

Kinton, Jack, ed. 1975. *American Community: Creation and Revival.* Aurora, Ill.: Social Sciences and Sociological Resources.

Klaassen, Walter. 1981a. *Anabaptism in Outline.* Scottdale: Herald Press.

———. 1981b. *Neither Catholic nor Protestant.* Waterloo: Conrad Press.

———. 1982. *Sixteenth-Century Anabaptism: Defences, Confessions, Refutations.* Waterloo: Conrad Grebel College.

Klassen, A. J. 1976. *Confession of Faith of the General Conference of Mennonite Brethren Churches.* Hillsboro, Kans.: Mennonite Brethren Publishing House.

Klassen, John. 1986. "Women and the Family among Dutch Anabaptist Martyrs." *Mennonite Quarterly Review* 60:548–71.

Klassen, Peter James. 1964. *The Economics of Anabaptism.* The Hague: Mouton.

Klassen, William. n.d. "The Mennonite Syndrome." Unpublished paper, Mennonite Historical Library, Goshen College, Goshen, Ind.

―――. 1980. "The Role of the Child in Anabaptism." In Harry Loewen 1980a.

Klingelsmith, Sharon. 1980. "Women in the Mennonite Church, 1900–1930." *Mennonite Quarterly Review* 54:163–207.

Koop, P. Albert. 1981. "Some Economic Aspects of Mennonite Migration with Special Emphasis on the 1870s Migration from Russia to North America." Ibid. 55:143–56.

Krahn, Cornelius. 1955. "Agriculture among the Mennonites in Russia." *Mennonite Encyclopedia*, 1:24–27.

―――. 1956a. "Elder." Ibid., 2:178–81.

―――. 1956b. "Family." Ibid., 2: 293–95.

―――. 1957. "Muenster Anabaptists." Ibid., 3:777–82.

―――. 1959. "Pietism." Ibid., 4:176–79.

―――. 1968. *Dutch Anabaptism*. The Hague: Martinus Nijhoff.

Kraus, C. Norman. 1979. *Evangelicalism and Anabaptism*. Scottdale: Herald Press.

―――. 1987. *Jesus Christ Our Lord: Christology from a Disciple's Perspective*. Scottdale: Herald Press.

Kraybill, Don, ed. 1978. *Mennonite Education: Issues, Facts, and Changes*. Scottdale: Herald Press.

―――. 1987. "Mennonite Women's Veiling: The Rise and Fall of a Sacred Symbol." *Mennonite Quarterly Review* 61:298–320.

―――. 1988. "Modernity and Identity: The Transformation of Mennonite Ethnicity." In Redekop and Steiner 1988.

Kraybill, Don, and Phyllis Good. 1982. *The Perils of Professionalism*. Scottdale: Herald Press.

Kraybill, Paul, ed. 1978. *Mennonite World Handbook*. Lombard, Ill.: Mennonite World Conference.

―――, ed. 1984. *Mennonite World Handbook Supplement*. Lombard: Mennonite World Conference.

Kreider, Robert. 1951. "Anabaptist Conception of the Church in the Russian Mennonite Environment." *Mennonite Quarterly Review* 25:17–33.

―――. 1952. "Anabaptism and Humanism." *Mennonite Quarterly Review* 26:123–41.

―――. 1984. *Mennonite World Conference Yearbook*. Lombard: Mennonite World Conference.

Kroeber, H. L., ed. 1953. *Anthropology Today*. Chicago: University of Chicago Press.

Larsen, Lyle E., ed. 1976. *The Canadian Family in Comparative Perspective*. Scarborough: Prentice-Hall.

Latourette, Kenneth. 1953. *A History of Christianity*. New York: Harper.

Laurence, Hugh Getty. 1980. "Changes in Religion, Economics, and Boundary Conditions among Amish Mennonites in South-West Ontario." Ph.D. dissertation, McGill University, Montreal.

Leadership and Authority in the Life of the Church. 1981. Scottdale: Mennonite Publishing House.

Leatherman, Quintus. 1956. "Christopher Dock." *Mennonite Encyclopedia*, 2:76–77.

Lenski, Gerhard. 1961. *The Religious Factor*. New York: Doubleday.

Liechty, Joseph. 1980. "Humility: The Foundation of Mennonite Religious Outlook in the 1890s." *Mennonite Quarterly Review* 54:5–31.

Lind, Millard. 1976. "Reflections on Biblical Hermeneutics." In Burkholder and Redekop 1976.

Linton, Ralph, ed. 1945. *The Science of Man in World Crisis*. New York: Columbia University Press.

Littell, Franklin. 1947. "Anabaptist Theology of Missions." *Mennonite Quarterly Review* 21:5–17.

———. 1957. "The Anabaptist Concept of the Church." In Hershberger 1957a.

———. 1960. "The Work of the Holy Spirit in Group Decisions." *Mennonite Quarterly Review* 34:75–96.

Loewen, Harry, ed. 1980a. *Mennonite Images*. Winnipeg: Hyperion Press.

———. 1980b. "The Anabaptist View of the World: The Beginning of a Mennonite Continuum?" In Harry Loewen 1980a.

———. 1980c. "Anabaptists in Gottfried Keller's Novellas." Ibid.

———. 1983. "Mennonite Literature in Canada: Beginning, Reception, and Study." *Journal of Mennonite Studies* 1:119–32.

———, ed. 1988. *Why I Am a Mennonite*. Scottdale: Herald Press.

Loewen, Harry, and Al Reimer. 1985a. "Origins and Literary Development of Canadian Mennonite Low German." *Mennonite Quarterly Review* 69:279–89.

———. 1985b. *Visions and Realities*. Winnipeg: Hyperion Press.

Loewen, Howard J. 1983. "One Lord, One Church, One Hope: Mennonite Confessions of Faith in America—An Introduction." *Mennonite Quarterly Review* 57:265–81.

———. 1985. *One Lord, One Church, One Hope: Mennonite Confessions of Faith in America—An Introduction*. Elkhart, Ind.: Institute of Mennonite Studies.

Lohrenz, J. H. 1928. "The Early Aims of Tabor College." Unpublished paper, Tabor College Library, Tabor College, Hillsboro, Kans.

———. 1957. "Mennonite Brethren Church." *Mennonite Encyclopedia*, 3:595–602.

MacMaster, Richard K. 1985. *Land, Piety, and Peoplehood*. Scottdale: Herald Press.

Mannheim, Karl. 1936. *Ideology and Utopia*. New York: Harcourt-Brace.

Marr, M. Lucille. 1987. "Anabaptist Women of the North: Peers in the Faith, Subordinates in Marriage." *Mennonite Quarterly Review* 61:347–62.

Marsden, George. 1980. *Fundamentalism and American Culture*. New York: Oxford University Press.

Martens, Hildegard. 1977. "The Relationship of Religions to Socio-economic Divisions among the Mennonites in Canada." Ph.D. dissertation, University of Toronto.

Martin, David. 1966. *Pacifism: An Historical and Sociological Study*. New York: Shocken Books.

Martin, Maurice. 1983. "The Pure Church: The Burden of Anabaptism." *Conrad Grebel Review* 1:29–41.

Maykovich, Minako. 1976. "Alienation of Mental Health of Mennonites in Western Ontario." In Ishwaran 1976.

Mead, Sidney. 1977. "Denominationalism: The Shape of Protestantism in America." In Richey 1977.

Mehl, Roger. 1970. *The Sociology of Protestantism*. Philadelphia: Westminster Press.

Mennonite Encyclopedia. 1957–59. 4 vols. Scottdale: New Mennonite Publishing House.

Mennonite Reporter. 1983. "Artists from Four Provinces meet in Winnipeg." 13, no. 10:9.

Mennonite Yearbook. 1905–. Scottdale: Mennonite Publishing House.

Merton, Robert K. 1957. *Social Theory and Social Structure*. Glencoe: Free Press.

Mierau, Eric. 1983. "Rehabilitating Ethnicity." *Direction* 12:7–14.

Miller, Elmer. 1985. "Marking Mennonite Identity: A Structural Approach to Separation." *Conrad Grebel Review* 3:251–63.

Miller, John. 1984. "The Contemporary Fathering Crisis, the Bible, and Research Psychology." *Conrad Grebel Review* 1:21–37.

Miller, Mary. 1959. *A Pillar of Cloud*. Newton: Mennonite Press.

Mininger, Paul. 1967. "Our World, Our Church, and Our College." *Mennonite Quarterly Review* 27:279–309.

Nafziger, Estel. 1965. "The Mennonite Ethic in the Weberian Framework." *Explorations in Entrepreneurial History* 2:187–204.

———. 1986. *Entrepreneurship, Equity, and Economic Development*. Greenwich, Conn.: JAI Press, 1986.

Neff, Christian. 1955a. "Berne." *Mennonite Encyclopedia*, 1:287–97.

———. 1955b. "Confessions of Faith." Ibid., 679–86.

———. 1955c. "Conference." Ibid., 669–70.

Neufeld, Vernon H. 1983. *If We Can Love: The Mennonite Mental Health Story*. Newton: Faith and Life Press.

Niebuhr, H. Richard. 1951. *Christ and Culture*. New York: Harper.

Nisbet, Robert A. 1966. *The Sociological Tradition*. New York: Basic Books.

O'Dea, Thomas F., and Janet Aviad. 1983. *The Sociology of Religion*. Englewood Cliffs, N.J.: Prentice-Hall.

Olson, Theodore. 1982. *Millennialism, Utopianism, and Progress*. Toronto: University of Toronto Press.

Ozment, Steven, ed. 1982. *Reformation Europe*. St. Louis: Center for Reformation Research.

Packull, Werner. 1985. "The Image of the 'Common Man' in Early Pamphlets of the Reformation (1520–1525)." *Historical Reflections* 12:253–77.

———. 1986. "In Search of the 'Common Man' in Early German Anabaptist Ideology." *Sixteenth-Century Journal* 17:51–57.

Palmer, Howard. 1972. *Land of Second Choice: A History of Ethnic Groups in Southern Alberta*. Lethbridge, Alberta: Lethbridge Herald.

Pannabecker, S. F. 1957. "Foreign Mennonite Missions." *Mennonite Encyclopedia*, 3:712–17.

———. 1977. *Open Doors: The History of the General Conference Mennonite Church*. Newton: Faith and Life Press.

Parsons, Talcott. 1951. *The Social System*. Glencoe: Free Press.

Pauls, Peter. 1980. "The Search for Identity: A Recurring Theme in Mennonite Poetry." In Harry Loewen 1980a.

Payne, Ernest. 1957. "The Anabaptist Impact on Western Christendom." In Hershberger 1957a.

Peachey, Paul. 1954. *Die soziale Herkunft der Schweizer Täufer*. Karlsruhe: Schneider Verlag.

———. 1968. "Identity Crisis among American Mennonites." *Mennonite Quarterly Review* 42:243–59.

Penner, Horst. 1978. *Die ost und westpreussischen Mennoniten*. Weierhof: Mennonitischer Geschichtsverein.

Peter, Karl. 1976a. "The Dialectic of Family and Community in the Social History of Hutterites." In Larsen 1976.

———. 1976b. "The Hutterite Family." In Ishwaran 1976.

———. 1987. *The Dynamics of Hutterite Society*. Edmonton: University of Alberta Press.

Peters, H. P. 1925. *History and Development of Education among the Mennonites in Kansas*. Hillsboro, Kans.: Private printing.

Peters, Jacob. 1986. "Organizational Change within a Religious Denomination: A Case Study of the Conference of Mennonites in Canada." Ph.D. dissertation, University of Waterloo, Waterloo, Ont.

Pike, E. Royston, ed. 1958. *Encyclopedia of Religion*. New York: Meridian Library.

Poettcker, Henry, and Rudy Regehr, eds. 1972. *Call to Faithfulness*. Winnipeg: Canadian Mennonite Bible College.

Ratzlaff, Erich. 1971. *Im Weichselbogen*. Winnipeg: Christian Press.

Redekop, Calvin. 1953. "The Cultural Assimilation of Mennonites in Mountain Lake, Minnesota." M.A. thesis, University of Minnesota, Minneapolis.

———. 1957. "Patterns of Cultural Assimilation among Mennonites." *Proceedings of the Conference on Mennonite Educational and Cultural Problems* 11:99–112.

———. 1959. "The Sectarian Black and White World." Ph.D. dissertation, University of Chicago.

———. 1961. "The Relation of Research to the Sectarian Self-Image." *Proceedings of the Conference on Mennonite Educational and Cultural Problems* 13:43–53.

———. 1963. *Brotherhood and Schism*. Scottdale: Herald Press.

———. 1969. *The Old Colony Mennonites*. Baltimore: Johns Hopkins University Press.

———. 1970. *The Free Church and Seductive Culture*. Scottdale: Herald Press.

———. 1973. "Religion and Society: A State within a Church." *Mennonite Quarterly Review* 47:339–57.

———. 1975. "The Communal Groups: Inside or Outside the Community." In Kinton 1975.

———. 1976. "Institutions, Power, and the Gospel." In Burkholder and Redekop 1976.

———. 1978a. "The Old Colony Mennonites in Central and South America." In P. Kraybill 1978, 273–79.

———. 1978b. "Future Options for Mennonite Brethren Higher Education." *Direction* 7:12–21.

———. 1980. *Strangers Become Neighbors*. Scottdale: Herald Press.

———. 1981. "The Embarrassment of a Religious Tradition." *Mennonite Life* 36:17–21.

———. 1982. "Mennonite Displacement of Indigenous Groups: An Historical and Sociological Analysis." *Canadian Ethnic Studies* 14:71–90.

———. 1984a. "Anabaptism and the Ethnic Ghost." *Mennonite Quarterly Review* 58:133–46.

———. 1984b. "The Emergence of Mennonite Leadership on the Frontier: A Case Study of H. W. Lohrenz." *Mennonite Life* 39:23–29.

———. 1984c. "The Mennonite Identity Crisis." *Journal of Mennonite Studies* 2:87–103.

———. 1985. "The Mennonite Romance with the Lord." In Loewen and Reimer 1985b.

———. 1988a. "Mennonite Faith and Economic Reality." Manuscript in progress.

———. 1988b. "The sociology of Mennonite Identity: A Second Opinion." In Redekop and Steiner 1988.

Redekop, Calvin, and Urie Bender. 1988. *Who Am I? What Am I? Searching for Meaning in Your Work*. Grand Rapids: Zondervan.

Redekop, Calvin, and John A. Hostetler. 1977. "The Plain People: An Interpretation." *Mennonite Quarterly Review* 51:266–77.

Redekop, Calvin, and Al Koop. 1988. "The Many Streams of Anabaptist/Mennonite Utopianism." Unpublished paper, Conrad Grebel College, Waterloo, Ont.

Redekop, Calvin, and Sam Steiner, eds. 1988. *Mennonite Identity: Historical and Contemporary Perspectives*. Lanham, Md.: University Press of America.

Redekop, Freda Pellman, ed. 1984. *The Redevelop Book*. Waterloo, Ont.: Benanna Tree Publishers.

Redekop, John. 1976. "The State and the Free Church." In Burkholder and Redekop 1976.

———. 1981. "The Interaction of Economics and Religion." *Direction* 10:48–68.

———. 1983. "Mennonites and Politics in Canada and the United States." *Journal of Mennonite Studies* 1:79–105.

———. 1987. *A People Apart: Ethnicity and the Mennonite Brethren*. Hillsboro, Kans.: Kindred Press.

Redekop, Magdalene. 1988. "Through the Mennonite Looking Glass." In Harry Loewen 1988.

Redfield, Robert. 1956. *Peasant Society and Culture*. Chicago: University of Chicago Press.

Regehr, Rudy. 1972. "A Century of Private Schools." In Poettcker and Regehr 1972.

Regehr, William. 1982. "Evangelical Mennonite Brethren." *Mennonite Life* 37:29–31.

Reimer, A. James. 1983. "The Nature and Possibility of a Mennonite Theology." *Conrad Grebel Review* 1:33–56.

Reimer, Al. 1980a. "The Creation of Arnold Dyck's 'Koop en Bua' Characters." In Harry Loewen 1980a.

———. 1980b. "The Russian-Mennonite Experience in Fiction." Ibid.

———. 1985. *My Harp Is Turned to Mourning.* Winnipeg: Hyperion Press.

———. 1988. "Coming in Out of the Cold." In Harry Loewen 1988.

Reimer, Margaret Loewen. 1983. *One Quilt, Many Pieces.* Waterloo: Mennonite Publishing Service.

Reimer, Margaret Loewen, and Paul Tiessen. 1985. "The Poetry and Distemper of Patrick Friesen and David Waltner Toews." In Loewen and Reimer 1985b, 243–54.

Reitz, Jeffrey G. 1980. *The Survival of Ethnic Groups.* Toronto: McGraw-Hill.

Rempel, David C. 1933. "The Mennonite Colonies in New Russia: A Study of Settlement and Economic Development from 1789 to 1914." Ph.D. dissertation, Stanford University, Palo Alto, Calif.

Rempel, Kevin. 1982. "The Evangelical Mennonite Brethren: In Search of a Religious Identity." Unpublished paper, Fresno, Calif.

Richey, Russell E., ed. 1977. *Denominationalism.* Nashville: Abingdon.

Rimland, Ingrid. 1977. *The Wanderers.* St. Louis: Concordia.

———. 1980. *"The Wanderers Revised."* In Harry Loewen 1980a.

Rose, Marilyn Preheim. 1982. "On the Move: A Study of Migration and Ethnic Persistence among Mennonites from East Freeman, South Dakota." Ph.D. dissertation, University of Iowa, Iowa City.

Ruether, Rosemary. 1970. *The Radical Kingdom.* New York: Harper.

Rushby, William, and John C. Thrush. 1973. "Mennonites and Social Compassion: The Rokeach Hypothesis Reconsidered." *Review of Religious Research* 15:16–28.

Ruth, John. 1978. *Mennonite Identity and Literary Art.* Scottdale: Herald Press.

Sandeen, Ernest R. 1970. *The Roots of Fundamentalism: British and American Millennialism.* Chicago: University of Chicago Press.

Sauder, Menno. 1945. *The True and False Church.* 3rd ed. Privately published in Canada (n.p.).

Sawatsky, Rodney. 1973. "The Influence of Fundamentalism on Mennonite Nonresistance, 1908–1944." M.A. thesis, University of Minnesota, Minneapolis.

———. 1977. "History as Ideology: The Identity Struggle of an American Minority—the Mennonites." Ph.D. dissertation, Princeton University.

———. 1983. "Commitment and Critique: A Dialectical Imperative." *Conrad Grebel Review* 1:1–12.

———. 1987. *Authority and Identity.* North Newton, Kans.: Bethel College.

Sawatzky, Harry Leonard. 1971. *They Sought a Country.* Berkeley and Los Angeles: University of California Press.

Schäufele, Wolfgang. 1962. "The Missionary Vision and Eternity of the Anabaptist Laity." *Mennonite Quarterly Review* 35, no. 2:99–115.

Schlabach, Theron. 1980. *Gospel versus Gospel: Mission and the Mennonite Church.* Scottdale: Herald Press.

———. 1988. *Peace, Faith, Nation.* Scottdale: Herald Press.

Schluderman, S., and E. Schluderman. 1969. "Factor Analysis of Semantic Structures on Hutterite Adults." *Journal of Psychology* 73:263–73.

Schowalter, Otto. 1957. "Mennonites in Literature." *Mennonite Encyclopedia*, 3:360–66.

Schowalter, Paul. 1957. "Martyrs." Ibid. 3:521–25.

Séguy, Jean. 1977. *Les Assemblées Anabaptistes-Mennonites de France*. Paris: Mouton.

Seibt, Ferdinand. 1972. *Utopica*. Dusseldorf: Verlag L. Schwann.

Shenk, Wilbert. 1978. "Growth through Missions." In P. Kraybill 1978.

———. 1984. *Anabaptism and Mission*. Scottdale: Herald Press.

Siegel, Bernard. 1970. "Defensive Structuring and Environmental Stress." *American Journal of Sociology* 76:11–32.

Simmel, Georg. 1955. *The Web of Group Affiliations*. Glencoe: Free Press.

Simons, Menno. 1956. *The Complete Writings of Menno Simons*. Scottdale: Herald Press.

Smith, C. Henry. 1950. *The Story of the Mennonites*. Newton: Mennonite Publishing Office.

———. 1962. *Mennonite Country Boy*. Newton: Faith and Life Press.

Smith, Timothy L. 1977. "Congregation, State, and Denomination: The Forming of the American Religious Structure." In Richey 1977.

Smucker, Donovan. 1945. "The Theological Triumph of the Early Anabaptist-Mennonites." *Mennonite Quarterly Review* 19:5–26.

———. 1976. "Gelassenheit, Entrepreneurs, and Remnants: Socioeconomic Models among the Mennonites." In Burkholder and Redekop 1976.

———. 1977. *The Sociology of Canadian Mennonites, Hutterites, and Amish*. Waterloo: Wilfrid Laurier Press.

Spaulding, Lloyd. 1953. "Profile of a Mennonite Community: A Survey of Moundridge, Kansas." *Proceedings of the Conference on Mennonite Educational and Cultural Problems* 9:78–88.

Springer, Nelson, and A. J. Klassen. 1977. *Mennonite Bibliography, 1631–1961*. Vols. 1–2. Scottdale: Herald Press.

Sprunger, Keith. 1984. "C. C. Regier: Progressive Mennonite Historian." *Mennonite Life* 39:10–18.

Stahl, John Daniel. 1981. "Conflict, Conscience, and Community in Selected Mennonite Children's Stories." *Mennonite Quarterly Review* 55:62–74.

Stambaugh, Sara. 1984. *I Hear the Reaper's Song*. Intercourse, Pa.: Good Books.

Stayer, James. 1972. *Anabaptists and the Sword*. Lawrence, Kans.: Coronado Press.

———. 1982. "The Anabaptists." In Ozment 1982.

———. 1984. "Neue Modelle eines gemeines Lebens." In Goertz 1984.

———. 1988. "Anabaptist Community of Goods." Unpublished manuscript, Queens University, Kingston, Ont.

Stayer, James, and Werner Packull, eds. 1980. *The Anabaptists and Thomas Müntzer*. Dubuque: Kendall-Hunt Publishing Co.

Stayer, James; Werner Packull; and Klaus Depperman. 1975. "From Monogenesis to Polygenesis: The Historical Discussion of Anabaptist Origins." *Mennonite Quarterly Review* 49:83–121.

Steiner, Sue. 1984. "To John Miller: The Contemporary Fathering Crisis, the Bible, and Research Psychology." *Conrad Grebel Review* 2:56–59.

Stucky, Solomon. 1983. *For Conscience' Sake*. Scottdale: Herald Press.

Swartley, Willard, ed. 1984a. *Essays on Biblical Interpretation: Anabaptist Mennonite Perspectives*. Elkhart, Ind.: Institute of Mennonite Studies.

————. 1984b. *Explorations of Systematic Theology from Mennonite Perspectives*. Elkhart, Ind.: Institute of Mennonite Studies.

Studer, Gerald. 1970. "Toward a Theology of Servanthood." In Hernley 1970, 227–96.

Swatos, William. 1979. *Into Denominationalism*. Norwich, Conn.: Society for the Scientific Study of Religion.

Tawney, R. H. 1926. *Religion and the Rise of Capitalism*. New York: New American Library.

Teichrau, Allan. 1983. "Gordon Friesen: Writer, Radical, and Ex-Mennonite!" *Mennonite Life* 38 (June): 4–17.

Thielman, George. 1955. "The Canadian Mennonites: A Study of an Ethnic Group in Relation to State and Community." Ph.D. dissertation, Western Reserve University, Cleveland.

Thiessen, Irmgard. 1966. "Values and Personality Characteristics of Mennonites in Manitoba." *Mennonite Quarterly Review* 40:48–61.

Tiessen, Hildi. 1988. "The Role of Art and Literature in Mennonite Self-Understanding." In Redekop and Steiner 1988.

Tillich, Paul. 1963. *Systematic Theology*. Vol. 3. Chicago: University of Chicago Press.

Tönnies, Ferdinand. 1957. *Community and Society*. New York: Harper Torchbooks.

Toews, J. B. 1977. "Mennonite Brethren Identity and Theological Diversity." In Paul Toews 1977, 133–57.

Toews, John A. 1975. *A History of the Mennonite Brethren: Pilgrims and Pioneers*. Fresno, Calif.: Board of Christian Literature.

Toews, John B. 1979. "Cultural and Intellectual Aspects of the Mennonite Experience in Russia." *Mennonite Quarterly Review* 53:137–159.

————. 1982. *Czars, Soviets, and Mennonites*. Newton: Faith and Life Press.

Toews, John E. 1978. "Mennonite Brethren Higher Education: Perspectives and Proposals." *Direction* 7:22–23.

Toews, Paul, ed. 1977. *Pilgrims and Strangers: Essays in Mennonite Brethren History*. Fresno: Center for Mennonite Brethren Studies.

————. 1983. "Fundamentalist Conflict in Mennonite Colleges: A Response to Cultural Transitions?" *Mennonite Quarterly Review* 57:241–56.

Tolstoy, Leo. 1952. *War and Peace*. Chicago: Encyclopedia Britannica.

Troeltsch, Ernst. 1960. *The Social Teachings of the Christian Churches*. New York: Harper Torchbooks.

Unruh, John R. 1952. *In the Name of Christ*. Scottdale: Herald Press.

Urry, James. 1978. "The Closed and the Open: Social and Religious Change among the Mennonites in Russia." Ph.D. dissertation, Oxford University.

————. 1983. "'The Snares of Reason: Changing Attitudes to 'Knowledge' in Nineteenth-Century Russia." *Comparative Studies in Society and History* 25:306–22.

Van Braght, Tieleman. 1950. *Martyrs' Mirror*. Scottdale: Herald Press.

Van der Zijpp, N. 1957a. *"Martyrs' Mirror." Mennonite Encyclopedia*, 3:527–29.

———. 1957b. "War of the Lambs." Ibid., 271.

Van der Zijpp, N., and Harold S. Bender. 1955. "Business among the Mennonites in Holland." *Mennonite Encyclopedia* 1:483.

Vogt, Roy. 1972. "Economic Questions and the Mennonite Conscience." In Poettcker and Regehr 1972.

———. 1980. "The Impact of Economic and Social Class on Mennonite Theology." In Harry Loewen 1980a.

———. 1983. "Mennonite Studies in Economics." *Journal of Mennonite Studies* 2:64–78.

Vogt, Virgil. 1983. *Coming Together*. Elkhart, Ind.: Fellowship of Hope.

Wach, Joachim. 1946. *Church, Denomination, and Sect*. Evanston, Ill.: Seabury-Western Theological Seminary.

———. 1951. *Sociology of Religion*. Chicago: University of Chicago Press.

Waltner, Erland. 1958. *Studies in Church Discipline*. Newton: Mennonite Publication Office.

———. 1962. "Foreword." In C. J. Dyck 1962.

Weaver, J. Denny. 1984. "Perspectives on a Mennonite Theology." *Conrad Grebel Review* 2:189–210.

Weber, Max. 1946. *From Max Weber: Essays in Sociology*. New York: Oxford University Press.

———. 1958. *The Protestant Ethic and the Spirit of Capitalism*. New York: Scribners.

———. 1964. *The Sociology of Religion*. Boston: Beacon.

Wenger, John C. 1947. *Glimpses of Mennonite History and Doctrine*. Scottdale: Herald Press.

———. 1954. *Introduction to Theology*. Scottdale: Herald Press.

———. 1956. "Doctrinal Writings of the Anabaptists." *Mennonite Encyclopedia*, 2:77–79.

———. 1966. *The Mennonite Church in America*. Scottdale: Herald Press.

Wenger, John C., and Harold S. Bender. 1957. "Nonconformity." *Mennonite Encyclopedia*, 3:890–96.

Wiebe, Don. 1980. "Philosophical Reflections on Twentieth-Century Mennonite Thought." In Harry Loewen 1980a.

Wiebe, Katie Funk. 1983. "Ten Years Later." *Report* vol. 50. Akron, Pa: Mennonite Central Committee.

———. 1985. "The Mennonite Woman in Mennonite Fiction." In Loewen and Reimer 1985b.

Wiebe, Rudy. 1962. *Peace Shall Destroy Many*. Toronto: MacClelland and Stewart.

———. 1970. *The Blue Mountains of China*. Grand Rapids: Eerdmans.

Wieswedel, Wilhelm. 1955. "Bible." *Mennonite Encyclopedia*, 1:322–28.

Williams, George H. 1962. *The Radical Reformation*. Philadelphia: Westminster Press.

Williams, Robin M. 1955. *American Society*. New York: Knopf.

Wilson, Bryan. 1970. *Religious Sects*. New York: McGraw-Hill.

Winter, Gibson. 1961. *The Suburban Captivity of the Churches*. Garden City, N.Y.: Doubleday.

Wirth, Louis. 1945. "The Problem of Minority Groups." In Linton 1945.

Wittlinger, Carlton O. 1978. "General Conference of the Brethren in Christ." In P. Kraybill 1978.

Yinger, J. Milton. 1970. *The Scientific Study of Religion*. New York: Macmillan.

Yoder, Edward. 1985. *Pilgrimage of a Mind*. Scottdale: Mennonite Publishing House.

Yoder, John Howard. 1954. "Introduction." *Concern* 1:3–7.

———. 1967. "Binding and Loosing." *Concern* 14:2–32.

———. 1972. *The Politics of Jesus*. Grand Rapids: Eerdmans.

Yoder, Gideon. 1956. *The Nurture and Evangelism of Children*. Scottdale: Herald Press.

Yoder, Michael. 1983. "1982 Mennonite Census: A Summary of Findings." Mimeo. Mennonite Historical Library, Goshen College, Goshen, Ind.

———. 1985. "Findings from the 1982 Mennonite Census." *Mennonite Quarterly Review* 59:307–49.

Yoder, Perry. 1982. *From Word to Life: A Guide to Bible Study*. Scottdale: Mennonite Publishing House.

Yoder, Walter, 1959. "Singing Schools." *Mennonite Encyclopedia*, 4:533–34.

Zschäbitz, Gerhard. 1958. *Zur mitteldeutschen Wiedertäuferbewegung nach dem grossem Bauernkrieg*. Berlin: Rutten & Loening.

Name Index

Dawson, C.A., 319
Denck, Hans, 4, 16, 55, 57, 105
Depperman, Klaus, 34, 279, 311, 313
Dock, Christopher, 177, 183
Dodd, C.H., 130
Driedger, Leo, 138, 169, 187, 189, 228,
    245–46, 303, 307, 319, 331
Dueck, Al, 98, 300
Duerksen, Menno, 120
Durkheim, Emil, 61, 131
Durnbaugh, Don, 35
Dyck, Arnold, 91, 99–100
Dyck, Bill, 96, 97
Dyck, C.J., 4, 32, 55, 231, 247, 250,
    255, 275

Eaton, Joseph, 27, 95, 165
Eberle, Hypoloytus, 8
Eby, John, 209, 257
Ehrenstrom, Nils, 62
Epp, David, 198
Epp, Frank, 138–39, 232, 278
Erasmus, 108
Erb, Alta, 245

Fathauer, George, 243
Felstead, Clair, 74, 268
Flinck, Govert, 110
Francis, E.K., 19, 22, 35, 69, 80, 81,
    132, 160, 278, 292, 319, 332–33
Franz, Werner, 325
Fretz, J.W., 137, 141, 194, 197, 200,
    221, 245–46, 248–49, 280
Friedmann, Robert, 35, 109, 281–82
Friesen, Gordon, 120
Friesen, Martin, 227, 325
Friesen, P.M., 42, 59, 112, 198, 222

Gardner, E. Clinton, 192
Gingerich, Melvin, 182, 199, 208
Goertz, Hans Jürgen, 7, 49, 98, 193,
    278, 311
Good, Phyllis, 303
Gordon, Milton, 139–40, 333
Graber, J.D., 243–44
Graber, Robert, 59, 74, 269
Grebel, Conrad, 4
Groenveld, S., 110, 116–17, 197
Gross, Leonard, 9, 34, 37, 175

Haas, Martin, 316, 319
Hallowell, A. Irving, 91, 94
Halverson, Martin, 283
Harder, David, 119, 177
Harder, Leland, 43, 88, 199, 200, 219–
    20, 224, 226, 230, 242, 255, 273,
    286–87, 288, 292–93, 301, 305, 334,
    340
Harder, Menno S., 176, 177, 180, 190
Hartzler, J.E., 179, 190
Haury, Dave, 285
Hege, Fritz, 8
Heidebrecht, Darrell, 325
Herberg, Will, 278
Hernley, Ralph, 280
Hershberger, Guy F., 125, 141, 194,
    195–97, 202, 207, 208, 217, 218, 224,
    225, 228–29, 231, 250, 300–301
Hiebert, Clarence, 42, 60, 97–98, 270–
    71, 331
Hobhouse, Walter, 216
Hoffman, Melchoir, 10, 16, 17, 49, 107
Horsch, John, 175, 284
Hostetler, Beulah, 75, 273, 281–82, 287–
    89, 290
Hostetler, John A., 9, 10, 16, 22–23, 28,
    36–37, 38, 75–79, 84, 95, 107, 132–
    34, 160–62, 164–65, 175–76, 189,
    208, 221, 264–66, 270, 325
Hubmaier, Balthasar, 4, 16
Hunsberger, Bruce, 97
Huntington, Gertrude, 162
Hut, Hans, 4, 16
Hutter, Jacob, 4, 9, 16, 57

Jacobsz, Lambert, 110
Jacobszoon, J.P., 110, 116–17, 197
Juhnke, James, 34, 217, 223, 224, 226,
    232, 245, 246, 291

Kauffman, Ivan, 306
Kauffman, J. Howard, 43, 86, 88, 160,
    164, 166–68, 169, 199, 200, 219–20,
    224, 226, 230, 255, 286–87, 288,
    292–93, 334
Kaufman, E.G., 41, 235, 241
Kautsky, Karl, 311, 313, 319
Keeney, William, 231
Klaassen, Walter, 35, 49, 107
Klassen, A.J., 60

Subject Index

Acculturation: through education, 189; of faith, 300–301; of Mennonites, 325–26; and schism, 265; of values, 293

Achievement, and secularization, 209–10

Affluence, dangers of, 213

Altona, Manitoba, described, 204–5

Amish, Old Order, history of, 37–38

Anabaptism: 3, 4; in diaspora, 316–17; as ethical system, 320; becoming ethnic, 319–21; mellowing of, 325–26; as movement, 7–8, 319; oppressed, 318–19; spread of, through missions, 234–35; as utopian, 311–17

Anabaptist dispersion, 6, 13–16

Anabaptist hunters, 10, 15

Anabaptist Movement: spread of, 8; reception of, 10

Appenzell, 6

Artists, Mennonite, 110–112

Arts, expressive: among Mennonites, 110–113; and dualism, 119; cooptation of, 121; receptivity of, 120

Assimilation, in Mennonite society, 338

Augsburg, as early Anabaptist center, 8

Ausbund: earliest songbook, 109; in Mennonite story, 138

Authority, secular, and Mennonite life, 81

Authority, Mennonite: of bible, 75; and congregation, 65, 67; and family, 172–73; and power, 69; and tradition, 75

Baptism: adult, 319; of children, 159

Beachy Amish, 38

Beliefs: importance of, 60; of Mennonites, 51–59; role of, 336; and schism, 269

Bern: spread of Anabaptism to, 8; flight of Anabaptists from, 15

Bethel College: and faculty purges, 285; founding of, 180; and fundamentalism, 290; and liberalism, 283–84

Biblicism, and legalism, 299

Biological growth: of Hutterites, 27; of Mennonites, 26–27; of Old Colony Mennonites, 27

Bishop: nature of, 70; and Rome, 74; source of, 69
Businesspeople, Mennonite, 203

Change, 259; in Mennonite family, 167–73; in Mennonite occupations, 204–6; nature of, 276–78; of remnant, 317; and Utopia, 311; of values, 292–93
Character, Mennonite: aspects of, 92–93; selectivity of, 93–94
Children, 159
Chiliasm: among early Anabaptists, 9
Church, Mennonite: and institutionalization, 256–58; pure, 55
Church, Roman Catholic: and empire, 216; corruption of, 312–13; renewal of, 314; restitution of, 312–13
Church, state, 279
Churches, Federal Council of, and General Conference of Mennonites, 284
Colleges, Mennonite, 180–82; and liberalism, 283–85; and MCC, 253
Concern Movement: and Mennonite church, 304; and renewal, 305
Common man, and sectarian impulse, 330
Commonwealth: in Belize, 82; in Bolivia, 83; defined, 80; as Kingdom of God, 221; in Manitoba, 82; in Mexico, 82; in Paraguay, 82; in Russia, 74; in Saskatchewan, 83; and two-Kingdom theology, 222; in United States, 83
Communism: of contemporary Mennonites, 322; of early Anabaptists, 313
Community, Mennonite: as community of saints, 141; and congregation, 77, 83–85; defined, 83–84, 129–30, 130–32; and effect on economics, 206; and ethnicity, 307; and family, 168–69; function of, 133–34; as *Gemeinde*, 132; as ideology, 136; in Lancaster County (Pa.), 84; meaning of, 136–37; as peoplehood, 131, 137–39; religious nature of, 134; as social community, 135; structure and network, 134, 308; as theocracy, 78; as total community, 135
Conferences, Mennonite: and authority, 65–67; described, 39–44; and individualism, 87; and organization, 256–57

Confession of Faith, 66–67; Dortrecht, 34, 217; Schleitheim, 65, 217
Conflict: and ethnicity, 323–25; of Flemish-Frisian, 261–62; caused by fundamentalism, 289; fundamentalist-modernist, 272–73; over growth and discipline, 246; ideological, 272; and leadership, 306; in Mennonite community, 325; of mission and separation, 241; in Old Colony, 262; paradigm of, 339; over purity, 331; and schism, 270; with society, 339
Congregation, 320; authority of, 313; autonomy of, 66; and family, 172–73; function of, 63–64; and fundamentalism, 88, 289–90; and leadership, 306; lifestyles of, 88–89; as organizing principle, 62; as social institution, 71
Conservatism, and schism, 268, 271
Consciousness, false, 314
Contradiction, in Mennonite society, 340–42
Credit Unions, 250
Crisis, Mennonite Identity: 276–78
Culture: and Christ, 114–15, defined by Mennonites, 116; and identity, 338; and pluralism, 338; versus faith, 300

Defection, of Hutterites, 28; of Mennonites, 28–29
Denomination, Mennonites as, 334–36
Dialects, 64; Amish, 64; Hutterite, 64; low German, 31; Pennsylvania Dutch, 31; Plattdeutsch, 64
Differentiation, Mennonite, types of, 34–35
Differentiation, social: and schism, 271–73; and strain, 272–74
Dilemmas: of aesthetics and faith, 126; belief versus structure, 302–6; of institutionalization, 297–302
Discipline: and legalism, 298; in Mennonite church, 280; as world view, 295
Division: classic elements in, 266–71; among conservative groups, 265; among Hutterites, 265–66; and "sheep stealing," 270
Divorce, among Mennonites, 169
Dortrecht Confession, 217
Doukhobors, theocracy of, 79

Dualism: of Mennonite beliefs, 217; in Mennonite theology, 296

Eastern District General Conference, 40
Economics: brotherhood of, 196–97; change in, 204–7; and community support, 210; confrontation of, 195; conventional, 197–98; effect of, on religion, 192; Hutterite view of, 194–95; and Mennonites, 193; of Mennonites, 198; and political activity, 230
Education: of children, 175; and future of Mennonites, 187; as *Gelassenheit*, 175; history of, 106–13, 175–78; among Hutterites, 175–76; of Mennonite leadership, 175, 185; among Old Orders, 177–78; not understood, 187; service to church, 188
Empire, Holy Roman, 312
Entrepreneurship, 203, 209
Equilibrium, of faith and structure, 273
Established Church, corruption of, 48–49
Ethnicity: change to, 319; and faith, 323; as *Gemeinde*, 316; and ideology, 333–34; Mennonite outreach through, 241–42; as network, 308; and peoplehood, 318; portable, 307; as self-fulfilling prophecy, 320; and suffering, 319–20; "trap of," 319; versus faith, 307
Ethics: Anabaptist stress of, 320; as lifestyle, 321
Evangelical Mennonite Brethren, and modernism, 285
Evangelicalism, and schism, 270–71
Evangelism, 24–26, 27
Evangelization: hindered by organization, 257–58; and separation, 242
Excommunication, 4

Faith: versus culture, 300; and economics, 207–14; loss of, 278; and service, 253–54; and suffering, 317; supported by ethnicity, 323–24
Faith, and arts: dilemma of, 122–23, 126; discussed, 117–18; future of, 122–23, and identity, 123; and Mennonite life, 123; and socialization, 124–25
Faithfulness, to original Christianity, 323

Family, Mennonite: accommodation of, 168–69; and community, 160–61, 163–64; and congregation, 158–59; conventional, 161–62; and divorce, 169; historical review of, 157–61; and marriage, 158; outside of covenant, 159–60; theocratic type, 162; tendency to authoritarianism, 168; and urbanization, 168–69
Farm, Mennonite: movement from, 204–5
Fellowship, disruption of, 264–65
Fiction: and Mennonite personality, 100; of Mennonite writers, 99–100; of Rudy Wiebe, 100; and women, 103
Fundamentalism: cause for schism, 288–89; defined, 286–87; and liberalism, 287; in Mennonite community, 287–90; and pacifism, 288; source of, 286–87; spread of, 288–89

Gelassenheit: cited, xi, 53; and aesthetics, 106; and artistic expression, 118–19, 122; in congregation, 73–74; and personality, 92
Gemeinschaft-Gesellschaft: defined, 129; as *Gemeinde*, 140
General Conference Mennonites, 40–41
God, City of: relation to, 215–16; and city of Man, 216
Goods, Community of: in Hutterite model, 195; in secularization, 208–14
Goshen College: closing of, 182–84; founding of, 180; and fundamentalism, 290; and liberalism, 283–84; and Rokeach Value Scale, 97
Grace Bible Institute, and modernism, 285
Growth, of Mennonites, 28

Health and welfare: as Mennonite goal, 253–55
Health, mental: of Mennonites, 96, 102–3; organizations, 255
Hesston College, founding of, 181
Holdeman Mennonites: described, 40–42; personality of, 97–98; schisms in, 270–71; worldliness of, 331
Hostility, and schism, 269

Humility: xi; of Christ, 116; and ideology, 333; of Mennonite personality, 99
Hussite Rebellion, 312
Hutterites: 36, 95
Hymnary, Mennonite: 109–10

Income, Mennonite: comparative, 199–200
Identity Crisis: and aesthetics, 125; ambivalence to, 324; and community, 137–38; and loss of boundaries, 125; among Mennonites, xi, 98; as search for identity, 125–26, 276–78; secular pressures, 301; supported by ideology, 333; threats to, 302
Ideology: and ethnicity, 333; and protest, 314–15; and Utopia, 311
Inferiority, of Mennonites over outreach, 241
Instability, of Mennonite economic system, 212
Institution, 257–58; Mennonite church as, 72
Institutionalization: dilemmas of, 273, 297–302; Mennonite, 298–302; stages of, 336–41
Integration, 303, 309
Intellectual life: Anabaptist-Mennonite, 107–8; analyzed, 113; rationale for, 114–16; religious limitations of, 109; retreat from, 119

Judaism, as theocracy, 79

Kingdom of God: xii, 9, 17; and culture, 116; in Paraguay, 221

Lambs' War, in Holland, 261
Leadership: ambiguity of, 74–75; and congregation, 67–70; reaction against, 306–7
Legalism, versus discipline, 298
Liberalism: defined, 283; and Mennonite colleges, 283–85
Lifestyle: and ethnicity, 324; of Anabaptists, 320–21
Limmat River, 8

Manz, Felix, 4, 8
Marriage, in Mennonite community, 160
Martyrdom, of Anabaptists, 318
Martyrs, 8, 10
Martyrs' Mirror: and Jan Luyken, 110; function of, 316–18; role of, 92, 138
Martyrs' Synod, 8
Mennonite Central Committee (MCC): Mennonite support of, 85–86; and mutual aid, 247; and service, 251–55
Mennonite Disaster Service (MDS), 250
Mennonite Economic Development Associates (MEDA), 204; role of, 213; service of, 256
Melchiorites, 4
Menists, 4, 10
Mennonite Brethren, described, 40–43
Mennonite Brethren in Christ, described, 40–43
Mennonite Old Orders, personality traits of, 95
Mennonite World Conference, 256
Mennonites: as cult, 334; as denomination, 334; as distinct group, 335; as ethnic group, 29, 322–23; expelled from France, 16; Germanic, xii, 30; as minority, 334; non-Germanic, xii, 31; as religious-utopian movement, 336; traditional, 29; various names of, 10
Migration, of Mennonites, 15–17, 19–23; and schism, 268
Missions: contemporary motives of, 241; cooperation in, 242; dormancy period of, 235; in early Anabaptism, 233; early dynamics of, 234–44; forms of, 244–46; functions of, 243–44; home, 245; Mennonites and, 233; non-denominational, 244; rebirth of, 235; versus self-preservation, 299; statistics of, 235–41
Models, of economics: community of goods, 193; Hutterite view of, 194
Models, of Mennonite life: and Mennonite conferences, 87; of modern Mennonites, 86
Modernism; conflict over, 284–85; history of, 283; impact of, on Mennonites, 283–91
Moravia, 4; emigration to, 15
Mormons, as theocracy, 79
Mountain Lake, Minn., described, 204–5

Music, tradition of, among Mennonites, 109–10
Muenster Rebellion: and migration, 16; and Peasants Revolt, 9
Mutual Aid: central to Anabaptism, 321–22; in congregations, 280; described, 248–50; in Dutch church, 321–22; among Hutterites, 247; and life insurance, 249; for Russian Mennonites, 247; through MCC, 247; as world view, 295

Nationalism: pull of, 229; effects of, 232
Networks, 308–9
Nonresistance, and military service, 225–26

Obbenites, 4
Oberschulze, in Mennonite Commonwealth, 82
Occupations, changes in, 200–201
Old Colony Mennonites, 41; and pride, 118
Old Mennonites, 40
Oppression: and peoplehood, 318–19, and revolution, 315, story of, 317
Organization, social, in Mennonite community, 81–82
Organization: for church life, 256; and institutionalization, 257–58; of Mennonite disaster service, 250; and Mennonite society, 256; of Mental health, 255; of Mutual Aid, 249–50; and power, 305; and secularization, 257; of welfare and health, 254–55
Officeholding: among Mennonites, 223; versus informal influence, 227

Paraguay, Mennonites in, 221
Parish, Roman Catholic, and commonwealth, 82
Participation, Mennonite: in economics, 230; in informal activities, 227; in military service, 224; in office holding, 224; selective, 220, 231; in state, 220; in voting, 226
Peoplehood, Mennonite: consciousness of, 324; defined, 139–40; hope for, 341; marking Mennonites, 322–23;

and restitution, 318–19; tradition of, 138, 326
Peasants Revolt: as millinarian movement, 8; influence of, on Muenster, 9, 50
Persecution, of Anabaptists, 8, 15
Personality, Mennonite: basic traits of, 96–97; context of, 95–102; defined, 91; discussed, 93–105; and normality, 102; outsiders' view of, 101–2; and schism, 268; stereotype of, 100–102; structure of, 92–93; and women, 103–4
Philosophy, political, and Mennonite voting, 226
Pietism: among Old Mennonites, 281–2; influence of, 56, 281–82
Pluralism, of Mennonite society, 338–39
Police, and Mennonite community, 222
Politics: changes in, 229–32; and economics, 230; interpretation of, 228; participation in, 219
Power: concentration of, 69; in organizations, 305; and personality, 74; rejected by Mennonites, 116; and schism, 268
Practice, Orthodox, in Mennonite community, 279–81
Pride, 118
Priesthood, of Believers, congregation as, 65
Privilegien (privileges): and Mennonites, 80; defined, 80; earliest, 176; role of, 325
Protest, Anabaptist: aspects of, 48; of institutional church, 49–50
Purity: in church, 55; of sect, 331; versus worldliness, 298

Reformation, protest of, by Catholics, 216
Reformed Church, persecutions by, 8, 10, 15
Reformed Mennonites, 40
Reformers, 314
Reinlander Mennonites, 41
Relief service, 250, 251, 254
Religion: affected by economics, 192; affected by success, 209, and stratification, 192

Religion, civil, in Mennonite community, 278

Renewal: of life in Christ, 321; movements of, 304–5; during Renaissance, 311; and schism, 263–64; through Utopia, 313

Restitutionists, and utopians, xiii

Rokeach Value Scale, discussed, 97

Roman Catholic Church, 4, 6

Russia, Mennonite migration to, 19

Saint Gall, spread of Anabaptism to, 8

Schism: analysis of, 264–71; Flemish-Friesian, 59–60; among Hutterites, 58; among Mennonites, 261; Muenster, 58; among Old Orders, 263; origins of, 56; and renewal, 263–4; review of, 261–4

Schleitheim Confession, 217, 312

Schools: elementary, 176–78; secondary, 178

Schwertler split, 58, 314

Sect, Mennonites defined as, 329–32

Sectarian Protest, Mennonites as, 35; and mission, 241; and two worlds, 119

Secularization: evaluated, 294–95; in economics, 197; of Mennonite future, 211–13; of Mennonite youth, 303; and missions, 241–43; and organizations, 257–58; and science, 302; and success, 213; and urbanization, 211

Seduction, by world, 326–27

Self-consciousness, of Anabaptism, 320

Self-hatred, of Mennonites, 300

Self-preservation: through memory, 326; versus mission, 299

Seminaries: and secularization, 79–80; purpose of, 179–80

Separation: and economic forces, 228–30; and ethnicity, 332–33; and informal politics, 227; as Mennonite trait, 280; and missions, 241; and political factors, 231; and stagnation, 298; from world, 34, 319–21; as world view, 294

Service: opportunity for, 253; through MCC, 251–53

Service, military, Mennonites and, 224

Singing, Mennonite, tradition of, 109–10

Socialization, 123–24

Society of Brothers, 36

Society, Mennonite: described, 336–39

Sommerfelder Mennonites, 41

Spirit, life of the, and Mennonites, 116

Stability, versus change, 259

Staebler split, 58

Stagnation, by separation, 298

State, the: antipathy toward, 215; and economic forces, 230; and ethnicity, 332; and Mennonite commonwealth, 216; office holding in, 223; participation in, 218; rejection of, 279; separation from, 332; world view of, 294

State: churchly: as dilemma, 222; defined, 220; Mennonites in Paraguay as, 221

Stauffer Mennonites, 40

Stewardship, Mennonite concept of, 210

Stille im Lande: Mennonites as, 317–18

Story, and survival, 226–27; as form of utopia, 316–17

Strain, structural: in Mennonite society, 273, 340

Strasbourg, 8

Students, Mennonite, 97

Suffering, of Anabaptists, 316

Switzerland: 4; Appenzell in, 6; St. Gall, 6

Sword, in Anabaptist thought, 215

Sword and Trumpet, The, and modernism, 284

Syndrome, Mennonite, defined, 96–97

Tabor: and fundamentalism, 290; founding of, 181

Theocracy, 78

Theology: in colleges, 290–91; and dualism, 296; and ethnicity, 333; and fundamentalism, 286; and liberalism, 283; of missions and separation, 241; and renewal, 313; and schism, 270–71; Two-Kingdom, 217; and unity, 270–71; and world-view, 294–95

Theology, Anabaptist: and service, 253; as orthodox, 51; derived from Europe, 51

Tourette's Disease, 103

Tradition: and consciousness, 326–27; and deterioration, 299; and leadership, 306; and schism, 265–66

Truth: of Anabaptists, 314; of Anabaptist story, 326–27

Two Kingdoms: gradient of, 218; and informal influence, 227; and lobby-

ing, 227; in Paraguay, 221; and political stance, 231; typology of, 218
Tyrol: 4; emigration to, 15; refuge for Anabaptists, 8; severity of persecution in, 9

Unity: lack of, 56; in one region, 274; theological, 272–73
Utopia: death of, 326; dynamics of, 313; and faithful, 317; Mennonites as, 310, 336–38; origins of, 315; as story, 316

Values: in America, 291–92; of Anabaptists, 291–93
Vision, Anabaptist: and polygenetics, 279; described, 279; retention of, 324–25
Vitality, spiritual, loss of, 278
Volkskirche, 279
Voluntarism: of Mennonite church, 319; and faith, 319–20
Voting: conservative, 226; by Mennonites, 226

Wealth: and defection, 209; and secularization, 213; of Mennonites, 200
Wisler Mennonites, 40
Women, Mennonite: in missions, 244; and personality, 103–4; and relation to family, 169; and status in community, 169–71
Work, Mennonite attitudes toward, 210
World: influence of, 294, relation of Mennonites to, 295
Worldliness: analyzed, 294–95; as cause for schism, 268–71; and culture, 115; and education, 189–90; and liberalism, 288; and purity, 298; and separation, 115–16; power of, 326–27
World view: American, 291; elements of Mennonite, 291, 294
Writers, Mennonite, 110–11

Zentralschule, purpose of, 180
Zurich: flight from, 15; as origin of Anabaptism, 4, 23

Designed by Chris L. Smith
Composed by the Composing Room of Michigan, Inc.,
in Plantin text and display
Printed by the Maple Press Company, Inc.,
on 50-lb. MV Eggshell Cream Offset paper and
bound in Joanna's Arrestox A and Kennett